THE DERRIDA–HABERMAS READER

Edited by
Lasse Thomassen

EDINBURGH UNIVERSITY PRESS

Edinburgh University Press Ltd
22 George Square, Edinburgh

Typeset in Sabon and Gill Sans
by TechBooks, New Delhi, India, and
printed and bound in Great Britain by
MPG Books, Bodmin, Cornwall

A CIP record for this book is available from
the British Library

ISBN-10 0 7486 2249 7 (hardback)
ISBN-13 978 0 7486 2249 8 (hardback)
ISBN-10 0 7486 2250 0 (paperback)
ISBN-13 978 0 7486 2250 4 (paperback)

CONTENTS

Acknowledgements viii

Introduction: Between Deconstruction and Rational Reconstruction 1

PART I PHILOSOPHY AND LITERATURE

Introduction 11

1. Leveling the Genre Distinction between Philosophy and Literature 13
   Jürgen Habermas
2. Is There a Philosophical Language? 35
   Jacques Derrida
3. Habermas, Derrida and the Functions of Philosophy 46
   Richard Rorty

PART II ETHICS AND POLITICS

Introduction 69

4. An Allegory of Modernity/Postmodernity: Habermas and Derrida 71
   Richard J. Bernstein

5. Frankfurt Impromptu – Remarks on Derrida and Habermas 98
Simon Critchley

6. Performative Powerlessness – A Response to Simon Critchley 111
Jacques Derrida

7. How to Respond to the Ethical Question 115
Jürgen Habermas

8. Democracy and Difference: Reflections on the Metapolitics of Lyotard and Derrida 128
Seyla Benhabib

PART III IDENTITY/DIFFERENCE: RIGHTS, TOLERANCE AND POLITICAL SPACE

Introduction 159

9. Dead Rights, Live Futures: On Habermas's Attempt to Reconcile Constitutionalism and Democracy 161
Bonnie Honig

10. 'A Bizarre, Even Opaque Practice': Habermas on Constitutionalism and Democracy 176
Lasse Thomassen

11. Religious Tolerance – The Pacemaker for Cultural Rights 195
Jürgen Habermas

12. Hostipitality 208
Jacques Derrida

13. Between Deliberation and Deconstruction: The Condition of Post-National Democracy 231
Martin Morris

PART IV BEYOND THE NATION-STATE: EUROPE, COSMOPOLITANISM AND INTERNATIONAL LAW

Introduction 257

14. For a Justice to Come: An Interview with Jacques Derrida 259
Jacques Derrida and Lieven De Cauter

15. February 15, or What Binds Europeans Together: A Plea for a Common Foreign Policy, Beginning in the Core of Europe 270
Jürgen Habermas and Jacques Derrida

16. Between Hope and Terror: Habermas and Derrida Plead for the Im/Possible 278
Martin Beck Matuštík

AFTERWORDS

Introduction 299

17. Honesty of Thought 300
Jacques Derrida

18. A Last Farewell: Derrida's Enlightening Impact 307
Jürgen Habermas

Bibliography 309

Copyright Acknowledgements 314

Notes on the Contributors 317

Index 319

ACKNOWLEDGEMENTS

This volume would not have been possible without the help of several people. I would like to thank first of all the contributors for their generous support for the project. In particular, I would like to thank Simon Critchley, Martin Beck Matuštík, Bonnie Honig and Jürgen Habermas, who helped steer me in the right direction at crucial points. At Edinburgh University Press, I would like to thank Nicola Ramsey and Eddie Clark for their continued support and for answering my endless queries in the process of putting together the volume. I would also like to thank Joanna Delorme at Galilée and Helen Tartar at Fordham University Press. Finally, I would like to thank Seth Hague for his help with the introductions and Chapter 7.

Lasse Thomassen

INTRODUCTION: BETWEEN DECONSTRUCTION AND RATIONAL RECONSTRUCTION

Jacques Derrida and Jürgen Habermas are great philosophers in both scope and influence. They have each written dozens of books on a variety of subjects, and they have been influential in many disciplines, Derrida most influential in the humanities and Habermas in the social sciences. Indeed, their influence is such that that we refer to 'Derridean' and 'Habermasian' strands of thought.

Jacques Derrida was born in Algeria in 1930 and died in 2004. His parents were Jewish and as a result he was expelled from school during World War II. This had a lasting impact on him, leaving him, as he often recounted, with a feeling of being neither Jewish nor French nor Algerian. This left him suspicious of discourses of identity, something clearly evident in his method of deconstruction. He later went on to Paris to study and become professor at École des Hautes Études en Sciences Sociales. He was also a frequent visitor to universities in the United States, where he held several visiting professorships.

Jürgen Habermas was born in Germany in 1929. The horrors of World War II and the Holocaust were formative for his adolescence. Later in his life, it led him to develop a defence of reason, modernity and Enlightenment, and to develop an account of normative reason in pluralist societies. In 1964, he became professor at the University of Frankfurt, eventually becoming the main representative of the second generation of the Frankfurt School of Critical Theory. Today he is Professor Emeritus at the University of Frankfurt and still writes books at the pace of one every one or two years.

What merits a book on Habermas and Derrida is their simultaneous differences and shared concerns. They are often taken as representatives of, respectively, modernity and postmodernism, universalism and particularism, and reason and the critique of reason. There are indeed important differences between them over the role of philosophy and reason. Nonetheless, they share in a critique of nationalism and xenophobia, and a concern for further European integration and the rule of law in international relations.

In the following, I shall first give a brief account of the relationship between Derrida and Habermas and then introduce their respective works on method, philosophy, ethics and politics.

THE HISTORY OF A FRIENDSHIP WITH OBSTACLES

The story of Derrida and Habermas starts in the first half of the 1980s. In 1984, Derrida visited Frankfurt on Habermas's invitation, and, in 1985, Habermas published *The Philosophical Discourse of Modernity* in German, which included two chapters on Derrida (see Chapter 1; Habermas 1987). The intellectual climate in Germany at the time was marked by an opposition between defenders of reason, modernity and Enlightenment, and what theorists like Habermas saw as a dangerous neo-conservative and postmodern critique of reason.

If Habermas's reading of Derrida in *The Philosophical Discourse of Modernity* was unsympathetic, so were Derrida's responses to it. As he later noted, he responded 'as far as possible with arguments, but admittedly a bit polemically' (see Chapter 17). Derrida's responses consist of two lengthy footnotes (Derrida 1988; 1989), some comments in a reply to Karl-Otto Apel (Derrida and Wetzel 1987), and an interview on the nature of philosophy (see Chapter 2). Derrida claimed that not only had Habermas got him wrong, but also that he had not even read him, something he attributed to the lack of references to his work in Habermas's texts. To Derrida, Habermas was engaged in blackmail: are you for or against reason? For or against Enlightenment?

Then, at a 'party' at Northwestern University in Chicago, where they were both teaching at the end of the 1990s, Habermas 'approached me [Derrida], laughing in a friendly manner, and suggested that we have a "discussion"' (see Chapter 17). Not only did Habermas now believe it possible to discuss and argue with Derrida, but the gesture was also mutual. Subsequently, there was a new tone that rang in Derrida and Habermas's comments on one another's work (see Chapter 6; Derrida 1998; Habermas 2004a). Later on, they would agree to have their interviews on the international situation after 9/11 published in the same volume (Borradori 2003). Habermas took part in a conference on 'Derrida's Judaism' (see Chapter 7), and they co-signed a piece on the role of Europe in the new world order (see Chapter 15). This is not to say that Derrida and Habermas are, today, arguing the same thing in the same way. As Derrida notes in his preface to their co-signed piece, which was written by Habermas: 'despite all obvious differences in our approaches and arguments, our aspirations converge regarding the future of the institutions of international law and the new challenges for Europe' (see Chapter 15). And Habermas (2004a): 'Apart from all the politics, it is the philosophical reference to an author like Kant that connects me to Derrida'. What bring them together, then, are a number of common *political* concerns: economic, social and political inequalities, international law, terrorism, migration, and Europe.

HABERMAS: COMMUNICATIVE ACTION, DISCOURSE ETHICS AND DELIBERATIVE DEMOCRACY

Habermas's work spans more than five decades and several disciplines.[1] If there is one thread running through it, it is the attempt to rescue the emancipatory potential of modernity and Enlightenment. Central to this task is to develop a theory of rationality with an account of normative rationality for pluralist and secular societies. Habermas argues that we must differentiate among different kinds of rationality, instrumental rationality being only one of them. To confuse instrumental rationality with reason as such would lead us to exclude rational resolution of normative issues. This is where Habermas parts company with the Critical Theory of Theodor Adorno and Max Horkheimer from the first generation of the Frankfurt School. Habermas argues that, in their critique of Enlightenment reason, Adorno and Horkheimer confuse instrumental reason with reason as such. While this leads them to a radical critique of contemporary society, Habermas seeks a way out of the iron cage of instrumental reason. He finds this in an alternative and differentiated account of rationality, in which communicative rationality is only one, but an essential, part of reason. Communicative rationality rests on the mutual agreement among participants in free dialogue rather than on the efficiency of an instrumental means-end relation.

To Habermas, the stakes are clear: without an account of rationality in normative questions, one can only instrumentalise or aestheticise normative relations, neither of which can form the basis for social critique. This is part of Habermas's problem with Derrida, who, according to Habermas, reduces all discourse to aesthetics and instrumental rationality where the only criterion is rhetorical success (see Chapter 1).

Habermas's method is one of rational reconstruction, by which he means the critical appropriation of the normative content of a practice or institution. Habermas argues that there are certain, mostly implicit, assumptions that one makes when engaged in social action and language use. He refers to these as universal or 'quasi-transcendental' structures to signify that they are unavoidable and beyond individual choice. He asks, first, what makes peaceful social interaction possible in the long run. His answer is that only an account of communicative action – action oriented towards mutual understanding – can explain it. Second, he asks what makes communicative action possible. His answer is that, when engaging in communicative action, one makes the – often implicit, but always unavoidable – assumption that it would be possible to reach agreement under certain idealised circumstances. More precisely, when putting forward validity claims to truth or normative rightness, these claims are put forward in a particular context. Yet, they transcend that context insofar as they imply that one would defend them in rational discourse (or in an 'ideal speech situation', a term Habermas uses in his earlier work). These are discourses where everybody possibly affected by a norm, for instance, has an equal say, and the outcome is a rational consensus.

The argument serves to show how these quasi-transcendental structures of language can be rationally reconstructed: they are not the mere contingent constructs of a philosopher, but reconstructions of what is actually the case when we communicate. Even if a rational consensus never actually occurs, we nonetheless presuppose it whenever we engage in communicative action, and it serves to explain how social interaction is possible. Moreover, it serves as an account of validity: our access to reality is always mediated by language, but the very structure of language gives us a way to judge validity claims. Truth and rightness are determined in rational discourse. This is Habermas's discourse ethics: an account of the discursive and intersubjective foundation of validity, whether cognitive (truth) or normative (rightness) validity.

Habermas's argument for deliberative democracy, which he developed in *Between Facts and Norms* (Habermas 1996b), is analogous to his argument for communicative action and discourse ethics. Again he rationally reconstructs the normative content and the quasi-transcendental structures of the practice of democracy. Given that legal norms are the only available medium for integrating modern, complex societies, he asks: how can laws contribute to social integration and still be legitimate in pluralist societies? His answer is autonomy, that is, rational self-legislation. If the addressees of the laws are able to understand themselves as simultaneously the authors of the laws, they will be able to relate to the laws not only strategically (fear of reprisals and so on) but also out of respect. This is a Kantian argument with a twist. The difference between Kant and Habermas is that, for the latter, the laws must be the result of public deliberation – hence, *deliberative* democracy. The legitimacy of the laws is determined in public deliberations where all those possibly affected by the laws have an equal say.

The legitimacy of democracy thus depends on the extent to which laws and decisions are the result of public deliberations characterised by equality and openness. Most important here is the public sphere, where citizens should be guided by the force of the better argument, not by instrumental or strategic gain. In his most recent work, Habermas has been concerned with the European public sphere or rather lack thereof (see Chapter 15).

He is concerned that, without a common public sphere, the decisions and laws of the European Union will be imposed on the citizens rather than the product of their free and equal opinion and will formation.

Modern societies are pluralist. They are a plurality of what Habermas, following John Rawls, calls ethical conceptions of the good: religious ideas, cultural ideas, and so on of what a good life is. Habermas argues that pluralist societies can only be integrated if we distinguish this level of ethical conceptions from a common level of political culture. As he argues in Chapter 7, the political level must be neutral vis-à-vis particular ethical conceptions of the good and not favour one over the other. The common political culture crystallises around a constitutional patriotism, which is a shared allegiance to the normative content of the constitution (basic individual rights, political rights, and so on).

Tolerance is also important in this respect, and it is a good example of Habermas's method of rational reconstruction (see Chapter 12). He argues that in traditional accounts of tolerance, tolerance is a hierarchical relationship between the tolerating and the tolerated parties where the former bestows tolerance on the latter as an act of grace. This does not lead Habermas to reject the concept of tolerance, as he argues that it is possible to appropriate a normative kernel of equal respect from it. Hence, he conceives of tolerance as a relationship between equal partners in a dialogue.

In his most recent work, Habermas has been preoccupied with what he calls 'the postnational constellation', and it is in this area that he has most in common with Derrida. Habermas believes that we must move beyond the nation-state and start thinking about politics at a European and global level as a response to globalisation (see Chapter 15; Habermas 1998a, 2001a).

DERRIDA AND DECONSTRUCTION

Derrida's work consists of readings of philosophical, literary and political texts using the method of deconstruction.[2] To refer to deconstruction as a method is a bit of a misnomer, since deconstruction *as* method is arguably also the deconstruction *of* method (Derrida 2002b; Gasché 1986). Deconstruction does not promise to provide a transparent set of tools or methodologies through which we can appropriate the object of study. Instead, deconstruction aims to expose the aporias of texts. 'Aporias' here refer to irresolvable contradictions, and 'texts' should be understood in a very general sense as meaningful structures. Thus, 'texts' are not just what we usually understand by that word (books, documents and so on), but includes any meaningful practice or part thereof, from official documents to political institutions, thus making it possible to study political phenomena as 'texts'.

A deconstructive analysis is always an intervention, so it does not leave fully intact the object of study. While deconstruction starts from a close reading of the text in question, the purpose is not to (re-)establish its coherence or unity in a hermeneutical fashion. Instead, the purpose is to show the limits of the text in order to subvert it. This is why Derrida has always insisted that deconstruction is political, even before he started engaging with explicitly political issues in the 1980s and 1990s.

According to Derrida, aporias paradoxically account for the functioning of texts and social practices. In short, what accounts for the functioning of a social practice simultaneously undermines it. In deconstructivist terminology this means that the condition of possibility of something is simultaneously its condition of impossibility (hence why we are dealing with an irresolvable aporia). An example of this is Derrida's deconstruction of hospitality (see Chapter 12; Derrida 2000 and 2001b). Hospitality is made possible by what simultaneously limits it: without a home where I am sovereign, I cannot welcome or show hospitality towards the other. So, Derrida concludes, hospitality is always conditional hospitality, that is, conditional upon the other's acceptance of my sovereignty in my home.

The fact that deconstruction is not simply applied but also rearticulated in the process of applying it means that there is a limit to its systematisation. Every deconstructive reading is to some extent singular, and, as a result, Derrida's work cannot be as easily summed up or systematised in the way it is possible to summarise Habermas's work. Yet, there are certain terms or quasi-concepts that occur across Derrida's texts. They are terms like *différance*, iterability and undecidability (see Gasché 1986 for an overview). With these and other terms, Derrida puts into question discourses that rely on given and coherent identities. For instance, he has warned against thinking of 'Europe' as a coherent unity (see Chapter 15; Derrida 1992). Generally speaking, Derrida argues that meaning and identity – for instance, the identity of Europe – are inherently contingent and unstable. As a consequence, language is not a transparent medium but itself a site of political struggle, because it matters which concepts and distinctions we use, how we describe things, and so on. Derrida calls attention to these exclusions and shows the history of current concepts and vocabularies.

A good example is Derrida's questioning of the definition of terrorism, where he shows that there is a multiplicity of definitions of terrorism. The dominance of one definition therefore rests on the suppression of other possible definitions, which, as the so-called 'war on terror' has shown, is not without consequence for policies (Borradori 2003). This view of language sets Derrida off from Habermas. For Derrida, language can never be transparent, which problematises Habermas's belief in rational discourse and rational consensus.

In the areas of ethics and politics, Derrida has deconstructed concepts such as hospitality (see Chapter 12), friendship, responsibility, forgiveness, sovereignty and cosmopolitanism (see Chapter 14). In each case, he does so through a critical engagement with the Western philosophical tradition, especially Kant. And in each case, he shows how these concepts are marked by inherent aporias.

A final important part of Derrida's work on politics is his idea of a democracy to come (or justice to come). A democracy to come is not a democracy that will be realised sometime in the future. Instead the idea is that no instantiation of democracy or justice – in any present, including a future one – is perfect, and that democracy and justice are therefore always deferred and *to come*. So, unlike Habermas, Derrida believes that, however fair and inclusive, the procedures and norms of democracy and justice can always be improved.

THE STRUCTURE OF THE BOOK

The eighteen chapters of the book have been carefully selected to give a flavour of the affinities and differences between Derrida's and Habermas's respective works. The book is divided into four Parts, each covering an important area of these similarities and/or differences: Philosophy and literature; Ethics and politics; Identity/difference; and Beyond the nation-state. At the end of the book are two Afterwords, by Derrida and Habermas respectively, which are their most recent statements on one another's works. In order to facilitate navigation of the book, each chapter is preceded by a short introduction to the context and argument of the chapter. In addition, each Part starts with a brief preface to the issues at stake and suggestions for further reading. Finally, the bibliography at the back of the book contains references to all existing literature on Derrida and Habermas and to the works cited in the introductions.

NOTES

1. The best introductions to Habermas's work are McCarthy (1978) for his earlier work, Rasmussen (1990) for communicative action and discourse ethics, and Eriksen and Weigård (2003) for his political philosophy. See also Thomassen (2005) for a brief introduction to Habermas.
2. The best introductions to Derrida's work are Lucy 2004 (for a basic introduction), and Gasché 1986 for a formidable interpretation of deconstruction. Derrida 2002b is easily accessible and gives a good idea of Derrida's method of deconstruction. Beardsworth 1996 provides an introduction to the politics of Derrida.

PART I
PHILOSOPHY AND LITERATURE

INTRODUCTION

The 1980s saw heated debates over modernity and postmodernity – debates that are often presented as for or against reason, and sometimes as debates between German and French thinking. In Germany at the time, there was an increasing interest in French post-structuralist or 'post-modern' thought, although there was resistance from thinkers who cast themselves as the defenders of reason, among them Jürgen Habermas.

Habermas's contribution to this debate was *The Philosophical Discourse of Modernity*, first published in German in 1985 and translated into English in 1987. The book was one long attack on philosophers associated with the term 'postmodernism': Nietzsche, Heidegger, Foucault, Deleuze – and, of course, Jacques Derrida. The book contains two chapters on Derrida. The first deals with Derrida's critiques of the metaphysics of presence and logocentrism (Habermas 1987). Habermas argues that the philosophical tradition has already dealt with these issues, and that there is therefore no reason to reject the philosophical tradition as such, as he took Derrida to be doing. The second chapter is the one reprinted in the present volume as Chapter 1. In it, Habermas argues that Derrida levels important distinctions between philosophy and literature, logic and rhetoric, normal and abnormal language use, and the problem-solving and world-disclosive functions of language. As a result, Derrida is unable to provide a foundation for social critique.

Derrida's response to Habermas can be found in Chapter 2. He claims that Habermas has misread him to the extent that he has even read him at all, and that he – Derrida – does not level the distinction between philosophy and literature but enquires into its conditions of possibility and impossibility.

A number of commentators have written about Habermas's critique of Derrida and about the dispute between the two. One of them is Richard Rorty (Chapter 3), who argues that, if conceived correctly, Derrida and Habermas are complementary rather than competing. For Rorty, Derrida is useful for 'private concerns, in the sense of idiosyncratic projects of self-overcoming', and Habermas is useful for 'public concerns, namely, those having to do with the suffering of other human beings'.

FURTHER READING

For an overview of the debate on modernity and postmodernity, see Bowie 2001. For various positions in this debate, see d'Entrèves and Benhabib 1996 and McCumber 2000; and Frank 1989 for a critique of the French 'postmodernists'.

For Habermas's contribution to this debate, see also Habermas 1996a and his companion piece to his critique of Derrida's levelling of the genre distinction between philosophy and literature, 'Philosophy and Science as Literature?', on the work of the Italian novelist Italo Calvino (Habermas 1992). For Derrida's response to Habermas, see also Derrida 1988, 1989, and 2001a, and Derrida and Wetzel 1987. For Habermas and Derrida on the nature of language, see Culler 1988, Bohman 1988, Jay 1992, and Martin 1992.

Rorty has extended his reading of Derrida in his introduction to deconstruction (1995) and in pieces on Derrida (1991 and 1996). Derrida's response to Rorty can be found in Derrida 1996.

Some of the commentators on the Derrida-Habermas debate divided themselves according to their allegiance to either Habermas and critical theory (Fraser 1984; McCarthy 1988 and 1990; Dews 1995) or Derrida and deconstruction (Culler 1988; Trey 1989; Martin 1992; Coole 1996). A number of commentators, while no doubt more sympathetic to one than the other, argue that the opposition between Habermas and Derrida rested on misunderstandings. For instance, Rodolph Gasché (1988), Christopher Norris (1989) and Marie Fleming (1996) argue that both Derrida and Habermas are modern philosophers and should both be seen as inheritors of Kant, and that Habermas's reading of Derrida as a total critic of reason is therefore misplaced. Like Rorty, David Couzens Hoy (1996) argue that Derrida and Habermas are complementary in some respects, and, in the context of aesthetics, Pieter Duvenage (2003) has made a similar argument.

1

Jürgen Habermas

LEVELING THE GENRE DISTINCTION BETWEEN PHILOSOPHY AND LITERATURE

In this chapter, taken from The Philosophical Discourse of Modernity, *Jürgen Habermas alleges that Jacques Derrida treats everything as one big, general text, thereby levelling four important distinctions. The first is, as the title of the chapter suggests, the distinction between philosophy and literature. The second is the distinction between logic and rhetoric: 'Derrida', Habermas writes, 'is particularly interested in standing the primacy of logic over rhetoric, canonized since Aristotle, on its head.' The third distinction is that between, what Habermas, following J. L. Austin's and John Searle's theories of speech acts, calls normal and abnormal language use. The former refers to serious and literal language use in everyday, communicative contexts, and the latter to non-serious or 'parasitic' language use as in fiction. Finally, Habermas claims that Derrida obscures the distinction between the problem-solving and world-disclosive functions of language, that is, between solving questions of what is true and right, and opening up new horizons of meaning thereby making us see things differently.*

In each of these four cases, it is important for Habermas to uphold clear distinctions, even if this does not lead him to reject the importance of rhetoric, world-disclosure, and so on: 'Literary criticism and philosophy have a family resemblance to literature . . . in their rhetorical achievements. But their family relationship stops right there, for in each of these enterprises [that is, philosophy and literary criticism] the tools of rhetoric are subordinated to the discipline of a distinct *form of argumentation.' When Derrida generalises literature, rhetoric, world-disclosure, and so on, he thereby overlooks the distinctiveness of everyday communicative practices and their contribution to social integration. In short, Habermas argues that Derrida cannot explain how language works in everyday, problem-solving contexts.*

To Habermas, there is more than the distinction between philosophy and literature at stake here. He concludes that 'Whoever transposes the radical critique of reason into the domain of rhetoric... also dulls the sword of the critique of reason itself.' Like other critics of reason, Derrida's deconstruction has nothing to contribute to social critique, according to Habermas.

I

Adorno's 'negative dialectics' and Derrida's 'deconstruction' can be seen as different answers to the same problem. The totalizing critique self-critique of reason gets caught in a performative contradiction since subject-centered reason can be convicted of being authoritarian in nature only by having recourse to its own tools. The tools of thought, which miss the 'dimension of nonidentity' and are imbued with the 'metaphysics of presence', are nevertheless the only available means for uncovering their own insufficiency. Heidegger flees from this paradox to the luminous heights of an esoteric, special discourse, which absolves itself of the restrictions of discursive speech generally and is immunized by vagueness against any specific objections. He makes use of metaphysical concepts for purposes of a critique of metaphysics, as a ladder he casts away once he has mounted the rungs. Once on the heights, however, the late Heidegger does not, as did the early Wittgenstein, withdraw into the mystic's silent intuition; instead, with the gestures of the seer and an abundance of words, he lays claim to the authority of the initiate.

Adorno operates differently. He does not slip out of the paradoxes of the self-referential critique of reason; he makes the performative contradiction within which this line of thought has moved since Nietzsche, and which he acknowledges to be unavoidable, into the organizational form of indirect communication. Identity thinking turned against itself becomes pressed into continual self-denial and allows the wounds it inflicts on itself and its objects to be seen. This exercise quite rightly bears the name negative dialectics because Adorno practices determinate negation unremittingly, even though it has lost any foothold in the categorical network of Hegelian Logic – as a fetishism of demystification, so to speak. This fastening upon a critical procedure that can no longer be sure of its foundations is explained by the fact that Adorno (in contrast to Heidegger) bears no elitist contempt for discursive thought. Like exiles, we wander about lost in the discursive zone; and yet it is only the insistent force of a groundless reflection turned against itself that preserves our connection with the utopia of a long since lost, uncoerced and intuitive knowledge belonging to the primal past.[1] Discursive thought

---

Jürgen Habermas (trans. Frederick G. Lawrence), *The Philosophical Discourse of Modernity, Twelve Lectures* (Cambridge: Polity Press, 1987).

cannot identify itself as the decadent form of this knowledge by means of its own resources; for this purpose, the aesthetic experience gained in contact with avant-garde art is needed. The promise for which the surviving philosophic tradition is no longer a match has withdrawn into the mirror-writing of the esoteric work of art and requires a negativistic deciphering. From this labor of deciphering, philosophy sucks the residue of that paradoxical trust in reason with which negative dialectics executes (in the double sense of this word) its performative contradiction.

Derrida cannot share Adorno's aesthetically certified, residual faith in a deranged reason that has been expelled from the domains of philosophy and become, literally, utopian [having no place]. He is just as little convinced that Heidegger actually escaped the conceptual constraints of the philosophy of the subject by using metaphysical concepts in order to 'cancel them out'. Derrida does, to be sure, want to advance the already forged path of the critique of metaphysics; he, too, would just as soon break out of the paradox as broodingly encircle it. But like Adorno, he guards against the gestures of profundity that Heidegger unhesitatingly imitates from his opposite number, the philosophy of origins. And so there are also parallels between Derrida and Adorno.

This affinity in regard to their thought gestures calls for a more precise analysis. Adorno and Derrida are sensitized in the same way against definitive, totalizing, all-incorporating models, especially against the organic dimension in works of art. Thus, both stress the primacy of the allegorical over the symbolic, of metonomy over metaphor, of the Romantic over the Classical. Both use the fragment as an expository form; they place any system under suspicion. Both are abundantly insightful in decoding the normal case from the point of view of its limit cases; they meet in a negative extremism, finding the essential in the marginal and incidental, the right on the side of the subversive and the outcast, and the truth in the peripheral and the inauthentic. A distrust of everything direct and substantial goes along with an intransigent tracing of mediations, of hidden presuppositions and dependencies. The critique of origins, of anything original, of first principles, goes together with a certain fanaticism about showing what is merely produced, imitated, and secondary in everything. What pervades Adorno's work as a materialist motif – his unmasking of idealist positings, his reversal of false constitutive connections, his thesis about the primacy of the object – even for this there is a parallel in Derrida's logic of the supplement. The rebellious labor of deconstruction aims indeed at dismantling smuggled-in basic conceptual hierarchies, at overthrowing foundational relationships and conceptual relations of domination, such as those between speech and writing, the intelligible and the sensible, nature and culture, inner and outer, mind and matter, male and female. Logic and rhetoric constitute one of these conceptual pairs. Derrida is particularly interested in standing the primacy of logic over rhetoric, canonized since Aristotle, on its head.

It is not as though Derrida concerned himself with these controversial questions in terms of viewpoints familiar from the history of philosophy. If he had done so, he would have had to relativize the status of his own project in relation to the tradition that was shaped from Dante to Vico, and kept alive through Hamann, Humboldt, and Droysen, down to Dilthey and Gadamer. For the protest against the Platonic-Aristotelian primacy of the logical over the rhetorical that is raised anew by Derrida was articulated in this tradition. Derrida wants to expand the sovereignty of rhetoric over the realm of the logical in order to solve the problem confronting the totalizing critique of reason. As I have indicated, he is satisfied neither with Adorno's negative dialectics nor with Heidegger's critique of metaphysics – the one remaining tied to the rational bliss of the dialectic, the other to the elevation of origins proper to metaphysics, all protestations to the contrary notwithstanding. Heidegger only escapes the paradoxes of a self-referential critique of reason by claiming a special status for *Andenken*, that is, its release from discursive obligations. He remains completely silent about the privileged access to truth. Derrida strives to arrive at the same esoteric access to truth, but he does not want to admit it as a privilege – no matter for what or for whom. He does not place himself in lordly fashion above the objection of pragmatic inconsistency, but renders its *objectless*.

There can only be talk about 'contradiction' in the light of consistency requirements, which lose their authority or are at least subordinated to other demands – of an aesthetic nature, for example – if logic loses its conventional primacy over rhetoric. Then the deconstructionist can deal with the works of philosophy as works of literature and adapt the critique of metaphysics to the standards of a literary criticism that does not misunderstand itself in a scientistic way. As soon as we take the *literary* character of Nietzsche's writings seriously, the suitableness of his critique of reason has to be assessed in accord with the standards of rhetorical success and not those of logical consistency. Such a critique (which is more adequate to its object) is not immediately directed toward the network of discursive relationships of which arguments are built, but toward the figures that shape style and are decisive for the literary and rhetorical power of a text. A literary criticism that in a certain sense merely *continues* the literary process of its objects cannot end up in a science. Similarly, the deconstruction of great philosophical texts, carried out as literary criticism in this broader sense, is not subject to the criteria of problem-solving, purely cognitive undertakings.

Hence, Derrida *undercuts* the very problem that Adorno acknowledged as unavoidable and turned into the starting point of his reflectively self-transcending identity-thinking. For Derrida, this problem has no object since the deconstructive enterprise cannot be pinned down to the discursive obligations of philosophy and science. He calls his procedure deconstruction because it is supposed to *clear away* the ontological *scaffolding* erected by philosophy in the course of its subject-centered history of reason. However, in his business of deconstruction, Derrida does not proceed analytically, in the sense of identifying hidden presuppositions or implications. This is just the way in which each successive generation has critically reviewed the works of the preceding ones. Instead, Derrida proceeds by a critique of style, in that he finds something like indirect communications, by which the text itself denies its manifest content, in the rhetorical surplus of meaning inherent in the literary strata of texts that present themselves as nonliterary. In this way, he compels texts by Husserl, Saussure, or Rousseau to confess their guilt, against the explicit interpretations of their authors. Thanks to their rhetorical content, texts combed against the grain contradict what they state, such as the explicitly asserted primacy of signification over the sign, of the voice in relation to writing, of the intuitively given and immediately present over the representative and the postponed-postponing. In a philosophical text, the blind spot cannot be identified on the level of manifest content any more than it can in a literary text. 'Blindness and insight' are rhetorically interwoven with one another. Thus, the constraints constitutive for knowledge of a philosophical text only become accessible when the text is handled as what it would not like to be – as a literary text.

If, however, the philosophical (or scholarly) text were thereby only *extraneously turned* into an apparently literary one, deconstruction would still be an arbitrary act. Derrida can only attain Heidegger's goal of bursting metaphysical thought-forms from the inside by means of his essentially rhetorical procedure if the philosophical text is *in truth* a literary one – if one can *demonstrate* that the genre distinction between philosophy and literature dissolves upon closer examination. This demonstration is supposed to be carried out by way of deconstruction itself; in every single case we see anew the impossibility of so specializing the language of philosophy and science for cognitive purposes that they are cleaned of everything metaphorical and merely rhetorical, and kept free of literary admixtures. The frailty of the genre distinction between philosophy and literature is evidenced in the practice of deconstruction; in the end, *all* genre distinctions are submerged in one comprehensive, all-embracing context of texts – Derrida talks in a hypostatizing manner about a 'universal text'. What remains is self-inscribing writing as the medium in which each text is woven together with everything else. Even before it makes its appearance, every text and every particular genre has already lost its autonomy to an all-devouring text production. This is the ground of the primacy of rhetoric, which is concerned with the qualities of texts in general, over logic, as a system of rules to which only certain types of discourse are subjected in an exclusive manner – those bound to argumentation.

II

This – at first glance inconspicuous – transformation of the 'destruction' into the 'deconstruction' of the philosophical tradition transposes the radical critique of reason into the domain of rhetoric and thereby shows it a way out of the aporia of self-referentiality: Anyone who still wanted to attribute paradoxes to the critique of metaphysics after this transformation would have misunderstood it in a scientistic manner. This argument holds good only if the following propositions are true:

1. Literary criticism is not primarily a scientific (or scholarly: *wissenschaftliches*) enterprise but observes the same rhetorical criteria as its literary objects.
2. Far from there being a genre distinction between philosophy and literature, philosophical texts can be rendered accessible in their essential contents by literary criticism.
3. The primacy of rhetoric over logic means the overall responsibility of rhetoric for the general qualities of an all-embracing context of texts, within which all genre distinctions are ultimately dissolved; philosophy and science no more constitute their own proper universes than art and literature constitute a realm of fiction that could assert its autonomy vis-à-vis the universal text.

Proposition 3 explicates propositions 2 and 1 by despecializing the meaning of 'literary criticism'. Literary criticism does serve as a model that clarifies itself through a long tradition; but it is considered precisely as a model case of something more universal, namely, a criticism suited to the rhetorical qualities of everyday discourse as well as of discourse outside the everyday. The procedure of deconstruction deploys this generalized criticism to bring to light the suppressed surpluses of rhetorical meaning in philosophical and scientific texts – against their manifest sense. Derrida's claim that 'deconstruction' is an instrument for bringing Nietzsche's radical critique of reason out of the dead end of its paradoxical self-referentiality therefore stands – or falls – with thesis number 3.

Just this thesis has been the centerpoint of the lively reception Derrida's work has enjoyed in the literature faculties of prominent American universities.[2] In the United States, literary criticism has for a long time been institutionalized as an academic discipline, that is, within the scholarly-scientific enterprise. From the very start, the self-tormenting question about the scholarly-scientific character of literary criticism was institutionalized along with it. This endemic self-doubt forms the background for the reception of Derrida, along with the dissolution of the decades-long domination of New Criticism, which was convinced of the autonomy of the literary work of art and drew nourishment from the scientific pathos of structuralism. The idea of 'deconstruction' could catch on in this constellation because it opened up to literary criticism a task of undoubted significance, under exactly the opposite premises: Derrida disputed the autonomy of the linguistic work of art and the independent meaning of the aesthetic illusion no less energetically than he does the possibility of criticism's ever being able to attain scientific status. At the same time, literary criticism serves him as the model for a procedure that takes on an almost world-historical mission with its overcoming of the thinking of the metaphysics of presence and of the age of logocentrism.

The leveling of the genre distinction between literary criticism and literature frees the critical enterprise from the unfortunate compulsion to submit to pseudo-scientific standards; it simultaneously lifts it above science to the level of creative activity. Criticism does not need to consider itself as something secondary; it gains literary status. In the texts of Hillis Miller, Geoffrey Hartman, and Paul de Man we can find the new self-awareness: 'that critics are no more parasites than the texts they interpret, since both inhabit a host-text of pre-existing language which itself parasitically feeds on their host-like willingness to receive it.' Deconstructionists break with the traditional Arnoldian conception of criticism's function as a mere servant: 'Criticism is now crossing over into literature, rejecting its subservient Arnoldian stance and taking on the freedom of interpretive style with a matchless gusto.'[3] Thus, in perhaps his most brilliant book, Paul de Man deals with critical texts by Lukács, Barthes, Blanchot, and Jakobson with a method and finesse that are usually reserved only for literary texts: 'Since they are not scientific, critical texts have to be read with the same awareness of ambivalence that is brought to the study of non-critical texts.'[4]

Just as important as the equation of literary criticism with creative literary production is the increase in significance enjoyed by literary criticism as sharing in the business of the critique of metaphysics. This upgrading to the critique of metaphysics requires a counterbalancing supplement to Derrida's interpretation of the leveling of the genre distinction between philosophy and literature. Jonathan Culler recalls the strategic meaning of Derrida's treatment of philosophical texts through literary criticism in order to suggest that, in turn, literary criticism treat literary texts also as philosophical texts. Simultaneously maintaining and relativizing the distinction between the two genres 'is essential to the demonstration that the most truly philosophical reading of a philosophical text . . . is one that treats the work as literature, as a fictive, rhetorical construct whose elements and order are determined by various textual exigencies.' Then he continues: 'Conversely, the most powerful and opposite readings of literary works may be those that treat them as philosophical gestures by teasing out the implications of their dealings with the philosophical oppositions that support them.'[5]

Proposition 2 is thus varied in the following sense:

> 2′. Far from there being a genre distinction between philosophy and literature, literary texts can be rendered accessible in their essential contents by a critique of metaphysics.

Of course, the two propositions 2 and 2′ point in the direction of the primacy of rhetoric over logic, which is asserted in proposition 3. Consequently, American literary critics are concerned to develop a concept of *general* literature, equal in overall scope to rhetoric, which would correspond to Derrida's 'universal text'. The notion of literature as confined to the realm of the fictive is deconstructed at the same time as the conventional notion of philosophy that denies the metaphorical basis of philosophical thought: 'The notion of literature of literary discourse is involved in several of the hierarchical oppositions on which deconstruction has focussed: serious/non-serious, literal/metaphorical, truth/fiction.... Deconstruction's demonstration that these hierarchies are undone by the working of the texts that propose them alters the standing of literary language.' There now follows, in the form of a conditional statement, the thesis on which everything depends – both the self-understanding of a literary criticism upgraded to the critique of metaphysics and the deconstructionist dissolution of the performative contradiction of a self-referential critique of reason: 'If serious language is a special case of non-serious, if truths are fictions whose fictionality has been forgotten, then literature is not a deviant, parasitical instance of language. On the contrary, other discourses can be seen as cases of a generalized literature, or archi-literature.'[6] Since Derrida does not belong to those philosophers who like to argue, it is expedient to take a closer look at his disciples in literary criticism within the Anglo-Saxon climate of argument in order to see whether this thesis really can be held.

Jonathan Culler reconstructs in a very clear way the somewhat impenetrable discussion between Derrida and Searle in order to show by the example of Austin's speech-act theory that any attempt to demarcate the ordinary domain of normal speech from an 'unusual' use of language, 'deviating' from the standard cases, is doomed to failure. Culler's thesis is expanded and indirectly confirmed in a study of speech-act theory by Mary Louise Pratt, who wants to prove, by the example of the structuralist theory of poetics, that even the attempt to delimit the extraordinary domain of fictive discourse from everyday discourse fails (see section III below). But first let us take a look at the debate between Derrida and Searle.[7]

From this complex discussion, Culler selects as the central issue the question of whether Austin does in fact, as it seems he does, make a totally unprejudiced, provisory, and purely methodical move. Austin wants to analyze the rules intuitively mastered by competent speakers, in accordance with which typical speech acts can be successfully executed. He undertakes this analysis with respect to sentences from *normal* everyday practice that are uttered *seriously* and used as *simply* and *literally* as possible. Thus, the unit of analysis, the standard speech act, is the result of certain abstractions. The theoretician of speech acts directs his attention to a sample of normal linguistic utterances from which all complex, derivative, parasitic, and deviant cases have been filtered out. A concept of 'usual' and normal linguistic practice underpins this isolation, a concept of 'ordinary language' whose harmlessness and consistency Derrida puts in doubt. Austin's intention is clear: He wants to analyze the universal properties of 'promises', for example, with respect to cases in which the utterance of corresponding sentences actually *functions* as a promise. Now there are contexts in which the same sentences lose the illocutionary force of a promise. Spoken by an actor on the stage, as part of a poem, or even in a monologue, a promise, according to Austin, becomes 'null and void in a unique manner'. The same holds true for a promise that comes up in a quotation, or one merely mentioned. In these contexts, there is no *serious* or *binding* use, and sometimes not even a *literal* use, of the respective performative sentence, but a derivative or parasitic use instead. As Searle constantly repeats, these fictive or simulated or indirect modes of use are 'parasitic' in the sense that logically they presuppose the possibility of a serious, literal, and binding use of sentences grammatically appropriate for making promises. Culler extracts what are in essence three objections from Derrida's texts; they point toward the impossibility of such an operation and are meant to show that the common distinctions between serious and simulated, literal and metaphorical, everyday and fictional, usual and parasitic modes of speech break down.

(a) In his initial argument, Derrida posits a not very clear link between quotability and repeatability on the one hand, and fictionality on the other. The quotation of a promise is only apparently something secondary in comparison to the directly made promise, for the indirect rendition of a performative utterance in a quote is a form of repetition, and as quotability presupposes the possibility of repetition in accord with a rule, that is, conventionality, it belongs to the nature of any conventionally generated utterance (including performative ones) that it can be quoted – and fictively imitated, in a broader sense: 'If it were not possible for a character in a play to make a promise, there could be no promise in real life, for what makes it possible to promise, as Austin tells us, is the existence of a conventional procedure, of formulas one can repeat. For me to be able to make a promise in real life, there must be iterable procedures or formulas such as are used on stage. Serious behavior is a case of role-playing.'[8]

In this argument, Derrida obviously already presupposes what he wants to prove: that any convention which permits the repetition of exemplary actions possesses from the outset not only a symbolic, but also a fictional character. But it must first be shown that the conventions of a game are ultimately indistinguishable from norms of action. Austin introduces the quotation of a promise as an example of a derivative or parasitic form because the illocutionary force is removed from the quoted promise by the form of indirect rendition; it is thereby taken out of the context of which it 'functions', that is, in which it coordinates the actions of the different participants in interaction and has consequences relevant to action. Only the actually performed speech act is *effective as action*; the promise mentioned or reported in a quote depends grammatically upon this. A setting that deprives it of its illocutionary force constitutes the bridge between quotation and fictional representation. Even action on the stage rests on a basis of everyday action (on the part of the actors, director, stage-workers, and theater people); and in the context of this framework, promises can function *in another mode* than they do 'on stage', that is, with obligations and consequences relevant for action. Derrida makes no attempt to 'deconstruct' this distinctive functional mode of ordinary speech within communicative action. In the illocutionary binding force of linguistic utterances Austin discovered a mechanism for coordinating action that places normal speech, as part of everyday practice, under constraints different from those of fictional discourse, simulation, and interior monologue. The constraints under which illocutionary acts develop a force for coordinating action and have consequences relevant to action define the domain of 'normal' language. They can be analyzed as the kinds of idealizing suppositions we have to make in communicative actions.

(b) The second argument brought forward by Culler, with Derrida, against Austin and Searle relates to just such idealizations. Any generalizing analysis of speech acts has to be able to specify general contextual conditions for the illocutionary success of standardized speech acts. Searle has been especially occupied with this task.[9] Linguistic expressions, however, change their meanings depending on shifting contexts; moreover, contexts are so constituted as to be open to ever wider-reaching specification. It is one of the peculiarities of our language that we can separate utterances from their original contexts and transplant them into different ones – Derrida speaks of 'grafting'. In this manner, we can think of a speech act, such as a 'marriage vow', in ever new and more improbable contexts; the specification of universal contextual conditions does not run into any natural limits: 'Suppose that the requirements for a marriage ceremony were met but that one of the parties were under hypnosis, or that the ceremony were impeccable in all respects but had been called a "rehearsal", or finally, that while the speaker was a minister licensed to perform weddings and the couple had obtained a license, that three of them were on this occasion acting in a play that, coincidentally, included a wedding ceremony.'[10] These variations of context that change meaning cannot in principle be arrested or controlled, because contexts cannot be exhausted, that is, they cannot be theoretically mastered once and for all. Culler shows clearly that Austin cannot escape this difficulty by taking refuge in the intentions of speakers and listeners. It is not the thoughts of bride, bridegroom, or priest that decide the validity of the ceremony, but their actions and the circumstances under which they are carried out: 'What counts is the plausibility of the description: whether or not the features of the context adduced create a frame that alters the illocutionary force of utterances.'[11]

Searle reacted to this difficulty by introducing a qualification to the effect that the literal meaning of a sentence does not completely fix the validity conditions of the speech act in which it is employed; it depends, rather, on tacit supplementation by a system of background assumptions regarding the normality of general world conditions. These parareflective background certainties have a holistic nature; they cannot be exhausted by a countably finite set of specifications. Meanings of sentences, however well analyzed, are thus valid only relative to a shared background knowledge that is constitutive of the lifeworld of a linguistic community. But Searle makes clear that the addition of this relational moment does not bring with it the relativism of meaning that Derrida is after. As long as language games are functioning and the preunderstanding constitutive of the lifeworld has not broken down, participants rightly count on world conditions being what is understood in their linguistic community as 'normal'. And in cases where individual background convictions do become problematic, they assume that they could reach a rationally motivated agreement. Both are strong, that is to say idealizing, suppositions; but these idealizations are not arbitrary, logocentric acts brought to bear by theoreticians on unmanageable contexts in order to give the illusion of mastery; rather, they are presuppositions that the participants themselves have to make if communicative action is to be at all possible.

(c) The role of idealizing suppositions can also be clarified in connection with some other consequences of this same state of affairs. Because contexts are changeable and can be expanded in any desired direction, the same text can be open to different readings; it is the text itself that makes possible its uncontrollable effective history. Still, Derrida's purposely paradoxical statement that any interpretation is inevitably a false interpretation, and any understanding a misunderstanding, does not follow from this venerable hermeneutic insight. Culler justifies the statement 'Every reading is a misreading' as follows: 'If a text can be understood, it can in principle be understood repeatedly, by different readers in different circumstances. These acts of reading or understanding are not, of course, identical. They involve modifications and differences, but differences which are deemed not to matter. We can thus say that understanding is a special case of misunderstanding, a particular deviation or determination of misunderstanding. It is a misunderstanding whose misses do not matter.'[12] Yet Culler leaves one thing out of consideration. The productivity of the process of understanding remains unproblematic only so long as all participants stick to the reference point of possibly achieving a mutual understanding in which the *same* utterances are assigned the same meaning. As Gadamer has shown, the hermeneutic effort that would bridge over temporal and cultural distances remains oriented toward the idea of a possible consensus being brought about in the present.

Under the pressure for decisions proper to the communicative practice of everyday life, participants are dependent upon agreements that coordinate their actions. The more removed interpretations are from the 'seriousness of this type of situation', the more they can prescind from the idealizing supposition of an achievable consensus. But they can never be wholly absolved of the idea that wrong interpretations must in principle be criticizable in terms of consensus to be aimed for ideally. The interpreter does not impose this idea on his object; rather, with the performative attitude of a participant observer, he takes it over from the direct participants, *who can act communicatively only under the presupposition of intersubjectively identical ascriptions of meaning*. I do not mean to marshal a Wittgensteinian positivism of language games against Derrida's thesis. It is not habitual linguistic practice that determines just what meaning is attributed to a text or an utterance.[13] Rather, language games only work because they presuppose idealizations that transcend any particular language game; as a necessary condition of possibly reaching understanding, these idealizations give rise to the perspective of an agreement that is open to criticism on the basis of validity claims. A language operating under these kinds of constraints is subject to an ongoing test. Everyday communicative practice, in which agents have to reach an understanding about something in the world, stands under the need to prove its worth, and it is the idealizing suppositions that make such testing possible in the first place. It is in relation to this need for standing the test within ordinary practice that one may distinguish, with Austin and Searle, between 'usual' and 'parasitic' uses of language.

III

Up to this point, I have criticized Derrida's third and fundamental assumption only to the extent that (against Culler's reconstruction of Derrida's arguments) I have defended the possibility of demarcating normal speech from *derivative* forms. I have not yet shown how fictional discourse can be separated from the normal (everyday) use of language. This aspect is the most important for Derrida. If 'literature' and 'writing' constitute the model for a universal context of texts, which cannot be surpassed and within which all genre distinctions are ultimately dissolved, they cannot be separated from other discourses as an autonomous realm of fiction. For the literary critics who follow Derrida in the United States, the thesis of the autonomy of the linguistic work of art is, as I mentioned, also unacceptable, because they want to set themselves off from the formalism of the New Criticism and from structuralist aesthetics.

The Prague Structuralists originally tried to distinguish poetic from ordinary language in view of their relations to extralinguistic reality. Insofar as language occurs in *communicative functions*, it has to produce relations between linguistic expression and speaker, hearer, and the state of affairs represented. Bühler articulated this in his semiotic scheme as the sign-functions of expression, appeal, and representation.[14] However, when language fulfills a poetic function, it does so in virtue of a reflexive relation to the linguistic expression itself. Consequently, reference to an object, informational content, and truth-value – conditions of validity in general – are extrinsic to poetic speech; an utterance can be poetic to the extent that it is directed to the linguistic medium itself, to its own linguistic form. Roman Jakobson integrated this characterization into an expanded scheme of functions; in addition to the basic functions – expressing the speaker's intentions, establishing interpersonal relations, and representing states of affairs – which go back to Bühler, and two more functions related to making contact and to the code, he ascribes to linguistic utterances a poetic function, which directs our attention to 'the message as such'.[15] We are less concerned here with a closer characterization of the poetic function (in accord with which the principle of equivalence is projected from the axis of selection to the axis of combination) than with an interesting consequence that is important for our problem of delimiting normal from other instances of speech: 'Any attempt to reduce the sphere of the poetic function would be a deceptive oversimplification. The poetic function is not the only function of verbal artistry, merely a *predominant* and *structurally determinative* one, whereas in all other linguistic activities it plays a subordinate and supplementary role. Inasmuch as it *directs our attention to the sign's perceptibility*, this function deepens the fundamental dichotomy between signs and objects. For this reason, linguistics should not, when it studies the poetic function, restrict itself solely to the field of poetry.'[16] Poetic speech, therefore, is to be distinguished only in virtue of the primacy and structure-forming force of a certain function that is always fulfilled together with other linguistic functions.

Richard Ohmann makes use of Austin's approach to specify poetic language in this sense. For him, the phenomenon in need of clarification is the fictionality of the linguistic work of art, that is, the generation of aesthetic illusion by which a second, specifically de-realized arena is opened up on the basis of a continued everyday practice. What distinguishes poetic language is its 'world-generating' capacity: 'A literary work creates a world . . . by providing the reader with *impaired* and incomplete speech acts which he completes by supplying the appropriate circumstances.'[17] The unique *impairment* of speech acts that generates fictions arises when they are robbed of their illocutionary force, or maintain their illocutionary meanings only as in the refraction of indirect repetition or quotation: 'A literary work is a discourse whose sentences lack the illocutionary forces that would normally attach to them. Its illocutionary force is mimetic. . . . Specifically, a literary work purportedly imitates a series of speech acts, which in fact have no other existence. By doing so, it leads the reader to imagine a speaker, a situation, a set of ancillary events, and so on.'[18] The bracketing of illocutionary force virtualizes the relations to the world in which the speech acts are involved due to their illocutionary force, and releases the participants in interaction from reaching agreement about something in the world on the basis of idealizing understandings in such a way that they coordinate their plans of action and thus enter into obligations relevant to the outcomes of action: 'Since the quasi-speech acts of literature are not *carrying on the world's business* – describing, urging, contracting, etc. – the reader may well attend to them in a non-pragmatic way.'[19] Neutralizing their binding force releases the disempowered illocutionary acts from the pressure to decide proper to everyday communicative practice, removes them from the sphere of usual discourse, and thereby empowers them for the playful creation of new worlds – or, rather, for the pure demonstration of the world-disclosing force of innovative linguistic expressions. This specialization in the world-disclosive function of speech explains the unique self-reflexivity of poetic language to which Jakobson refers and which leads Geoffrey Hartman to pose the rhetorical question: 'Is not literary language the name we give to a diction whose frame of reference is such that the words stand out as words (even as sounds) rather than being, at once, assimilable meanings?'[20]

Mary L. Pratt makes use of Ohmann's studies[21] to refute, by means of speech-act theory, the thesis of the independence of the literary work in Derrida's sense. She does not consider fictionality, the bracketing of illocutionary force, and the disengagement of poetic language from everyday communicative practice to be adequate selective criteria, because fictional speech elements such as jokes, irony, wish-fantasies, stories, and parables pervade our everyday discourse and by no means constitute an autonomous universe apart from 'the world's business'. Conversely, non-fiction works, memoirs, travel reports, historical romances, even *romans à clef* or thrillers that, like Truman Capote's *In Cold Blood*, adapt a factually documented case, by no means create an unambiguously fictional world, even though we often relegate these productions, for the most part at least, to 'literature'. Pratt uses the results of studies in sociolinguistics by W. Labov[22] to prove that natural narratives, that is, the 'stories' told spontaneously or upon request in everyday life, follow the same rhetorical laws of construction and exhibit structural characteristics similar to literary narratives: 'Labov's data make it necessary to account for narrative rhetoric in terms that are not exclusively literary; the fact that fictive or mimetically organized utterances can occur in almost any realm of extraliterary discourse requires that we do the same for fictivity or mimesis. In other words, the relation between a work's ficitivity and its literariness is indirect.'[23]

Nonetheless, the fact that normal language is permeated with fictional, narrative, metaphorical, and, in general, with rhetorical elements does not yet speak against the attempt to explain the autonomy of the linguistic work of art by the bracketing of illocutionary forces, for, according to Jakobson, the mark of fictionality is suited for demarcating literature form everyday discourses only to the degree that the world-disclosing function of language predominates over the other linguistic functions and determines the structure of the linguistic artifact. In a certain respect, it is the refraction and partial elimination of illocutionary validity claims that distinguishes the story from the statement of the eyewitness, teasing from insulting, being ironic from misleading, the hypothesis from the assertion, wish-fantasy from perception, a training maneuver from an act of warfare, and a scenario from a report of an actual catastrophe. But in none of these cases do the illocutionary acts lose their binding force for coordinating action. Even in the cases adduced for the sake of comparison, the communicative functions of the speech acts remain intact insofar as the fictive elements cannot be separated from contexts of life practice. The world-disclosive function of language does not gain independence over against the expressive, regulative, and informative functions. By contrast, in Truman Capote's literary elaboration of a notorious and carefully researched incident, precisely this may be the case. That is to say, what grounds the *primacy* and the structuring force of the poetic function is not the deviation of a fictional representation from the documentary report of an incident, but the exemplary elaboration that takes the case out of its context and makes it the occasion for an innovative, world-disclosive, and eye-opening representation in which the rhetorical means of representation depart from communicative routines and take on a life of their own.

It is interesting to see how Pratt is compelled to work out this poetic function against her will. Her sociolinguistic counterproposal begins with the analysis of a speech situation that poetic discourse shares with other discourses – the kind of arrangement in which a narrator or lecturer turns to a public and calls its attention to a text. The text undergoes certain procedures of preparation and selection before it is ready for delivery. Before a text can lay claim to the patience and discretion of the audience, it has also to satisfy certain criteria of relevance: it *has to be worth telling*. The tellability is to be assessed in terms of the manifestation of some significant exemplary experience. In its content, a tellable text reaches beyond the local context of the immediate speech situation and is open to further elaboration: 'As might be expected, these two features – contextual detachability and susceptibility to elaboration – are equally important characteristics of literature.' Of course, literary texts share these characteristics with 'display texts' in general. The latter are characterized by their special communicative functions: 'They are designed to serve a purpose I have described as that of verbally representing states of affairs and experiences which are held to be *unusual* or *problematic* in such a way that the addressee will respond affectively in the intended way, adopt the intended evaluation and interpretation, take pleasure in doing so, and *generally find the whole undertaking worth it*.'[24] One sees how the pragmatic linguistic analyst creeps up on literary texts from outside, as it were. The latter have still to satisfy a final condition; in the case of literary texts, tellability must gain a preponderance over other functional characteristics: 'In the end, tellability can take precedence over assertability itself.'[25] Only in this case do the functional demands and structural constraints of everyday communicative practice (which Pratt defines by means of Grice's conversation postulates) lose their force. The concern to give one's contribution an informative shape, to say what is relevant, to be straightforward and to avoid obscure, ambiguous, and prolix utterances are idealizing presuppositions of the communicative action of *normal speech*, but not of poetic discourse: 'Our tolerance, indeed propensity, for elaboration when dealing with the tellable suggests that, in Gricean terms, the standards of quantity, quality and manner for display texts differ from those Grice suggests for declarative speech in his maxims.'

In the end, the analysis leads to a confirmation of the thesis it would like to refute. To the degree that the poetic, world-disclosing function of language gains primacy and structuring force, language escapes the structural constraints and communicative functions of everyday life. The space of fiction that is opened up when linguistic forms of expression become reflexive results from suspending illocutionary binding forces and those idealizations that make possible a use of language oriented toward mutual understanding – and hence make possible a coordination of plans of action that operates via the intersubjective recognition of criticizable validity claims. One can read Derrida's debate with Austin also as a denial of this independently structured domain of everyday communicative practice; it corresponds to the denial of an autonomous realm of fiction.

IV

Because Derrida denies both, he can analyze any given discourse in accord with the model of poetic language, and do so as if language generally were determined by the poetic use of language specialized in world-disclosure. From this viewpoint, language as such converges with literature or indeed with 'writing'. This *aestheticizing of language, which is purchased with the twofold denial of the proper senses of normal and poetic discourse*, also explains Derrida's insensitivity toward the tension-filled polarity between the poetic-world-disclosive function of language and its prosaic, innerworldly functions, which a modified version of Bühler's functional scheme takes into consideration.[26]

Linguistically mediated processes such as the acquisition of knowledge, the transmission of culture, the formation of personal identity, and socialization and social integration involve mastering problems posed by the world; the independence of learning processes within the world are embedded in a *world-constituting* context that prejudices everything; they are fatalistically delivered up to the unmanageable happening of text production, overwhelmed by the poetic-creative transformation of a background designed by archewriting, and condemned to be provincial. An aesthetic contextualism blinds him to the fact that everyday communicative practice makes learning processes possible (thanks to built-in idealization) in relation to which the world-disclosive force of interpreting language has in turn to prove its worth. These learning processes unfold an independent logic that transcends all local constraints, because experiences and judgments are formed only in light of criticizable validity claims. Derrida neglects the potential for negation inherent in the validity basis of action oriented toward reaching understanding; he permits the capacity to solve problems to disappear behind the world-creating capacity of language; the former capacity is possessed by language as the medium through which those acting communicatively get involved in relations to the world whenever they agree with one another about something in the objective world, in their common social world, or in the subjective worlds to which each has privileged access.

Richard Rorty proposes a similar leveling; unlike Derrida, however, he does not remain idealistically fixated upon the history of metaphysics as a transcendent happening that determines everything intramundane. According to Rorty, science and morality, economics and politics, are delivered up to a process of language-creating protuberances *in just the same way* as art and philosophy. Like Kuhnian history of science, the flux of interpretations beats rhythmically between revolutions and normalizations of language. He observes this back-and-forth between two situations in all fields of cultural life: 'One is the sort of situation encountered when people pretty much agree on what is wanted, and are talking about how best to get it. In such a situation there is no need to say anything terribly unfamiliar, for argument is typically about the truth of assertions rather than about the utility of vocabularies. The contrasting situation is one in which everything is up for grabs at once – in which the motives and terms of discussions are a central subject of argument. . . . In such periods people begin to toss around old words in new sense, to throw in the occasional neologism, and thus to hammer out a new idiom which initially attracts attention to itself and only later gets put to work.'[27] One notices how the Nietzschean pathos of a *Lebensphilosophie* that has made the linguistic turn beclouds the sober insights of pragmatism; in the picture painted by Rorty, the renovative process of linguistic world-disclosure no longer has a *counterpoise* in the testing processes of intramundane practice. The 'Yes' and 'No' of communicatively acting agents is so prejudiced and rhetorically overdetermined by their linguistic contexts that the anomalies that start to arise during the phases of exhaustion are taken to represent only symptoms of waning vitality, or aging processes analogous to processes of nature – and are not seen as the result of *deficient* solutions to problems and *invalid* answers.

Intramundane linguistic practice draws its power of negation from validity claims that go beyond the horizons of any currently given context. But the contextualist concept of language, laden as it is with *Lebensphilosophie*, is impervious to the very real force of the counterfactual, which makes itself felt in the idealizing presuppositions of communicative action. Hence Derrida and Rorty are also mistaken about the unique status of discourses differentiated from ordinary communication and tailored to a single validity dimension (truth or normative rightness), or to a single complex of problems (questions of truth or justice). In modern societies, the spheres of science, morality, and law have crystallized around these forms of argumentation. The corresponding cultural systems of action administer *problem-solving capacities* in a way similar to that in which the enterprises of art and literature administer *capacities for world-disclosure*. Because Derrida overgeneralizes this one linguistic function – namely, the poetic – he can no longer see the complex relationship of the ordinary practice of normal speech to the two extraordinary spheres, differentiated, as it were, in opposite directions. The polar tension between world-disclosure and problem-solving is held together within the functional matrix of ordinary language; but art and literature on the one side, and science, morality, and law on the other, are specialized for experiences and modes of knowledge that can be shaped and worked out within the compass of *one* linguistic function and *one* dimension of validity at a time. Derrida holistically levels these complicated relationships in order to equate philosophy with literature and criticism. He fails to recognize the special status that both philosophy and literary criticism, each in its own way, assume as mediators between expert cultures and the everyday world.

Literary criticism, institutionalized in Europe since the eighteenth century, has contributed to the differentiation of art. It has responded to the increasing autonomy of linguistic works of art by means of a discourse specialized for questions of taste. In it, the claims with which literary texts appear are submitted to examination – claims to 'artistic truth', aesthetic harmony, exemplary validity, innovative force, and authenticity. In this respect, aesthetic criticism is similar to argumentative forms specialized for prepositional truth and the rightness of norms, that is, to theoretical and practical discourse. It is, however, not merely an esoteric component of expert culture but, beyond this, has the job of mediating between expert culture and everyday world.

This *bridging function* of art criticism is more obvious in the case of music and the plastic arts than in that of literary works, which are already formulated in the medium of language, even if it is a poetic, self-referential language. From this second, exoteric standpoint, criticism performs a translating activity of a unique kind. It brings the experiential content of the work of art into normal language; the innovative potential of art and literature for the lifeworlds and life histories that reproduce themselves through everyday communicative practice can only be unleashed in this maieutic way. This is then deposited in the changed configuration of the evaluative vocabulary, in a renovation of value orientations and need interpretations, which alters the color of modes of life by way of altering modes of perception.

Philosophy also occupies a position with two fronts similar to that of literary criticism – or at least this is true of modern philosophy, which no longer promises to redeem the claims of religion in the name of theory. On the one hand, it directs its interest to the foundations of science, morality, and law and attaches theoretical claims to its statements. Characterized by universalist problematics and strong theoretical strategies, it maintains an intimate relationship with the sciences. And yet philosophy is not simply an esoteric component of an expert culture. It maintains just as intimate a relationship with the totality of the lifeworld and with sound common sense, even if in a subversive way it relentlessly shakes up the certainties of everyday practice. Philosophical thinking represents the lifeworld's interest in the whole complex of functions and structures connected and combined in communicative action, and it does so in the face of knowledge systems differentiated out in accord with particular dimensions of validity. Of course, it maintains this relationship to totality with a reflectiveness lacking in the intuitively present background proper to the lifeworld.

If one takes into consideration the two-front position of criticism and philosophy that I have only sketched here – toward the everyday world on the one side, and on the other toward the specialized cultures of art and literature, science and morality – it becomes clear what the leveling of the genre distinction between philosophy and literature, and the assimilation of philosophy to literature and of literature to philosophy, as affirmed in propositions 2 and 2′, mean. This leveling and this assimilation confusedly jumble the constellations in which the rhetorical elements of language assume *entirely different* roles. The rhetorical element occurs in its *pure form* only in the self-referentiality of the poetic expression, that is, in the language of fiction specialized for world-disclosure. Even the normal language of everyday life is ineradicably rhetorical; but within the matrix of different linguistic functions, the rhetorical elements recede here. The world-disclosive linguistic framework is almost at a standstill in the routines of everyday practice. The same holds true of the specialized languages of science and technology, law and morality, economics, political science, etc. They, too, live off of the illuminating power of metaphorical tropes; but the rhetorical elements, which are by no means expunged, are tamed, as it were, and enlisted for special purposes of problem-solving.

The rhetorical dimension plays a different and far more important role in the language of literary criticism and philosophy. They are both faced with tasks that are paradoxical in similar ways. They are supposed to feed the contents of expert cultures, in which knowledge is accumulated under one aspect of validity at a time, into an everyday practice in which all linguistic functions and aspects of validity are intermeshed to form one syndrome. And yet literary criticism and philosophy are supposed to accomplish this task of mediation with means of expression taken from languages specialized in questions of taste or of truth. They can only resolve this paradox by rhetorically expanding and enriching their special languages to the extent that is required to link up indirect communications with the manifest contents of statements, and to do so in a deliberate way. That explains the strong rhetorical strain characteristic of studies by literary critics and philosophers alike. Significant critics and great philosophers are also noted writers. Literary criticism and philosophy have a family resemblance to literature – and to this extent to one another as well – in their rhetorical achievements. But their family relationship stops right there, for in each of these enterprises the tools of rhetoric are subordinated to the discipline of a *distinct* form of argumentation.

If, following Derrida's recommendation, philosophical thinking were to be relieved of the duty of solving problems and shifted over to the function of literary criticism, it would be robbed not merely of its seriousness, but of its productivity. Conversely, the literary-critical power of judgment loses its potency when, as is happening among Derrida's disciples in literature departments, it gets displaced from appropriating aesthetic experiential contents into the critique of metaphysics. The false assimilation of one enterprise to the other robs both of their substance. And so we return to the issue with which we started. Whoever transposes the radical critique of reason into the domain of rhetoric in order to blunt the paradox of self-referentiality, also dulls the sword of the critique of reason itself. The false pretense of eliminating the genre distinction between philosophy and literature cannot lead us out of this aporia.[28]

Notes

1. H. Schnädelbach, 'Dialektik als Vernunftkritik,' in L. von Friedeburg and J. Habermas, eds, *Adorno-Konferenz 1983* (Frankfurt, 1983), pp. 66ff.
2. This is especially true of the Yale Critics, Paul de Man, Geoffrey Hartman, J. Hillis Miller, and Harold Bloom. See J. Arac, W. Godzich, and W. Martin, eds, *The Yale Critics: Deconstruction in America* (Minneapolis, 1983). In addition to Yale, important centers of deconstructionism are located at Johns Hopkins and Cornell universities.
3. Christopher Norris, *Deconstruction: Theory and practice* (New York and London, 1982), pp. 93, 98.
4. Paul de Man, *Blindness and Insight*, 2d ed. (Minneapolis, 1983), p. 110.
5. Jonathan Culler, *On Deconstruction* (London, 1983), p. 150.
6. Ibid., p. 181.
7. In his essay 'Signature Event Context,' in *Margins of Philosophy* (Chicago, 1982), pp. 307–330, Derrida devotes the last section to a discussion of Austin's theory. Searle refers to this in 'Reiterating the Differences: A Reply to Derrida,' *Glyph* 1 (1977): 198ff. Derrida's response appeared in *Glyph* 12 (1977): 202ff. under the title 'Limited Inc.'
8. Culler, *On Deconstruction*, p. 119.

9. John Searle, *Speech Acts* (Cambridge, 1969), and *Expression and Meaning* (Cambridge, 1979).
10. Culler, *On Deconstruction*, pp. 121ff.
11. Ibid., p. 123.
12. Ibid., p. 176.
13. Compare ibid., pp. 130ff.
14. Karl Bühler, *Semiotic Foundations of Language Theory* (New York, 1982).
15. Roman Jakobson, 'Linguistics and Poetics,' in Thomas A. Sebeok, editor, *Style in Language* (Cambridge, MA, 1960), pp. 350–358.
16. Ibid.
17. R. Ohmann, 'Speech-Acts and the Definition of Literature,' *Philosophy and Rhetoric* 4 (1971): 17.
18. Ibid., p. 14.
19. Ibid., p. 17.
20. Geoffrey Hartman, *Saving the Text* (Baltimore, 1981), p. xxi.
21. See also 'Speech, Literature, and the Space between,' *New Literary History* 5 (1974): 34ff.
22. William Labov, *Language in the Inner City* (Philadelphia, 1972).
23. Mary Louise Pratt, *A Speech-Act Theory of Literary Discourse* (Bloomington, 1977), p. 92; I am grateful to Jonathan Culler for his reference to this interesting book.
24. Ibid., p. 148.
25. Ibid., p. 147.
26. See Jürgen Habermas, *Theory of Communicative Action*, volume 1 (Boston, 1984), pp. 273ff.
27. Richard Rorty, 'Deconstruction and Circumvention' (manuscript, 1983) [Editor's note: Subsequently published in Richard Rorty, *Essays on Heidegger and Others: Philosophical Papers Volume* 2 (Cambridge: Cambridge University Press, 1991), pp. 85–106]; and *Consequences of Pragmatism* (Minneapolis, 1982), especially the introduction and chapters 6, 7 and 9.
28. Our reflections have brought us to a point from which we can see why Heidegger, Adorno, and Derrida get into this aporia at all. They all still defend themselves as if they were living in the shadow of the 'last' philosopher, as did the first generation of Hegelian disciples. They are still battling against the 'strong' concepts of theory, truth, and system that have actually belonged to the past for over a century and a half. They still think they have to arouse philosophy from what Derrida calls 'the dream of its heart.' They believe they have to tear philosophy away from the madness of expounding a theory that has the last word. Such a comprehensive, closed, and definitive system of propositions would have to be formulated in a language that is self-explanatory, that neither needs nor permits commentary, and thus that brings to a standstill the effective history in which interpretations are heaped upon interpretations without end. In this connection, Rorty speaks about the demand for a language 'which can receive no gloss, requires no interpretation, cannot be distanced, cannot be sneered at by later generations. It is the hope for a vocabulary which is intrinsically and self-evidently final, not only the most comprehensive and fruitful vocabulary we have come up with so far' (Rorty, *Consequences of Pragmatism*, pp. 93ff.).

    If reason were bound, under penalty of demise, to hold on to these goals of metaphysics classically pursued from Parmenides to Hegel, if reason as such (even after Hegel) stood before the alternative of either maintaining the strong concepts of theory, truth, and system that were common in the great tradition or of throwing in the sponge, then an *adequate* critique of reason would really have to grasp the roots at such a depth that it could scarcely avoid the paradoxes of self-referentiality. Nietzsche viewed the matter in this way. And, unfortunately, Heidegger, Adorno, and Derrida all still seem to confuse the universalist *problematics still maintained* in philosophy with the long since *abandoned status claims* that philosophy once alleged its answers to have. Today, however, it is clear that the scope of universalist questions – for instance, questions of the necessary conditions for the rationality of utterances, or of the universal pragmatic presuppositions of communicative action and argumentation – does indeed have to be reflected in the grammatical form of universal propositions – but not in any unconditional validity or 'ultimate foundations' claimed for themselves or their theoretical framework. The fallibilist consciousness of the sciences caught up with philosophy, too, a long time ago.

With this kind of fallibilism, we, philosophers and nonphilosophers alike, do not by any means eschew truth claims. Such claims cannot be raised in the performative attitude of the first person other than as transcending space and time – precisely as claims. But we are also aware that there is no zero-context for truth claims. They are raised here and now and are open to criticism. Hence we reckon upon the trivial *possibility* that they will be revised tomorrow or someplace else. Just as it always has, philosophy understands itself as the defender of rationality in the sense of the claim of reason endogenous to our form of life. In its work, however, it prefers a combination of strong propositions with weak status claims; so little is this totalitarian, that there is no call for a totalizing critique of reason against it. On this point, see my 'Die Philosophie als Platzhalter und Interpret', in *Moralbewusstsein und kommunikatives Handeln* (Frankfurt, 1983), pp. 7ff. (English translation forthcoming) [Editor's note: Subsequently published as 'Philosophy as Stand-In and Interpreter', in Jürgen Habermas, *Moral Consciousness and Communicative Action*, trans. Christian Lenhardt and Shierry Weber Nicholson (Cambridge, Mass.: MIT Press, 1990), pp. 1–20].

2

Jacques Derrida

IS THERE A PHILOSOPHICAL LANGUAGE?

In this interview, Derrida addresses the accusations Habermas launched in the previous chapter. Derrida claims that Habermas has not really read him and that he misrepresents his work. With regard to the distinction between philosophy and literature, Derrida makes three points. First, he argues that he does not confuse philosophy and literature. Second, he points out that the distinction between the two is conventional rather than natural, and that there are elements of what is usually called literature in what is usually called philosophy, and vice versa. Finally, he argues that there is no single or unitary philosophical tradition. Historically, philosophy has even been divided over what philosophy is. This is the reason why Derrida examines non-canonical texts from the philosophical tradition, thereby putting the latter's unity into question.

Derrida is not only interested in the limits of distinctions or what he refers to as their conditions of impossibility; he is also interested in what makes them possible. Hence, he is not seeking to do away with distinctions, but to examine the way they have been constructed historically. In the case of the distinction between philosophy and literature, Derrida asks whether the question 'what is philosophy?' is itself philosophical. He argues that the identity of that question itself is undecidable, because we can only decide it as philosophical (or non-philosophical) if we already know the answer to the question; yet, that would render the question pointless in the first place. Insofar as the philosophical tradition has asked what philosophy is, there is a part of philosophy that is undecidable as either philosophical or non-philosophical, namely the question 'what is philosophy?'

Q.: You have suggested several times that the philosophical text should be taken as is, before moving beyond it toward the thinking that directs it. You have in this way been led to read philosophical texts with the same eye as you read texts generally considered to be 'literary', and to take up again these latter texts from within a philosophical problematic. Is there a specifically philosophic writing, and in what way is it distinct from other forms of writing? Does not the concern with literality distract us from the demonstrative function of philosophic discourse? Do we not risk in this way effacing the specificity of the genres, and measuring all texts on the same scale?

J. D.: All texts are different. One must try never to measure them 'on the same scale'. And never to read them 'with the same eye'. Each text calls for, so to speak, another 'eye'. Doubtless, to a certain extent, it also responds to a coded, determined expectation, to an eye and to an ear that precede it and dictate it, in some way, or that orient it. But for certain rare texts, the writing also tends, one might say, to trace the structure and the physiology of an eye that does not yet exist and to which the event of the text destines itself, for which it sometimes invents its destination no less than it regulates itself by that destination. To whom is a text addressed? Just how far can this be determined, on the side of the 'author' or on the side of the 'readers'? Why is it that a certain 'play' remains irreducible and even indispensable in this very determination? These questions are also historical, social, institutional, political.

To restrict myself to the *types* you evoke, I have never assimilated so-called philosophical text to a so-called literary text. The two types seem to me irreducibly different. And yet one must realize that the limits between the two are more complex (for example, I don't believe they are *genres*, as you suggest) and especially that these limits are less natural, ahistorical, or given than people say or think. The two types can be interwoven in a same corpus according to laws and forms that it is not only interesting and novel to study but indispensable if one wants to continue to refer to the identity of something like a 'philosophic discourse' while having some idea what one is talking about. Must one not be interested in the conventions, the institutions, the interpretations that produce or maintain this apparatus of limitations, with all the norms and thus all the exclusions they imply? One cannot approach this set of questions without asking oneself at some moment or other: 'What is philosophy?' and 'What is literature?' More difficult and more wide open than ever, these questions in themselves, by definition

Jacques Derrida (trans. Peggy Kamuf, ed. Elisabeth Weber), 'Is There a Philosophical Language?', *Points... Interviews, 1974–1994* (Stanford: Stanford University Press, 1995).

and if at least one pursues them in an effective fashion, are neither simply philosophical nor simply literary. I would say the same thing, ultimately, about the texts I write, at least to the extent that they are worked over or dictated by the turbulence of these questions. Which does not mean, at least I hope, that they give up on the necessity of *demonstrating*, as rigorously as possible, even if the rules of the demonstration are no longer altogether, and above all constantly, the same as in what you call a 'philosophic discourse'. Even within the latter, you know, the regimes of demonstrativity are problematic, multiple, mobile. They themselves form the constant object of the whole history of philosophy. The debate that has arisen as regards them is indistinguishable from philosophy itself. Do you think that for Plato, Aristotle, Descartes, Hegel, Marx, Nietzsche, Bergson, Heidegger, or Merleau-Ponty, the rules of demonstrativity had to be the same? And the language, the logic, the rhetoric?

To analyze 'philosophic discourse' in its form, its modes of composition, its rhetoric, its metaphors, its language, its fictions, everything that resists translation, and so forth, is not to reduce it to literature. It is even a largely philosophical task (even if it does not remain philosophical throughout) to study these 'forms' that are no longer just forms, as well as the modalities according to which, by interpreting poetry and literature, assigning the latter a social and political status, and seeking to exclude them from its own body, the academic institution of philosophy has claimed its own autonomy, and practiced a disavowal with relation to its own language, what you call 'literality' and writing in general; it thereby misrecognized the norms of its own discourse, the relations between speech and writing, the procedures of canonization of major or exemplary texts, and so forth. Those who protest against all these questions mean to protect a certain institutional authority of philosophy, in the form in which it was frozen at a given moment. By protecting themselves against these questions and against the transformations that the questions call for or suppose, they are also protecting the institution against philosophy. From this point of view, it seemed interesting to me to study certain discourses, those of Nietzsche or Valéry for example, that tend to consider philosophy as a species of literature. But I never subscribed to that notion and I have explained myself on this point. Those who accuse me of reducing philosophy to literature or logic to rhetoric (see, for example, the latest book by Habermas, *The Philosophical Discourse of Modernity*[1]) have visibly and carefully avoided reading me.

Conversely, I do not think that the 'demonstrative' mode of even philosophy in general is foreign to literature. Just as there 'literary' and 'fictional' dimensions in any philosophical discourse (and a whole 'politics' of language, a politics period generally contained there), likewise there are philosophemes at work in any text defined as 'literary', and already in the finally altogether modern concept of 'literature'.

This explanation between 'philosophy' and 'literature' is not only a difficult problem that I try to elaborate as such, it is also that which takes the form of writing in my texts, a writing that, by being neither purely literary nor purely philosophical, attempts to sacrifice neither the attention to demonstration or to theses nor the fictionality or poetics of languages.

In a word, and to respond to the very letter of your question, I don't believe that there is 'a specifically philosophical writing', a sole philosophical writing whose purity is always the same and out of reach of all sorts of contaminations. And first of all for this overwhelming reason: philosophy is spoken and written in a natural language, not in an absolutely formalizable and universal language. That said, within this natural language and its uses, certain modes have been forcibly imposed (and there is here a relation of force) as philosophical. These modes are multiple, conflictual, inseparable from the philosophical content itself and from its 'theses'. A philosophical debate is also a combat in view of imposing discursive modes, demonstrative procedures, rhetorical and pedagogical techniques. Each time a philosophy has been opposed, it was also, although not only, by contesting the properly, authentically philosophical character of the other's discourse.

Q.: Your recent work seems to be marked by a growing concern for the question of the signature, the proper name. In what way does this question have weight in the field of philosophy where for a long time the problematics were considered to be impersonal and the proper names of philosophy were considered the emblems of these problematics?

J. D.: From the outset, a new problematic of writing or of the trace was bound to communicate, in a strict and strictly necessary fashion, with a problematic of the proper name (it is already a central theme in *Of Grammatology*)[2] and of the signature (especially since *Margins of Philosophy*[3]). This is all the more indispensable in that this new problematic of the trace passes by way of the deconstruction of certain metaphysical discourses on the constituting subject, with all the traits that traditionally characterize it: identity to itself, consciousness, intention, presence or proximity to itself, autonomy, relation to the object. The point was, then, to resituate or to reinscribe the function said to be that of the subject or, if you prefer, to re-elaborate a thinking of the subject which was neither dogmatic or empiricist, nor critical (in the Kantian sense) or phenomenological (Cartesian-Husserlian). But simultaneously, while taking into account the questions that Heidegger addresses to the metaphysics of the *subjectum* as the support of representations and so forth, I thought that this gesture of Heidegger's called for new questions.

All the more so since, despite many complications that I have tried to take into account, Heidegger in fact most often reproduces (for example in his 'Nietzsche') the classical and academic gesture that consists of dissociating, *on the one hand*, an 'internal' reading of the text or of 'thinking', or even an immanent reading of the system from, *on the other hand*, a 'biography' that remains finally secondary and external. This is how in general, in the university, a sort of classical, 'novelized' narrative of the 'life of the great philosophers' is opposed to a systematic, or even structural, philosophical reading, which is organized either around a unique and ingenious intuition (this motif is finally common to Bergson and to Heidegger) or else around an 'evolution' – in two or three stages.

I have tried to analyze the presuppositions of this gesture and to undertake analyses around the borders, limits, frames, and marginalizations of all sorts that in general have authorized these dissociations. The questions of the signature and of the proper name seem to me in fact to offer advantages for this re-elaboration. The signature in general is neither simply internal to the immanence of the signed text (here, for example, the philosophical corpus), nor simply detachable and external. If either of these hypotheses were the case, then it would disappear as signature. If your signature did not belong in a certain manner to the very space that you sign and that is defined by a symbolic system of conventions (the letter, the post card, the check, or any other attestation), it would not have any value as commitment. If, on the other hand, your signature were simply immanent to the signed text, inscribed in it as one of its parts, it again would not have the performative force of a signature. In the two cases (inside and outside), you would be doing no more than indicating or mentioning your name, which is not the same thing as signing. The signature is neither inside nor outside. It is situated on a limit defined by a system and a history of conventions; I am still using these three words, system, history, and convention, in order to save time, but in the problematic I am talking about they cannot be accepted unquestioned.

It was necessary, then, to take a look at these problems: the 'convention' and 'history' of a topology, the borders, the framings, but also performative responsibility and force. It was also necessary to remove them from the oppositions or alternatives that I have just mentioned. How does a signature operate? The thing is complicated, always different, precisely, from one signature and from one idiom to another, but this was the indispensable condition for preparing a rigorous access to the relations between a text and its 'author', a text and its conditions of production, whether they be, as one used to say, psychobiographical or socio-historico-political. This is valid in general for any text and any 'author', but then requires many specifications according to the types of texts considered. The distinctions do not fall only between philosophical and literary texts, but also within these types and, at the limit – the limit of the idiom – between all texts, which may also be juridical, political, scientific (and differently according to the different 'regions', and so forth). While tracing this analysis in, for example, Hegel or Nietzsche, Genet, Blanchot, Artaud, or Ponge, I proposed a certain number of general axioms even as I tried to take account of the idiom or of the desire for idiom in each case. I cite here these examples because the work concerning the signature also passes by way of the proper name in the ordinary sense, I mean the patronym in the form I have just cited. But without being able to reconstitute this work here, I would like to specify a few points and recall several precautions.

a. Even when the signifier of the proper name, in its public and legal form, exposes itself to this analysis of the signature, the latter cannot be reduced to the name. It has never consisted in writing, simply, one's proper name. That is why, in my texts, the references to the signifier of the proper name, even if they seem to occupy center stage, remain preliminary and have a finally limited importance. As often as possible, I signal my distrust of the facile, abusive, or self-satisfied games to which this can give rise.

b. The 'proper name' is not necessarily to be confused with what we commonly designate as such, that is, the official patronym, the one inscribed by a civil status. If one calls 'proper name' the singular set of marks, traits, appellations by means of which someone can identify him- or herself, call him- or herself, or still yet be called, without having totally chosen or determined them him- or herself, you begin to see the difficulty. It is never certain that this set gathers itself together, that there is only one of them, that it does not remain secret for some, or even for the 'consciousness' of the bearer of the name, and so forth. This opens up a formidable field for analysis.

c. A possibility thus remains open: the proper name may not exist in all purity and the signature may finally remain impossible in all strictness, if at least one still supposes that a proper name must be absolutely proper, a signature absolutely autonomous (free) and purely idiomatic. If, for reasons that I try to analyze, there is never a pure idiom, in any case an idiom that I can give *to myself* or invent in its purity, then it follows that the concepts of signature and of proper name, without being necessarily ruined, have to be re-elaborated. This re-elaboration, it seems to me, can give rise to new rules, to new procedures of reading, notably as concerns the relations of the philosophical 'author' with his or her text, society, the institutions of teaching and publication traditions, inheritances, but I am not sure it can give rise to a general theory of the signature and the proper name, on the classical model of theory or of philosophy (formalizable, constative, and objective metalanguage). For the very reasons I have just mentioned, this new discourse on the signature and the proper name must once again be signed and carry with it *in itself* a mark of the performative operation that one cannot simply and totally remove from the set under consideration. This does not lead to relativism but imprints another curvature on theoretical discourse.

Q.: You have inscribed your works under the title of "deconstruction", while explicitly opposing this thematic to the Heideggerian thematic of destruction. From '*retrait*' to '*pas*', from 'the post card' to 'the envoi', from 'margins', to '*parages*', deconstruction weaves a tighter and tighter network of names that are neither concepts, nor metaphors, but rather seem to be landmarks or roadsigns.[4] Does deconstructive activity resemble that of the surveyor or geometer? Does not this 'spatialization' of the relation to tradition reinforce the idea of a 'closure' of this tradition to the detriment of a more differentiated perception of the plurality of filiations?

J. D.: Yes, the relation of 'deconstruction' to Heideggerian 'destruction' has always, for more than twenty years now, been marked by questions, displacements, or even, as is sometimes said, by criticisms. I pointed this out once again at the beginning of *Of Spirit* (1987)[5], but this has been the case since *Of Grammatology* (1967). Heidegger's thought remains nonetheless for me one of the most rigorous, provocative, and necessary of our time. Permit me to recall these two things in order to say how shocking and ridiculous I find all the simplistic classifications, the hasty homogenizations that certain people have indulged in over the last few months (I am not speaking only of the newspapers). These abuses and this rudeness are as threatening as obscurantism itself, and this threat is equally moral and political, to say nothing of philosophy itself.

To pick up on your words, while the 'network' you evoke is reducible neither to a weave of concepts nor to a weave of metaphors, I am not sure that it consists only in 'landmarks' or 'roadsigns'. I would have been tempted to ask you what you mean by that. The next sentence, in your question, seems to indicate that with these words you are privileging the relation to space and, within space, to the experience of the 'geometer' or the 'surveyor'. But you realize of course that the geometer is no longer a 'surveyor' (see my translation and introduction to Husserl's *Origin of Geometry*)[6] and that there are many other experiences of space besides those two.

But first of all I would like to return to this question of the concept and the metaphor to which you just alluded. Two clarifications: I have never reduced the concept to metaphor or, as I was accused again recently of doing by Habermas, logic to rhetoric (no more than I reduced philosophy to literature, as we were just saying). This is clearly said in numerous places, in particular in 'The White Mythology',[7] which proposes an altogether different 'logic' of the relations between concept and metaphor. I can only refer to this here. Whatever may be in fact the attention I give to questions and to the experience of space – whether we're talking about *The Origin of Geometry*, or about writing, painting, drawing (in *The Truth in Painting*)[8] – I don't think that the 'spacing [*espacement*]' I talk about is simply 'spatial' or 'spatializing'. It doubtless permits the rehabilitation, so to speak, of the spatiality that certain philosophical traditions had subordinated, marginalized, or even ignored. But, on the one hand, spac*ing* also says the becoming space of time itself; it intervenes, with differance, in the movement of temporalization itself; spacing is also time, one might say. On the other hand, irreducible by virtue of being a differential interval, it disrupts presence, the self-identity of any presence, with all the consequences that this can have. One may trace these consequences in the most diverse fields.

I confess now I am not sure I see how this gesture, which is certainly not a 'spatialization', could mark the 'closure' of 'tradition'. Differential spacing indicates on the contrary the impossibility of any closure. As for the 'plurality of filiations' and necessity of a 'more differentiated perception', this will always have been my 'theme' in some way, in particular as signaled by the name 'dissemination'. If one takes the expression 'plurality of filiations' in its familial literality, then this is virtually the very 'subject' of 'Dissemination',[9] 'Plato's Pharmacy',[10] and especially *Glas*[11] and *The Post Card*.[12] If one steps back a bit farther (I am trying to understand the thinking behind your question), I have always distinguished 'closure' from end (*Of Grammatology*) and have often recalled that the tradition was not homogeneous (which explains my interest in non-canonical texts that destabilize the representation a certain dominant tradition gave of itself). I have often said how problematic I find the idea of Metaphysics, capital M, and the Heideggerian schema of the epochality of Being or of the reassembled unity of a history of Being, even if the claim, the desire, the limit, or the failure of this 'auto'-interpretation has to be taken into account. I put 'auto' in quotation marks because it is always this identity and especially this self-identity, this power of transparent, exhaustive, or totalizing reflexivity that is found to be in question here.

Q.: Your recent research concerns 'philosophical nationality'. In what way does language seem to you to be constitutive of an identity? Is there a French philosophy?

J. D.: Everything depends obviously on what one means by language. And also, if you will pardon my saying so, by 'identity' and constitution. If, as I seem to understand, by identity you mean identity of a 'philosophical nationality' or in a larger sense of a philosophical tradition, I would say that language, of course, plays a very important role there. Philosophy finds its element in so-called natural language. It has never been able to formalize itself integrally in an artificial language despite several fascinating attempts to do so in the history of philosophy. It is also true that this formalization (according to artificial codes constituted in the course of a history) is always, up to a certain point, at work. This means that philosophical language or languages are more or less well defined and coherent subsets within natural languages or rather the uses of natural languages. And one may find equivalents and regulated translations between these subsets from one natural language to another. Thus German and French philosophers can refer to more or less ancient and stable conventions in order to translate their respective uses of certain words that have a high degree of philosophical content. But you know all the problems this provokes, problems which are not distinguishable from the philosophical debate itself.

If, on the other hand, there is no thinking outside of some language (a proposition that would nevertheless have to be accompanied by many precautions that I cannot enumerate here), then, of course, an identity and especially a national identity in philosophy is not constituted outside of the element of language.

That said, I don't believe one can establish a simple correspondence between a national philosophical tradition and a language, in the ordinary sense of this term. The so-called Continental and Anglo-Saxon (or analytic) traditions, to use these very crude and imprecise labels, are divided, and in a very uneven fashion, among English, German, Italian, Spanish, and so forth. The philosophical 'language' (by which I mean the subcode) of analytic philosophy or of some tradition or other (Anglo-American, e.g., Austin; Austro-Anglo-American, e.g., Wittgenstein) is caught up in a number of overdeterminations in relation to the so-called national language, which is itself spoken by citizens of different countries (the English of Americans, the French spoken outside of France). This explains why there sometimes develops outside of the so-called language of origin (of the original text) a tradition of reading that is reassimilated only with difficulty by the very people who speak or think they speak this language of origin. This is true in very different ways for both Wittgenstein and Heidegger. The French 'readings' or 'reception' of Heidegger encounter a strong resistance in Germany (as does Heidegger himself, and for reasons that are not only political). As for French specialists of Wittgenstein, neither Germanophones nor Anglophones are very interested in it, to the point that one cannot even say they resist it.

Is there, then, a French philosophy? No, less than ever if one considers the heterogeneity, as well as the conflictuality, that marks all manifestations called philosophical: publications, teaching, discursive forms and norms, the relations to institutions, to the socio political field, to the power of the media. One would even have trouble establishing a typology, since every attempt at typology would presuppose precisely an interpretation that takes sides in the conflict. It would encounter right away a predictable hostility from almost all sides. Therefore, although I do have my own little idea about this, I will not risk it, here, now. On the other hand, despite all the debates and battles over philosophical 'positions' or 'practices', who can deny that there is a configuration of French philosophy, and that over its history, despite the succession of hegemonies, despite the mobility of dominant strains, this configuration constitutes a tradition, which is to say a relatively identifiable element of transmission, memory, heritage? In order to analyze it, one would have to take into account a very large number of always overdeterminable givens – historical, linguistic, social – across very specific institutions (which are not only the institutions of teaching and research), but without ever forgetting that rather capital overdetermination which we call philosophy, if there is any! This is too difficult and too touchy for me to risk getting into it here in a few sentences. I think that the identity of French philosophy has never been more severely tested than it is today. The signs of this are a growing rigidity of the power of the University as exercised in its official capacities as well as, and often going in the same direction, a certain journalistic aggressivity. To take only one current example, I will cite the decision handed down just recently (by the CNU) that prevents [Philippe] Lacoue-Labarthe and [Jean-Luc] Nancy, which is to say two philosophers whose work has been recognized and respected in France and abroad for many years, from becoming full professors in the university.[13] Through these sometimes laughable signs of war, which finally paralyze nothing but what is already inert and paralyzed, the severe test I mentioned a moment ago confers its singularity on this thing we call 'French philosophy'. It belongs to an idiom which is, as always, more difficult to perceive at home than abroad. The idiom, if there is one, is never pure, chosen, or manifest on its own side, precisely. The idiom is always and only for the other, in advance expropriated (exappropriated).

Notes

Published in *Autrement* 102 (November 1988), 'A quoi pensent les philosophes?' (What are the philosophers thinking about?), edited by J. Roman and E. Tassin. The text was introduced as follows: 'In rethinking the texts that have constituted it as a tradition, philosophy discovering its alliance with writing. What of the limits, what of the closure of philosophical discourse? Jacques Derrida wrote four replies to this question.'

1. *The Philosophical Discourse of Modernity: Twelve Lectures*, trans. Frederick Lawrence (Cambridge, Mass.: MIT Press, 1987).
2. [Editor's note: Jacques Derrida, *Of Grammatology*, trans. Gayatri Chakravorty Spivak, 2nd edn (Baltimore: Johns Hopkins University, 1997).]
3. [Editor's note: Jacques Derrida, *Margins of Philosophy*, trans. Alan Bass (Chicago: University of Chicago Press, 1982).]
4. All the terms in quotation marks figure in titles of texts by Derrida.—Trans.
5. [Editor's note: Jacques Derrida, *Of Spirit: Heidegger and the Question*, trans. Geoffrey Bennington and Rachel Bowlby (Chicago: The University of Chicago Press, 1989).]
6. [Editor's note: Jacques Derrida, *Edmund Husserl's Origin of Geometry: An Introduction*, trans. John Leavey, Jr (New York: Harvester Press, 1978).]
7. In *Margins–of Philosophy*. [Editor's note: Jacques Derrida, 'White Mythology: Metaphor in the Text of Philosophy', in Jacques Derrida, *Margins of Philosophy*.]
8. [Editor's note: Jacques Derrida, *The Truth in Painting*, trans. Geoff Bennington and Ian McLeod (Chicago: University of Chicago Press, 1987).]

9. [Editor's note: Jacques Derrida, *Dissemination*, trans. Barbara Johnson (Chicago: University of Chicago Press, 1981).]
10. [Editor's note: In ibid.]
11. [Editor's note: Jacques Derrida, *Glas*, trans. John P. Leavey, Jr and Richard Rand (Lincoln: University of Nebraska Press, 1986).]
12. [Editor's note: Jacques Derrida, *The Post Card: From Socrates to Freud and Beyond*, trans. Alan Bass (Chicago: University of Chicago Press, 1987).]
13. The GNU is the Conseil National des Universités. Appointed by the government for each discipline, it has the power of final approval over nominations to a full professorship. When Philippe Lacoue-Labarthe and Jean-Luc Nancy were recommended for professorships in philosophy by the University of Strasbourg, the GNU preferred another candidate each time. These decisions, as well as many others in philosophy and other disciplines, were publicly contested and drew much criticism of the sectarian, partisan procedures of the GNU. Both Lacoue-Labarthe and Nancy have since been named professors of philosophy at Strasbourg.—Trans.

3

Richard Rorty

HABERMAS, DERRIDA AND THE FUNCTIONS OF PHILOSOPHY

Richard Rorty, whose reading of Derrida Habermas refers to in Chapter 1, is one of the most prolific and influential contemporary philosophers and literary theorists. He is also one of Derrida's most important interlocutors, although he has a philosophical and political project of his own inspired by American pragmatism.

Rorty accepts Habermas's account of Derrida as a philosopher of rhetoric and world-disclosure who has nothing to contribute to social justice. Derrida is useful for what Rorty calls 'private' concerns, because he gives us tools to rearticulate the vocabularies in which we describe ourselves and the world around us. We can therefore treat Derrida's philosophical texts as literature. Habermas, on the other hand, is useful for what Rorty calls 'public' purposes in that he can contribute to pragmatic solutions to social injustice. However, Rorty rejects Habermas's attempt to found his political philosophy in a philosophy of language; such foundationalism, he argues, is neither possible nor necessary. Habermas and Derrida thus correspond to the two parts of the position Rorty calls the 'liberal ironist'. The liberal ironist is someone who is a liberal insofar as she believes that human suffering is the most pressing political problem, but that the basic political institutions and principles are already in place in Western liberal democracies. She is an ironist and non-foundationalist insofar as she takes an ironic distance to the vocabularies she uses to describe herself and the world around her. Like problem-solving and world-disclosure, liberalism and irony are complementary but must be distinguished. In this light, Rorty argues, Derrida and Habermas are different but complementary thinkers.

I see Jacques Derrida as the most intriguing and ingenious of contemporary philosophers, and Jürgen Habermas as the most socially useful – the one who does the most for social democratic politics. Admiring both men as I do, I should like to iron out some of the differences between them. In this paper, I want to examine Habermas' criticisms of Derrida in his *Der Philosophische Diskurs der Moderne*, and then go on to a discussion of Habermas' attempt to put philosophy in the service of human emancipation. My strategy will be to urge that Derrida and Habermas complement, rather than oppose, each other.

I argued in my *Contingency, Irony and Solidarity*[1] that Derrida's books are just what you need if you have been impressed and burdened by Heidegger – if you feel the power of Heideggerian language, but want to avoid describing yourself in terms of it. A text like 'Envois' (the initial section of Derrida's *La Carte Postale*[2]) is an edifying account of how one reader of Heidegger wrestled with an overweening grandfather, and won. On the other hand, Habermas's *Philosophische Diskurs* is just what you need if you find Heidegger and Derrida equally pointless. Habermas helps you feel justified in circumventing the Nietzsche-Heidegger-Derrida genre of ironist theorizing, in going around it rather than through it. If you remain unimpressed by Heidegger's litanies and Derrida's fantasies, Habermas gives you good reasons for saying that, at least for purposes of doing some public good, you can just *ignore* both.

Habermas sees Heidegger and Derrida as belonging to the tradition he calls 'the philosophy of subjectivity', and which he traces back to Kant and Hegel. Using my own jargon, I should describe this tradition as one more misguided metaphysical attempt to combine the public and the private. It is an attempt to synthesize activities which it would be better to keep distinct – the effort of an individual thinker to free himself from his predecessors on the one hand, and the collective political enterprise of increasing freedom and equality on the other. The 'egoism' which Santayana remarked in German philosophy from Fichte onwards was typically combined, until Nietzsche, with an attempt at greater social justice.

But, as Habermas rightly says, 'With Nietzsche the criticism of modernity dispenses for the first time with its retention of an emancipatory content'.[3] Since Nietzsche's time, the philosophy of subjectivity has been taken over by the ironists – by people who are interested in their own autonomy and

Richard Rorty, 'Habermas, Derrida, and the Functions of Philosophy', *Revue Internationale de Philosophie*, 4 (1995), pp. 437–59.

individuality rather than in their social usefulness, and whose excursions into politics are incidental to their principal motives. What I call 'ironist theorizing' – theorizing which emphasizes its own contingency – remained a sub-text in Hegel (emerging only at odd moments, such as the end of the 'Introduction' to *The Philosophy of Right*[4] and then thrust back out of sight). But after Nietzsche this sort of theorizing began to crowd out other genres.

Habermas thinks that the philosophy of subjectivity was a false start, and that the political uselessness of this sort of philosophy became increasingly obvious in our century, as we watched philosophers concentrating more and more on the 'game of mutually out doing' each other. As ironist theorizing shoved a concern for human solidarity aside, concern for the emancipation of the individual philosopher from his predecessors replaced concern for the emancipation of the oppressed. So Habermas wants to replace this tradition with something of greater social utility: what he calls a 'philosophy of intersubjectivity'. This sort of philosophy will keep what is still usable in Enlightenment rationalism while jettisoning both metaphysical attempts to 'ground' this rationalism in 'the nature of the subject' and ironist attempts to 'subvert' it.

This philosophy of intersubjectivity centers around a practise characteristic of liberal societies – treating as true whatever can be agreed upon in the course of free discussion, and waving aside the question of whether there is some metaphysical object to which the result of such discussion might or might not correspond. Such a philosophy politicizes epistemology, in the sense that it takes what matters to the search for truth to be the social (and in particular the political) conditions under which that search is conducted, rather than the deep inner nature of the subjects doing the searching. Habermas says that he

> conceives of intersubjective understanding as the telos inscribed into communication in ordinary language, and of the logocentrism of Western thought, heightened by the philosophy of consciousness, as a systematic foreshortening and distortion of a potential always already operative in the communicative practice of everyday life but only selectively exploited.[5]

In other words, what is wrong with what Heidegger calls 'metaphysics' and Derrida 'logocentrism' is that it has hoped to do by reflection – by looking inward – what can only be done by expanding the scope and membership of a conversation. It has delved into the privacy of 'the subject' instead of going public. If we do go public, we shall identify the rational with the procedures, and the true with the results, of 'undistorted communication' – the sort of communication characteristic of an ideally democratic society. What stands in the way of such communication has nothing much to do with 'logocentrism', and everything to do with practical politics. All that the philosopher, in his or her professional capacity, can do for social justice is to point out present obstacles to 'undistorted communication'. These obstacles do not include the esoteric matters with which Heidegger and Derrida are obsessed (e.g., the confusion of Being with the most general features of beings, the presupposed primacy of speech over writing). Rather, they include such things as the control of mass-circulation magazines by people who want to safeguard their own wealth and power at the expense of the poor and weak.

Habermas is certainly right that if we look to the texts commonly identified as 'philosophical' for help in realizing the ideals of the liberal democracies, we can just skip Nietzsche, Heidegger, Derrida and (most of) Foucault.[6] But I think that he goes one step too far when he says that

> A more viable solution suggests itself if we drop the somewhat sentimental presupposition of metaphysical homelessness, and if we understand the hectic to and fro between transcendental and empirical modes of dealing with issues, between radical self-reflection and an incomprehensible element prior to all production – that is to say, when we understand the puzzle of all these doublings for what it is: a symptom of exhaustion. The paradigm of the philosophy of consciousness is exhausted. If this is so, the symptoms of exhaustion should dissolve with the transition to the paradigm of mutual under standing.[7]

Habermas is right in saying that the ironists' quest for ever deeper irony and ever more ineffable sublimity has little direct public utility. But I do not think that this shows that 'the paradigm of the philosophy of consciousness is a symptom of exhaustion'. What he sees as symptoms of exhaustion, I see them as symptoms of vitality. This is because I read people like Heidegger and Nietzsche as good *private* philosophers, and he reads them as bad public philosophers.

I argue in *Contingency, Irony and Solidarity* that Heidegger's and Derrida's only relevance to the quest for social justice is that, like the Romantic poets before them, they make more vivid and concrete our sense of what human life might be like in a democratic utopia – a utopia in which the quest for autonomy is impeded as little as possible by social institutions. They do little or nothing to justify the choice of such a utopia, or to hasten its arrival. But they do show how the creation of new discourses can enlarge the realm of possibility. They thereby help free us from the picture which gave rise to the philosophy of subjectivity in the first place – the metaphysician's picture of something deep within us, at the center of every human self, uncaused by and unreachable by historically-conditioned processes of acculturation, something which privileges one vocabulary of moral deliberation over all the others.

Because Habermas reads these writers as unsuccessful public philosophers – philosophers who still aim at the 'self-reassurance of modernity', at giving the modern age something which will replace religion – he makes a move which I do not want to make. He demands that writers like Heidegger and Derrida provide a public justification of their own practise – an intersubjectively arguable account of what they are doing. He wants to treat them as claiming what he calls 'universal validity', whereas I regard the question of universal validity as irrelevant to their practices.[8] Whereas I want to see the line of thought that runs from Nietzsche to Heidegger to Derrida as (even if this was not the intent of these writers themselves) opening up new private possibilities, possibilities only incidentally and contingently relevant to liberal social hope, Habermas sees this line of thought as a public danger, as a threat to democratic society. When discussing Heidegger, he puts Heidegger's diagnosis of the state of the modern world – his crusade against technology, giantism, and Americanism – in the foreground. I would treat this crusade as epiphenomenal. When discussing Derrida, he insists that Derrida not just exhibit a new kind of writing, but justify writing that way by argument. Derrida, he says,

> can only attain Heidegger's goal of bursting metaphysical thought-forms from the inside by means of his essentially rhetorical procedure if the philosophical text is in truth a literary one – if one can demonstrate that the genre distinction between philosophy and literature dissolves upon closer examination.[9]

In what follows, I shall confine myself to this last claim.[10] Examining it will, I hope, let me clarify my own sense of the distinct functions fulfilled by Habermas' public sort of philosophy and by Derrida's privatized sort of philosophy.

Habermas rightly says that 'Derrida does not belong to those philosophers who like to argue'.[11] He therefore looks to Derrida's American admirers for the arguments which he thinks Derrida needs. He finds what he wants in Jonathan Culler's claim that

> If serious language is a special case of non-serious, if truths are fictions whose fictionality has been forgotten, then literature is not a deviant, parasitical instance of language. On the contrary, other discourses can be seen as cases of a generalized literature, or archi literature.[12]

Putting aside for a moment the question of whether one needs to put forward any such large, metaphysical-sounding theses to defend Derrida's practise,[13] let us see what Habermas says in reply to Culler's claim.

In the course of an intricate argument, which I shall not try to summarize, he makes two principal points. The first is that one can distinguish between 'ordinary' and 'parasitical' uses of language by distinguishing between language which operates under the constraint of being 'open to criticism on the basis of making validity claims' and language which is free from this constraint.[14] The second point, which undergirds and clarifies the first, is that there is a distinction between the 'world-disclosing' and the 'problem-solving' functions of language. Habermas thinks that Derrida denies the existence both of an 'independently structured domain of everyday communicative practise' and of an 'autonomous realm of fiction.' He says:

> Because Derrida denies both, he can analyze any given discourse in accord with the model of poetic language, and do so as if language generally were determined by the poetic use of language specialized in world-disclosure. From this viewpoint, language as such converges with literature or indeed with 'writing'. *This aestheticizing of language, which is purchased with the twofold denial of the proper senses of normal and poetic discourse*, also explains Derrida's insensitivity toward the tension-filled polarity between the poetic-world disclosive function of language and its prosaic, innerworldly functions... An aesthetic contextualism blinds him to the fact that everyday communicative practice makes learning processes possible (thanks to built-in idealizations) in relation to which the world disclosive force of interpreting language has in turn to prove its worth... He permits the capacity to solve problems to disappear behind the world-creating capacity of language.[15]

On my reading of Derrida, he does not 'deny' the existence of any of the things to which Habermas accuses him of being blind. He knows perfectly well that there are communicative practises to which argumentation by reference to standard rules is essential, and that these are indispensable for public purposes. He does not need to say, with Culler, that 'the serious is a special case of the non-serious', though he and Habermas should be able to agree that 'other discourses can be seen as cases of a generalized literature' if some useful purpose is served by so seeing them. Derrida has developed a way of writing which enables us so to see them. But, *pace* Culler and Rodolphe Gasché),[16] this way of writing neither presupposes nor demonstrates any view about 'the nature of language', nor, *pace* Habermas, can it be criticized by reference to any such view.

It is one thing to 'analyze any given discourse in accord with the model of poetic language' – that is, to play around with it in the way Derrida plays around with texts from Heidegger, Hegel, and others – and another thing to claim that 'language generally is determined by the poetic use of language specialized in world-disclosure'. Derrida need not, and I take it would not, think in terms of 'language generally' being 'determined' by anything. But he might say, as I would, that lots of the expressions used in everyday public problem-solving were, once upon a time, startling metaphors – bits of world-disclosing discourse which nobody, at first, knew how to argue about, or with. Derrida could, I think, wholeheartedly agree with Habermas that 'the world-disclosing force of interpreting language has . . . to prove its worth' before such metaphors get literalized and made into socially useful tools. Lots of poetic achievements remain 'just' poetic achievements; they never get used by anybody but their creators. Lots of attempts at private autonomy – notably, I should argue, Nietzsche's and Heidegger's – remain 'merely' such attempts. Others turn out to have socially useful spin-offs. But there is no reason why recognizing the source of such useful products should cause 'the capacity to solve problems to disappear behind the world-creating capacity of language'.[17]

Habermas seems to me to beg all the important questions against Derrida when he assumes that treating X as Y requires an argument to show that X is 'a special case' of Y, or that there 'really' is no difference between X and Y – that one cannot simply treat X as Y in order to see what happens. But admirers of Derrida (e.g., Culler, Gasché, Paul de Man) set Derrida up for this question-begging treatment when they commit him to having 'demonstrated' something original and startling about the nature of language. His defenders make him into a quasi-metaphysician, and refuse to let him remain an ironist. Habermas takes them at their word and points out, correctly enough, that if language were what American 'deconstructive literary theory' says it is then it would be hard to use marks and noises as tools in solving our public problems. If 'philosophy' could indeed show that 'language' was something more than people manipulating marks and noises for various private and public purposes – if 'language' could be 'demonstrated' to be something which could (as deconstructive critics suggest) act on its own, go out of control, stab itself in the back, tear its own head off, etc. – then we really *would* be in trouble. But nothing except the urge to make Derrida into a man with a great big theory about a great big subject suggests that 'language' can do anything of the sort.

Derrida's American friends, the ones who want to make him into a theorist and are not content to let him remain an ironist about theory, exhibit just the sort of reverence for 'philosophy' which is satirized in 'Envois'. De Man, for example, thinks that 'the necessary immanence of reading in relation to the text' stands out as 'the irreducible philosophical problem raised by all forms of literary criticism', and that 'In France it took the rigor and intellectual integrity of a philosopher whose main concern is not with literary texts to restore the complexities of reading to the dignity of a philosophical question'.[18] Many of Derrida's fans can imagine nothing nicer than having a big bouncy child by Socrates.[19] Habermas is not this reverential about philosophy, but he still thinks that before anybody 'levels' the philosophy-literature distinction he is honor-bound to demonstrate some philosophical theses – and in particular to agree with Culler that

> Far from there being a genre distinction between philosophy and literature, philosophical texts can be rendered accessible in their essential contents by literary criticism and literary texts can be rendered accessible in their essential contents by a critique of metaphysics.[20]

But surely if there is one idea which Derrida has no use for it is that of 'essential contents'. Like Quine, Goodman, Wittgenstein, Bergson, Whitehead, and lots of other twentieth-century philosophers, Derrida dissolves substances, essences and all, into webs of relations. The result of his reading is not to get at essences but to place texts in contexts – placing books next to other books (as in *Glas*[21]) and weaving bits of books together with bits of other books. One result of this activity is to blur genres, but that is not because genres are not 'real'. It is because one way to create a new genre is to stitch together bits and pieces of old genres – an activity which would not produce interesting new effects if the old genres were not just as distinct as we had always thought they were. It is one thing to weave differently colored strands together in the hope of making something new, and another to think that 'philosophy' has 'demonstrated' that colors are *really* 'indeterminate' and 'ambivalent'.

Habermas wonders why Heidegger and Derrida are 'still battling against the "strong" concepts of theory, truth and system that have actually belonged to the past for over a century and a half', why they still think that 'they have to tear philosophy away from the madness of expounding a theory that has the last word'.[22] I am suggesting that they are not interested in tearing 'philosophy' away from this madness, but simply in tearing themselves away from their own past – from the particular words which threatened to be, for them, the last ones. (Viz., the words of Nietzsche in the case of Heidegger, the words of Heidegger in the case of Derrida.) They are not as public-spirited as Habermas assumes every philosopher must be, nor (any more than Nietzsche) are they easily understood as stages in the attempt of 'modernity' to achieve 'self-reassurance' – the drama within which Habermas tries to situate them.

Habermas does not feel he has done justice to a philosopher unless he places him within a religio-political context, and has connected his work up with the need to 'regenerate the unifying power of religion in the medium of reason'.[23] So when he says that in Derrida and Foucault the 'philosophy of subjectivity' has exhausted its possibilities, it is possibilities of public usefulness that he has in mind. Where Habermas sees a contrast between a socially useless, exhausted, philosophy of subjectivity and a socially unifying philosophy of rationality-as-intersubjectivity, I see a contrast between the private need for autonomy and the public need for a synoptic view of the goals of a democratic society, a society held together by an agreement, in Rawls' words, to give 'the right priority over the good', to make justice 'the first virtue'.

I have argued elsewhere[24] that part of the force of these Rawlsian slogans is that democratic societies need not concern themselves with 'the subject' or 'human nature' – that such a society privatizes questions concerning such topics. This claim chimes with Habermas' view that the only 'universals' which a philosophy of intersubjectivity will come up with will be procedural ones, not decisions on such matters of 'substance' as the point of human life. So perhaps Habermas would not have to modify anything very fundamental to his view in order to make room for Heidegger and Derrida, viewed as people engaged in enterprises irrelevant (at least so far as we can presently see) to the public life of our society. Such enterprises are useful only to that quite small group of people for whom 'the tradition of Western metaphysics' still looms large – the people whose self-image is stated in terms of the quarrel between the ironists and the metaphysicians. The extent to which these ways of articulating that self-image – Heidegger's litanies, or Derrida's puns – eventually spill over into the public realm is unpredictable, and usually irrelevant to their private aims.

* * *

One obstacle to my treatment of Habermas and Derrida as complementary is that these two philosophers appear to disagree over the nature and function of philosophy. Such a disagreement, it is easy to think, must be profound. In my view, however, 'the nature and function of philosophy' is a pseudo-topic, as much so as 'the nature and task of the novel'. Talk of 'the end of philosophy' is as easy, but as empty, as talk of 'the end of the novel'. The term 'the novel' by now covers so many different kinds of things (from *Tristram Shandy* to *Gone With the Wind*, from *Lolita* to *Malone Dies*, from *Oliver Twist* to *The Executioner's Song*) that everyone knows that 'the death of the novel' means no more than 'the death of a certain kind of novel'. The same cynicism should be felt about announcements of 'the end of philosophy', which typically mean something like 'the end of metaphysical system-building' or 'the end of empiricism' or 'the end of Cartesianism'. No definition of 'philosophy' can cover Carnap and Rawls, early Hegel and late Wittgenstein, Derrida and Habermas, and still isolate something coherent enough to have an 'end'.

Still there is something – something which, unlike the question about 'the nature of philosophy', is not merely verbal – which Derrida and Habermas disagree about, and which makes it hard to view them as complementary. The disagreement is hard to pin down, but it comes out when we find Habermas treating the Nietzsche-Heidegger-Derrida tradition as a 'critique of reason', and when he identifies his own view with a recovery of Enlightenment rationalism. Although Habermas says that his 'communications-theoretic concept of the lifeworld has been freed from the mortgages of transcendental philosophy',[25] and that 'the purism of pure reason is not resurrected again in communicative reason',[26] he has no intention of freeing 'communicative reason' from the ideal of 'universal validity'. He still wants an Archimedean point from which, for example, to criticize Foucault for 'relativism' and for being unable to give an account of 'the normative foundations of [theory's] own rhetoric'.[27] He still wants to say that 'the validity claimed for propositions and norms transcends spaces and times, "blots out" space and time'.[28]

This urge toward universal validity makes Habermas distrust what he calls "linguistic historicism" – the line of thought which, I have argued, unites Dewey and Heidegger, James and Nietzsche, Derrida and Davidson. He thinks this view results in "hypostasizing the world-disclosing force of language".[29] He thinks that such hypostatization confines discourse to the limits of that particular time and space in which a given language-game is played, excluding "any interaction between world-disclosing language and learning processes in the world".[30] But I can see no basis for Habermas' insistence that people like Castoriadis and Derrida must *exclude* such interaction, nor for the claim that they are 'criticizing reason'. If reason is interpreted not as a universal human faculty which somehow transcends the invention of new vocabularies, but a what Habermas calls 'communicative reason', none of us linguistic historicists has any interest whatever in 'criticizing' it.

Habermas sees an anti-democratic bogeyman – 'the subject' – hiding behind the 'linguistic' masks which Foucault, Derrida and Castoriadis assume. Yet all three men would be happy to grant Habermas' point that 'reason is by its very nature incarnated in contexts of communicative action and in structures of the life world',[31] nor are any of them interested in undertaking 'an explanation of the intersubjectivity of social praxis' that 'begins from the premise of isolated consciousness'.[32] It is one thing to say that the individual's unconscious is a 'unique and private world which runs up against the socially institutionalized world' – that there is a 'blind impress' on each of us which has nothing in particular to do with socializing 'learning processes' – and quite another to say that the 'psyche and society stand in a kind of metaphysical opposition to each other'.[33] There is no reason to think we have to choose between Dewey and Derrida, between public problem-solving and private struggles for autonomy. The two activities can co-exist peacefully. There is no reason why philosophy should have to choose between them, nor any need to assign one some sort of epistemic priority over the other. The choice between the two activities, in any given concrete case, is no more susceptible to application of general criteria than is any other painful conflict between duties to others and duties to self.

Habermas is disgusted, by every sign of the re-emergence of *Lebensphilosophie*, something he despises almost as much as Heidegger did.[34] This is because he over-dramatizes the contrast between 'subject-centered reason' and 'communicative reason', and looks for signs of 'subject-centeredness' in everything that claims the status of 'philosophy' without being socially useful. He thinks that in both Castoriadis and Heidegger, 'the "truth" of semantic world-disclosure also founds the propositional truth of statements; it prejudices the validity of linguistic utterances generally'.[35] But this criticism confuses the source of new ideas with the 'ground of their validity'. It confuses causes with reasons. It also confuses an initial stage, in which new metaphors are produced to satisfy private needs, with a later stage in which, after these metaphors are literalized, we have become able to argue about the truth of sentences formulated in terms of them. Derrida and Castoriadis can happily agree with Davidson that *nothing* 'founds the propositional truth of statements' except social practice, argument, intersubjective conversational exchange. But they would be right to insist that nothing could 'prejudice the validity of linguistic utterances generally' except the absence of freedom and leisure to engage in such free exchanges (thanks to, for example, illiteracy, hunger, or the secret police). The only other thing which might prejudice this validity would be the failure of new 'semantic world-disclosures' to provide fresh grist for the argumentative mill – the sort of novelties of which totalitarian regimes are rightly fearful.

Habermas' suspicions of *Lebensphilosophie*, of Romanticism, and of 'world-disclosure', can be traced back to his continuing commitment to the claim that there is something called 'critical reason' which can detect the difference between 'invariant regularities of social action as such' and 'ideologically frozen relations of dependence that can in principle be transformed'.[36] This claim contrasts with the view of us linguistic historicists: that 'ideologically frozen relations of dependence' become detectable only when somebody suggests concrete alternatives to them. Our main argument for this view is that there is no way to tell in advance whether any given regularity is 'invariant', since the conditions of the possibility of social action are forever being enlarged by 'semantic world-disclosure'. We linguistic historicists think that there is no such thing as 'humanity' to be emancipated by being ushered from an age of 'distorted' to one of 'undistorted' communication – no common core to men and women of all ages and climes, other than their shared susceptibility to pain and humiliation.[37]

On the view of a naturalistic historicist like Dewey – a philosopher who was as remote from the philosophy of subjectivity as Mead, and as remote from ironism as Habermas – every form of social life is likely, sooner or later, to freeze over into something which the more imaginative and restless spirits of the time will see as 'repressive' and 'distorting'. What is wrong with these forms of life is not that they are 'ideological' but just that they have been used to justify the systematic administration of pain and humiliation. Typically, they once played a role in liberation – in freeing people from some still worse alternative.[38] So to say that this pain and humiliation is now unnecessary is to say that now an alternative form of social life has become available – one which we could not have envisaged had not a brave new possible world been disclosed by a linguistic innovation, an innovation which may have been caused by some merely private turbulence. From this point of view 'distorted communication' is a relative term – one which is given sense by contrast with a proposed alternative communication situation, the disclosure of an alternative social world. As Marx and Foucault helped us see, today's chains are often forged from the hammers which struck off yesterday's. As Foucault was more inclined to admit than Marx, this sequence of hammers-into-chains is unlikely to end with the invention of hammers that *cannot* be forged into chains – hammers that are *purely* rational, with no ideological alloy. Still, the chains might, with luck, get a little lighter and more easily breakable each time.

If Habermas were content with this sort of historicism and contextualism, he would have little motive for his suspicions of 'subject-centered thinking'. But his attachment to the idea of 'universal validity' makes it impossible for him to accept it. I see this attachment as a species of the same temptation which made Plato, Augustine, Kant, Nietzsche and Heidegger try for affiliation or incarnation – for a relation to something larger than themselves and the contingent circumstances in which they find themselves (e.g., the Good, God, the Moral Law, the Will to Power, Being). As soon as the notion of 'emancipation' is separated from suggestions about how to break a particular set of manicles (e.g., chattel slavery, priestcraft, wage slavery, racial or gender discrimination, mindless bureaucracy) and made the aim of an ahistorical 'human interest', it gets connected with the idea that there is something called 'human nature' or 'humanity itself' which needs to be emancipated. On my view, Humanity and Critical Reason are (like God, the Good, The Subject, Language, *Ereignis* and *différance*) just more candidates for this position of Something Larger.

The best account of this use of the idea of 'humanity' with which I am familiar is given in Bernard Yack's *The Longing for Total Revolution*. In this book, Yack identifies the least common denominator of the sort of social theory which aims at 'enabling human beings to realize their humanity' as a Kant-style contrast between 'nature' and 'freedom', with its accompanying demand that 'our autonomy be realized in our institutions'.[39] He shows that, although this anti-naturalist, idealist, contrast is officially repudiated by both Marx and Nietzsche, both desert their official naturalism when they start to talk about a 'transformation of mankind'. Yack sees Hegel as having accepted contingency in a way in which neither Marx nor Nietzsche were able to accept it – as having been willing to admit that there would never be a political realization of the ideal which, Hegel thought, could be realized in the private activity of the philosopher who attains Absolute Knowledge.[40] By contrast, he sees Marx and Nietzsche as officially willing to accept the brute materiality of contingent conditions while remaining committed, unofficially, to a future state of humanity in which this materiality has been evaded. Yack concludes his book by saying that

> the premiss that suggests the identification of dehumanization ... as the obstacle to a world without social sources of dissatisfaction – a definition of the individual's humanity in terms of the individual's ability to resist external conditioning – rules out their realization of our humanity in the external world. Any institution that conditions our behavior will be dehumanizing, as long as we hold this understanding of man's humanity.[41]

This idea of people having an 'inside' – a central core – which 'resists external conditioning' is one of those which we linguistic historicists reject. If we drop this idea, then we shall need the sort of private-public distinction upon which I have been insisting. For then we shall view autonomy not as the actualization of a common human potentiality but as self-creation: the process of fighting free of very particular inheritances in order to work out the consequences of idiosyncratic 'blind impresses'. The ideal liberal community will be one in which respect for such particularity and idiosyncrasy is widespread, one in which the only sort of human liberty which is hoped for is Isaiah Berlin's 'negative liberty' – being left alone.

For such a community, 'universal validity', freedom from a limited spatio-temporal context, is not to the point. That ideal community would see the task of social theory as what Rawls calls 'attaining reflective equilibrium' between our old moral principles (the generalities we invoke to justify old institutions) and our reactions to new developments, our sense of the desirability or undesirability of various recently-disclosed possibilities. Out of this attempt there will come initiatives to reform old institutions, or to replace them with new ones. The question of the intrinsic validity of the principles would not arise. In particular, the question of whether they were 'universally valid' or 'merely ours' would not. So there would be continual social *criticism*, but no *radical* social *theory*, if 'radical' means appealing to something beyond inherited principles and reactions to new developments.

What would guard such a society from feeling comfortable with the institutionalized infliction of pain and humiliation on the powerless? From taking such pain for granted? Only detailed descriptions of that pain and humiliation – descriptions which brought home to the powerless the contrast between their lives and the lives of others (thus inciting revolution), and brought the same contrast home to the privileged (thus inciting reform). Instead of a general theoretical test for the presence of 'ideology' and 'distortion of communication' of the sort Habermas envisages, there would be only particular descriptions of injury and concrete suggestions about ways of avoiding injury.

Who provides such descriptions? In contemporary liberal society, a vast range of people: journalists, anthropologists, sociologists, novelists, dramatists, moviemakers, painters. Providing a continual supply of such descriptions is one of the things liberal societies do best. Think of books like *Uncle Tom's Cabin* and *Les Misérables*, of stretches of Dickens and Zola, of *The Story of an African Farm*, *All Quiet on the Western Front*, *The Well of Loneliness*, *The People of the Abyss*, *Black Boy*, and *Animal Farm*. These novels are continuous with non-fiction like *The Drapier Letters*, *The Children of Sanchez*, *The Road to Wigan Pier*, and *The Gulag Archipelago*, and also with articles and columns written by muck-raking reporters or social scientists, and with reports written by committees of do-gooders or bureaucrats. Such books both mobilize those who are being injured and unsettle those who are doing, or countenancing, injury. They provide the intuitions – the strong reactions to novel stimuli – which theoretical attempts at reflective equilibrium take into account.

The expectation of getting something more than this constant provision of new stimuli – the desire for a theory which supersedes the search for reflective equilibrium by offering '*radical* criticism of society' – has been the most exciting feature of intellectual life since the Revolution. It is exciting for the same reasons that the promise of affiliation with or incarnation of Something Larger has always been exciting: it suggests that we may get taken behind the scenes, behind the appearances to a hidden place where we may, for the first time, become what we really are. Such a theory, if it existed, would do *wholesale*, for everybody, what one might have thought could only be done by each person for himself, one at a time – it would give us autonomy.

The dangers of the search for such autonomy have been exhibited in detail by analysts of fascism, by historians of Marxism like Kolakowski, and by many others who have written on the sociology of radical movements, and on the psychological roots of what Yack calls 'the longing for total revolution'. The question of whether this longing has, so far, done more harm than good – a question which divides, e.g., Kolakowski from E. P. Thompson, as it divided Orwell from Isaac Deutscher – is not one about which I feel any certainty, though I incline to Kolakowski's and Orwell's side. All I feel able to do is to try to spell out what the intellectual world might look like if the desire for 'radical' social theory were absent. In that world, the switch from an ideal of universal validity to linguistic historicism would encourage irony at the expense of metaphysics – encourage a sense of the contingency of final vocabularies rather than attempts to escape this contingency. For such a switch would make it difficult to invoke the reality-appearance distinction in the contexts in which metaphysicians have sought to deploy it. More specifically, it would make it impossible to think of autonomy as 'release from repressive external forces' or 'as the distortion by social institutions of the essentially human'. It would make it impossible to run together the diminution of pain and humiliation with the idea of 'transforming the nature of man'. To be bluntly chauvinist about it: this switch would emphasize the Anglo-Saxon utilitarian-reformist brand of social thought and de-emphasize the German *Ideologiekritik* brand. It would set aside the 'ideology-nonideology' distinction for the same reason that it sets aside the 'humanizing-dehumanizing' distinction.[42]

In such an intellectual world, there would be an ever-recurring need to restore reflective equilibrium between old platitudes and reactions to new stimuli. But it would be evident that the impetus to social change came from those stimuli, not from theoretical discoveries. So neither the analogy between social theory and natural science, nor the metaphor of penetrating to ever deeper levels in order to expose ever deeper roots, would any longer seem attractive. Social theory would be analogized rather to literary criticism and to jurisprudence – areas of culture in which metaphors of depth and radicality are not of much use.

In *Contingency, Irony and Solidarity* I put forward a contrast between an intellectual world dominated by the 'German' longing for some higher destiny than that of Nietzsche's 'last men', and one dominated merely by the 'Anglo-Saxon' desire to avoid the infliction of unnecessary pain and humiliation in terms of the distinction between the sublime and the beautiful.[43] Radicals want sublimity, but liberals just want beauty. Liberals in the Mill-Dewey tradition dream of a utopia in which everybody has a chance at the things which only the richer citizens of the rich North Atlantic democracies have been able to get – the freedom, wealth and leisure to pursue private perfection in idiosyncratic ways. This utopia is just a lot more of the same kind of thing as we have had a little of already – not a transfiguration but a redistribution. Radicals, by contrast, want a world in which all things have been made new, and in which the rearrangement of little private things, the pursuit of idiosyncratic autonomy, is subsumed under some higher, larger, more thrilling communal goal. They want a public version of the sublimity which, I have been urging in this chapter, is by its nature private – the sublimity one attains by breaking out of some particular inheritance (a vocabulary, a tradition, a style) which one had feared might bound one's entire life.

Because they despise the prospect of a world of 'last men', radicals treat 'bourgeois society' and 'bourgeois ideology' in the way in which ironist theorists treat metaphysics – as an insidious temptation which it is our duty to surmount. This has often produced the illusion that to criticize metaphysics *is* to criticize bourgeois ideology, and conversely. This casual assimilation produces, among radicals, the illusion that there is an important connection between ironist theory and radical politics. Among liberals, it produces the view that the ironists' sense of contingency rots the moral fabric of democratic societies. Both illusions are encouraged by memories of Nietzsche's occasional anti-democratic frothings, Heidegger's attempt to climb on Hitler's bandwagon, Sartre's period of mindless allegiance to Stalin, and Foucault's quasi-anarchism.

The wide variety of political views with which the first of these illusions is compatible – fascism, Stalinism, anarchism – confirms Yack's view that the common element of radical politics is the craving for a sublime Otherness, something to which the everyday predicates in terms of which we describe the difference between the beautiful and the ugly, the pleasant and the painful, do not apply. It seems strange to associate Habermas – the most sensible, temperate, and effective spokesman for social democracy among contemporary philosophers – with such a craving. Yet from the perspective of my linguistic historicism, Habermas' distrust of contextualism, his search for 'universal validity', is one more symptom of that craving. His conviction that there is an 'emancipatory interest' distinct from the merely 'technical interest' in how to rearrange things so as to produce less pain and more happiness is another. Further, there is his conviction that mere Anglo-Saxon 'positivism' and 'scientism' are insufficient for an understanding of contemporary society, and his suspicion that they are somehow 'complicit' with what is worst in that society.[44] As I see it, this conviction represents a residual acceptance of Kant's nature-freedom distinction and of Marx's contrast between 'ideology' and a mode of thought which, because it represents 'human freedom' rather than any 'external constraints', succeeds in being non-ideological. To this extent, at least, I view Habermas himself as still enmeshed in what he calls 'the philosophy of subjectivity'.

If one starts off from the view that freedom is the recognition of contingency rather than of the existence of a specifically human realm exempt from natural necessity, then one will be more dubious about the social utility of philosophy than Habermas is. One will hope for less from philosophy, at least from the sort of philosophy characterized by what Habermas calls 'universalist problematics and strong theoretical strategies'.[45] Instead, one will put most of one's hopes for the relief of unnecessary, socially-countenanced, pain and humiliation in two things. First, the sorts of writing I listed above: novels, articles and reports by those who are able to make specific kinds of pain and humiliation visible. Second, proposals for specific changes in social arrangements – e.g., in laws, company regulations, administrative procedures, educational practises, etc., etc. This means that terms like 'late capitalism', 'modern industrial society', and 'conditions of the production of knowledge' will be employed less frequently and terms like 'worker representation', 'laws against unproductive financial manipulation', and 'journalists' union' more.

A preference for this level of concreteness rather than characteristic of large-scale German-style 'social theory' is, of course, not simply a deduction from large philosophical premises. It is justified, if at all, not simply by a desire for the recognition of contingency but by a political judgment:

namely, that the rich democracies of the present day already contain the sorts of institutions necessary to their own reform, and that communication among the citizens of those democracies is not 'distorted' by anything more esoteric than greed, fear, ignorance, and resentment. This amounts to saying that the instruments of perfectibility are already, in the rich North Atlantic constitutional democracies, in place – that the principal institutions of contemporary democratic societies do not require 'unmasking' but rather strenuous utilization, supplemented by luck. Such a judgment is risky, and perhaps mistaken. But if it is mistaken, it will not be shown to be so by 'universalist problematics and strong theoretical strategies', but by continued trial and error.

NOTES

1. This paper is a reworking of material which I had intended to include in that book, but left out of the final version for organizational reasons. So it sometimes contains bits of the jargon which I developed in that book – e.g., a contrast between the 'ironist' and the 'metaphysician'. I define these terms at pp. 73–75 of *Contingency, Irony and Solidarity* [Editor's note: (Cambridge: Cambridge University Press, 1989)]. Roughly, the ironist is a nominalist and historicist who strives to retain a sense that the vocabulary of moral deliberation he or she uses is a product of history and chance – to his or her having been born at a certain time at a certain place. The metaphysician, by contrast, is someone who believes that there is one right vocabulary of moral deliberation, one which is in touch with reality (and, in particular, with our essential humanity). The heroine of my book is the 'liberal Ironist' – someone devoted to social justice who nevertheless takes her own devotion to this cause as merely contingent. I discuss Habermas at pp. 61–69 as a 'liberal who is unwilling to be an ironist'. I discuss Derrida's 'Envois' in chapter 6. The core of my book is a distinction between private concerns, in the sense of idiosyncratic projects of self-overcoming, and public concerns, those having to do with the suffering of other human beings. This distinction is emphatically not the one with which some readers have identified it: the distinction between the domestic hearth and the public forum, between οικος and πόλις.
2. [Editor's note: Jacques Derrida, *The Post Card: From Socrates to Freud and Beyond*, trans. Alan Bass (Chicago: University of Chicago Press, 1987).]
3. *Der Philosophische Diskurs der Moderne*, (Frankfurt: Suhrkamp, 1985), p. 117. [Editor's note: Subsequently published as Jürgen Habermas, *The Philosophical Discourse of Modernity: Twelve Lectures*, trans. Frederick G. Lawrence (Cambridge: Polity Press, 1987), p. 94. All subsequent references in square brackets refer to the English translation.]
4. [Editor's note: G. W. F. Hegel, *Philosophy of Right*, trans. S. W. Dyde (Amherst: Prometheus, 1996).]
5. Ibid., p. 362 [311].
6. Foucault is the one person on this list who might be thought to have reversed Nietzsche's inclination to disengage philosophy from projects of human emancipation. Foucault certainly said a lot of useful things about contemporary institutions, but I agree with Habermas' criticism of Foucault in chapters 9–10 of *Philosophische Diskurs*, and in particular with his claim that Foucault's notion of emancipation turns on a contrast between 'power' and 'the implicit knowledge of the people' upon whom power is exercised – a contrast to which Foucault is not, given his view of the interconnection of truth and power, entitled. Some readers of Derrida, such as

Richard Bernstein, have attempted to attribute ethico-political, egalitarian, motives to his work; Derrida himself obviously believes that deconstruction has some sort of political relevance. I am dubious about such claims, but I shall not try to argue the issue here. Derrida's own attempt to make deconstruction relevant to politics is ably criticized by Thomas McCarthy in 'On the Margins of Politics', *Journal of Philosophy*, vol. 86 (1989), pp. 645–648.

7. *Philosophische Diskurs*, p. 346 [296].
8. Habermas says that 'the transcendent moment of universal validity bursts every provinciality asunder; the obligatory moment of accepted validity claims renders them carriers of a *context-bound* everyday practice'. (Ibid., p. 375 [322]). But no provincial context is going to burst before somebody has recontextualized current everyday practise by dreaming up new words in which to express alternative possibilities. Revolutionary recontextualization is the sort of thing both poets and ironist theorists like Heidegger and Derrida are good at. Sometimes Habermas talks as if he had adopted the metaphysician's assumption that all the alternative candidates for belief and desire are already available, and the only problem were making sure that they get thrashed out freely. That sort of assumption is suggested, for example, in his discussion of Schiller's *Aesthetic Education of Man* [Editor's note: Friedrich Schiller (trans. Elizabeth M. Wilkinson and L. A. Willoughby), *On the Aesthetic Education of Man* (Oxford: Clarendon Press, 1967).]; he takes Schiller to be treating 'art as primarily a form of communication' (*Philosophische Diskurs*, pp. 62–63 [48]) and to be sowing the germ of the Weberian idea of 'the independent logics of the value spheres of science, morality and art' (p. 64 [50]). Habermas seems to made nervous by Romanticism. He does not discuss Schiller's exaltation of "play" nor is he inclined to follow Shelley (as Dewey did) in thinking of poets as unacknowledged legislators. Still, I take it he might agree with me that all social institutions can do is give you freedom of discussion; you still need the poetic imagination, still need revolutionary recontextualizers, to give you new alternatives to discuss. For he remarks that 'the specialized languages of science and technology, law and morality, economics, political science, etc.... live off the illuminating power of metaphorical tropes'.
9. *Philosophische Diskurs*, p. 223 [189].
10. This means that I shall not go into the interesting, but large and tangled, question, much discussed ever since the days of *Knowledge and Human Interests* [Editor's note: Jürgen Habermas (trans. Jeremy J. Shapiro) (Cambridge: Polity Press, 1987)], of the respective roles of ahistoricist universalist 'transcendentalism' and of pragmatic kibitzing in Habermas' thought. To discuss this topic adequately would involve getting into the further question of whether Habermas wants a theory of rationality which 'grounds' democratic institutions in an ahistorical foundation or simply one which summarizes the tendencies of those institutions – whether Habermas' metaphilosophy is or is not, like Rawls', explicitly historicist. I have mooted this latter question briefly in "Habermas and Lyotard on Post-Modernity" (in my *Essays on Heidegger and Others*, Cambridge: Cambridge University Press, 1991) and in a review of *Philosophische Diskurs* (London Review of Books, September 3, 1987).
11. Habermas, *Philosophical Discourse*, p. 193.
12. Culler, *On Deconstruction* [Editor's note: *Theory and Criticism after Structuralism* (London: Routledge, 1983).], p. 181, quoted by Habermas, *Philosophische Diskurs*, pp. 227–228 [193].
13. I argue, in various essays included in Part II of my *Essays on Heidegger and Others* (Cambridge: Cambridge University Press, 1991), that no such need exists. See also my 'Deconstruction', forthcoming in volume 8 of *The Cambridge History of Literary Criticism* [Editor's note: subsequently published as Richard Rorty, 'Deconstruction', in Raman Selden (ed.), *The Cambridge History of Literary Criticism.*

Volume 8: From Formalism to Poststructuralism (Cambridge: Cambridge University Press, 1995), pp. 166–96.]

14. *Philosophische Diskurs*, pp. 233–234 [199]. Habermas backs up this distinction by saying 'Language games only work because they presuppose idealizations that transcend any particular language game; as a necessary condition of possibly reaching understanding, these idealizations give rise to the perspective of an agreement that is open to criticism on the basis of validity claims. A language operating under these kinds of constraints is subject to an ongoing test. Everyday communicative practise, in which agents have to reach an understanding about something in the world, stands under the need to prove its worth, and it is the idealizing suppositions that make such testing possible in the first place'. I agree with the gist of this, though I should argue, against Habermas and Apel, that the relevant idealizations need not involve the notion of 'universal validity'.
15. Ibid., pp. 240–241 [205]. Emphasis in the original.
16. See my criticisms of Gasché's interpretation of Derrida in 'Is Derrida a Transcendental Philosopher?', included in my *Essays on Heidegger and Others* (cited above).
17. *Philosophische Diskurs*, p. 241 [205].
18. Paul de Man, *Blindness and Insight*, p. 110. De Man's respect for the power of philosophy is so great that he thinks 'Derrida's work is one of the places where the future possibility of literary criticism is being decided'. He takes the Kantian idea of 'conditions of possibility' with full seriousness, and thinks that philosophers might discover that critics could not continue to do what they had apparently been doing. But when Kant showed that metaphysics was 'impossible' his argument was that it was always possible to 'demonstrate' antithetical propositions once one trespassed across the bounds of sense. It is hard to see what the analogue for literary criticism might be; nobody would be surprised, or disturbed, to hear that critics are unable to resolve disputes over antithetical interpretations of a text. De Man could not really have supposed that literary criticism must meet Northrop Frye's demands for 'scientific status', yet only some such presupposition could make sense of his tributes to Derrida.
19. 'The attempt to have a child by Socrates' is one of Derrida's figures, in *La Carte Postale*, for doing the sort of thing which the metaphysical tradition has always tried to do – produce one more candidate for the role of all-powerful, all-encompassing vocabulary. It is an attempt Derrida explicitly repudiates.
20. I here conflate 'Proposition 2' on p. 224 [190] of Habermas' book with 'Proposition 2' on p. 227 [193].
21. [Editor's note: Jacques Derrida, *Glas*, trans. John P. Leavey, Jr and Richard Rand (Lincoln: University of Nebraska Press, 1986).]
22. Ibid., pp. 246–247 [210, note 28].
23. Ibid., p. 31 [20]. See also p. 166 [139]: 'Since the close of the eighteenth century, the discourse of modernity has had a single theme under ever new titles: the weakening of the forces of social bonding, privatization and diremption – in short, the deformations of a one-sidedly rationalized everyday praxis which evoke the need for something equivalent to the unifying power of religion'.
24. See my 'The Priority of Democracy to Philosophy' in my *Objectivity, Relativism and Truth* (Cambridge: Cambridge University Press, 1991).
25. Op. cit., p. 416 [358].
26. Ibid., p. 351 [301].
27. Ibid., p. 344 [294]; compare p. 333 [284].
28. Ibid., p. 375 [323].
29. Ibid., p. 372 [320].
30. Ibid., p. 371 [319].
31. Ibid., pp. 374–375 [322].
32. Ibid., p. 387 [333].

33. Ibid., p. 388 [333 and 334].
34. See ibid., p. 371 [318]: 'Castoriadis ends where Simmel began: with *Lebensphilosophie*'. Compare p. 242 [206] where, commenting on my view that 'science and morality, economics and politics, are delivered up to a process of language-creating protuberances *in just the same way* as art and philosophy' Habermas says: 'One sees how the Nietzschean pathos of a *Lebensphilosophie* that has made the linguistic turn beclouds the sober insights of pragmatism'.
35. Ibid., p. 385 [331].
36. Appendix to *Knowledge and Human Interests*, p. 310.
37. For some attempts to defend this claim about the non-existence of 'humanity', see my 'Cosmopolitanism Without Emancipation: A Reply to Jean-Francois Lyotard' in my *Objectivity, Relativism and Truth* [Editor's note: (Cambridge: Cambridge University Press, 1991).] See also my 'Pragmatism and Feminism', *Michigan Quarterly Review* (Spring, 1991).
38. We linguistic historicists tend to agree with Dewey that 'The worse or evil is a rejected good. In deliberation and before choice no evil presents itself as evil. Until it is rejected, it is a competing good. After rejection, it figures not as a lesser good, but as the bad of that situation'. *Nature and Conduct* (*Middle Works*, vol. 14), p. 193. See also Dewey's 'Outlines of a Critical Theory of Ethics' (*Early Works*, vol. 3, p. 379): 'Goodness is not remoteness from badness. In one sense, goodness is based upon badness; that is, good action is always based upon action good once, but bad if persisted in under changing circumstances'.
39. See Bernard Yack, *The Longing for Total Revolution: Philosophical Sources of Social Discontent from Rousseau to Marx and Nietzsche* (Princeton: Princeton University Press, 1985), p. 365.
40. See chapter 5 of ibid., pp. 209–210, in the course of which Yack cites Dieter Henrich's claim that Hegel's 'is the only philosophic theory which recognizes absolute contingency.'
41. Op. cit., p. 366.
42. See Raymond Geuss, *The Idea of Social Theory* [Editor's note: *Habermas and the Frankfurt School* (Cambridge: Cambridge University Press, 1981).] on 'ideology-critique'.
43. Nietzsche had another way of putting it: 'Man does not live for pleasure; only Englishmen do that'. *The Twilight of the Idols* ('Maxims and Arrows', no. 12).
44. See *Knowledge and Human Interests*, p. 5: 'Positivism . . . has regressed behind the level of reflection represented by Kant's philosophy'. For the Habermas of that early book, Kant's nature-freedom distinction remains an essential propaeduetic to Hegel's discovery of what Habermas called 'the emancipatory power of reflection, which the subject experiences in itself to the extent that it becomes transparent to its own genesis' and to a denial of the 'positivist' doctrine that 'knowledge is a mere instrument of an organism's adaptation to its environment' (ibid., p. 197) – a doctrine Dewey thought entirely compatible with the criticism of contemporary institutions. Although Habermas has changed his views a great deal in the ensuing twenty years, I think he remains faithful to the conviction that social theory can do something for contemporary societies analogous to what individuals can do privately (in, e.g., psychoanalysis): viz., become 'transparent to their own genesis'. For a good critical discussion of Habermas' theory of 'the emancipatory interest' see Thomas McCarthy, *The Critical Theory of Jürgen Habermas* (Cambridge, Mass.. MIT Press, 1978), section 2.5, esp. pp. 99ff. McCarthy is very helpful on Habermas' attempt to bring Kant together with Marx.
45. *The Philosophical Discourse of Modernity*, p. 208. On this topic, see an exchange between Thomas McCarthy and myself in *Critical Inquiry*, vol. 16 (1990).

PART II
ETHICS AND POLITICS

INTRODUCTION

At the end of Chapter 1, Habermas argues that the dispute between Derrida and himself is not only over the distinction between philosophy and literature but also, and more importantly, concerns the possibility of social critique. The chapters in this Part focus on the affinities and differences between Derrida and Habermas on questions of ethical and political critique.

Some commentators have suggested that Derrida's work took an ethical and political turn during the 1980s, when Derrida started addressing ethical and political issues directly. Derrida and some of his followers have responded that Derrida's work was ethical and political from the very beginning, even when it did not address ethical and political issues directly. This is so since deconstructive readings question established authorities and totalitarian closures, whether of philosophical texts or political systems.

Generally speaking, Critical Theorists and Habermasians, including Habermas himself, have argued that Derrida's deconstruction is ethically and politically vacuous, if not dangerous. Derrida and other deconstructionists have responded that the Habermasian approach risks reifying the institutions and practices of existing liberal democracies, and that the approach excludes difference, disagreement and otherness because it conceives of ethics and politics in a rationalistic and consensual fashion.

At issue in the five chapters in this Part are first of all how to conceive of the relationship to the other, something addressed in particular by Simon Critchley, Derrida and Habermas. While central to both Derrida and Habermas, they nonetheless conceive of the relation to the other – or intersubjectivity – in very different ways. Habermas argues that a symmetrical and inclusive relation to the other is possible; Derrida that symmetry and inclusion is only made possible by a simultaneous asymmetry and exclusion. Another issue, broached by Richard J. Bernstein and Seyla Benhabib in particular, is what should be the focus of a theory of ethics and politics: the exceptional and marginal (Derrida), or the communicative contexts of ordinary politics (Habermas)? In Critchley and Derrida's terms, can justice be achieved through the right norms (Habermas), or does justice – and, hence, ethics, politics and democracy – exceed any positive norm (Derrida)?

Further Reading

For an overview of the debates surrounding the politics of postmodernism, including Derrida and Habermas, see White 1991. For Habermasian critiques of Derrida on ethics and politics, see Fraser 1984 and McCarthy 1988 and 1990. For a critique of Habermas, see Coole 1996.

Like Bernstein in Chapter 4, some commentators have argued that Derrida and Habermas are more or less complementary when it comes to ethics and politics, thus suggesting that even if there are philosophical disagreements, it may be possible for Derrideans and Habermasians to engage in a meaningful dialogue at the level of ethics and politics. Some of these commentators have argued that, while there are differences between Derrida and Habermas, one can supplement Derrida with Habermas (Critchley 1999; Devenney 2004), or Habermas with Derrida (Honneth 1995). Others have argued that, on concrete political issues, there are affinities, while incommensurable differences remain with regard to underlying philosophical assumptions of their politics (van Reijen 1994). For an attempt to go beyond the 'either Derrida or Habermas', see also Landry 2000.

For comparisons and uses of Derrida and Habermas in other contexts, see Hoy 1985 (law), Mendieta 2003 (human cloning), Myerson 1995 (the university), and Purdon 2003 and Reader 2004 (environment and ecology).

4

Richard J. Bernstein

AN ALLEGORY OF MODERNITY/POSTMODERNITY: HABERMAS AND DERRIDA

This chapter serves as a bridge to Parts I and II, moving from a consideration of issues surrounding philosophy and reason to issues concerning ethics and politics. Richard J. Bernstein is inspired by Hannah Arendt and, like Rorty, American Pragmatism. In addition he has written extensively on both Critical Theory, including Habermas, and so-called postmodern theory, including Derrida.

In this chapter, Bernstein looks at Habermas and Derrida as representatives of modernity and postmodernity respectively. While they cannot be reconciled, their different foci complement one another. Derrida is useful for thinking about difference and the singularity of the other in relation to ethics and politics; yet, he claims, his writings remain too abstract and philosophical. Derrida does not consider how the empirical social sciences may inform philosophy (and vice versa), and Derrida does not say enough about what is to be done about, for instance, the political decisions one should take and how one should take them. In this regard, Bernstein argues, Habermas is more insightful.

During the past decade – in virtually every area of cultural life – there has been an explosion of discourses about 'modernity' and 'postmodernity'. These discourses and the endless symposia dealing with this problematic have been at once heady and confusing. Heady, because they are signs of a

Richard J. Bernstein, The New Constellation: *The Ethical-Political Horizons of Modernity/Postmodernity* (Cambridge: Polity Press, 1991).

prevailing mood – what Heidegger calls a *Stimmung* – one which is amorphous, elusive, protean. It is difficult to pin down and to characterize. Nevertheless it exerts a powerful influence. For there is a prevailing sense that something is happening that radically calls into question entrenched ways of thinking, acting and feeling. Consider the following description of the postmodern movement as a movement of 'unmaking' by the literary critic, Iban Hassan.

> It is an antinomian moment that assumes a vast unmaking of the Western mind – what Michel Foucault might call postmodern *epistēmē*. I say 'unmaking' though other terms are now *de rigueur*: for instance, deconstruction, decentering, disappearance, demystification, discontinuity, *différance* dispersion, etc. Such terms express an ontological rejection of the traditional full subject, the *cogito* of Western philosophy. They express, too, an epistemological obsession with fragments, and a corresponding ideological commitment to minorities in politics, sex and language. To think well, to feel well, to act well, to read well according to this *epistēmē* of unmaking, is to refuse the tyranny of wholes: totalization in human endeavour is potentially totalitarian.'[1]

Consider also the way in which Jean-Francois Lyotard defined 'modern' and 'postmodern' in his polemical monograph, *The Post-modern Condition: A Report on Knowledge* – a tract that draws upon many 'postmodern' themes and which has provoked extensive discussion:

> I will use the term modern to designate any science that legitimates itself with reference to a metadiscourse of this kind making explicit appeal to some grand narrative, such as the dialectics of Spirit, the hermeneutics of meaning, the emancipation of the rational or working subject, or the creation of wealth.
>
> Simplifying to the extreme I define postmodern as incredulity toward metanarratives. This incredulity is undoubtedly a product of progress in the sciences; but that progress in turn presupposes it. To the obsolescence of the metanarrative apparatus of legitimation corresponds most notably, the crisis of metaphysical philosophy and of the university institution which in part relied on it. The narrative function is losing its functors, its great hero, its great voyages, its great goal.[2]

Although these passages give some indication of the 'postmodern' mood, it is becoming increasingly evident that the terms 'modern' and 'postmodern' are not only vague, ambiguous and slippery, they have been used in conflicting and even contradictory ways. Even when this confusion is acknowledged there has been a strong temptation to go on using them, to slide into a quasi-essentialism where we talk as if there are a set of determinate features that mark off the 'modern' from the 'postmodern'. The trouble is that nobody seems to agree about what these distinguishing characteristics are. My own conviction is that we have reached a stage of discussion where these labels (and their cognates) obscure more than they clarify – that it is better to drop these terms from our 'vocabularies', and to try to sort out the relevant issues without reifying these labels.

So I want to do something different, but something that is relevant to these debates. I want to play off against each other two thinkers whose names are frequently invoked in the so-called quarrel of 'moderns' and 'postmoderns', a quarrel that seems to have displaced the venerable quarrel of the 'ancients' and the 'moderns'. Habermas, for whom the concept of modernity is central, is frequently taken to be the boldest defender of the unfinished project of modernity, a forceful champion of the Enlightenment legacy. Derrida, who rarely even mentions 'modernity' or 'postmodernity', is nevertheless taken to be the 'postmodern' thinker par excellence.[3] Initially, the differences between them – differences in focus, style, tone, and the legacies upon which they draw, *seem* so striking that one wonders if they share any common ground. When one turns to the ways in which they write about each other, one may despair of bridging what appears unbridgeable.[4] It is all too easy to think that an abyss separates them, that if ever there were vocabularies that are incommensurable then the vocabularies of Habermas and Derrida qualify as paradigmatic examples. I do not think that there is some theoretical perspective in which their crucial differences can be reconciled, *aufgehoben*. They cannot. But I want to show some of the ways in which they supplement each other, how we can view them as reflecting two intertwined strands of the 'modern/postmodern' *Stimmung*. The 'logic' of my argument is Both/And rather than Either/Or. This Both/And exhibits unresolved, perhaps unresolvable tensions and instabilities.

Drawing upon two metaphors used by Adorno – the metaphors of a force-field and constellation – I intend to show how Habermas/Derrida enable us to gain a deeper grasp of our present cultural and philosophical situation. By a 'force-field' Adorno means 'a relational interplay of attractions and aversions that constitute the dynamic, transmutational structure of a complex phenomenon.'[5] By 'constellation' – a metaphor that Adorno borrowed from Benjamin – he means 'a juxtaposed rather than integrated cluster of changing elements that resist reduction to a common denominator, essential core, or generative first principle.'[6] To refer to Benjamin once again, the force-field and constellation that I will be sketching may be read as an *allegory* of the 'modern/postmodern' condition.

My approach to Habermas and Derrida may appear slightly unorthodox. I want to show what they are 'up to'. I share William James' conviction when he shrewdly remarked:

> If we take the whole history of philosophy, the systems reduce themselves to a few main types which under all technical verbiage in which the ingenious intellect of man envelops them, are just so many visions, modes of feeling the whole push, and seeing the whole drift of life, forced on one by one's total character and experience and on the whole *preferred* – there is no other truthful word – as one's best working attitude.[7]

I reject the approach to Habermas and Derrida that reads them as if they consisted only in a collection of disembodied texts with little regard to their flesh and blood experiences. We cannot gain a nuanced understanding of what they are 'up to', to their 'modes of feeling the whole push' unless we pay some attention to the vital formative personal experiences that have shaped even their most theoretical writings. Specifically, I am concerned with the ways in which they have experienced the threats, dangers and challenges of the horrendous – almost incomprehensible – events of the twentieth century.

THE UNFINISHED PROJECT OF THE ENLIGHTENMENT

For Habermas, one of these central formative experiences was his shock as a young adolescent when he discovered the full horrors of Nazism. It is in the background of almost everything he has written. Habermas, who was born in 1929, tells us:

> At the age of 15 or 16, I sat before the radio and experienced what was being discussed before the Nuremberg tribunal, when others, instead of being struck by the ghastliness, began to dispute the justice of the trial, procedural questions, and questions of jurisdiction, there was that first rupture, which still gapes. Certainly, it is only because I was still sensitive and easily offended that I did not close myself to the fact of a collectively realized inhumanity in the same measure as the majority of my elders.[8]

The painful awareness of 'the ghastliness', of 'a collectively realized inhumanity', a sharp sense of 'rupture' were the traumatic experiences of the young Habermas. A question began to take shape – a question that has haunted Habermas ever since: how could one account for the 'pathologies of modernity'? How could one explain that rupture in the cultural tradition of Kant, Hegel and Marx in which the ideals of reason, freedom and justice had been so prominent? As a university student, Habermas, like many of his contemporaries, experienced the intellectual power of Heidegger's *Sein und Zeit* (1927), but he was also deeply affected by Lukács' *History and Class Consciousness* (1922), and especially Horkheimer and Adorno's *Dialectic of Enlightenment* (1944). Before he became Adorno's assistant, Habermas perceived the challenge posed by the *Dialectic of Enlightenment* when in its opening sentence the authors declared:

> In the most general sense of progressive thought, the Enlightenment has always aimed at liberating men from fear and establishing their sovereignty. Yet the fully enlightened earth radiates disaster triumphant.[9]

In the *Dialectic of Enlightenment* the authors relentlessly sought to highlight the 'dark side' of the Enlightenment legacy and indeed all of social and cultural modernity – the way in which the Enlightenment gave rise to and promoted a 'totalitarian' instrumental rationality that infected every aspect of cultural, social and personal life – even reaching into the inner recesses of the human psyche. In this respect, Horkheimer and Adorno were deepening and extending the concept of reification that Lukács had so brilliantly analyzed in *History and Class Consciousness*. But contrary to Lukács, they categorically rejected the idea that a proletarian revolution would 'solve' the problem of reification, or that with development of the proletarian class consciousness, there would be a 'final reconciliation' of Subject and Object. Horkheimer and Adorno were at once much closer, and certainly more extreme than, Max Weber – at least the Weber who was read as prophesying that the twentieth century would be the epoch of the triumph of *Zweckrationalität* and bureaucratic normalization creating an 'iron cage' from which there is no escape.

Habermas realized that one could not underestimate the growth and spread of instrumental, strategic, and systems rationality in the economic, social, and political structures of the modern world, and their powerful tendencies to reshape and colonize our everyday life-world. But at first, almost instinctively, and later, with increasing theoretical finesse, Habermas argued that this monolithic portrait of the totalitarian character of Enlightenment rationality was over drawn. It failed to do justice to those philosophic and historical tendencies – also rooted in the Enlightenment – that gave rise to democratic public spaces in which a different type of communal rationality was manifested.[10] At a deeper level there was a failure to do justice to what Habermas first called symbolic interaction (and later called communicative action), and its distinctive type of rationality – the type of action that is oriented to mutual understanding and consensual action rather than to the goals of efficiency and success.

Gradually it became clear to Habermas that a proper response to all those – whether they were associated with the political left or right – who claimed that our modern destiny is one in which there is an ineluctable triumph of instrumental, technological 'rationality' (what Heidegger called *Gestell*) is to reopen and rethink the entire problematic of rationality. In this rethinking – this reconstructive project – one needs to draw crucial and categorical distinctions between different types of action, rationality, rationalization processes, and their complex dynamic interrelations. Although Habermas' terminology has shifted and has become more differentiated, he has consistently maintained that there is a categorical distinction between the varieties of instrumental, strategic, systems, and technological rationality *and* communicative, dialogical rationality. Furthermore he has argued that instrumental rationality pre supposes and is dependent upon communicative rationality. All attempts to reduce or translate communicative action to monological, teleological, goal-oriented action and rationality fail – or so Habermas argues. Once we make a categorical distinction between communicative and purposive-rational action, we can sharply distinguish what the rationalization of these different action-types means.

'Purposive-rational actions can be regarded under two different aspects – the empirical efficiency of technical means and the consistency of choice between suitable means.'[11] 'Rationalization' as it pertains to purposive-rational actions means increasing efficiency or the consistency of 'rational' choices. This is the type of rationalization that has been privileged by neoclassical economists and those influenced by models of economic rationality.

But 'rationalization' of the communicative action has a radically different meaning:

> Rationalization here means extirpating those relations of force that are inconspicuously set in the very structures of communication and that prevent conscious settlement of conflicts . . . Rationalization means overcoming such systematically distorted communication in which action supporting consensus concerning the reciprocally raised validity claims . . . can be sustained in appearance only, that is counterfactually.'[12]

The position expressed in this passage is rich in its consequences. I want to emphasize that Habermas' theoretical reconstructive project of elucidating the universal conditions for communicative action is not merely 'theoretical': it has strong practical consequences for orienting our ethical and political activity. It directs us to the normative task of overcoming those material obstacles that prevent or inhibit undistorted and non-coerced communication. Positively stated, it means working toward the cultivation of practices that bring us closer to the ideal of seeking to resolve conflicts through discourses where the only relevant force is the 'force of the better argument'. Habermas is frequently misread as if he were proposing an ideal form of life in which all conflicts would be settled by rational discussion – an ideal form of life where all violence would disappear. But this is a caricature. Our concrete historical forms of life are always shaped by traditions, social practices and communal bonds that are more concrete and complex than our rational discursive practices. Without these traditions there would be no *substance* to our ethical and political convictions. Violence and distortion may be uneliminable, but they can be diminished. Habermas' limited but all-important thesis is that:

> In action oriented to reaching understanding, validity claims are 'always already' implicitly raised. Those universal claims (to the comprehensibility of the symbolic expression, the truth of the propositional content, the truthfulness of the intentional expression, and the rightness of the speech act with respect to existing norms and values) are set in the general structures of possible communication. In these validity claims communicative theory can locate a gentle, but obstinate, a never silent although seldom redeemed claim to reason, a claim that must be recognized *de facto* whenever and wherever there is to be consensual action).[13]

Habermas rejects any philosophy of history that is explicitly or implicitly committed to a grand teleological narrative. Nevertheless he does strongly affirm that, even though the claim to reason – to communicative dialogical reason – is silenced over and over again, it 'develops a stubbornly transcending power, because it is renewed with each act of unconstrained understanding, with each moment of living together in solidarity, of successful individuation, and of saving emancipation.'[14]

Habermas is a thoroughgoing fallibilist who rejects classical foundationalist and transcendental arguments. One of his criticisms of thinkers like Heidegger, Adorno and Derrida is that they still write in the 'shadow of the "last" philosopher, as did the first generation of Hegelian disciples. They still feel the need to battle against those "strong" concepts of system, totality, truth, and completed theory which belong to the past.'[15] Ironically, much of the *pathos* of their writings gains its force from the specter of the Grand System. 'They still think that they have to arouse philosophy from what Derrida calls "the dream of its heart." They believe they have to tear philosophy away from the madness of expounding a theory that has the last word.'[16] Despite their protests to the contrary, they are still entrapped in the *aporias* and *culs-de-sac* of what Habermas calls 'The Philosophy of Subjectivity'. Their failure, according to Habermas, is not to realize and fully appreciate that the 'fallibilist consciousness of the sciences caught up with philosophy too, a long time ago.'[17] When they declare that philosophy or metaphysics is over, their image of philosophy is still that of the Absolute System – the philosophy of 'the last word'. Each, in his way, wants to keep philosophy or thinking 'pure' – pure from any contamination by empirical social scientific research.

Habermas' fallibilism is not incompatible with making universal claims and seeking to redeem them with the strongest arguments we can give. This is the way in which he conceives of his own theory of communicative action. In *this* respect, Habermas sees no epistemological difference between a theory of communicative action and any other scientific theory. For in advancing any theory we are always making universal validity claims which are necessarily open to ongoing criticism and revision.[18]

Throughout his intellectual career, Habermas has relentlessly sought to track down, expose and defeat the varieties of nihilism, relativism, decisionism, historicism and neo-Aristotelian contextualism that have been so fashionable in the twentieth century. Here too his motivations are not exclusively theoretical – they are motivated by his practical concerns. For he argues that the logic of all these 'positions', when we think them through, undermines the possibility of critique that is rationally grounded and warranted. He criticizes all forms of totalizing critique, claiming that they lead to performative contradictions. What he says about Nietzsche applies equally to all those who work in his shadow (including Derrida): 'Nietzsche's critique consumes the critical impulse itself.' 'If thought can no longer operate in the realms of truth and validity claims, then analysis and critique lose their meaning.' One is left only with the seductions of a 'bad' aestheticism that 'enthrones *taste*, the "Yes" and "No" of the palate . . . as the sole organ of knowledge beyond Truth and Falsity, beyond Good and Evil.'[19]

Pervading all of Habermas' writings is his strong and unshakeable commitment to democracy. No less than John Dewey, Habermas is the philosopher of democracy. This is one of the reasons why he has been so drawn to the American pragmatic tradition, especially Peirce, Mead, and Dewey. From Peirce he appropriates the idea of an ongoing self-critical community of inquirers always open to criticizing its validity claims. Following Mead, he develops a theory of the genesis of the social self in which democratic individuality, and post-conventional morality are realizable achievements of practical intersubjectivity. With Dewey, Habermas believes in the normative ideal of a democratic society in which all share and participate. Like Dewey, who saw the most urgent problem of our time to be the cultivation of democratic public life, Habermas also believes that democratic participation is compatible with the complexity of advanced technological societies.

Habermas' entire project can be conceived of as a rethinking and rewriting of the *Dialectic of Enlightenment*. Habermas, like his mentors, has been alert to the self-destructive tendencies unleashed by the Enlightenment. But against them he argues that we need a more differentiated analysis of the conflicting tendencies of modernity and the Enlightenment legacy – one that does justice to the powerful tendencies of the growth and spread of systems rationality *and* those fragile practices in which we can still discern the transcending power of communicative rationality. Habermas is far more dialectical than Horkheimer and Adorno. For the overwhelming thrust of the *Dialectic of Enlightenment* is negative – it is a dark narrative of ineluctable self-destruction. But in a more dialectically nuanced manner, Habermas shows that our present situation, and the future possibilities open to us, are systematically ambiguous. Whether we will some day live in the cosmic night of nihilism *or* restore a proper balance between communicative and systems rationality is still an open question. The 'colonization of the life world by systems rationality' is the most powerful tendency of advanced technological societies. But this tendency is not the manifestation of a logic of history that is working itself out 'behind our backs'. The promise of modernity is still an unfinished *project* – a project whose realization is dependent upon our present *praxis*.

Once we get a sense of Habermas' mode of 'feeling the whole push', his vision of 'the whole drift of life' then many aspects of his thinking and actions fall into place. We can understand why he is so suspicious of the ways in which the talk of 'postmodernity' and 'post-Enlightenment' slip into 'old' variations of counter- or anti-modern themes. We can understand his frequent political and journalistic interventions in a German context. For Habermas is hyper-sensitive to those aspects of the pernicious cultural tendency to separate Germany's 'spiritual destiny' from the moral and political achievements of Western democracy. Despite Habermas' acknowledgment that Heidegger – the Heidegger of *Sein und Zeit* – is Germany's greatest twentieth-century philosopher, he is scathing in his exposure and criticism of the ideological biases that infect Heidegger's writings from 1929 on.[20] We can even understand why Habermas is so critical and deeply suspicious of the major tendencies in post-World War II French cultural life. He reads Derrida as little more than a latinized disciple of Heidegger who furthers some of the worst tendencies in the late Heidegger. For he thinks that Derrida seduces us into thinking we can confront contemporary political, ethical and juridical problems by endless deconstruction of texts. Habermas is impatient with anyone who disdains concrete empirical social scientific research – who still wants to keep thinking 'pure'.

Iris Murdoch once shrewdly remarked 'it is always a significant question to ask of any philosopher: what is he afraid of?' The answer for Habermas is clear. It is 'irrationalism' whatever guise it takes – whether ugly fascist forms, disguised neo-conservative variations, or the playful antics of those who seek to domesticate Nietzsche. In a time when it has become so fashionable to attack, mock, ridicule the claim to Reason, Habermas is not afraid to appear 'old-fashioned' – to insist on 'the stubbornness with which philosophy clings to the role of the "guardian of reason"' – a role that 'can hardly be dismissed as an idiosyncrasy of self-absorbed intellectuals, especially in a period in which basic irrationalist undercurrents are transmuted once again into a dubious form of politics.'[21]

The Elusiveness and Threat of Otherness

Let me turn abruptly to Derrida. The turn is abrupt because initially it appears to be crossing an unbridgeable chasm. If one can speak of an experience of incommensurability and radical otherness, the turn to Derrida seems to transport us to a different world with few if any points of contact with the problems, theses and concerns that so preoccupy Habermas. I have already suggested that the metaphors of a constellation and force-field are helpful to grasp the agonistic and antagonistic tensions between them. To show this I want to adumbrate a reading of Derrida that brings forth the ethical-political-juridical motifs that run through *all* his writings.[22]

Just as I began my analysis of Habermas by recollecting a formative experience in his intellectual development, I want to juxtapose this with what Derrida himself takes to be a crucial experience of his childhood. Habermas and Derrida are almost exact contemporaries (Habermas was born in 1929, Derrida in 1930). At the time when Habermas was growing up in Nazi Germany, Derrida was experiencing the war as a French Algerian Jew in El-Biar. In the fragments of his autobiography that Derrida weaves into his writings and from some of his interviews, we can gain a glimmer of his childhood experiences – or at least his *memory* of them.

> The war came to Algeria in 1940, and with it, already then, the first concealed rumblings of the Algerian war. As a child, I had the instinctive feeling that the end of the world was at hand, a feeling which at the same time was most natural, and in any case, the only one I ever knew. Even to a child incapable of analyzing things, it was clear that all this would end in fire and blood. No one can escape that violence and fear.[23]

Derrida came from a petit-bourgeois Jewish family which was partially assimilated. He was and was not a Jew. He was and was not an Algerian. As an Algerian Jew he was and was not a Frenchman. By his own testimony his primary experience was a 'feeling of non-belonging' – of 'otherness'.[24] And this continued when he went to France as a student at the age of nineteen. For Derrida has always characterized himself as working at the margins of philosophy and literature. The motifs of alterity, difference, supplementarity, marginality that weave in and out of all of his texts have their *correspondences* in those early experiences. He tells us:

> My central question is: from what site or non-site (*non-lieu*) can philosophy as such appear to itself, so that it can interrogate and reflect upon itself in an original manner? Such a non-site or alterity would be irreducible to philosophy. But the problem is that such a non-site cannot be defined or situated by means of philosophical language.[25]

The experience and obsessive concern with alterity, otherness – or more precisely, the singularity and otherness of the Other – haunt all of Derrida's texts. Furthermore his fascination with otherness (in all its modes) does have powerful ethical-political resonances – as we shall see. Deconstruction cannot be captured or reduced to a formula. Nevertheless, I can think of no more apt description than the one given by Derrida when he says 'deconstruction is, in itself, a positive response to an alterity which necessarily calls, summons or motivates it. Deconstruction is therefore a vocation – a response to a call.'[26] Deconstruction is 'an openness towards the other.'[27]

When I say that all the texts signed by Derrida are pervaded by ethical-political-juridical motifs, I do not simply mean that Derrida 'has' an ethics and politics. I mean something much stronger. An ethical-political-juridical reading of all his texts is a point of departure for understanding his 'mode of feeling the whole push'. His ethical-political concerns shape and are shaped by his deconstruction of logocentrism, phonocentrism, phallogocentrism, and especially what he – following Heidegger – calls 'the metaphysics of presence'.[28]

Derrida is acutely aware that we cannot question or shake traditional ethical and political claims without at the same time also drawing upon these traditional claims. The very dichotomy of 'inside–outside' is also deconstructed. We are never simply 'inside' or 'outside' metaphysics. Derrida has been read – I think seriously misread – as if he were advocating a total rupture with metaphysics, as if some apocalyptic event might occur that would once and for all release us from the metaphysical exigency. But he mocks the very idea of such an apocalyptic happening.[29] He tells us that 'the idea that we might be able to get outside of metaphysics has always struck me as naive', and that 'we cannot really say that we are "locked into" or "condemned to" metaphysics, for we are, strictly speaking, neither inside nor outside.'[30]

According to Derrida, memory and promise, repetition and rupture always *come* together.[31] Concerning history and tradition, concerning the complex temporality of past-present-future, Derrida, in a manner that is reminiscent of Benjamin, writes:

> My own conviction is that we must maintain two contradictory affirmations at the same time. On the one hand we affirm the existence of ruptures in history, and on the other we affirm that these ruptures produce gaps or faults (*failles*) in which the most hidden and forgotten archives can emerge and constantly recur and work through history. One must surmount the categorical oppositions of philosophic logic out of fidelity to these conflicting positions of historical discontinuity (rupture) and continuity (repetition), which are neither pure break with the past nor a pure unfolding or explication of it.[32]

There is a another prevalent misreading of Derrida – claiming that he is guilty of some sort of linguistic idealism in his linkage of the history of signification, metaphysics and the 'West'. The most common criticism of Derrida is that he 'reduces' everything to texts (and/or language) and declares that there is nothing beyond the text. But the key question is what does Derrida mean by a 'text'? He answers this question in many places, but one of his clearest and most forceful statements occurs in his polemical exchange about apartheid, 'Racism's Last Word'. He tells us that 'text' as he uses the term is not to be confused with the graphisms of a 'book'.

> No more than writing or trace, it is not limited to the *paper* which you can cover with your graphism. It is precisely for strategic reasons that I found it necessary to recast the concept of text by generalizing it almost without any limit that is. That's why there is nothing '*beyond* the text'. That's why South Africa and *apartheid* are, like you and me, part of this general text, which is not to say that it can be read the way one reads a book. That's why the text is always a field of forces: heterogeneous, differential, open, and so on. That's why deconstructive readings and writings are concerned not only with library books, with discourses, with conceptual and semantic contents. They are not simply analyses of discourse. . . . They are also effective or active (as one says) interventions that transform contexts without limiting themselves to theoretical or constative utterances even though they must also produce such utterances.[33]

Derrida claims that his 'strategic reevaluation of the concept of text allows [him] to bring together in a more consistent fashion, in the most consistent fashion possible, theoretico-philosophical necessities with "practical", political and other necessities of what is called deconstruction.'[34] He emphatically affirms that 'deconstructive practices are also and first of all political and institutional practices.'[35]

But what precisely does this mean? How are deconstructive practices 'first of all' political and institutional practices? The following passage provides an important clue.

> what is somewhat hastily called deconstruction is not, if it is of any consequence, a specialized set of discursive procedures, even less the rules of a new hermeneutic method, working on texts or utterances in the shelter of a given and stable institution. It is also, at the very least, a way of taking a position, in its work of analysis, concerning the political and institutional structures that make possible and govern our practice, our competences, our performances. Precisely because it is never concerned only with signified content, deconstruction should not be separable from this politico-institutional problematic and should

> seek a new investigation of responsibility, an investigation which questions the codes inherited from ethics and politics. This means that too political for some, it will seem paralyzing to those who only recognize politics by the most familiar road signs.[36]

Let me step back in order to comment on this dense passage and the controversial claims that Derrida makes here. Derrida is always concerned (obsessed) with the question of the otherness of the Other, with the differences that are presupposed by self-identity. He is always working on the margins, fascinated with the 'logic of supplementarity'. Metaphors of 'exile' and 'parasite' weave through his writings. Derrida is not only concerned with the receding limits that are presumably 'discovered' or stipulated, he is deeply suspicious of all forms of boundary-fixing – including the boundary-fixing between theoretical and practical-political-institutional 'domains'. Here too one must be sensitive to Derrida's precise point if we want to grasp what he is 'up to'. Contrary to what many of his critics (including Habermas) claim, Derrida does *not* seek to deny all distinctions and reduce everything to one confused homogeneous text. He does *not* deny there are important distinctions between philosophy and literature or logic and rhetoric. He scrutinizes the precise 'points' where distinctions, dichotomies, dualisms break down and are called into question. His deconstructive practices would not even make sense unless we initially take distinctions, negations, and oppositions 'seriously'. It is non-reducible heterogeneity and heterology that he makes manifest. He consistently opposes a 'logic of apartheid', radical separation into 'natural' kinds – whether we understand apartheid 'literally' or 'figuratively'. He sees the *logic* of apartheid at work not only in South Africa but in the 'homelands of academic culture'. In responding to the critics of his *appeal* concerning apartheid, he concludes with a declaration that has much broader significance:

> in the homelands of academic culture or of 'political action' you would favor instead reserved domains, the separate development of each community in the zone assigned to it.
>
> Not me.[37]

There is no fixed boundary between theoretical and practical domains, between texts and institutional contexts. Willy-nilly, all deconstruction for Derrida is always and also political. But there is a problem here that needs to be squarely confronted. Deconstruction may be 'too political for some' but why does it also 'seem paralyzing to those who only recognize politics by the most familiar road signs'? We need to probe further.

As a citizen, Derrida has taken strong admirable stands on a variety of political and ethical issues. He has fought against apartheid, written a moving homage to Mandela, actively participated in resisting the French government's attempt to reduce the teaching of philosophy in secondary schools, helped to start a new 'open' university in Paris, been an outspoken critic of infringements on human rights, addressed feminist issues, and was even arrested and interrogated on a framed-up charge in Czechoslovakia. He has been an engaged intellectual. But what do these activities have to do with deconstruction? He speaks about this when he was asked: 'Can the theoretical radicality of deconstruction be translated into a radical praxis?' He tells us 'I must confess that I have never succeeded in directly relating deconstruction to existing political programmes.'[38] The key terms here are 'directly' and 'existing', for Derrida declares 'all of our political codes and terminologies still remain fundamentally metaphysical, regardless of whether they originate from the right or the left.'[39] But this still leaves open the question whether it is even possible to imagine a 'political code' that is not metaphysical – at least in the 'objectionable' sense of metaphysical. Derrida himself is not clear whether this is possible. When asked again whether he thinks this implies inaction and non-commitment, he answers:

> Not at all. But the difficulty is to gesture in opposite directions at the same time: on the one hand to preserve a distance and suspicion with regard to the official political codes governing reality; on the other, to intervene here and now in a practical and engaged manner whenever the necessity arises. This position of dual allegiance, in which I personally find myself, is one of perpetual uneasiness. I try where I can to act politically while recognizing that such action remains incommensurate with my intellectual project of deconstruction.[40]

Although this is one of Derrida's most forthright statements on the relation (or non-relation) 'between' deconstruction and his politics, it is still open to different and conflicting interpretations. I want to suggest a reading that is consonant with many of his other texts. The danger with any political code is that it can become rigidified or reified – a set of unquestioned formulas that we rely on to direct our actions. More important, no code is ever *sufficient* to justify or legitimate a decision in any specific context. No code can close the gap or diminish the undecidability that confronts us in making an ethical-political decision or choice. '*This particular* undecidable opens the field of decision or of decidability.'

> It calls for decision in the order of ethical-political responsibility. It is even its necessary condition. A decision can only come into being in a space that exceeds the calculable program that would destroy all responsibility by transforming it into a programmable effect of determinate causes. There can be no moral or political responsibility without this trial and this passage by way of the undecidable.[41]

Derrida is echoing and reinforcing a point made by many critics of the modern bias that the primary task of moral and political philosophy is to specify and justify the universal rules that ought to govern our decisions and actions. But Derrida is also critical of those who think that an appeal to judgment or *phronēsis* gets us out of this bind.[42] He radicalizes the openness that he takes to be characteristic of responsibility and decision by emphasizing the *experience* of the undecidable. We have to think and act without banisters and barriers – or rather with the realization that it is 'we' who construct and deconstruct these barriers. Nevertheless, responsibility, action, and decision 'here and now' demand that we at least temporarily suspend constant questioning. (Otherwise we would slip into inaction and non-commitment which are also modes of action and commitment.) This is his point about gesturing 'in opposite directions'. We cannot escape from the responsibilities and obligations that are thrust upon us – thrust upon us by the Other. Given our radical contingency we can never know or control when we are called upon to respond. We must always be prepared to confront new unpredictable responsibilities.[43] So when Derrida speaks of his 'perpetual uneasiness' he is not merely expressing an idiosyncratic subjective state of mind but rather expressing a condition of undecidability which – to speak in a non-Derridean manner – is built into 'the human condition'.

Derrida has an acute sense that, at least since the 'rupture' we call Nietzsche, we can no longer be content with self-satisfied appeals to moral and political foundations, first principles and *archai*. We are compelled to question these. But he is equally acute in his realization that such a questioning doesn't 'solve' anything. We cannot assume a permanent frozen stance of *an-archē*. For this is another fixed metaphysical position. We cannot escape responsibility, decision, and choice. They are thrust upon us by the Other. Furthermore, we cannot simply dismiss or ignore those ethical and political principles that are constitutive of our traditions. The problem – and it is a problem for which there cannot be any final or permanent 'solution' – is to live this perpetual uneasiness in a way in which we 'gesture in opposite directions at the same time', where we keep alive the distance of questioning and are prepared to act decisively 'here and now' – where we do not hide in bad faith from the double binds that we always confront.

But still we want to know what sort of politics Derrida does favor. What is its substantive content? Derrida has been extremely tentative and hesitant, although not silent. Considering the subversive quality of all his thinking, and his questioning of all forms of authority (even the authority claimed by 'guardians of reason'), it is easier to discern what he is 'against' rather than what he is 'for'. One will not find in his writings a clear and explicit statement of a political program. But I do not think it is fair to say he is entirely negative – that his political views are nothing but a 'negative theology' translated into a political register. Derrida himself declares 'Deconstruction certainly entails a moment of affirmation. Indeed, I cannot conceive of a radical critique which would not be ultimately motivated by some sort of affirmation, acknowledged or not. Deconstruction always presupposes affirmation. . . .'[44] What then is Derrida affirming?

Let me approach the question of Derrida's normative ethical-political vision in what may seem to be an oblique manner. Already in *Of Grammatology*, Derrida linked phonocentrism, logocentrism, and the metaphysics of presence with phallogocentrism. Phallogocentrism and the question of sexual difference have been persistent iterated motifs throughout his writings – explored with subtle nuances, wit, and sometimes with raucous humor. (Derrida's playfulness – a powerful deconstructive strategy – has infuriated many of his critics and provided ammunition for claiming he is 'non serious'.) Derrida's concern with 'sexual difference' has been a vehicle for exploring and elaborating what he means by *différance* even for probing the blindness and insights of Heidegger's all-important notion of 'ontological difference'. His analyses of 'sexual difference' are intended to move us beyond the logic of binary oppositions so characteristic of metaphysics – or more accurately to complicate the logic of binary oppositions in a manner that makes us aware of differences that always elude our conceptual grids. In what may well be one of the most lyrical passages in his writings he dreams about what may be beyond our traditional gendered ways of thinking, acting, and feeling. He sketches the possibility of a different relationship with the other when he writes:

> This double dissymmetry perhaps goes beyond known or coded marks, beyond the grammar and spelling, shall we say (metaphorically) of sexuality. This indeed revives the following question: what if we were to reach, what if we were to approach here (for one does not arrive at this as one would at a determined location) the area of a relationship to the other where the code of sexual marks would no longer be discriminating? The relationship would not be a-sexual, far from it, but would be sexual otherwise: beyond the binary difference that governs the decorum of all codes, beyond the distinction masculine/feminine. . . . As I dream of saving the chance that his question offers I would like to believe in the multiplicity of sexually marked voices. I would like to believe in the masses, this indeterminable number of blended voices, this mobile of non-identified sexual marks whose choreography can carry, divide, multiply the body of each 'individual', whether he be classified as 'man' or as 'woman' according to the criteria of usage.[45]

The syntactical construction of this passage ('shall we say', 'if we were to reach', 'I would like to believe', etc.) is itself a sign of Derrida's tentativeness in elaborating what is 'beyond the binary difference'. But it can be read as an allegory of Derrida's 'ethical-political' vision. It also enables one to understand the power of Derrida's thinking for those – whether women, Blacks, or others who have experienced the pain and humiliation of being excluded and silenced. For whether Derrida writes about sexual difference, or the logic of apartheid, or a politics of friendship that is no longer infiltrated by fraternal metaphors, when he calls into question the dichotomy of friend and enemy that Carl Schmitt took to be the defining characteristic of all politics, he is envisioning the possibility of a state of affairs where the violence of discrimination – if not completely eliminated – is at least minimized, where difference is no longer taken to be a threat, but is affirmed and celebrated, difference where there is *both* symmetry and asymmetry, reciprocity and non-reciprocity.[46] He even speaks of this as 'a democracy to come' – a democracy not to be identified with any of its existing institutional forms. Here too we can locate Derrida's double gestures. For his tentativeness and hesitancy in elaborating his dream is itself an expression of his conviction that we never quite eliminate violence from our language, institutions, and practices – that it is always a self-deceptive illusion to think this has been achieved – that we can 'arrive at this as one would at a determined location'. But we can – and Derrida takes this to be a perpetual demanding task to be renewed over and over again

> – try to recognize and analyze [violence] as best we can in its various forms: obvious or disguised, institutional or individual, literal or metaphoric, candid or hypocritical, in good or guilty conscience. And if, as I believe, violence remains in fact (almost) ineradicable, its analysis and the most refined, ingenious account of its conditions will be the least violent gestures, perhaps even non-violent, and in any case those which contribute most to transforming the legal-ethical-political rules.[47]

THE *POLEMOS* OF 'MODERNITY/POST MODERNITY'

In order to show how 'the relational interplay of attractions and aversions' between Habermas and Derrida can be read as an allegory of our 'modern/postmodern' condition, I want to consider how they exemplify conflicting strands in the modern/postmodern *Stimmung*. Habermas, as we have seen, is not a naive *Aufklärer*. He is profoundly aware of the ambiguities, conflicts, and treacheries of the Enlightenment legacy. He is not an uncritical champion of modernity. His project has been one of systematically analyzing social and cultural modernity in order to specify and do justice to its conflicting and ambiguous tendencies. The Enlightenment legacy cannot be smoothed out into *either* a grand narrative of the progressive realization of freedom and justice *or* the cosmic night of ineluctable nihilistic self-destruction. With a stubborn persistence, he seeks to keep alive the memory/promise and hope of a world in which justice, equality and dialogical rationality are concretely realized in our everyday practices. He staunchly resists all those who claim this hope must be abandoned, that our most cherished dreams of creating and realizing norms of justice must inevitably turn into totalitarian nightmares. He rejects the all too fashionable view that discursive practices are only a meaningless displacement of power/knowledge regimes. He is a 'guardian of reason', but the reason he defends is dialogical, intersubjective, communicative. He is a fallibilist, but argues this stance is not only compatible with, but requires a serious attempt to ground critique in universal validity claims, and to engage in political *praxis* directed toward the material achievement of the norms of social critique. For Habermas, we can not avoid the question, critique 'in the name of what?' His quarrel with many so-called 'postmodern' thinkers is that they either fail to confront this question, obscure it, or get caught in performative contradictions. One reason why Habermas 'speaks' to so many of 'us' and is so relevant to the 'modern/postmodern' condition is because however feeble and fragile this aspect of the Enlightenment legacy has become, and despite the attacks on this legacy, it nevertheless will not die – the demand for freedom and *claim* to dialogical reasonableness does have a 'stubbornly transcending power' – as recent events from South Africa to Eastern Europe so vividly demonstrate.

Derrida, as I have tried to show, is not indifferent to this memory/promise and hope. He even, in his way, calls for a new *Aufklärung*.[48] But his 'center' – his mode of 'feeling the whole push' is very different from, but not necessarily incompatible with, Habermas' perspective. What is 'central' for Derrida is otherness, alterity, *différance*. His primary concern is with meticulously analyzing and deconstructing the ways in which we consciously or unconsciously exclude, marginalize, suppress, and repress the otherness and singularity of the Other – the Other that refuses to be contained, mastered, domesticated. This is the strand of the 'modern/postmodern' mood that Derrida has the genius for exhibiting.

Few contemporary thinkers have been as incisive and nuanced as Derrida in tracking the varieties of otherness, in *showing* how otherness ruptures, disrupts, threatens and eludes our logocentric conceptual grids. He seeks to show us why and how a 'logic' of opposition and negation requires to be complicated and supplemented by a 'logic' of *différance*. This 'logic' is not quite a *logos* that can bind together differences. For Derrida is also stubbornly persistent in analyzing and exposing the difference of difference. The 'Other' he speaks about is not a 'generalized other' that can be assigned a proper or common name. This is one reason he keeps returning to the question of naming. Translating this into an ethical-political idiom means that when we turn our attention to the singularity of the Other or *différance*, we must focus on the differences that 'make' a difference. Derrida avoids the facile 'postmodern' temptation to lump together all differences under the general rubric of *the* 'Other'.

Derrida 'speaks to' so many of 'us' because the question of otherness (in all its variations) has become a 'central' – if not *the* central – theoretical/practical question of our time.[49] How can we hope to be open to, and respond responsibly to the terror of otherness and singularity of the Other? This is primarily an ethical-political question for which there is not and cannot be a 'final solution'. Derrida is much closer in style and temperament to Adorno and Benjamin than he is to Habermas. Like Adorno, Derrida also seeks to expose the violence of what Adorno called 'identity logic' – the multifarious ways that institutionalized forms of rationality and conceptual grids violate singularity. Like Benjamin, Derrida is also obsessed with fragments, detritus, and the fissures that rupture 'smooth' historical continuities.

When we place Habermas/Derrida in a new constellation – view them as each other's other – then their strengths and weaknesses come into sharp relief. We can witness their symbiotic 'interplay of attractions and aversions'. For Habermas, communicative action and rationality are the powerful magnetic poles of his work. Everything he explores emanates from, and is drawn back to these poles. His reading of the philosophic discourse of modernity is that 'postmodern' philosophic discourses are caught within the *aporias* of 'a philosophy of subjectivity' which is now exhausting itself. These discourses – despite desperate protests to the contrary – have failed to break out of a philosophy of subjectivity or consciousness. They have failed to make the paradigm shift to a model of communicative dialogical action and rationality.[50]

Communicative action – action oriented to mutual reciprocal understanding – never becomes fully thematized in Derrida's writings. But his deconstructive practices bear on it. For Derrida, like Adorno and Benjamin, is far more sensitive to what Habermas acknowledges but does not closely analyze – the multifarious ways in which communication (even under 'ideal' conditions) goes awry. He is alert to the ways in which 'mutual understanding' so frequently turns into mutual misunderstanding, how appeals to dialogue can and do contain their own hidden violences, how communication – especially in the contemporary world – has become little more than an 'economy' of commodity exchange of information bits. He warns us that even appeals to face-to-face spoken communication can repress the heterogeneity and asymmetry of the other.

Abstractly there is something enormously attractive about Habermas' appeal to the 'force of the better argument' until we ask ourselves what this means and presupposes. Even under 'ideal' conditions where participants are committed to discursive argumentation, there is rarely agreement about what constitutes 'the force of the better argument'. We philosophers, for example, cannot even agree what are the arguments advanced in any of our canonical texts, whether Plato, Aristotle, Kant or Hegel, etc. – and there is certainly no consensus about who has advanced the better arguments.

Furthermore there isn't even any agreement about the *role* the argument does or should play in a philosophic 'vocabulary'. We should not be innocent about the ways in which 'tough minded' appeals to argumentation become ideological weapons for dismissing or excluding philosophical alternatives – for example, when analytic philosophers complain that Continental philosophers (including Habermas) do not argue, or indulge in 'sloppy' argumentation. Who decides what is and what is not an argument, by what criteria, and what constitutes the force of the better argument? Who really believes that philosophers can achieve a rational consensus, or even that this is desirable? In raising these issues, I am not suggesting that 'anything goes' or that there is never any way of sorting out better or worse arguments. On the contrary, we can and should debate about what constitutes an argument, how forceful it is, and how we are to evaluate competing arguments. But there are rarely (if ever) any algorithms or clear criteria for determining this in non trivial instances.[51] Think how much more intractable the problems become when we turn to specific ethical and political disputes. Does it even makes sense to think that there might even be a rational consensus about the force of the better argument in the current debates about abortion? Is the very idea of a 'rational consensus' in such concrete conflictual contexts even intelligible? Any society must have some procedures for dealing with conflicts that cannot be resolved by argumentation – even when all parties are committed to rational argumentation. But what precisely is the determinate (*bestimmt*) content of declaring that one ought to consider only the force of the better argument?

There are friends and foes of Derrida who think that he undermines and ridicules any appeal to rational argument – or that this is a consequence of his deconstructive practices. But this is a slander. It is not what he is doing when he analyzes the complex interplay of logic and rhetoric. He does *not* 'reduce' all logic and argumentation to disguised rhetorical tropes.[52] Rather he is showing us just how difficult and complex it is to ferret out argumentation and rhetorical strands even in the most apparently 'straightforward' and 'serious' speech acts.

Habermas is certainly aware of the pervasiveness of plurality, heterogeneity, and difference. Those who think his insistence on universal validity claims means he has no understanding of contingency and plurality are caricaturing him. He even tells us the 'pluralization of diverging universes of discourse belongs to specifically modern experience'. There has been a 'shattering of naive consensus'.[53] For Habermas the primary question is how one is to *respond* to this intensified pluralization. His worry is that the celebration of plurality and difference all too easily degenerates into a self-defeating relativism, contextualism, and 'bad' historicism. Habermas does provide an important corrective to those who uncritically celebrate contingency, plurality, difference and otherness. There are manifestations of otherness that we *legitimately* seek to eliminate and destroy – when we are convinced the other we are confronting is evil – like the evil of apartheid and fascism. One of the most obfuscating aspects of 'modern/postmodern polemics' is the way in which universality is pitted against plurality and alterity. Even those who celebrate plurality and difference – like Lyotard and Rorty – make an implicit appeal to universality – when, for example, they advocate a world in which there is a *universal* 'letting be' where difference is allowed to flourish.

Derrida is not guilty of some of these excesses. He is neither a relativist nor an irrationalist, but he is constantly showing us the treacheries of facile appeals to universals, principles, *archai*. Undecidability for Derrida is not indifference or a mask for nihilism, but rather a constant ethical-political reminder that 'a decision can only come into being in a space that exceeds the calculable program that would destroy all responsibility . . . [that] there can be no moral or political responsibility without this trial and this passage by way of the undecidable'.[54]

Nevertheless, for all Derrida's affirmation that deconstruction intervenes, that it is a way of taking an ethical-political 'position', and that it may be 'too political' for some, there is a certain 'abstractness' in his understanding of politics. Placing Derrida in constellation with Habermas helps to pinpoint this. Deconstruction, he tells us, 'should not be separable from [the] politico-institutional problematic and should seek a new investigation of responsibility'.[55] Derrida has shown – in a series of perceptive analyses ranging from Kant through Heidegger – how their discourses about the university cannot be separated from their discourses about the institutional structure of the modern university. He has developed a sharp and incisive critique of university institutions and practices. But suppose we step back and ask: what does Derrida mean by a 'politico-institutional structure'. Of course, there is no univocal answer to this question. But Derrida never quite rises to the level of *necessary* generality (as he does in telling us what he means by a 'text') where we can gain some perspective, some overview of the complex dynamics of institutional structures that shape politics and society in the contemporary world. We will simply not find in his writings anything resembling a social and political theory – as we do find in Habermas.

It is an important virtue to be vigilant – as Derrida is – about the ways in which *any* general social and political theory or code can go awry, how it can deconstruct itself. But it is just as important and necessary to seek, in a fallibilistic spirit, for a general understanding and explanation of the institutional dynamics of politics and society. Otherwise the specific ways in which we intervene 'here and now' can lack any orientation. Derrida's claims about a 'democracy to come' are powerfully evocative. He warns us against identifying this 'democracy to come' with any of its present institutional forms. Like Habermas he would insist that it is not the task of the philosopher or theorist – as some sort of 'master' intellectual – to lay out blueprints for such a democracy. This can and should be decided by participants. But still it is fair to ask for some determinate content. We want *some* understanding of what kinds of institutions and practices should be developed for 'a democracy to come'. Or even more minimally, we want some orientation about what changes 'here and now' are needed in our present institutional structures. Derrida, thus far, has very little to say about any of this.[56] Consequently there is a danger that, for all the evocative power of the very idea of a 'democracy to come', the idea of such a democracy can become an impotent, vague abstraction.

There is another curious lacuna in Derrida's prolific writings. Earlier I indicated Derrida's deep suspicion of 'boundary-fixing' and his incisiveness in exposing the precise points where boundaries and limits break down and/or recede. He has consistently maintained that philosophy itself is not a well-defined discipline or *Fach* neatly separable from other disciplines and discourses. But there is one lesson or consequence from this master strategy that he has not drawn – and this is the source of many of the sharpest differences between him and Habermas. Habermas argues that there is no fixed boundary between philosophy and the critical social sciences. There is – and ought to be – a symbiotic relationship between philosophy and the social sciences, although they are not reducible to each other. Pragmatically this means that the philosopher, especially the social and political philosopher, must be responsive and alert to what can be learned from the social disciplines. Whatever our final judgment of ways in which Habermas uses and criticizes Weber, Durkheim, Parsons, Mead, Piaget, Kohlberg (and many other social scientists), he has consistently sought to develop a subtle dialectical interplay between philosophical speculation and social scientific theoretically oriented empirical research. In this play, this to-and-fro movement between philosophy and the critical social sciences, he has *practiced* what one would think ought to be a consequence of Derrida's own deconstructive analyses.

Although Derrida does deal with what the French take to be the preeminent *sciences humaines* – especially linguistics and psychoanalysis – there are only casual references to the full range of the social disciplines. More important, Derrida's fundamental bias has been to move in one direction only – to show and expose the dubious 'philosophic' presuppositions that infect the social disciplines, rather than to ask what, if anything, philosophy might learn from them. He tells us:

> To say to oneself that one is going to study something that is not philosophy is to deceive oneself. It is not difficult to show that in political economy, for example, there is a philosophical discourse in operation . . . Philosophy, as logocentrism, is present in every scientific discipline and the only justification for transforming philosophy into a specialized discipline is the necessity to render explicit and thematic the philosophical subtext in every discourse. The principal function

> which the teaching of philosophy serves is to enable people to become 'conscious', to become aware of what exactly they are saying, what kind of discourse they are engaged in when they do mathematics, physics, political economy, and so on. There is no system of teaching or transmitting knowledge which can retain its coherence or integrity without, at one moment or another, interrogating itself philosophically, that is, without acknowledging its subtextual premises; and this may even include an interrogation of unspoken political interests or traditional values.[57]

Habermas would agree with everything that is said here, but he would (rightly, I think) ask: should this not be a two-way street? Should we not also ask what philosophy can learn from critical social scientific research?

The issue here is not just metatheoretical. For it conditions the very way in which Derrida deals with social and political themes. When Derrida examines questions of justice, law, violence he does not *primarily* deal with specific institutional practices, but with the written texts, specifically the writings of those who have addressed these issues – Aristotle, Kant, Hegel, Kafka, Benjamin, Levinas, etc. I do not want to denigrate this way – this *methodos*. His analyses are extraordinarily perceptive and rich in their consequences. But surely – as Derrida himself acknowledges – they need to be *supplemented* by the theoretical and empirical study of societal institutions and practices. But this is not what Derrida does. There is nothing in Derrida's writings that seeks to rule out the importance of critical theoretical and empirical research into the structural dynamics of society and politics. On the contrary, such an endeavor is what his own questioning of boundary-fixing demands. Nevertheless, his neglect of dealing more directly and explicitly with political and societal institutions in their historical complexity does have the consequence of making his own understanding of society and politics sound rather 'thin'.

There are many aspects and problems in the writings of Habermas and Derrida that I have not explored here. But by now I hope the thrust of my argument is clear, and why I believe we can (and should) read them as an *allegory* of the 'modern/postmodern' condition. I reiterate what I said earlier. I do not think there is a theoretical perspective from which we can reconcile their differences, their otherness to each other – nor do I think we should smooth out their 'aversions and attractions'. The nasty questions that they raise about each other's 'project' need to be relentlessly pursued. One of the primary lessons of 'modernity/postmodernity' is a radical skepticism about the possibility of a reconciliation – an *Aufhebung*, without gaps, fissures, and ruptures. However, *together*, Habermas/Derrida provide us with a force-field that constitutes 'the dynamic, transmutational structure of a complex phenomenon' – the phenomenon I have labeled 'modernity/postmodernity'. *Together* they form a new constellation – a 'juxtaposed rather than an integrated cluster of changing elements that resist reduction to a common denominator, essential core, or generative first principle'. I have spoken about Habermas/Derrida, but my primary concern here is not simply to focus on their texts – the texts that bear their signatures. The rationale for examining their texts is because, more rigorously and thoroughly than many others (including their 'followers'), they *show* the tangled intertwined strands of the 'modern/postmodern' *Stimmung*. My reading of Habermas/Derrida is intended to be an allegory of this *Stimmung*. The 'logic' of my allegory has been an unstable tensed Both/And rather than a determinate fixed Either/Or. This is what I believe to be – to use an old-fashioned but not outdated expression – the *truth* of the *polemos* of 'modernity/postmodernity'.

NOTES

1. This passage from Iban Hassan is cited by Albrecht Wellmer, 'The Dialectic of Modernity and Post-Modernity,' in *Praxis International* 4 (January 1985), p. 338.
2. Jean-François Lyotard, *The Postmodern Condition: A Report on Knowledge*, trans. G. Bennington and B. Massumi (Minneapolis: University of Minnesota Press, 1984), pp. xxiii–xxiv.
3. 'I have never been very happy with the term "modernity". Of course, I feel that what is happening in the world today is something unique and singular. As soon, however, as we give it the label of "modernity", we describe it in a certain historical system of evolution or progress (a notion derived from Enlightenment rationalism) which tends to blind us to the fact that what confronts us today is *also* something ancient and hidden in history. I believe that what "happens" in our contemporary world and strikes us as particularly new has in fact an essential connection with something extremely old which has been covered over (*archi-dissumulé*). So that the new is not so much that which occurs for the first time but that "very ancient" dimension which recurs in the "very modern"; and which indeed has been signified repetitively throughout our historical tradition, in Greece and in Rome, in Plato and in Descartes and in Kant, etc. No matter how novel or unprecedented a modern meaning may appear, it is never exclusively *modernist* but is also and at the same time a phenomenon of *repetition*.' 'Dialogue with Jacques Derrida,' in Richard Kearney, ed., *Dialogues with Contemporary Continental Thinkers* (Manchester University Press, 1984), pp. 112–13.
4. Habermas' most sustained discussion of Derrida occurs in *The Philosophical Discourse of Modernity*, trans. F. Lawrence (Cambridge, Mass.: MIT Press, 1987). See chap. 8, 'Beyond a Temporalized Philosophy of Origins: Jacques Derrida's Critique of Phonocentrism', and 'Excursus on Leveling the Genre Distinction between Philosophy and Literature'. Derrida has not systematically discussed Habermas' work. But see his brief and sharp reply to Habermas, p. 156, footnote 9, *Limited Inc.*, ed. Gerald Graff (Evanston: Northwestern University Press, 1988).
5. Martin Jay, *Adorno* (Cambridge, Mass.: Harvard University Press, 1984), p. 14.
6. Ibid., p. 15.
7. William James, *A Pluralistic Universe* (Cambridge, Mass.: Harvard University Press, 1977), pp. 14–15.
8. Jürgen Habermas, 'The German Idealism of the Jewish Philosophers,' *Philosophical-Political Profiles*, trans. Frederick Lawrence (Cambridge, Mass.: MIT Press, 1983), p. 41.
9. Max Horkheimer and Theodor W. Adorno, *Dialectic of Enlightenment*, trans. John Cumming (New York: Continuum, 1972), p. 3.

10. See Habermas' early book on the public sphere which has recently been translated into English by Thomas Burger and Frederick Lawrence, *The Structural Transformation of the Public Sphere: An Inquiry into a Category of Bourgeois Society* (Cambridge, Mass.: MIT Press, 1989).
11. Jürgen Habermas, 'Historical Materialism and the Development of Normative Structures,' in *Communication and the Evolution of Society*, trans. Thomas McCarthy (Boston: Beacon, 1979), p. 117.
12. Ibid., pp. 119–20.
13. Ibid., p. 97.
14. Jürgen Habermas, 'A Reply To My Critics,' in John B. Thompson and David Held, eds, *Habermas: Critical Debates* (London: MacMillan, 1982), p. 221.
15. Habermas, *The Philosophical Discourse of Modernity*, p. 408.
16. Ibid.
17. Ibid.
18. Habermas does think there is a categorical distinction between the natural sciences and the reconstructive critical social sciences. But both types of sciences are fallibilistic and make universal claims open to ongoing criticism.
19. Jürgen Habermas, 'The Entwinement of Myth and Enlightenment: Re-Reading *Dialectic of Enlightenment*,' in *New German Critique* 26 (1982), pp. 23, 25, 27.
20. See Jürgen Habermas, 'Work and Weltanschauung: The Heidegger Controversy from a German Perspective,' *Critical Inquiry* 15 (Winter 1989).
21. Jürgen Habermas, 'Questions and Counterquestions,' in Richard J. Bernstein, ed., *Habermas and Modernity* (Cambridge, Mass.: MIT Press, 1985), p. 195.
22. Derrida himself frequently uses such hyphenated expressions as 'ethical-political-juridical' or 'ethical-political'. The point of these hyphenated expressions is to mark the inseparability of the issues examined. In this respect Derrida acknowledges the ancient (Greek) tradition in which questions concerning *ēthos*, *polis*, and *nomos* are intertwined. This does not mean that one can ignore important differences between ethics, morality, and politics. For the purposes of this essay I will stress the interrelatedness of these 'domains' rather than the crucial differences and distinctions among them.
23. 'An Interview with Derrida' in David Wood and Robert Bernasconi, eds, *Derrida and Différance* (Evanston: Northwestern University Press, 1988), p. 74.
24. Ibid., p. 75.
25. 'Dialogue with Jacques Derrida,' p. 108.
26. Ibid., p. 118.
27. Ibid., p. 124.
28. See the previous essay, 'Serious Play: the Ethical-Political Horizon of Derrida', where I argue that an ethical-political orientation is a point of departure for reading virtually everything Derrida has written. During the past decade the 'themes' of violence, justice, law, responsibility have become even more prominent in his writings.
29. See Jacques Derrida, 'Of an Apocalyptic Tone Recently Adopted in Philosophy,' *Oxford Literary Review* 6 (1984).
30. 'Dialogue with Jacques Derrida,' p. 111.
31. 'I never separate promising from memory', Jacques Derrida, 'But beyond... (Open Letter to Anne McClintock and Rob Nixon),' *Critical Inquiry* 13 (Autumn 1986), p. 160.
32. 'Dialogue with Jacques Derrida,' p. 113.
33. Derrida, 'But beyond...,' pp. 167–8. See also Jacques Derrida, 'Racism's Last Word,' trans. Peggy Kamuf, *Critical Inquiry* 12 (Autumn 1985).
34. Derrida, 'But beyond...,' p. 168.
35. Ibid.
36. Jacques Derrida, 'The Conflict of Faculties: A *Mochlos*' (forthcoming). [Editor's note: Subsequently published as 'Mochlos; or, The Conflict of the Faculties,' in

R. Rand (ed.), *Logomachia: The Conflict of the Faculties* (Lincoln: University of Nebraska Press, 1992), pp. 1–34.]
37. Derrida, 'But beyond . . .,' p. 170.
38. 'Dialogue with Jacques Derrida,' p. 119.
39. Ibid., p. 120.
40. Ibid.
41. Derrida, Afterword, *Limited Inc.*, p. 116.
42. For a critical discussion of recent appropriations of the concept of *phronēsis*, see Richard J. Bernstein, *Beyond Objectivism and Relativism: Science, Hermeneutics and Praxis* (Philadelphia: University of Pennsylvania Press, 1983).
43. Almost every text of Derrida touches on questions of response, responsiveness, and responsibility. In his writings during the past decade the explicit discussion of responsibility has become more and more prominent. See 'The Principle of Reason: The University in the Eyes of its Pupils,' *Diacritics* 13 (Fall 1983), 'The Conflict of Faculties,' 'Like the Sound of the Sea Deep within a Shell: Paul de Man's War,' *Critical Inquiry* 14 (Spring, 1988). Few commentators on the latter essay have noted that it is not only an essay dealing with 'Paul de Man's War' but is also a meditation on the question, ambiguities, and double binds of *responsibility*.
44. 'Dialogue with Derrida,' p. 118.
45. Jacques Derrida, 'Choreographics,' *Diacritics* 12 (Summer 1982), pp. 66–7. See also 'Voice ii: Jacques Derrida et Verena Andermott Conley,' *Boundary* 2 12 (Winter 1984); and 'Geschlecht – Sexual Difference, Ontological Difference,' *Research in Phenomenology* 13 (1983).
46. See Jacques Derrida, 'The Politics of Friendship' (unpublished manuscript) [Editor's note: Subsequently published as *Politics of Friendship*, trans. George Collins (London: Verso, 1997).] See also 'Violence and Metaphysics: An Essay on the Thought of Emmanuel Levinas' in *Writing and Difference*, trans. Alan Bass (Chicago: University of Chicago Press, 1978).
47. Derrida, 'Afterword', *Limited Inc.*, p. 112.
48. See Derrida, 'The Principle of Reason'.
49. The 'problem' of the Other is just as fundamental for Habermas as it is for Derrida. Here too their approaches *supplement* each other. Habermas' primary concern is with the personal Other as it appears in communicative action, i.e., with reciprocal communication in achieving mutual understanding. All communication is dialogical where the right of the Other to assent or dissent freely to professed validity claims should prevail as a binding universal norm. Derrida typically focuses on the ways in which the Other eludes understanding and provides a site (non-site) for questioning that which strives to assimilate and master the Other. Whereas Habermas emphasizes reciprocity, symmetry, and mutual recognition, Derrida focuses on non-reciprocity, asymmetry, and the faults in mutual recognition.
50. See Habermas, *The Philosophical Discourse of Modernity*.
51. For a development of this point see my book, *Beyond Objectivism and Relativism*. See also my criticism of Habermas' understanding of his project of reconstructive science of communicative action in 'Interpretation and Solidarity: An Interview with Richard Bernstein by Dunja Melcié,' *Praxis International* 9, no. 3 (October, 1989).
52. 'Deconstruction, as I have practiced it, has always been foreign to rhetoricism – which, as its name indicates, can become another form of logocentrism – and this despite or rather because of the interest I have felt obliged to direct at questions of language and at figures of rhetoric. What is all too quickly forgotten is often what is most massively evident, to wit, that deconstruction, that at least to which I refer, begins by deconstructing logocentrism, and hence also that which rhetoricism might owe it. Also for the same reason I never assimilated philosophy, science, theory, criticism, law, morality, etc., to literary fictions.' (Derrida, 'Afterword', *Limited Inc.*, p. 156.)

53. Habermas, 'Questions and Counterquestions,' p. 192.
54. Derrida, Afterword, *Limited Inc.*, p. 116.
55. Derrida, 'The Conflict of Faculties'.
56. See Thomas McCarthy, 'The Politics of the Ineffable: Derrida's Deconstructionism,' *The Philosophical Forum* 21 (1989–90).
57. 'Dialogue with Jacques Derrida,' pp. 114–15.

5

Simon Critchley

FRANKFURT IMPROMPTU – REMARKS ON DERRIDA AND HABERMAS*

Simon Critchley has a longstanding interest in Derrida's deconstruction and, in particular, its relation to ethics and politics. In addition, he has written on other Continental philosophy traditions, including Habermas and Critical Theory. The present chapter was presented as an introduction at a seminar in 2000 where Derrida and Habermas discussed their different views of philosophy, ethics and politics.

Critchley is interested in the affinities and differences between Derrida and Habermas in relation to ethics and politics, and he focuses on two issues in particular: performativity and intersubjectivity. Both Derrida and Habermas are concerned with these issues, thus making an exchange of views possible. Their conceptualisations vary significantly, however. For instance, with regard to intersubjectivity – or, in Derrida's terms, the relation to the other – Habermas believes that symmetry is possible, whereas Derrida believes that there is no symmetry without asymmetry, no inclusion of the other without some simultaneous exclusion paradoxically making inclusion possible. More generally, according to Derrida, ethics and politics are marked by undecidability, and ethical and political decisions can therefore not simply follow a norm or procedure. Whereas for Habermas, this view ultimately leads to decisionism and arbitrariness, for Derrida it leads to infinite responsibility towards the other and the future. This is reflected in his idea of a justice and a democracy 'to come', that is, the idea that perfect justice and democracy are never present, but are forever deferred to an unreachable future.

Simon Critchley, 'Remarks on Derrida and Habermas', *Constellations*, 7: 4, 2000, pp. 455–65.

* A word on the context for these remarks. They were initially prepared, at the invitation of Axel Honneth, for a meeting between Jacques Derrida and Jürgen Habermas that was scheduled to take place at the Institute for Social Research, Frankfurt in February 1999, and then rescheduled for April 1999. Sadly, the meeting was postponed on both occasions due to illness. It finally took place at the Suhrkamp Haus in Frankfurt on June 24, 2000, where a version of this paper was delivered. The remarks were therefore drafted simply as an informal way of opening the discussion between Derrida and Habermas and should be read in that light. A French version was delivered at a conference in Paris in June 1999, to which Jacques Derrida responded.

INTRODUCTION

Let's begin by dispelling a few misconceptions about Derrida's work. Derrida is not and never was a postmodernist. He is not a private ironist, nor is he some sort of mystical or anarchic neo-Heideggerian. His work does not exacerbate nihilism, nor does it refuse or attempt to overcome the Enlightenment, the Subject, or whatever else. Deconstruction, in Derrida's hands, does not level the genre distinction between philosophy and literature (in fact, the opposite might be closer to the truth), nor does Derrida denigrate politics, society, and history to the status of the ontic.

On the contrary, at least on the reading that I have tried to develop over the years, Derrida's work is motivated by an overriding commitment, which I would call ethical, and which owes more than a small debt to Levinas (i.e., in Habermas's terms, the ethical as distinct from the moral). Furthermore, his work is animated by deep political concerns and has, I think, plausible and powerful political consequences. Although, to my mind, the ethical and political orientation of Derrida's work is evident in his early writing (cf. in particular, 'Violence and Metaphysics' (1964) and 'The Ends of Man' (1968)), and therefore talk of an ethical *Kehre* in deconstruction is misplaced, there is no doubt that this orientation has become much more strongly foregrounded in his work over the past ten years or so. This is particularly evident in 'Force of Law' (1992), *Specters of Marx* (1993), *Politics of Friendship* (1994), and *Adieu to Emmanuel Levinas* (1997).

To summarize crudely, thinking of 'Force of Law' and *Specters of Marx*, one might now say that what remains *undeconstructable* in any deconstruction is *justice*. One of the tasks of any proposed rapprochement between Derrida and Habermas would be to compare the meaning of justice in both of their projects, and specifically the relation between justice and law. As I see it, justice in Derrida's work is a moment of formal universality, a context-transcendent idealization in Habermasian terms. Very importantly, the *formal universality* of justice is not a regulative principle like the Moral Law in Kant, but is rather the making explicit or formalization of what is implicit in communicative action, in Habermas's terms, or the performative structure of speech acts, in terms closer to Derrida's. I will return to this point later in my remarks. Furthermore – and this is a central point for discussion – this formal universality of justice entails a commitment to a specific political form of society, namely democracy, or what Derrida calls *la démocratie á venir*, the meaning of which I will try and clarify below. An open question would concern the possible agreement or disagreement between *la démocratie á venir* and Habermas's procedural conception of democracy discussed, say, in 'Three Normative Models of Democracy'.

As can be seen from certain passages from *Politics of Friendship*, such an investigation of democracy and democratic reason is linked to a certain understanding of the project of Enlightenment, as Derrida remarks with seeming implicit reference to Habermas: 'For us there is no Enlightenment other than the one to be thought.'[1] One might say that for Derrida, as for Habermas, modernity is understood as the realization – and, moreover, the deformed realization – of Enlightenment in history, and is therefore an incomplete project, although the nature of this incompletion is undoubtedly approached differently in their writings. To my mind, this commitment to an Enlightenment 'to be thought' explains why Derrida can quite consistently state, as he does in 'Force of Law', that 'Nothing seems to me less outdated than the classical emancipatory ideal.'[2] A further open question for discussion concerns the relation between political action and social emancipation, i.e., what forms of political organization and intervention might be more adequate to the goal of social emancipation, which is something that Derrida expresses in *Specters of Marx* with the notion of 'The New International'.

So, pulling these initial thoughts together, we might say that Derrida's work is oriented around the quasi-normative axis of an emancipatory, democratic politics, based in the undeconstructible, context-transcendent, formal universality of justice. *Kurz gesagt*, Derrida sounds like Habermas, doesn't he? In a debate with Axel Honneth from 1994, I even jokingly suggested that they might get married.[3] Now, this is doubtless going too far too fast, but in the future we might at the very least be able to imagine a peaceful cohabitation, where they would occupy separate apartments in the same intellectual building, perhaps with a connecting door or two.

Before exploring two areas of possible agreement and disagreement, that I offer simply as a way of opening the discussion, two obvious and significant methodological differences between Habermas and Derrida might be noted.

1. I imagine that Derrida would be rather skeptical about the avowedly *post-metaphysical* orientation of Habermas's work, where all matters must be either empirically or normatively justified. To my mind, deconstruction is a genealogical operation animated by a thought of *heritage*, and the metaphysical tradition is an essential part of that heritage, even when – and arguably most importantly when – that tradition is being deconstructed. This is something admirably demonstrated in the intricate historical analyses of a text

like *Politics of Friendship*. Such a conception of heritage, where the very historicity of history emerges as a potentiality or possibility out of a reactivated (Husserl) or destroyed (Heidegger) tradition, is also, for Derrida, the condition of possibility for the present and future of philosophical thinking. From this perspective, therefore, the notion of the post-metaphysical would be doubtful because it risks throwing out the philosophical baby with the metaphysical bathwater.

2. Related to this first point, one would have to note the significant difference between Derrida's approach and that of Habermas and the entire Frankfurt School tradition, as concerns the understanding of the relation of philosophy to the social sciences. Adopting a Frankfurt School position on the necessary interdependence of philosophical and sociological reflection could lead to the perhaps justifiable criticism of Derrida, namely that his work is *too exclusively philosophical*, and belongs to what Horkheimer would call traditional rather than critical theory. That is, although it is not right to claim, as Habermas does in the *Philosophical Discourse of Modernity*, that Derrida reduces society, politics, and history to the status of the ontic, it is possible to argue that his theoretical categories lack sufficient sociological mediation insofar as they are derived too directly from an engagement with tradition conceived in exclusively metaphysical or logocentric terms.

For the remainder of my remarks, I would like briefly to outline two areas of more substantive agreement and disagreement between Habermas and Derrida. First, the question of intersubjectivity (a term that Derrida deliberately avoids) or the relation to the other; second, the question of the relation of ethics to politics in Derrida. I will conclude with some clarification of Derrida's use of the concept of democracy.

INTERSUBJECTIVITY, THE RELATION TO THE OTHER (SYMMETRY VERSUS ASYMMETRY)

So, both Habermas and Derrida are committed to an ideal of emancipation, but they are both anti-utopian thinkers.[4] This anti-utopianism is grounded in a certain understanding of the relation to the other, for Derrida, or intersubjectivity, for Habermas. For Habermas, the context-transcendent idealizations at the basis of discourse ethics are based in a formal or universal pragmatics of communication. Now, although this might *prima facie* seem an odd claim to make, I wonder whether there is something similar going on in Derrida's work. I think this can be brought out if we look at Derrida's comments on the concept of the messianic as an a priori structure that, as he puts it, 'belongs to all language': as that promisory, performative, or illocutionary dimension to our speech acts, which, as he describes it in an interview, is 'the universal dimension of experience'.[5] In his 'Remarks on Deconstruction and Pragmatism', Derrida says (although it should be pointed out that this was an improvised reply to Richard Rorty and not a written text):

> There is no language without the performative dimension of the promise, the minute I open my mouth I am in the promise. Even if I say that 'I don't believe in truth' or whatever, the minute I open my mouth there is a 'believe me' in play. And this 'I promise you that I am speaking the truth' is a messianic a priori, a promise which, even if it is not kept, even if one knows that it cannot be kept, takes place and qua promise is messianic.[6]

Derrida's discussion of the promise as that illocutionary dimension of speech acts whose denial would lead one into a performative contradiction has obvious Habermasian echoes. And despite Habermas's moral cognitivism and his insistence upon the symmetrical nature of intersubjectivity, it is clear at the very least that there is work to be done here and that possibly Habermas and Derrida share more with each other than they share with, say, Rorty, especially when it comes to political matters.

But if there is a similar and surprising proximity between Habermas and Derrida about the formal pragmatics of language, then in what does their difference consist? This brings me to the question of the symmetrical or asymmetrical nature of what is revealed in linguistic practice. Let me sketch Derrida's position with another quote from his 'Remarks on Deconstruction and Pragmatism', where he takes up the question of the need for *infinite responsibility*:

> I believe that we cannot give up on the concept of infinite responsibility, as Rorty seemed to do in his remarks, when he spoke of Levinas as a blind spot in my work. I would say, for Levinas and for myself, that if you give up the infinitude of responsibility, there is no responsibility. It is because we act and we live in infinitude that the responsibility with regard to the other is irreducible. If responsibility was not infinite, if every time that I have to take an ethical or political decision with regard to the other this was not infinite, then I would not be able to engage myself in an infinite debt with regard to each singularity. I owe myself infinitely to each and every singularity. If responsibility was not infinite, you could not have moral and political problems. There are only moral and political problems, and everything that follows from this, from the moment when responsibility is not limitable.[7]

To summarize very rapidly: to my mind the above passage describes something like the ethical (or quasi- or proto-ethical, if you are squeamish) moment in deconstruction. It is an experience of infinite responsibility, which can be qualified as undeconstructible, unconditional, a priori, and universal. However, infinite responsibility only arises within the context of a singular experience, that is, within the empirical event of a concrete speech act, the performative dimension of the promise.

However – and here we perhaps begin to see the limits to any rapprochement with Habermas – what takes place in the concrete linguistic event of the promise is a relation to an other, what Derrida calls a singularity, which is an experience of *infinite indebtedness*. Thus, the messianic a priori describes the structure of intersubjectivity in terms of an *asymmetrical* obligation that I could never meet, to which I would never be equal. Turning to Habermas, and thinking of 'Three Normative Models of Democracy': one wonders whether Derrida's emphasis on asymmetry and infinite responsibility would, for Habermas, suffer from a version of 'the ethical overload' problem that he criticizes in the republican model of democracy.[8] Does not infinite responsibility entail an ethical overload? To which Derrida might respond that ethics is always – and rightly – an experience of overload.

But let me try and clarify Habermas's position a little. Habermasian discourse ethics stands in the Kantian tradition of moral philosophy. However, unlike Kant, Habermas's understanding of morality does not begin from the individuality of Kantian moral self-consciousness, but rather from the recognition of the intersubjective constitution of moral norms and their embeddedness in shared forms of communicative praxis (thereby defusing the Hegelian critique of Kant). But, what Habermas shares with the Kantian tradition is the belief that the *de facto* incommensurability of values or pluralism about the nature of the good life in social modernity entails that moral theory cannot recommend particular values or a single account of the good life. As such, discourse ethics only claims to provide a *procedure* for moral argumentation; that is, a theory of justice capable of legitimating and testing moral norms and resolving the possible conflicts between them. Such a revised version of the Kantian categorical imperative procedure necessarily begins from the premise of equality of the equal treatment of all human beings. Thus, the Habermasian picture of intersubjectivity and the conception of justice connected to that picture is rooted in equality, reciprocity, mutuality, and symmetry.

So, it would seem that despite the formal universality and context-transcendent unconditionality that, on my reading, define both Habermas's and Derrida's approaches to the question of justice, there is a straightforward disagreement about the right picture of intersubjectivity or the relation to the other: symmetry in Habermas, asymmetry in Derrida. I would simply like to know how they view this issue. How do they both see the relation between the symmetrical and asymmetrical descriptions of intersubjectivity? Are they mutually exclusive, or could they supplement each other in an unexpected way?

With regard to the option raised by this last question, it has been argued by Axel Honneth that the symmetrical structure of intersubjectivity within Habermasian discourse ethics requires an additional moment of asymmetry. This is something that, for Honneth, can be achieved either through Winnicottian object-relations psychoanalysis or through a certain reading of Derrida and Levinas in terms of an ethics of care. For Honneth such an ethics of care articulates a moral counterpoint to Habermasian discourse ethics and shows that the experience of asymmetry and inequality must be granted a place in moral discourse if the goal of solidarity is not to remain an empty abstraction.[9]

A final thought in this connection: is the moment of asymmetry really absent from Habermas's work? At the end of the first appendix to *Between Facts and Norms*, Habermas writes, just after an allusion to Benjamin's notion of anamnesic solidarity with the dead of history:

> The fact that everyday affairs are necessarily banalized in political communication also poses a danger for semantic potentials from which this communication must still draw its nourishment. A culture without thorns would be absorbed by mere needs for compensation . . . it settles over the risk society like a foam carpet. No civil religion, however cleverly adjusted, could forestall this entropy of meaning. Even the moment of unconditionality insistently voiced in the transcending validity claims of everyday life does not suffice. *Another* kind of transcendence is preserved in the unfulfilled promise disclosed by the critical appropriation of identity-forming religious traditions, and *still another* in the negativity of modern art. The trivial and everyday must be open to the shock of what is absolutely strange, cryptic, or uncanny. Though these no longer provide a cover for privileges, they refuse to be assimilated to pregiven categories.[10]

This is a remarkable passage, where Habermas admits that another dimension of transcendence is required in order to supplement the transcending validity claims of discourse ethics. However, this transcendence of the strange, the cryptic, and the uncanny is a description of both aesthetic modernism (one inevitably thinks of Adorno) and religious transcendence. The question is: would the asymmetrical understanding of the relation to the other always be an aestheticizing or quasi-religious conception for Habermas? There is at least a question here, a question that is also provoked by Derrida's qualified use of Benjamin's notion of the messianic in recent writings, and also by his measured proximity to Levinas (I emphasize *measured*). So, keeping all of these thoughts in mind, let's go back to the framing question and ask – or suggest – whether both the symmetrical and asymmetrical dimensions of intersubjectivity are required in order to provide orientation in our moral and political lives? If so, then how? If not, then why not?

ETHICS AND POLITICS

Let me now turn to the second area of possible agreement or disagreement: the question of the relation of ethics to politics. In order to try and clarify what is at stake here, let me go back to Derrida's above-cited remark about infinite responsibility. It is on the basis of this undeconstructible infinite responsibility that one is propelled into moral and political problems, into the realm of decision. It is important to point out here that, for Derrida, the notion of the undeconstructible – justice, the messianic a priori, infinite responsibility – does not function as it does in the Kantian tradition that inspires Habermas, namely as the basis for a decision *procedure* in ethics, a categorical imperative mechanism in the light of which one might propose and test specific maxims. It remains for me an open question as to whether Derrida is justified in this suspicion of proceduralism, particularly as it seems to remove the possibility of *deliberation* from the taking of political decisions.

Be that as it may, let me try to clarify the relation of ethics to politics in Derrida by taking up the problem of foundationalism. I will do this in six argumentative steps, each of which might be seen as articulating a question to Habermas, although there would seem to be a basic agreement between Habermas and Derrida on the need to separate their conceptions of justice from any accusation of foundationalism.

1. For Derrida, it would seem, politics cannot be founded because such a foundation would limit the freedom of the decision. In politics there are no guarantees. Politics must be open to the dimension of the 'perhaps' or the 'maybe' which is the constant refrain of the early and central chapters of *Politics of Friendship*. For Derrida, nothing would be more irresponsible and totalitarian than the attempt *a priori* to exclude the monstrous or the terrible.[11] He writes: 'Without the possibility of radical evil, of perjury, and of absolute crime, there is no responsibility, no freedom, no decision.'[12]
2. So the relation of ethics to politics is that there is a gap or hiatus between these two domains. And here we confront a crucial qualification of the problem of ethics and politics: if politics is not founded in the classical manner, *then it is also not arbitrary*, for this would take us back to some *libertas arbitrarium* and its concomitant voluntaristic and sovereign conception of the will. That is, it would lead us back to an undeconstructed Schmittianism. One of the main burdens of the argument of *Politics of Friendship* is to try and think the notion of the decision outside of its traditional

voluntaristic determination, for example in Schmitt, where the possibility of the decision presupposes the existence of the sovereign subject, defined in terms of activity, freedom and the will.

3. To summarize the first two steps of the argument in a question: if politics is neither foundational (because that would limit freedom) nor arbitrary (because that would derive from a conception of freedom), then what follows from this? How does one think a non-foundational and yet non-arbitrary relation between ethics and politics? Derrida's claim would seem to be that there is indeed a link between ethics and politics. In *Adieu to Emmanuel Levinas*, Derrida puts the point more strongly, claiming that, '*This relation is necessary (il faut ce rapport)*, it must exist, it is necessary to deduce a politics and a law from ethics.'[13] Derrida tries, against Schmitt, to capture this sense of a non-foundational, yet non-arbitrary, relation between ethics and politics with the notion of *the other's decision in me*, a decision that is taken, but with regard to which I am passive.[14] That is to say, on my reading, particular political decisions are taken in relation to the formal universality of an ethical criterion: infinite responsibility to the other, justice, the messianic a priori.
4. Politics, then, is the task of invention in relation to the other's decision in me – non-foundationally and non-arbitrarily. But how does one do this exactly? Perhaps in the following way: in a quite banal sense, each decision is necessarily different. Every time I decide, I have to invent a new rule, a new norm, which must be absolutely singular in relation to both the other's infinite demand made on me and the finite context within which this demand arises. I think this is what Derrida means, in 'Force of Law' and elsewhere, by his qualified Kierkegaardian emphasis on the madness of the decision, namely that each decision is like a leap of faith made in relation to the singularity of a context. Such a position might be linked to one of Wittgenstein's more cryptic remarks in the *Philosophical Investigations*, where he writes that in following a rule, 'It would almost be more correct to say, not that an intuition was needed at every stage, but that a new decision was needed at every stage.'[15]
5. So, the political decision is made, experientially as it were, *ex nihilo*, and is not deduced or read off procedurally from a pre-given conception of justice or the moral law, and yet it is not arbitrary. It is the demand provoked by the other's decision in me that calls forth political invention, that provokes me into inventing a norm and taking a decision. The *singularity* of the context in which the demand arises provokes an act of invention whose criterion is *universal*.

6. So, to summarize, what we seem to have here is a relation between ethics and politics which is both non-foundational and non-arbitrary, that is, which leaves the decision open for invention while acknowledging that the decision comes from the other. The other's decision in me is not so much a Kantian *Faktum der Vernunft* as what one might call a *Faktum des Anderen.* If the 'fact of reason' is the demand of the good that must, for Kant, be consistent with the principle of autonomy, then the 'fact of the other' would be the demand of the good experienced as the heteronomous opening of autonomy, the heteronomous ethical source for autonomous political action (which does not at all mean that autonomy is abandoned).

   To conclude: there is a universal criterion for action but I am passive in relation to this criterion, I have a non-subsumptive relation to this *Faktum*, and the specific form of political action and decision-taking must be singular and context-dependent.

For Derrida, what has to be continually deconstructed in political thinking is the guarantee of a full *incarnation* of the universal in the particular, or the privileging of a specific particularity because it *embodies* the universal; for example, the classical idea of the state. However, it is hugely important to point out that Derrida does not make this move in order to avoid concrete political issues, that is, questions of the specific content of political decisions, but on the contrary to *defend* what he has elsewhere called in relation to Marx, 'The New International'; that is, a non-state-based form of internationalist political intervention. In response to the Leninesque question that Derrida raises in his reading of Blanchot in *Politics of Friendship*, 'Que faire?',[16] we might say that what is required is, as Derrida writes, 'another international law, another politics of frontiers, another humanitarian politics, even a humanitarian engagement that would hold itself *effectively* outside the interest of nation states.'[17] Another interesting area of discussion between Derrida and Habermas would be around the necessity for the state-form in our political thinking, where Habermas, in *Between Facts and Norms*, has defended the notion of the constitutional state.

DEMOCRACY-TO-COME

Let me close by trying to clarify the theme of democracy in Derrida's work, specifically what Derrida calls *la démocratie á venir*, 'democracy-to-come'. On the last page of *Politics of Friendship*, Derrida concludes with the following question, which picks up the discussion of the problem of foundationalism. He writes:

> If one wishes to retranslate this pledge into a hypothesis or a question, it would, then, perhaps, – by way of a temporary conclusion – take the

> following form: is it possible to think and to implement democracy, that which would keep the old name 'democracy', while uprooting from it all these figures of friendship (philosophical and religious) which prescribe fraternity: the family and the androcentric ethnic group? Is it possible, in assuming a certain faithful memory of democratic reason and reason *tout court* – I would even say, the Enlightenment of a certain *Aufklärung* (thus leaving open the abyss which is again opening today under these words) – not to found, where it is no longer a matter of founding, but to open out to the future, or rather, to the 'come', of a certain democracy (*non pas de fonder, là où il ne s'agit sans doute plus de fonder, mais d'ouvrir á l'avenir, ou plutôt au 'viens' d'une certaine démocratie*).[18]

Of course, these are rhetorical questions in the best French style and the answer is '*oui*'. As Derrida admits a few lines further on, this is '*Juste une question, mais qui suppose une affirmation*' ('Just a question, but one that presupposes an affirmation'). The affirmation here is that of 'democracy-to-come', but my question is: *how* might such a notion of democracy be understood?

'Democracy-to-come' is much easier to describe in negative rather than positive terms. Recalling the deconstruction of the idea of presence in his earlier work, Derrida is particularly anxious to distinguish democracy-to-come from any idea of a *future* democracy, where the future would be a modality of presence, namely the not-yet-present. Democracy-to-come is *not* to be confused with the living present of liberal democracy, lauded as the end of history by Fukuyama, but *neither* is it a regulative idea or an idea in the Kantian sense; *nor* is it even a utopia, insofar as all these conceptions understand the future as a modality of presence. For Derrida, and this is something particularly clear in *Specters of Marx*, it is a question of linking democracy-to-come to the messianic experience of the *here and now* (*l'ici-maintentant*), without which justice would be meaningless. Namely, what was described above as 'the universal dimension of experience' that 'belongs to all language'. So, the thought here is that the experience of justice as the here and now is the *á venir* of democracy. In other words, the temporality of democracy is *advent*, it is futural, but it is arrival happening *now*, it happens – and one thinks of Benjamin – as the messianic now blasting through the continuum of the present.

Democracy-to-come is a difficult notion to get hold of because it has a deliberately contradictory structure: that is, it has both the structure of a promise, of something futural 'to come', and it is something that takes place, that happens right *now*. In terms that Derrida uses in 'Force of Law', democracy-to-come has the character of 'the incalculable', an irreducible *Faktum* or remainder that cannot simply become the source of a deduction, or the object of a determinate judgment. As such I think, democracy-to-come has the character of an ethical demand or injunction, an incalculable fact that takes place now, but which permits the profile of a promisory task to be glimpsed.

Finally, and this is a step that Derrida suggests but does not really take, it would be a question of thinking the ethical imperative of democracy-to-come together with more concrete forms of democratic political deliberation, action, and intervention: the very political stuff of democratic life.[19] But for me, democracy should not be understood as a fixed political form of society, but rather as a process or, better, processes of democratization. Such processes of *democratization*, evidenced in numerous examples (the new social movements, NGOs, Greenpeace, Amnesty International, *médecins sans frontières*, the battle in Seattle), work within, across, above, beneath, and within the territory of the democratic state, not in the vain hope of achieving some sort of 'society without the state', but rather as providing constant critical pressure upon the state, a pressure of emancipatory intent aiming at its infinite amelioration, the endless betterment of actually existing democracy.[20]

NOTES

1. Derrida, *Politics of Friendship*, tr. G. Coffins (London and New York: Verso, 1997), pp. 42, cf. 43, 305–6.
2. Derrida, 'The Force of Law: The "Mystical Foundation of Authority,"' in D. Cornell et al., eds, *Deconstruction and the Possibility of Justice* (London and New York: Routledge, 1992), p. 28.
3. 'Habermas und Derrida werden verheiratet: Antwort auf Axel Honneth,' *Deutsche Zeitschrift für Philosophie* 42, no. 6 (1994): pp. 981–92. [Editor's note: Subsequently translated as 'Habermas and Derrida Get Married', in *The Ethics of Deconstruction: Derrida and Levinas*, 2nd edition (Edinburgh: Edinburgh University Press, 1999), pp. 267–80.]
4. For Derrida's suspicions of utopia, see his 'Remarks on Deconstruction and Pragmatism,' in Chantal Mouffe, ed., *Deconstruction and Pragmatism* (London and New York: Routledge, 1996), pp. 82–83.
5. Derrida, 'The Deconstruction of Actuality,' *Radical Philosophy* 68 (1994): p. 36.
6. Derrida, 'Remarks on Deconstruction and Pragmatism,' p. 82.
7. Ibid., p. 86.
8. Habermas, 'Three Normative Models of Democracy,' *Constellations* 1, no.1 (1994): p. 3.
9. Axel Honneth, 'The Other of Justice: Habermas and the Challenge of Postmodernism,' in *The Cambridge Companion to Habermas*, ed. Stephen White (Cambridge: Cambridge University Press, 1995), pp. 288–323.
10. Habermas, *Between Facts and Norms*, tr. W. Rehg (Cambridge, MA: MIT Press, 1996), p. 490.
11. Derrida, *Adieu a Emmanuel Levinas* (Paris: Galilée, 1997), p. 201.
12. Derrida, *Politics of Friendship*, p. 219.
13. Derrida, *Adieu à Emmanuel Levinas*, p. 198.
14. Derrida, *Politics of Friendship*, pp. 67–70.
15. Wittgenstein, *Philosophical Investigations*, tr. G. E. M. Anscombe (Oxford: Blackwell, 1958), p. 186.
16. Derrida, *Politics of Friendship*, p. 217.

17. Derrida, *Adieu a Emmanuel Levinas*, p. 176.
18. *Politics of Friendship*, p. 306.
19. For a Habermasian account of deliberation, see chs 9 and 10 of *The Inclusion of the Other* (Cambridge, MA: MIT Press, 1999).
20. A more detailed and scholarly presentation of many of the arguments in this text can be found in my *Ethics-Politics-Subjectivity* (London and New York: Verso, 1999). Those wishing to explore the relation between Derrida and Habermas would do well to look at the following two exemplary articles: Richard Rorty, 'Habermas, Derrida and Functions of Philosophy,' in *Truth and Progress: Philosophical Papers Volume 3* (Cambridge: Cambridge University Press, 1998) and Richard J. Bernstein, 'An Allegory of "Modernity/Postmodernity": Habermas and Derrida,' in *The New Constellation* (Cambridge: Polity, 1991), pp. 199–229.

6

Jacques Derrida

PERFORMATIVE POWERLESSNESS – A RESPONSE TO SIMON CRITCHLEY[1]

This chapter by Jacques Derrida is a response to an earlier version of Critchley's argument. Derrida confirms Critchley's view of the affinities and differences between his and Habermas's thinking on performativity, the relation to the other, responsibility and norms. Moreover, he adds the concept of sovereignty to those issues of concern to both Habermas and himself, but, as with the other issues, he also points to their potential differences in conceptualising it.

To thank Simon, I am going to say at what point I find what he said just in the sense of rightness (*justesse*) and of justice. I must all the same recount a little story in which Simon is mixed up. After a long debate, direct, indirect, through intermediaries or not, Habermas and I promised each other – and I will return to the promise – to meet and discuss. And this promise was probably so overdetermined that we fell ill, one after the other. At the moment of the meeting, which had been set for two days at Axel Honneth's seminar – two or three days before, I fell ill. It was the first time in my life that I canceled a meeting of this kind. We set another date, another meeting, for two or three months later, and the day before, on the eve, there was Mrs Habermas on the phone; Habermas was very sick, he had problems with

Jacques Derrida, 'Performative Powerlessness – A Response to Simon Critchley', trans. James Ingram, *Constellations*, 7: 4, 2000, pp. 466–8.

his inner ear, and we had to cancel for a second time the meeting we had promised each other, one and the other.

But what I wanted to say above all, then, is that what reassured me in the prospect of this troubling subject was that Simon would be there. I told myself that he at least knows the two contexts and will open a discussion, and it is with this text that you have begun the discussion here in Paris. And so what reassured me was that I knew that Simon would be there, and that he would open and would probably clarify the discussion – which you have done, in my opinion, magnificently – and I hope that the occasion will present itself for us to renew this difficult debate.

About the debate, I would just like to say that – I am not going to repeat all that you have very well said to open the question – at the point where I am now, the point at which an agreement, a discussion, would appear possible in what you have reconstructed is at bottom – on both sides – to develop together this question of formal pragmatics, of performativity. The question or the logic of performativity could be a ground, at least potentially, of possible discussion, for all of the reasons you have evoked. But I would say, more and more now, in a way that is rather new for me, I am more and more suspicious, whatever its fecundity, its necessity may be, of the theory of performativity. Why? Let me explain. I am going to take a certain angle on this to come back to what you said in your intervention. I believe that this logic of performativity, so necessary, so new in Western and academic discourses, so fertile also, has a certain limit, which is not only the limit I have tried several times to mark in complicating this discourse in its Austinian-Searlian tradition. It is not only that. It is that everywhere a given ethical, juridical, political space is given to performative acts, which is to say to languages which produce events, and which insofar as they produce events also give rise to institutions – a vast field. Each time, therefore, that we suppose that these performative languages, performative communications, produce events, then, to the same extent, they neutralize the event.

To put it another way, performativity for me is – I have this impression more and more – that which produces events, all institutions and acts in which responsibility is to be assumed; but it is also that which neutralizes the event, that is to say, what happens (*ce qui arrive*). Wherever there is the performative, whatever the form of communication, there is a context of legitimate, legitimizing, or legitimized convention that permits it to neutralize what happens, that is, the brute eventness of the arrivant (*l'événementialité brute de l'arrivant*). Put another way, if in a certain manner performativity encounters the event produced by language, it is also that which neutralizes the eventness of the event.

When you spoke of the empirical event, and the concrete act of language, I would say that it is exactly *that* which is too easily assimilated. That which unforeseeably affects us implies a retreat of all performative authority. At present I would claim that if there is performative authority, and consequently something of the event, of singularity, which is neutralized by the performative, then performativity always remains protective. And I suppose that at the same time the academic investment in the Western universities – where there is thinking, where things are happening – the investment in this theory of performativity, the investment in political theory (because the juridical is at work in the performative) has fertile, liberating effects, but also protectionist effects. I believe that a politics, as well as an ethics or a law, which regulates itself solely on performative power – the performative is a power – is not only a power, but also a legitimizing and legitimized power. And so, in a certain way, theories of the performative are always at the service of powers of legitimation, of legitimized or legitimizing powers. And consequently, in my view, the ethical must be exposed to a place where constative language as well as performative language is in the service of another language.

And there the question is posed of infinite responsibility. Habermas thinks that in the idea of infinite responsibility there is an ethical overload (*surcharge*), but the ethical overload has to be overwhelming (*surchargeant*), it overwhelms (*surcharge*), and the arrival of the other *is* the overload. One cannot eliminate the overload and control things by norms within discourse. When there are norms, it is finished, everything is done, everything follows from the norms. There is no more responsibility when there are norms. Thus, if one wants to normalize, to norm the ethical overload, it is finished, there is no more ethics. There is ethics precisely where I am in performative powerlessness.

It is at this point that I will say very, very quickly, much too quickly, naturally – since you have evoked Habermas's text on popular sovereignty, I would raise, I would distinguish, a thought of the unconditional, such as I have pursued here and there for a long time, and distinguish it from a thought of sovereignty. The two are very close, sovereignty and the unconditional. But there is an unconditional that is without sovereignty, an unconditionality that is without power, while sovereignty, in its secularized theological legacy – sovereignly naturally, of God and the king of divine right, popular sovereignty, democratic sovereignly in Rousseau's sense – remains a theological legacy. And thus, to this inherited theological fantasy of sovereignty, I would oppose an unconditionality without power. And it is there, in this 'without power', that I expose myself to the event, to the arrival of an event for which no performative is ready. For which no legitimating convention is provided. And it is to this arrival that the ethical question presents itself, that the call of the other, the arrival of the other, of an event, is a burden (*charge*), an infinite responsibility. This is not to say that I assume it myself. *I cannot assume responsibility*. I know simply that I cannot assume the responsibility that overwhelms me. I am infinitely overwhelmed as a finite being by a responsibility that cannot but be infinite – and impossible to assume. But at least I *think* this impossibility, and it is there that I *think* what my responsibility should be, which is to say, infinite. All the same, I cannot assume it. There, concerning responsibility, performativity is a luxury of authority. To be able to have the right and the power to produce the performative, there must naturally exist a right and a condition. If I provide these conditions, then it is finished.

(Simon Critchley: So, to return to the question of the other's decision in me, is this decision taken in the face of an event?)

This question of the decision of the other in me is an absurdity, it is inconceivable. As such, it has to be connected to that which I just said about the event – which undoes itself. The decision of the other in me means that the other who arrives to me is in some sense before me. It does not mean that I have someone in me, like a sort of little machine, a ventriloquist, who takes action in my place. It means that the decision itself corresponds to the other, and that I am myself only from this infinite responsibility which the other places in me. The other who is in me is greater than I. I can only gain access to my selfhood (*ipséité*), my egoity, etc., from this relation to the other in me, but the other in me can nevertheless not be incorporated or introjected – who is in me, greater than I. And this also happens through mourning, the experience of mourning from which I constitute myself, I establish myself. Thus, the decision comes to me: there it is, it is a thought, a simple decision, a decision that comes to me. I must take responsibility for the decision that comes to me. It comes to me (*Elle m'arrive . . .*).

Translated by James Ingram

TRANSLATOR'S NOTE

1. These remarks were offered in response to the May 1999 presentation of the French version of Simon Critchley's 'Remarks on Derrida and Habermas,' in this issue [Editor's note: reprinted here as Chapter 5]. The translation has not sought to efface their improvised character. Thanks to Simon Critchley, Veronica Coleman, Kyra Holland, and Jacques Derrida for their invaluable assistance.

7

Jürgen Habermas

HOW TO RESPOND TO THE ETHICAL QUESTION

The concerns raised by Critchley and Derrida in Chapters 5 and 6 are reflected in this one by Habermas. The context of Habermas's intervention was a conference in Paris that took place on 3–5 December 2000, under the title Judaities: Questions for Jacques Derrida, *which reflects the increasing importance of religion in Derrida's later work.*

Habermas is interested in how Derrida would respond to 'the ethical question', which, for Habermas, is raised by the fact of pluralism in modern societies. How is 'the inclusion of the other', to quote a title by Habermas, possible in societies divided along ethical – for instance, religious – lines? The reader should be aware that, while this is how Habermas conceives of the ethical question, for Derrida the ethical question concerns the relationship to an other who ultimately escapes inclusion because she cannot be included and *remain other at the same time.*

Habermas proposes how Derrida might answer 'the ethical question' considering the latter's relationship to Martin Heidegger. While critical of aspects of Heidegger's thought, Derrida's deconstruction is nonetheless strongly influenced by Heidegger. Habermas, too, is critical of aspects of Heidegger, especially his politics, and he asks where Derrida would depart from Heidegger. Is there, Habermas wants to know, something in Derrida's deconstruction of Heidegger that separates the French thinker from Heidegger's philosophy and politics on the important question of the substantive unity or pluralism of modern societies?

Jürgen Habermas, *Judéités. Questions pour Jacques Derrida*, eds Joseph Cohen and Raphael Zagury-Orly (Paris: Galilée, 2003).

(1) I am grateful for the opportunity to participate in the exploration of the Jewish background of Derrida's thought, though my role will be marginal in several aspects. Using a third language, I am painfully aware of an incapacity that excludes me from most of this philosophical exchange. An even greater obstacle is my distance from its major topics. In spite of a longstanding relation with Gershom Scholem, I am in no way an expert in the field of Judaism. And in view of this distinguished circle, I am certainly the one with the poorest knowledge of Derrida's oeuvre. Derrida would, of course, be the first to explain why a marginal position is not necessarily a disadvantage. Nevertheless, there are two reasons for accepting the invitation to speak here: I want to express my respect for an exciting work, in which I recognise, across a certain distance that separates us, allied motives and shared intentions. And I cannot resist the opportunity to 'put questions to Derrida'. For a while now I have been interested in the question as to at which point exactly the thoughts of Heidegger and Derrida part company. This is not meant as a philological question; it is as much a philosophical as a political one.

In a lecture that he gave at Frankfurt University last summer, Derrida talked about what we in Germany are used to calling 'the Idea of the University'. He passionately explained the unconditional commitment of the academic community to freedom and truth. A university that does not betray its own idea has to provide the institutional space for the 'profession' of such a faith. And it is up to the work of professors to express the performative meaning of that faith – in the sense of 'the setting-into-work of the truth'. This phrase – in German, '*das ins-Werk-setzen der Wahrheit*' – reminds us of the world-disclosing function that Heidegger attributes to great books and works of art. Therefore, it did not come as a surprise that Derrida, with due irony, devoted the last part of his lecture to an act of evocation – imploring what he called the 'arrival of an event' (*l'arrivée d'un événement*).

Speaking from within the walls of the university, this self-reflexive gesture was intended to make the audience, gathered in a university hall, aware of the very purpose that those walls are supposed to protect:

> It is too often said that the performative produces the event of which it speaks. One must also realise that, inversely, where there is the performative, there an event worthy of the name cannot arrive. If what arrives belongs to the horizon of the possible . . . of the 'I can' or 'I may', it does not arrive, it does not happen, in the full sense of the word . . . Only the impossible can arrive . . . The force of the event is always stronger than the force of a performative'.[1]

Derrida's words resonate with Heidegger's voice that we know from his notes on the event in *Vom Ereignis*. In the years between 1936 and 1938,

Heidegger first revealed his devotion to overcome the totalitarian features of a power-ridden subjectivism. It was not until 1946 that Heidegger made this turn fully public. In his *Letter on Humanism*, he explains his wholesale rejection of both the terms and the meaning of the humanist tradition insofar as they feed the normative self-understanding of modernity. By contrast, Derrida wishes to save the substance of this 'humanism', though he at the same time adopts Heidegger's attitude toward the 'arrival of an event'.

Human rights and the prosecution of crimes against humanity, a democracy that transcends national boundaries, sovereignty freed from misleading connotations, repeated reference to autonomy and the encouragement of resistance, disobedience or dissidence – in other words, everything that Derrida invokes in his interpretation of the purpose of our profession – are slaps in the face of Heidegger's verdicts on humanism. My question is simply the following: How do Heidegger and Derrida differ in their understanding of the arrival of what both posit as an undetermined 'event'? That difference would explain the difference in attitude for and against 'humanism'. We should not mistake the substantive question that I have in mind for a terminological issue. It does not matter whether we use the term 'humanism' in an affirmative or pejorative sense. Either way it is difficult to bring Derrida's purpose in line with the object of Heidegger's deep contempt. I have the suspicion that we face a division here between a neo-pagan betrayal of, and an ethical loyalty to, the monotheistic heritage.[2] Let us remember what Scholem said about such loyalty: 'Authentic tradition remains hidden; only when it goes to ruin tradition is it turned into an object, but comes its decline comes to the fore and can then be perceived in its greatness.'[3]

Being aware of my own limits with regard to Derrida's work, I will proceed in a round about way, starting from a rather distant place. You must expect neither an exegetic nor a deconstructive exercise, much less a close reading of any kind. In what follows, I will first explain the modern differentiation between moral and ethical theory (2); then present Kierkegaard's postmetaphysical, yet religious answer to the ethical question (3); and interrogate various attempts to appropriate Kierkegaard's ethical insights in philosophical or post-religious terms (4); and finally provide the arguments for specifying the question with which I would like to confront Derrida (5).

(2) Ethics was once the doctrine that could tell us how to lead 'the right kind of life'. Writing during and immediately after World War II, Adorno had, however, good reasons to present his *Minima Moralia* as a 'sad science' that delivers reflections from a 'damaged life'. As long as conceptions of the whole of nature and history were still available, philosophy could in good faith present a frame in which the life of individuals and communities were expected to fit. The design of the cosmos and human nature, the sequence of the stages of sacred or worldly history, were taken as value-laden facts that provided guidelines for the right life – for, in other words, 'what to do

with the time of our lives' (Max Frisch). In this context, the term 'right' had the meaning of an exemplary way of life worthwhile of being imitated by individuals and communities. 'Rightness' included the value of both the *good* and *just* life. But the more rapidly and ever more complex society changed, the shorter became the half-life period and expiry date of ethical models, never mind the Greek polis model of an ethical life as it had served for Aristotle, the social strata of medieval *societas civilis* of Thomas, and Hegel's state and society of the Prussian monarchy.

Political Liberalism marks the end of the line. It reacts with abstention to the facts of pluralism and individualisation. John Rawls' just society cannot prescribe a specific mode of life anymore, so it grants everybody the equal freedom to develop and pursue an ethical self-understanding or a 'conception of the good life' of her own. Modern philosophy by no means withdraws from all normative questions, but it confines itself to the sharply defined issues pertaining to justice. We consider norms and actions from the moral point of view if we are concerned with what is in the equal interest of all, or what is equally good for everybody affected.

'What is the right thing to do?' only appears at first sight to constitute the guiding question for both classical ethics and modern theories of justice. The 'should' of an ethical question must not be confused with the 'ought' of a moral question. In the first case we take care of our own well-being, whereas in the second case equal concern is given to the well-being of every one. A first-person reference is inscribed in the *selective* perspective of the first question – what in the long run would be *for me* or *for us* the best thing to do – whereas the moral point of view is an *inclusive* we-perspective, from which we discover the rights and duties *everybody* expects from *everybody else*. Ethical questions, in the classical sense, change their meaning with the particular context, from which they arise; they refer to an individual life-history or a shared form of cultural life. They are intertwined with questions of identity – who we are and would like to be, without blushing.

This logical differentiation has led to a schism within moral and ethical theories. Since each individual is absolutely different from everybody else and has a right to remain an 'other' to others, the search for what is equally good for everybody requires a careful abstraction from the exemplary images of a happy, good or succeeding life that are no longer shared by all. Our own existential self-understanding may still be nourished by the substance of religious narratives, metaphysical world views, and 'strong traditions' (MacIntyre) in general. But modern philosophy has lost the authority and competence to intervene in the struggle between comprehensive doctrines, and to offer an impartial judgement on their competing claims. Philosophy has withdrawn to the meta-level of an inquiry in the formal properties of ethical discourse. It thereby abstains from taking a stand on just those issues that are certainly the most relevant for our personal and communal life.

However, moral and political theories have to pay a high price for their division of labour concerning ethics proper. One consequence is the disconnection between moral judgement and moral action. Moral insights can effectively bind the will of an actor only as long as they are embedded in an ethical self-understanding that puts a person's concern for her own well-being in the service of motivating an equal interest in justice. Deontological theories, while they may well explain the justification and application of norms, lack moving arguments for 'why to be moral' at all. Political theories of justice face a similar problem. Once it comes to the question, why citizens should, in relevant conflicts, act according to constitutional principles rather than subjective preferences, they have no more than hope for the emergence of the right patterns of political culture and socialisation.

Philosophy not only pays a high price for its withdrawal; one might question the decision to withdraw itself, and ask why philosophy should leave the field to clinical theories, such as psychoanalysis, that claim to be competent for treating disturbed and damaged life. The conception of mental health is by no means an unproblematic analogy for physical health. Compared with the body, the soul and mind lack the same sort of clearly observable parameters for states of 'sickness'. A normative interpretation of what may count as an undisturbed mode of human life must all the more fill the place of lacking somatic indicators of health and illness, once socially wide-spread and inconspicuously normalised pathologies cause pains that do not even pass the threshold of people's consciousness. Why should philosophy abstain from a business that clinical psychology has to carry out in a conceptually more or less confused way anyway? Why should philosophy not contribute to explaining the intuitions and glimpses of what we sometimes yet dare, however hesitatingly, to recognise as 'wrong' or 'misspent' ways of life?

(3) Kierkegaard was the first to give a postmetaphysical answer to the ethical question in terms of how 'to be oneself'. This level of abstraction appropriately corresponds to the challenge of pluralism. In *Either/Or*, Kierkegaard contrasts the ethical way of life with a hedonistic masquerade of life. He paints this kind of 'aesthetic life', with some sympathy, in the attractive colours of early romanticism – as a sensuous mode of a leisurely, but dispersed life that is driven by the self-centred pleasures the ego draws from accidental and short-lived encounters. The ethical self, by contrast, pulls itself together and achieves a consciousness of its own freedom and individuality. Ethical life gains continuity and transparency through self-reflection, since 'he who lives ethically has himself as his task'.[4] Only a person, who has developed a deep concern for her own spiritual well-being and has thus become aware of the historicity of her existence, has also acquired the strength to make responsible commitments to others.

Kierkegaard analyses the structural, temporal and modal features of an authentic mode of 'being oneself'. The continued self-choice is guided by the infinite interest in the endangered success of one's own life project. Only through a self-critical appropriation of one's own past life history, recollected and retrieved in light of future possibilities, can a person become a unique, irreplaceable individual and an autonomous subject at the same time. The ethical self can continuously give an account of her life and thus *become* the person she *is*, only in light of the moral Sermon of the Mount, which Kierkegaard always tacitly presupposes. The individual develops an ethical self-understanding by repenting problematic elements of the past, of which she is ashamed, and by affirming only those mental attitudes and actual habits, with which she wants to be identified in the future: 'Everything that is posited in his freedom belongs to him essentially, however accidental it may seem to be.'

But Kierkegaard is far from Sartre's existentialism, when he adds:

> This distinction is not a product of his arbitrariness so that he might seem to have absolute power to make himself into what pleased him to be... The ethical individual dares to employ the expression that he is his own editor, but he is also fully aware that he is responsible – responsible for himself personally, responsible to the order of things in which he lives, responsible to God.[5]

For Kierkegaard, an ethical life cannot be stabilised but in relation to God. His conception is without any roots in a speculative interpretation of the whole of Being, and, in that sense, it is *post-metaphysical*, but not *post-religious*. Faith must come to complement moral knowledge, if the ethical question shall find a *compelling* answer.

Kierkegaard, the radical critic of contemporary culture, passionately denounces the ubiquity of, at worst, a frivolous and cynical, and, at best, a conformist and self-righteous attitude towards the normalisation of blatant injustice, humiliation and suffering. It is this phenomenon, he argues, that cannot be explained by a *lack of knowledge*, but only by a *corruption of will*. Those who *know* better are not *willing* to understand the disastrous state of mankind. Therefore, Kierkegaard speaks of 'sin' rather than 'guilt'. As soon as we interpret guilt as sin, however, we come to realise that we must hope for an absolute power of forgiveness – a power that intervenes in and reverses the course of history for the purpose of resurrecting the integrity of the innocent victims. (This was, by the way, at issue in the famous controversy between Walter Benjamin and Max Horkheimer during the thirties – even before the Holocaust.) For Kierkegaard, the promise of redemption is the motivating connection between the infinite concern for oneself and the moral commands of a post-conventional conscience. Faith in God, the Saviour, requires one 'to go beyond' Socrates and Kant.

Climacus, the author of the *Philosophical Fragments*, is still satisfied with considering the 'god in time' as a kind of 'thought project'; in the end he remains undecided, whether faith in the possibility of salvation is 'more true' than the Socratic project of ethical knowledge.[6] Kierkegaard therefore introduces an Anti-Climacus who presents the striking phenomenology of a 'sickness to death', which leads to a final reversal of consciousness. He first describes the disquieting state of a person who acquires awareness of the destination of 'becoming a self', yet turns his back on this existential imperative and flees into equally despairing alternatives: not to will to be oneself, not to be a self, or to will to be someone else – that is, to wish for a new self. The person, however, who then discovers that the failed attempts of his own, and not any circumstances, are the source of despair, that person must face the challenge of becoming oneself. In desperately willing to be oneself, he mobilises all his resources for an act of extreme self-assertion. What does that lead to?

The phenomena of an ever more intensive despair are as many manifestations of an ever clearer recognised failure to reach a balance that alone would make an authentic mode of existence possible. The failure of the last, *defiant* act of the ethical self to resolutely achieve this goal exclusively in virtue of its own powers marks the end of the therapeutic curriculum – the overturn of a secular self-understanding. It motivates the finite mind to transcend itself and to recognise the dependence on an Other in whom its own freedom is rooted. Kierkegaard describes this condition of rebirth with a formula, reminiscent of, but turning upside down the first few paragraphs of Fichte's *Wissenschaftslehre*: 'in relating itself to itself, and in willing to be itself, the self rests transparently in the power that established it'.[7] Though the literal reference to a 'power', in which the self is founded ('*gründet das Selbst in der Macht, die es setzte*': grounds the self in the power that established it) does not signify more than the finitude of a human existence in history, Kierkegaard prefers a much stronger, a religious reading. It is only through a consciousness of sin that the self can reach an awareness of his own finitude in the right way – so that 'this self takes on a new quality by being a self directly before God'.[8]

Kierkegaard's ethical subject survives its hopeless despair only in the shape of a religious self who, in its relation to itself, receives its freedom by *devoting* itself to an 'absolute Other' to whom 'it owes everything'. Kierkegaard, who was obsessed throughout his life by the Lutheran question as to how to conceptualise a merciful god, is a radical Protestant. This orthodoxy must be, of course, an annoyance for his *philosophical* followers. He himself acknowledges that there is no way to form a consistent *conception* of God – neither via *eminentiae* nor via *negationis*. Every idealisation remains parasitic on the basic predicates from which it starts; for the same reason the attempt to encircle the absolute Other via negations does not fare better: 'Understanding cannot even think the absolutely different; it cannot absolutely negate itself but uses itself for the purpose and therefore thinks the difference in itself.'[9] The gap between knowledge and faith cannot be bridged by reason. This situation presents a dilemma to philosophers who want to inherit Kierkegaard's post-metaphysical ethics, but must deny any recourse to a revealed truth. Let us quickly consider the responses of Karl Jaspers and Jean-Paul Sartre, and then move on to Heidegger and Adorno.

(4) Jaspers maintained that philosophical knowledge must be conceived as another faith – faith in reason. Philosophy rejects revelation as a source of truth, yet competes with religious doctrines for the right normative self-understanding of individuals, communities, and mankind in general. Socrates is juxtaposed with Jesus.[10] This strategy raises the difficult question of explaining the paradoxical epistemic status of such a hybrid enterprise. Though it is still supposed to abide by normal standards of rational discourse, philosophy is said to share that domain of transcendental problems and that kind of dogmatic claims we only know from the great world religions.[11] This resemblance of post-metaphysical thought with faith is as implausible as the assumed gap between modern philosophy and science. A different, straightforward atheistic strategy is adopted by Jean-Paul Sartre. His conception of existential freedom lacks, however, the warning against confusing a self-conscious ethical life with defiant self-assertion, which was the whole point of Kierkegaard's suggestive phenomenology of despair. Like Kierkegaard, Sartre wants to take into account both the fallibilism of the human mind and the unconditionality of the moral claims with which he is confronted. But he does not face the argument that the self cannot hope to satisfy its infinite ethical concern on these postmetaphysical conditions, unless it becomes aware of its specific finitude – the dependence on an enabling power that escapes one's own control.

Any philosophy that strives to be an heir to Kierkegaard has to offer an interpretation of this enabling power. A naturalist interpretation is ruled out, because the experience of a 'transparent' dependency is bound to the dimension of an interpersonal relation. Defiant self-assertion is directed against an other whom the self encounters as a second person. But it is far from obvious that this 'other' to whom the self, with her self-relation, must relate itself, is identical with 'the god in time'. The linguistic turn offers a deflationist interpretation. Interacting speakers are others to one another.

As historical and social beings, we find ourselves within a linguistically structured form of life. Caught in the restless concern not to fail our life, we face in everyday communication a surpassing power on which we, indeed, 'transparently rest'. Language, the medium of our communicative practices, is no one's private property. No one individually disposes over an intersubjectively shared language. No single participant is capable of controlling the course and dynamics of the interpenetrating processes of *mutual* understanding and *self*-understanding. How speakers and hearers make use of their respective communicative freedoms is not a matter of arbitrary choice. The logos that is embodied in ordinary language reaches speakers through the individual freedoms of its users, who raise validity claims with their speech-acts, and hearers who meet them with either a 'Yes' or a 'No'. Both are free only in virtue of being subject to the *binding power* of the reasons that they offer to one another, and take from one another.

This reading of the dependence on an 'Other' saves the fallibilist but anti-sceptic meaning of 'unconditionality' in a weak, or proceduralist sense. We know how to learn what we owe to one another; and each of us, respectively, as members of a community, can self-critically appropriate our past histories, in light of such moral obligations, for the sake of articulating a proper ethical self-understanding. Yet the communication remains 'ours', though it is ruled by a logos that escapes our control. The unconditionality of truth and freedom is a necessary presupposition of our practices and lacks an ontological guarantee beyond the cultural constituents of our forms of life. The right ethical self-understanding is neither revealed, nor in any other way 'given' to us, but achieved in a joint effort. From this perspective, the enabling power built into language is of a trans-subjective, rather than an absolute, quality.

This modest interpretation does not fit Kierkegaard's idea that binding moral norms must be anchored in faith, that is to say, in some ethical self-understanding that unconditionally grants to our life a 'meaning'. This is the sense in which we must understand Horkheimer's sentence, which has it that any attempt to save, without God, 'an unconditional meaning', is in vain. For everybody who, like Horkheimer, is convinced that 'together with God, eternal truth is dying',[12] philosophy faces an uneasy alternative. It must either give in to a desperate scepticism, or appropriate the theological substance of sin and salvation. Though I do not accept this alternative myself,[13] I would like to focus on an interesting consequence that has left its traces in the most important philosophical works of our century. On this premise philosophy cannot overcome the nostalgic defeatism that is reflected in Horkheimer's remarks, unless it provides a reasonable translation of the 'god in time' – 'reasonable' here means a translation of the God of Moses in terms of an impersonal conception of a temporalised absolute. This is the key, I think, for the works of Adorno and Derrida – and that of Heidegger as well?

Let me briefly compare Adorno with Heidegger in terms of their loyalty to the tradition of monotheism. While the first draws on messianic sources of Western Marxism, the other seems to follow Nietzsche in the attempt to reach back behind both the Jewish beginnings of monotheism and the Platonist beginnings of metaphysics.

(5) *Negative Dialectics* can be understood as the elaboration of the Kierkegaardian thought that Adorno first expressed in the final aphorism of his *Minima Moralia*: 'The only philosophy which can be responsibly practised in face of despair is the attempt to contemplate all things as they would present themselves from the standpoint of redemption ... Perspectives must

be fashioned that displace and estrange the world, reveal it to be . . . as indigent and distorted as it will appear one day in the messianic light.'[14] The counterfactual reference to such perspectives is justified in words that remind us of Kierkegaard's famous formula for becoming aware of a finitude that does not bar the human mind from its relation to the infinite, the possible, and the transcendent. Adorno appears to interpret the self-transcending insight of the despairing self who 'is restlessly and tormentedly engaged in willing to be itself', when he continues: 'The more passionately thought denies its conditionality for the sake of the unconditional, the more unconsciously, and so calamitously, it is delivered up to the world. Even its own impossibility it must at last comprehend for the sake of the possible.'[15]

With this concluding sentence Adorno takes back the theological allusion and makes the reader aware of the inner-worldly context from which Adorno speaks: 'beside the demand thus placed on thought, the question of the reality or unreality of redemption itself hardly matters.'[16] What matters, however, is the strong moral implication of the revoked allusion to God, the Saviour and the Reconciler. Adorno indirectly communicates that his critical perspective remains loyal to the egalitarian universalism that is inscribed in the very conception of God, the *Deus absconditus*. When we, at Judgement Day, individually step forward and see 'Him' face-to-face, God will, by his comprehensive and charitable evaluation of the unique features of every single life, do justice to each of us equally. It is this normative substance of monotheism that Adorno wants to keep – and that gets lost with Heidegger.

Kierkegaard's existential analysis of what it would require to live a life beyond despair has certainly never found a more convincing philosophical explication than in *Being and Time*.[17] It is, however, just the ontologising translation of Kierkegaard's modalities of an ethical life that deprives Heidegger's conception of authenticity of its normative core: 'In the end, Heidegger and Kierkegaard move in opposite directions. Unlike Kierkegaard's ethical life which constitutes a precondition of moral and social responsibility, Heidegger's methodological conception of authenticity is deeply anti-normative.'[18] The empty appeal to a resoluteness that lacks any substance anticipates the emptiness of an arrival of Being – an empty arrival that is nevertheless implored. In his later writings Heidegger retains this ontological perspective when he interprets the defiant self-assertion of the will to be oneself in terms of the subjectivism of the mentalist paradigm, and when he goes on to substitute a history of Being for Kierkegaard's 'god in history'.

This history manifests itself in a contingent series of fateful, yet overwhelming happenings – of shifts in world disclosure that are revealed through the pen of distinguished poets and thinkers like Hölderlin and Heidegger himself. The conversion from the Socratic self-understanding of an ethical self to the awareness of one's dependence on the grace and judgement of the Saviour, is replaced by the turn from the totalising thought of metaphysics to a submission under something superior. The anonymity of a withdrawn and impersonal power demands from us the obedient attitude of someone listening to the uncertain arrival of an indeterminate message. The only content we know in advance is what we get from Heidegger's critical reading of the history of metaphysics. But in this regard, the *Letter on Humanism* only repeats what Heidegger had extracted from his earlier interpretation of Nietzsche: that we have 'to eliminate all conceptions of justice, which stem from Christian, humanist, enlightenment, liberal and socialist morality.'[19] The assimilation of ethics to ontology leads Heidegger, in 1946, to answer the ethical question with a hint to the hollow ethos of 'Schicklichkeit': He asks man to fit to whatever might come from some superior power – an absent power that so far has had nothing to say.

The evacuation of all moral content from a temporalised Being results from decisions on which Heidegger's conception of a history of Being rests. Heidegger first includes, under the title of ontotheology, the monotheist tradition as part of the history of metaphysics. Judaism and Christianity thus fall under the critique of that history. The critique itself is driven, secondly, by a search for archaic origins that are 'earlier', and supposedly more telling, than Socrates and Jesus – those two sources of Western thought and civilization that Kierkegaard appreciates and Nietzsche detests. As a result of this strange impetus Heidegger likes to talk about 'Gods' rather than God as a singular. You remember the headline of his last interview in *Der Spiegel*: 'Nur *ein* Gott kann uns retten'.[20] Adorno's critique of 'Ursprungsdenken' is the antithesis to Heidegger's 'anfänglichem Denken'.

Echoing Nietzsche's 'last man', there is also a 'last God'. Heidegger declares that with the death of that poor guy all kinds of 'theisms' are definitely finished. No surprise then that there is neither a moral trace left in Heidegger's Being, nor in the anticipation of its arrival – no leftover from the egalitarian universalism that is inscribed in the monotheistic tradition. From this point of view it is interesting to follow the dialogue that Derrida imagines at the end of his book on Heidegger, a dialogue among Heidegger and Christian theologians.[21]

The theologians ask Heidegger for a revision of his rejection of the monotheist tradition. He should better recognise his own critique of ontotheology as the best possible interpretation of the experience of Christians, Jews and Muslims in their encounter with the actuality of God in history. Derrida's Heidegger responds to this invitation as we would expect. He insists on the fundamentalist claim of his search for first origins, reaching back far behind the beginnings of metaphysics and eschatology. Derrida, of course, fashions Heidegger's rebuke in cautious terms so that no suspicion about a regression into paganism can arise on the side of the theologians. But Derrida does not leave the dialogue at that. The most remarkable aspect of the exchange is the fact that he gives the last word to Heidegger's unwavering opponents and allows them to restate their conciliatory interpretation. In the end they embrace a reluctant Heidegger who is presented as having unintentionally captured what faith can mean for Jews and Christians alike.

This surprising end seems to indicate that Derrida's own appropriation of Heidegger's later philosophy rests on a theological, rather than pre-Socratic, background – a Jewish, rather than Greek, background. Moreover, his loyalty to Levinas reveals the tendency to answer the ethical question from the perspective of the self-reflective relation of the self to an Other 'who' speaks in each case through a second person. If I am not mistaken in this assumption, I can put my question as follows:

Can Derrida leave the normative connotations of the uncertain 'arrival' of an undefined 'event' as indeterminate as Heidegger does?

And, what burdens of justification would follow from accepting the demand of making explicit those normative connotations that – and this is no accident – remind us of a specific religious tradition, whatever they are?

NOTES

1. Jacques Derrida, 'The Future of the Profession', Ms. (2000), p. 43. Subsequently published as Jacques Derrida, 'The University without condition', in Jacques Derrida, *Without Alibi*, trans. and ed. Peggy Kamuf (Stanford: Stanford University Press, 2002), pp. 202–37 (p. 234).
2. Jürgen Habermas, *The Philosophical Discourse of Modernity: Twelve Lectures*, trans. Frederick C. Lawrence (Cambridge, Mass.: MIT Press, 1987), pp. 181ff.
3. Gershom Scholem, 'Zehn unhistorische Sätze über Kabbala', in Gershom Scholem, *Judaica 3* (Frankfurt am Main: Suhrkamp, 1973), p. 264, my translation.
4. Søren Kierkegaard, *Either/Or: Part II*, edited and translated by Howard V. Hong and Edna H. Hong (Princeton: Princeton University Press, 1987), p. 256.
5. Ibid., p. 260.
6. Søren Kierkegaard, *Philosophical Fragments*, edited and translated by Howard V. Hong and Edna H. Hong (Princeton: Princeton University Press, 1985), p. 111.
7. Søren Kierkegaard, *The Sickness unto Death*, edited and translated by Howard V. Hong and Edna H. Hong (Princeton: Princeton University Press, 1980), pp. 14 and 131.
8. Ibid., p. 79.
9. Kierkegaard, *Philosophical Fragments*, p. 45.
10. Karl Jaspers, *Die Grossen Philosophen, Bd. 1* (Munich: Piper, 1957).
11. Karl Jaspers, *Der philosophische Glaube angesichts der Offenbarung* (Munich: Piper, 1962), pp. 100f.: 'Da steht nicht Wissen gegen Glaube, sondern Glaube gegen Glaube . . . Offenbarungsglaube und Vernunftglaube stehen polar zueinander, sind betroffen voneinander, verstehen sich zwar nicht restlos, aber hören nicht auf im Versuch, sich zu verstehen. Was der je einzelne Mensch in sich für sich selbst verwirft, kann er im Anderen als dessen Glauben doch anerkennen.'
12. Max Horkheimer, *Theismus-Atheismus, Gesammelte Schriften Bd. 7* (Frankfurt am Main: Fischer), p. 184.
13. Compare Jürgen Habermas, 'To Seek to Salvage an Unconditional Meaning Without God Is a Futile Undertaking: Reflections on a Remark of Max Horkheimer', in Jürgen Habermas, *Justification and Application*, trans. C. Cronin (Cambridge: Polity Press, 1993), pp. 133–46.

14. Theodor W. Adorno, *Minima Moralia* (London: Verso, 1984), p. 247. [Editor's note: the reference to *Negative Dialects* is Theodor Adorno, *Negative Dialects*, trans. E. B. Ashton (London: Routledge, 1973).]
15. Ibid.
16. Ibid.
17. [Editor's note: Martin Heidegger, *Being and Time*, trans. John Macquarrie and Edward Robinson (Oxford: Blackwell, 1967).]
18. Patricia J. Huntington, 'Heidegger's Reading of Kierkegaard Revisited', in M. J. B. Matuštík and M. Westphal (eds), *Kierkegaard in Post/Modernity* (Bloomington: Indiana University Press, 1995), pp. 43–65.
19. Martin Heidegger, *Nietzsche, Bd. II* (Pfullingen: Neske, 1961), p. 325: 'Wir müssen freilich . . . alle Vorstellungen über die Gerechtigkeit, die aus der christlichen, humanistischen, aufklärerischen, bürgerlichen und sozialistischen Moral stammen, ausschalten.'
20. [Editor's note: 'Nur noch ein Gott kann uns retten – Spiegel-Interview mit Martin Heidegger', *Der Spiegel*, 31 May 1976 (the interview was conducted on 23 September 1966). English translation as 'Only a God Can Save Us – *Der Spiegel* Interview', trans. Maria P. Alter and John D. Caputo, in Richard Wolin (ed.) *The Heidegger Controversy: A Critical Reader* (New York: Columbia University Press, 1991).]
21. Jacques Derrida, *Of Spirit: Heidegger and the Question*, trans. Geoffrey Bennington and Rachel Bowlby (Chicago: The University of Chicago Press, 1989), pp. 109–13.

8

Seyla Benhabib

DEMOCRACY AND DIFFERENCE: REFLECTIONS ON THE METAPOLITICS OF LYOTARD AND DERRIDA[1]

Although critical of aspects of Habermas's work, Seyla Benhabib here criticises Derrida from a perspective largely informed by Habermas's work on communicative action and deliberative democracy. She argues that Derrida's focus on the exceptional – on the original institution of the polity, for instance – leaves him with no theory of ordinary politics. Despite Derrida's attempts, such a theory cannot be understood in terms of the exceptional politics of revolution. Moreover, and echoing Bernstein in Chapter 4, Benhabib argues that Derrida's analyses are too abstract and formal, thereby overlooking the concrete history of political and social institutions and practices. As a result, Derrida ignores the normative content of the democratic tradition, a normative content that, although not fully realised in the present, can nonetheless form the basis for a critique of present injustices. So, according to Benhabib, Derrida's analyses of politics lack both relevance and critical force.

The text, which was written during the early 1990s, is followed by a short afterword written shortly after Derrida's death. In it, Benhabib notes how the issues she raised in the original text are no less topical today than they were when it was first published.

Seyla Benhabib, 'Democracy and Difference: Reflections on the Metapolitics of Lyotard and Derrida', *The Journal of Political Philosophy* 2: 1, 1994, pp. 1–23.

I. THE DEMOCRATIC MOMENT

In his 1848 Preface to *Democracy in America*, Alexis de Tocqueville wrote,

> However sudden and momentous be the events which have just taken place so swiftly, the author of this book can claim that they have not taken him by surprise. This work was written fifteen years ago with a mind constantly preoccupied by a single thought: the thought of the approaching irresistible and universal spread of democracy throughout the world. On reading it again, one finds on every page a solemn warning that society is changing shape, that mankind lives under changing conditions, and new destinies are impending.[2]

In view of the momentous transformations which have occurred in the countries of Central and Eastern Europe and the former Soviet Union since 1989, and even prior to them, with the transition from dictatorships to democracy in the Philippines, Argentina, Chile, and Brazil, 'the thought of the approaching irresistible and universal spread of democracy throughout the world' sounds more true today than ever. Yet, as Tocqueville also reminds us, 'It is not force alone, but rather good laws, which make a new government secure. After the battle comes the lawgiver. The one destroys; the other builds up. Each has his function.'[3] As we watch the aftermath of these bloodless peoples' revolutions, with their wonderful sensual images of velvet and carnations, in Poland, Hungary, Czechoslavakia and the Philippines, we observe their colors fading and their scent diminishing as the routine of everyday as opposed to revolutionary politics settle in; in others such as the new Commonwealth of Independent Republics of the former Soviet Union and in the former Yugoslavia civil war conditions, violent upheavals, social chaos and nuclear perils darken the future.

These momentous transformations have caught the political thought of the present breathless and adrift. With very few exceptions, neither empirical nor normative political theory was prepared to deal with the magnitude of these changes with the self-confidence of Tocqueville.[4] This may not necessarily be lamentable; perhaps the 'owl of Minerva' truly flies at dusk and reflective thought can only paint its 'grey on grey'. It is my deep sense, however, that the lack of orientation in political theory in view of the transformations of the present is not due to the inevitable gap between political action and political reflection alone. There is a profound lack of simultaneity between the time of theory and the time of political action of such magnitude that Ernst Bloch's phrase of 'non-simultaneous simultaneities' ('ungleichzeitige Gleichzeitigkeiten')[5] strikes me as being quite apt to capture the mood of the present. While almost all so-called western industrial capitalist democracies are caught in a *fin de siècle* mood – consider some of the bewildering array of theoretical prefixes which have come to dominate our intellectual and cultural lives, postmodern, postindustrial, post-fordist, post-Keynesian, post-histoire, post-feminist – the efforts of the countries of Central and Eastern Europe appear as 'nachholende' revolutions,[6] as revolutions which are catching up with or making good for processes that others have already been through. For normative political theory, this unusual concatenation of historical circumstances has meant that the postmodernist *critique of western democracy* with which we have become so familiar in the last two decades and the Central and Eastern European as well as Latin American *aspirations to democracy* coexist in the same intellectual and political space. Postmodernist skepticism toward 'really existing western democracies', and at times the naively apologetic confirmation of western capitalism and democracy by their new aspirants are contemporaries of our current political and cultural horizon. It is this proximity and distance which is so disorienting as well as explosive.

In the present article I want to explore the question: what, if anything, has the postmodernist critique of normative thinking contributed to the current task of understanding and reconstructing democracy on a world-scale? My argument is that although the set of issues suggested by the vague terminology of 'difference', 'otherness', 'heterogeneity' or 'le differend' are crucial for the ethos of contemporary democratic communities, theorists of difference have not indicated where the line is to be drawn between forms of difference which foster democracy and forms of difference which reflect anti-democratic aspirations. In the transformed world political context of today, it is more essential than ever that the critique of democracy in the name of difference developed by oppositional intellectuals be formulated so carefully that these thoughts cannot be exploited for nationalist, tribalist, and xenophobic purposes. It is imperative that the politics of the 'differend' and 'la différance' not be settled beyond or at the margins of democratic politics.

In a recent article entitled 'The Other Heading: Reflections on Today's Europe', Jacques Derrida voices the following concerns and fears:

> Hope, fear, and trembling are commensurate with the signs that are coming to us from everywhere in Europe, where, precisely, in the name of identity, be it cultural or not, the worst violences, those that we recognize all too well without yet having thought them through, the crimes of xenophobia, racism, anti-Semitism, religious or national fanaticism, are being unleashed, mixed up, mixed up with each other, but also, and there is nothing fortuitous in this, mixed in with the breath, with the respiration, with the very 'spirit' of the promise.[7]

The question is whether the 'meta-politics' which follow from certain theories of 'différence', Derrida's not excluded, and in particular their undermining of the universalist premises of liberal-democratic theory, do not reduce such concerns about xenophobia, racism, anti-Semitism to good moral and political intentions which cannot be supported by philosophical arguments and strong reasons.[8] May it be that the critique of the universalist political tradition, developed by Jean-François Lyotard and Jacques Derrida, is so radical that it undermines the rational defensibility of these ideals and reduces them to sheer existential choices for which we cannot give reasons with good grounds? May it also be that this critique claims to be radical but is, in effect, curiously powerless to deal with the radical power of history and the historicity of political modernity since the American and the French Revolutions? May it be that the price of a certain kind of hyper-radicalism is an aloofness from institutional and social critique?[9]

Let me be very clear what my questions are not intended to imply. I am not suggesting that there is any deductive or conceptual link between certain philosophical positions and political practices and movements which we may consider objectionable.[10] To put it bluntly, theorists of difference are not responsible for the degenerate form of the politics of difference pursued at the present in Bosnia-Herzegovina for example and it would be tendentious to suggest so. One cannot criticize philosophical positions for their imputed, real or imaginary, political consequences in the hands of others. Neither am I suggesting that we should judge, evaluate, or question the commitment of theorists of difference to democratic ideals and aspirations. What I will be arguing instead is that Jean-François Lyotard and, to some extent, Jacques Derrida, privilege in their writings on the political *a certain perspective, a certain angle, a certain heuristic framework,* which itself has deep and ultimately, I think, misleading consequences for understanding the rational foundations of the democratic form of government. They attempt to illuminate political phenomena through an experience which is a limit condition: an extraordinary and foundational moment. In doing so, they repeat an epistemic and ultimately meta-political problem which Richard Wolin has very aptly characterized with reference to another group of thinkers, at a different time:

> . . . a general fascination with 'limit situations' (*Grenzsituationen*) and extremes; an interest in transposing the fundamental experiences of aesthetic modernity – shock, disruption, experiential immediacy; an infatuation with the sinister and the forbidden, with the 'flowers of evil' – to the plane of everyday life, thereby injecting an element of enthusiasm and vitality in what had otherwise become a rigid and lifeless mechanism.[11]

It is this fascination with the 'limit situation' in republican politics that I want to document in the writings of Lyotard and Derrida, and which I wish to criticize for its inadequacy for understanding democratic politics.

II. THE SITE OF LE DIFFEREND: THE REPUBLICAN ACT OF FOUNDATION IN LYOTARD'S AND DERRIDA'S WRITINGS

In Jean-François Lyotard's writings on politics[12] and in Jacques Derrida's recent essays repeatedly, a theme, a *problematique*, returns. This is the preoccupation with the *originary* or *foundational political* act. From Derrida's writings celebrating the bicentenary of the American Declaration of Independence[13] to Lyotard's linguistic analysis of republicanism in *le Differend and* to the reflections of both on Pascal and the 'foundations of law',[14] a fascination with the paradoxes and aporias of the foundational moment in republican politics is apparent.

For Lyotard the paradoxes of republican acts of foundating, as for Derrida, become the event, the moment, when the differend is revealed in politics, when in fact politics is revealed as 'le differend'. Lyotard writes:

> In a republic, the pronoun of the first-person plural is in effect the linchpin of the discourse of authorization. Substitutable for a proper name, We, the French people . . ., it is supposedly able to link prescriptions (such as articles in codes, court rulings, laws, decrees, ordinances, circulars, and commandos) onto their legitimation 'in a suitable way.' . . . [T]he republican regimen's principle of legitimacy is that the addressor of the norm, y, and the addressee of the obligation, x, are the same. The legislator ought not to be exempt from the obligation he or she norms. And the obligated one is able to promulgate the law that obligates him or her . . . *We decree as a norm that it is an obligation for us to carry out act a*. This is the principle of autonomy.[15]

Lyotard analyzes the paradoxical aspect of these foundational formulations: the puzzle emerges with the supposed 'identity' of the two 'we's' invoked, one in the normative which constitutes the act of founding, as in 'we the people decree as a norm that'; the second, in the case of the 'we' that is the addressee of the obligation, as 'we ought to obey the decreed laws'. The 'we' of the normative, 'we the people', and the 'we' of the declarative, 'we ought to obey the decreed laws', are not and may not be the same. There is a justifiable suspicion that the one who speaks the law and the one to whom the law applies do not overlap perfectly. The logic of republican identity here obfuscates and covers up an important political asymmetry, namely, the asymmetry between the law-givers and the constituents to whom the law applies.

This republican formula of autonomy disguises the 'differend' in politics, insofar as what is heterogeneous, incommensurable, other and irreducible to a common denominator is here subsumed under a formula of identity – 'we, the people'. What remain absolutely heterogeneous are the two moments of the 'we': the we who promulgates the law, and the we to whom the law applies. The formula of republican politics, 'we, the people declare that we shall obey x', makes the 'differend' disappear by reducing it to bland commensurability and identity.

Politics for Lyotard, in its authentic rather than the run-of-the-mill version, which he attributes to intellectuals and politicians, resides in the problem of 'linkage'.[16] The politics of language as well as the language of politics are the sites where the heterogeneous, other, different, incongruent, and unfamiliar are rendered homogeneous, the same, identical, congruent and familiar – 'heimisch'. To uncover and unmask this logic which homogenizes and imposes sameness over difference is the task of philosophical politics; but, and this is the crux of the matter, this process of rendering 'le differend', homogeneous, compatible, congruent, the same, is due to an absolute spontaneity; it just 'happens'. Lyotard here refers to Heidegger:

> No matter what its regimen, every phrase is in principle what is at stake in a differend between genres of discourse. This differend proceeds from the question, which accompanies any phrase, of how to link onto it. And this question proceeds from the nothingness that 'separates' one phrase from the 'following.' There are differends because, or like, there is *Ereignis*. But that's forgotten as much as possible: genres of discourse are modes of forgetting the occurrence, they fill the void between the phrases. This 'nothingness' is, nevertheless, what opens up the possibility of finalities proper to genres . . .[17]

Spontaneity, arbitrariness, linkage, the happening, heterogeneity versus the power that links, that binds, that organizes and moulds: this is the site of the civil war of language as well as of the language of politics.[18]

In his reflections on 'Declarations of Independence', Jacques Derrida likewise drives home the arbitrariness of all republican beginnings via the use of linguistic means of analysis. The statements of the American Declaration of Independence, 'We hold these truths to be self-evident: that all men are created equal; that they are endowed by their creator with certain inalienable Rights . . . ' indicate, according to Derrida, a confusion of the 'constative' with the 'performative'.[19] The signatories of the Declaration speak in the name of 'the laws of Nature and Nature's God'. Thus, they understand themselves to be stating a constative; whereas the utterance, 'we hold these truths to be self-evident', is a performative. It establishes the validity of the principles to which the adverb 'self-evident' refers in the very act of formulating them. For if it is the Laws of Nature and Nature's God which show these truths to be 'self-evicent', then their self-evidence should be apparent to all; but precisely because this self-evidence is not evident, the Revolutionaries break with the King of England and establish themselves as *holding* these truths to be self-evident. The performative of the revolutionary declaration mistakes itself to be a declarative.

Furthermore, who is the 'we' that is invoked as the signer of the Declaration? The representatives of the thirteen colonies? Thomas Jefferson, the author of the Declaration? Or the 'American people', whose presence is anticipated at a moment when it is still absent. It authorizes the Declaration only ex post facto.

For Derrida, revolutionary acts of foundations *confuse* their own performativity via appeals to the constative; for Lyotard revolutionary acts *present* the performative in the form of a constative. The point is quite the same: Derrida sees revolutionary acts of foundation as concealing their own lack of foundations, their historical contingency, by false hypostatization; Lyotard maintains that revolutionary acts of foundation hide the differend, that is the moment of spontaneity and creativity, when the 'gap', the 'hiatus' in language is bridged.

Lyotard and Derrida return here to the problem of republican and revolutionary justice which Hegel had first brilliantly analyzed in *The Phenomenology of Spirit* in the section on 'Absolute Freedom and Terror'.[20] If freedom meant accepting as legitimate only those principles and institutions which the will could have given itself, argued Hegel, then there would be no possible constraints on the content of what the will could legislate to bind itself legitimately. Neither the dictates of reason, nor the dictates of existing institutions and tradition could constrain the striving of the will toward absolute autonomy. Absolute, meaning unconditional, freedom, could only end in terror; for any content which the will would give itself, and any institutional specification which it would establish could always be subject to further criticism. The consequence is perpetual destruction, denunciation and dismantling of the existent. Absolute freedom cannot institutionalize itself; the revolution must devour its children. After Hegel, in her reflections on revolution, Hannah Arendt gave these perplexities of revolutionary legitimacy noted by Hegel their sharpest formulation.[21] Recalling her analysis will also suggest a different manner of thinking through the linguistic-political puzzles of revolutionary justice set identified by Lyotard and Derrida.

III. Hannah Arendt and the Antinomies of Revolutionary Acts of Beginning

According to Arendt 'the need for an absolute', for an absolute source of authority and legitimacy, manifests itself in the political sphere in two ways. The invocation of an absolute is needed 'to break two vicious circles, the one apparently inherent in human law-making, and the other inherent in the *petitio principii* which attends every new beginning, that is politically speaking, in the very task of foundation.'[22] The first of these needs expresses the puzzle of the legitimacy of the law: the source of authority of all human-made laws is thought to reside in an instance outside them, bestowing legitimacy upon them. Legality and legitimacy are distinguishable;

the promulgated law does not automatically carry its source of legitimacy within it. Hence this legitimacy is located in a source beyond the human-made law, be it in God, the Holy Scripture, in Nature or Reason.

The second need reflected in this search for an absolute in the political realm derives from the circularity inherent in the foundational act or in every beginning. If the will of the people united is the source of all legitimacy, then whence does this people derive its authority? If it is the constitution which a united people gives itself that forms and declares it as a body politic, whence does the constitution itself derive its authority? The act of foundation seems to send us in a circle: the revolutionary will of the people is said to be the foundational act which lends legitimacy to the constitution; on the other hand the will of the people is declared the highest law of the land because the constitution legitimizes it to bear this authority. Abbé Sieyès's distinction between *pouvoir constituant* and *pouvoir constitué* was an attempt to solve this paradox of foundational republicanism; the pouvoir constitué, constituted power, would have to derive its authority from the constituant power, *le pouvoir constituant*; but this constituting power was no other than the will of the nation, 'which itself remained outside and above all governments and all laws.'[23]

Hannah Arendt's reflections on these perplexities of revolution lead her to draw a distinction between the legitimacy of power and the legitimacy of the law.[24] It is the mark of successful revolutions, as opposed to those which enter the perpetual dialectic of the creation and destruction of freedom, that they succeed in stabilizing themselves through acts of constitution giving. Via these acts the 'government of laws replaces that of men.' The legitimacy of the laws can now be traced back to their being grounded in the constitution; whereas the legitimacy of the constitution itself remains indeterminate: particularly for those nations who are not fortunate enough to have retained some form of political organization prior to the moment of revolutionary upheaval, the mysterious authority of the political act at the beginning remains. Arendt's diagnosis here is that whereas none of the constituent assemblies of the French Revolution could command enough authority to lay down the law of the land, in the case of the American colonies it was otherwise because the Constitutional Assembly owed its own authority to the already existing political self-organization of the thirteen colonies.

IV. Antinomies of Revolutionary Foundations in Lyotard and Derrida

Let me return to Derrida's and Lyotard's analysis of the paradoxes of revolutionary beginnings in light of Arendt's analysis in *On Revolution*. They both maintain that the 'we' of the normative, as in 'we, the people', and the 'we' of the declarative, as in 'all residents of the Thirteen colonies', may not be the same. Through a series of reductions to identity, the moment of difference which is politically significant is covered over. To speak with Adorno, the logic of identity does violence to those whose otherness places them beyond the homogenizing logic of the 'we'. This violence at the origin, this forcible exclusion is concealed in every republican foundation, but it returns in the form of the political disjunction between those who speak in the name of the 'we' and those who are spoken about. Republican justice is based on this disjunction.

This insight appears to me absolutely fundamental. Every act of foundation and every act of constitution conceal a moment of exclusionary violence which constitute, define, and exclude the other. In the case of the American Declaration of Independence, this moment of exclusion is visible most prominently in the erasure of the Black American slave population of the colonies and of native American Indians. They are included in the second 'we', in the we to whom the law of the land applies, but they have no voice in the articulation of the law of the land. The subsequent history of the United States of America has shown that this moment of exclusion, this moment of violence to otherness, has never been completely obliterated: the violence of the revolutionary beginning in condoning slavery returns with the Civil War, when the status of the 'other' beyond the 'we' splits the republican community of citizens around the abolition of slavery. For Native American Indians the republican 'we' is the voice of a strange, alien law that decimates their own communities, disregards their tribal practices, confiscates their lands, and ultimately subjugates and conquers them. The question – 'who is the we?' – is a fundamental political question; in the name of whom do you speak and for whom do you think you are entitled to speak? Since every act of identity entails difference and differentiation, we can concede that there may be no act of republican founding that does not carry its own violence and exclusion within.

Yet to leave matters here would be to tell less than half the story. For Derrida this 'sin' at the origin indicates an absolute black, an absence, at the center of republican, and perhaps all, politics.[25] For Lyotard this original sin is also the site of that moment of spontaneity and freedom when le differend can appear. This obsession with the origin, with the act of foundation, however, is also exceedingly formalistic. The use of formal terms of linguistic analysis such as the performative, the constative and the normative already indicates the problem. Nothing is said about the *content* of the acts of declaration and independence; it is as if the content of the American Declaration of Independence for Derrida and the content of the French Declaration of the 'Droits de l'Homme et du Citoyen' for Lyotard were fully irrelevant to the formal logic of the problem of authority and legitimacy. But they are not. In the first place, only within the confines of a secular and rationalistic natural law tradition can we understand that the equivocation between 'the laws of nature' and the 'self-evident moral truths' which the American Founding fathers write of is not simply a linguistic, categorical confusion, but expresses the beginnings of an intellectual process when modern conceptions of democratic legitimacy emancipate themselves from earlier theological and cosmological underpinnings in a philosophy of nature.[26] To reduce this complex problem of the emergence of democratic conceptions of legitimation out of the natural law tradition to a linguistic mistake is to reduce the flesh and blood of history to a series of cruel jokes. This method of analysis is not only formalistic, it is also sterile because it does not allow us to come to grips with political thought in its historical context.

Perhaps even more significant is a second problem. The content of the declarative, to use Lyotard's language, which obliges us to obey certain kinds of principles is by no means insignificant. For between the *formal structure* of the original act of identity constitution and exclusion, and the *normative content* of the declarative which obliges us to obey certain laws a contradiction exists. Although it is 'we', the white, propertied, Christian, North American male heads of household, who hold these truths to be self-evident, 'that all men are created equal', and 'endowed by the law of nature with the rights of life, liberty, and the pursuit of happiness', between our contingent historical identity which affirm these truths and the content of these truths a tension, a dialectic of momentous historical proportions unfolds.[27] The abolitionists asked, 'If all men are created equal, how come the black slaves who labor for you, whom you whip, who raise your children, whom you rape are not also human?' Subsequently the Suffragettes asked, 'If you could contemplate that your own black slaves were humans like you, how could you not contemplate the full citizenship of the women whom you pledge to honor, love, and cherish, who run your homes, bear you children and take care of your body?' To paraphrase George Orwell, the paradox of modern democratic politics is that 'all pigs are equal; but some are more equal than others.' It is the ethos of democratic politics that the privilege of being counted an equal is always contested and essentially contestable. The American and French Declarations of Independence for the first time introduce a logic of universalist legitimation into history, and this logic subverts the exclusions and identity reductions posited by the revolutionaries themselves. Potentially there is a tension between the revolutionary constitution of the 'we' at a certain point in time, subject to sociological and historical vagueries, and the moral and political content of the revolutionary declarations which transcend the historical specificity of these declarations themselves.

The constitution of collective identity is indeed the site of the appearance of the 'differend' in history.[28] But all great social movements of modernity, from anti-Slavery to the Suffragettes, to the socialist and the anti-imperialist movements have not only pleaded for the formal inclusion of previously excluded groups under the 'we'; they have also suggested other modes of being, thinking, acting, and doing which have clashed with the republican-democratic conception of the citizen as the warrior-hero or the *paterfamilias*.

If one recalls Derrida's early works about the 'dissemination' of meaning,[29] and the impossibility of ever fixing multivocity in language, then my point that a dialectic would exist between the historically given meaning horizon of a text like the American Constitution, for example, and its subsequent interpretations is perfectly compatible with his position. The difficulty, however, lies in Derrida's hyperbolic vacillations between an ethical hermeneutic of the law and politics, on the one hand, and a political decisionism which entails a form of legal positivism on the other. According to the first view, Derrida's position would be that the meaning of justice always transcends and must transcend insofar as it embodies an ethical imperative individual acts of legislation, judgments rendered, and codifications encountered in history. Furthermore, none of these acts of legislation, judgment and codification could once and for all 'fix' their meaning; the meaning and the justice that would ensue from them would have to reside in the ever new appropriation of these principles. Derrida writes

> This 'fresh judgment' can very well – must very well – conform to pre-existing law, but the reinstituting, reinventive and freely decisive interpretation, the responsible interpretation of the judge requires that his 'justice' not just consist in conformity, in the conservative and reproductive act of judgment. In short, for a decision to be just and responsible, it must, in its proper moment if there is one, be both regulated and without regulation: it must conserve the law and also destroy it or suspend it enough to have to reinvent it in each case . . .[30]

Compare now this passage with the following in which the slip into political decisionism and legal positivism becomes visible:

> A constative can be *juste* (right or correct), in the sense of *justesse*, never in the sense of justice. *But as a performative cannot be just, in the sense of justice* ['justice' as opposed to 'justesse' in French S. B.], *except by founding itself on conventions and so on other anterior performatives, buried or not, it always maintains within itself some irruptive violence, it no longer responds to the demands of theoretical rationality* [my emphasis S. B.]. Since every constative utterance itself relies, at least implicitly, on a performative structure . . . , the dimension of *justesse* or truth of the theoretico-constative utterance (in all domains, particularly in the domain of the theory of law) always thus presupposes the dimension of justice ['justice' in French S. B.] of the performative utterances, that is to say their essential precipitation, which never proceeds without certain dissymmetry and some quality of violence.[31]

Whereas in the first set of considerations Derrida is addressing the hermeneutic problem of how, in the absence of clearly articulable and codifiable rules, rule-governed activity can nonetheless result, in the second passage cited there is a transition to the view of the 'irruptive violence' of the performative. The 'creative hermeneutic' which all legal understanding and interpretation displays is sharply distinguished from the 'irruptive violence' which 'no longer responds to the demands for theoretical rationality' but to which all constatives ultimately lead. One has to ask: in what does this violence consist? In Derrida's prioritizing of the performative is there not a regression to a thinking of origins, to the thought that there is a 'first' convention which precedes all conventions and from which subsequent performatives derive their power? Isn't Derrida suggesting that behind the law stands a moment of decision, a moment of sheer power, a moment of violent positing which 'no longer responds to the demands of theoretical rationality'? What is it that we are asked to remember in recalling this moment of 'originary', 'foundational' violence? What is it about politics and the political that this reflection upon the possible 'irruptive violence' at the beginning is supposed to reveal?

To deny the presence of violence, conquest, defeat, brute power, and subjugation in political history would be more than naïve. So, Derrida's point cannot be that simple. Rather, his analysis of the ultimate, 'non-rational', conventionality of the performative on which every constative 'relies', is intended to reveal something about the 'metaphysical abyss', the 'metaphysical beginning', *das Ereignis*, in Heideggerian language, across which and over which the mantle of law, legality, legitimacy, and consensual political power is thrown. It is only when we focus on this limit case of revolutionary beginnings that we can confront the arbitrariness, the sheer 'willfulness' of all power, which 'no longer responds to the demands of theoretical rationality.'

It is in their methodological fixation upon the 'arbitrariness' at the beginning in republican politics, that Lyotard as well as Derrida ultimately reduce the historical and socio-cultural problems of revolutionary violence, modern constitutionalism and nation-building to a set of metaphysical puzzles. The issue is not the philosophical interpretation of the political per se, but rather those philosophical presuppositions themselves in the light of which politics is thought about. On the one hand, both share the premises of a legal positivism which is not even so much argued for; it is simply posited that the law, as a performative grammatical enunciation, must also bear the metaphysical fate of all performatives, that is, either of resting itself upon another performative, thus leading to an infinite regress, or of establishing the conditions of its own performativity through a sheer act of positing. In terms of legal theory this means that either the legitimacy of the law rests with the law itself alone or with a moment of 'revolutionary', and ultimately arbitrary positing to which the law refers back. This means that it is illicit to question the law in the name of a further normative instance, such as morality or even rationality, which lies beyond the law. *Auctoriat facit legem*; 'And Covenants, without the Sword, are but Words, and of no strength to secure a man at all' as Thomas Hobbes has told us.[32] But how convincing is this 'performative' philosophy of the law which recycles the old theses of legal positivism in the garb of Austinian language analysis?

More significantly, what really follows for our understanding of democratic politics from this meta-critique of revolutionary foundings? What have we gained through their perspective? I want to suggest that at a formal level of analysis there is no solution to the paradoxes of the constitution of revolutionary authority; yet there are both historical and institutional ways of thinking about these issues that may lead to a more fruitful and less aporetic path than those followed by Lyotard and Derrida. Arendt can be our guide here: for Arendt, as faulty as her comparative analysis of the French and the American Revolutions was, the crucial historical question remained: What allowed the stabilization of the Constitution to become the supreme law of the land in the case of the United States and why, in the case of the French Revolution, constitutionalism did not become a tradition but was displaced by revolutionary republicanism? Unlike Lyotard and Derrida, Arendt translates the puzzle of the search for 'absolutes' in politics into a historical question concerning constitutional traditions.[33]

Furthermore, even if the conceptual aporias of foundational authority may be formally insoluble, democracies have developed a series of institutional mechanisms for controlling and self-correcting the arbitrariness of original positings of authority. In a constitutional democracy, there is no final seat of sovereignty. If the land has adopted a constitution, a Basic Law, the will of the legislature is itself subject to interpretation and analysis in light of the constitution. The legislature may promulgate a law but the procedure of 'constitutional review' allows a further instance to judge the 'will of the people' in light of the principles of the constitution. This mechanism of interplay between the legislature and an independent judicial instance with respect to interpretations of the constitution may ultimately be the sole guarantee preventing the democratic 'we's' of many nations from reverting back to the originary violence which accompanied their birth as nations, thus excluding the 'other' from their polity.[34] Lyotard and Derrida disregard the institutional dynamics whereby constitutional traditions enable democracies to correct, to limit and to ameliorate moments of unbridled majority rule, exclusionary positings of identity, and the arbitrary formation of normatives.

What attracts Lyotard, Derrida and Carl Schmitt before them to revolutionary 'limit situations',[35] is the view that constitutional democratic politics is mere humbug, mere routine. But there is an aspect of rationality in the interlocking and self-correcting institutional cycle between legislatures and constitutional instances. Constitutional democratic politics means that no instance is supreme; although the people are nominally sovereign, even the will of the people must submit itself to, and accept to bind itself by, a set of rules which are constantly interpreted, reappropriated and contested.[36] This is the historical and institutional solution to Hegel's critique of the revolutionary will and to Abbé Sieyès's disjunction between the 'pouvoir constituant' and the 'pouvoir constitué'. If the Supreme Court is the 'constitution in session', then democratic politics is the process whereby the meaning, the scope, and the prerogative of the interpretations delivered in this session are constantly challenged.

Certainly the closed circuit of institutional democratic politics can stifle the differend, it can even make it disappear. Perhaps, though, there is a form of democratic politics which lets the differend appear and which does not oppress and stifle it. Must such politics be located at the origin, at the margins, at the limits and extremes of the process alone? Can we conceive in everyday politics a process of the transfiguration of the commonplace? Let me suggest a few candidates of such processes from recent memory: think of the peace movements which nearly a decade ago swept across the face of Europe and the United States and which expressed loudly and clearly that the use of nuclear weapons among nations was morally and politically abhorrent; think of the Argentine movements of the mothers, the 'Desapareceidos', who with their pots and pans and tenacity, courage and imagination kept alive the meaning of human rights under the dictatorship; think, of course, of Nelson Mandela and the recent historic vote in South Africa for an end to apartheid.

Yet there is an important objection to this list as well. Although South Africa is abolishing apartheid, all across Europe a new form of apartheid against political refugees, economic refugees and foreigners is emerging. Eastern Europe did not only produce Vaclav Havel and Solidarnōszc but also the civil war in Yugoslavia and the ethnic massacres in Armenia and Azerbaijan. What conceptual means do we have for sorting out different instances of 'le differend'?

In conclusion I want to summarize in the form of three epistemic-political theses the conceptual shift from republican foundationalism to a deliberative model of democracy which is needed in political theory such as to enable us to think through some of these issues.

V. From Republican Foundationalism to a Deliberative Model of Democracy

Identity vs. Sovereignty

I would like to call the perspective from which Lyotard and Derrida illuminate political phenomena in their recent writings that of 'republican foundationalism'. Methodologically they choose to focus on one aspect of modern politics more than any other, precisely because the act and the event of founding a body politics seems to them to highlight the paradoxes and aporias at the heart of *all* political life. The republican act of foundation is not considered the *exception*, rather it becomes the *norm* in the light of which to judge all political life. But this focus on the act of foundation is extremely distorting for it ignores the institutional and historical learning processes which 'really existing democracies' have gone through.

The first contrast which I would like to establish between the perspectives of republican foundationalism and that of a deliberative model of democracy is around the problem of sovereignty in the body politic. For the foundationalist republicans, beginning with Jean-Jacques Rousseau, the act of sovereignty signifies that moment through which the political identity of the community is formed and its highest seat of authority posited. The metaphors of the 'body politics' and of the 'body of the people' suggest here a conflation of two distinct processes: the constitution of the political community as a unit on the one hand and that of the form of authority according to which this political community will be governed on the other.

To distinguish between the formation of political identity and the constitutional cum institutional form of sovereign authority is essential for the following reasons: the identity of a body politic refers not only, and not primarily, to the political process through which it is governed but rather to other criteria such as the linguistic, ethnic, racial, and religious make-up of its people. The concept of the 'nation' and the phenomenon of 'nationalism' have allowed the silent and historically disastrous identification of these two processes with each other, since the nation is thought to be not only the self-identical and homogeneous body politic but also to be the source of all sovereign authority.[37]

By contrast, the deliberative democratic model distinguishes between the *ethnos* and the *demos*, between the ethnic, cultural, linguistic, and religious identity of a people, and the political constitution of the people as an organized, self-governing body. A demos can consist of more than one ethnos; the sovereign political community may encompass and usually does encompass more than one ethnic, religious, and linguistic community. What makes such an ethnically diverse body politic one is not some mystical act of sovereign will-formation, but the constitutional and institutional principles through which such a people enter into the world-historical arena and demand recognition from others. No nation is the seat of an ultimate, mystical sovereignty. Democracies are not formed through the mystical sovereignty of nations but through the constitutional principles which peoples adopt in order to govern themselves by and through the institutional arrangements which they set into motion. Perhaps the events of recent history in the heart of Europe, unfolding with the Civil War in Yugoslavia, will have taught us how disastrous it is to conflate the aspirations of different groups to cultural and ethnic self-expression with the demands of political sovereignty.

Sovereignty vs. Democratic Legitimation

How can this distinction between sovereignty and identity be maintained? Neither Lyotard's philosophy nor Derrida's method of deconstruction have the conceptual resources to allow us to set the terms of the problem correctly. If we view the American and French Declarations of Independence not merely as harboring the conflation of the performative with the constative and the normative, but also as ushering a new principle of political legitimation into history, then a first step will have been made in this direction. It is the hallmark of political modernity that the legitimation of laws no longer derives from a theologically or cosmologically grounded *Weltanschauung*. The modern natural right and natural law traditions are hybrid conceptual movements of thought which, through paradoxical appeals to the concept of nature, legitimize a secular and ultimately man-made form of political authority. The loss of absolute and fundamental points of recourse in the political and ethical sphere always calls forth the question of legitimation. Modernized, secular societies repeatedly pose the question of political legitimacy and attempt to answer it under conditions of a postmetaphysical universe.

The American and the French Revolutions, despite their different paths and fortunes, introduced into history the idea that the source of all legitimation is the will of the people, insofar as this people adopts a set of universal moral and legal precepts guaranteeing it a set of inalienable rights. But between the belief in the sovereignty of the nation and the belief that this nation is sovereign only insofar as it chooses to abide by certain principles, a clash, a tension exists, which unfolded in subsequent history.

The question which future history posed was: what is the legitimacy of the sovereignty of the nation? From within a secular political context the only answer to this question can be: it is the set of universalist moral and legal principles which constitute moral imperatives transcending specific political-constitutional acts that legitimize an act of popular sovereignty. This is what Kant named the idea of a 'republican constitution from a cosmopolitan point of view'.[38] For Lyotard and Derrida the metaphysical baggage of these appeals to humanity and morality appear all too indefensible.

In his reflections on today's Europe entitled 'The Other Heading', Derrida expresses concern about nationalism and the mystified claims to identity on which it rests. 'No cultural identity,' he writes, 'presents itself as the opaque body of an untranslatable idiom, but always, on the contrary, as the irreplaceable *inscription* of the universal in the singular, the *unique testimony* to the human essence and to what is proper to man.'[39] Derrida observes that all claims to cultural and national identity have a homogenizing logic, in that they level out differences, create imaginary and purified forms of identities, and eliminate the non-identical and the differend from their midst. But the 'inscription of the universal in the singular', which accompanied the various declarations of the rights of man during the time of the bourgeois revolutions, can mean two very different things: on the one hand, this can refer to the homogenizing logic of cultural identity mentioned above; on the other hand, it is also the paradox of modern revolutions that they take place in the name of another universal, that is, of humanity and human rights which in turn have a context-transcending power. Like Hannah Arendt, between the claims of nationalism and those of the universalistic declaration of human rights I see the tragic conflict between ethnos and demos.[40] By not distinguishing between national and cultural searches for purity in the name of a 'universal human essence' and the universalistic claims of bourgeois revolutions, as encoded in their human rights declarations, Derrida assimilates both to a single problem, namely 'the inscription of the universal in the singular'. This, in his view, is the illicit move toward essentialism which must be deconstructed. Yet the only institutional and conceptual way to criticize nationalism and claims of cultural purity is *in the name* of universalistic human rights. If there is another conceptual and institutional strategy, certainly neither Derrida (nor Lyotard) have so far told us what this could be. Derrida cannot have it both ways: on the one hand he criticizes and condemns nationalism, racism, xenophobia and anti-Semitism, and, on the other hand, he undermines the conceptual bases for holding on to those universalistic moral and political principles in the name of which alone such critique can be carried out. The famous 'double gesture' of deconstruction, which parasitically feeds upon what it deconstructs, faces us here as well.

By contrast, from the perspective of deliberative democratic politics the struggle becomes articulating the normative bases of cosmopolitan republicanism in an increasingly decentered, fragmented and anti-metaphysical universe. The increasing globalization of the world-economy, legal systems, cultures and communication networks are now creating a world-wide political public sphere, such that the cosmopolitical point of view has ceased to be an ideal of reason alone and has become, in however distorted a fashion, a politically actual possibility. We need a new *jus gentium* for a new world; for 'the common opinion of mankind', that fictional posit of eighteenth century political thought, is still the only instance which can transcend the self-centered narcissism of nations and force them into recognizing the rights of others like them.

Democratic Legitimacy and the Public Sphere

Modern collective political identities in a disenchanted universe are fragile achievements, constantly prone to crises. To maintain a democratic constitutional form of government in the face of the combined pressures of the capitalist market, new forms of social modernization, and the ever-growing fluidity of cultural traditions is an extremely difficult task. To even have a chance of succeeding at this task, it is essential that politics allow in their midst the formation of an independent public sphere in which questions of identity, legitimacy and sovereignty can be perpetually debated and discussed. Only through the continuous asking and answering of the relevant questions through publicly accessible channels can new identities come to the fore, delegitimization processes be aired and the meaning of sovereignty be re-established.

Of course, I do not mean here a free-for-all constitutional discussion and even convention. Participation in the public sphere has its own rules; even challenging these rules, which may be, and often are, exclusionary and distortive, requires first respecting them.[41] The democratic public sphere is like Otto Neurath's boat: you cannot throw all the planks into the water and hope to be able to stay afloat; at any one time, you can only throw some plans overboard and still continue to float. Likewise, you cannot participate in the democratic public sphere if you do not respect universal civil and political rights; as a participant, however, you can challenge the very meaning, scope and legitimacy of rights which have allowed the process to unroll.[42]

The ability of citizens of modern democratic politics to participate in such processes requires us to think of their linguistic and epistemic capacities in a fashion quite different than that proposed by Jean-François Lyotard.[43] Such participation in the democratic public sphere demands certain hermeneutic skills which can indeed yield 'lawfulness without law' ('Gesetzmäessigkeit ohne Gesetz'). Individuals must be able to move through various levels of communication with fluidity, they must be able to shift levels of discursive reflection, they must be able to challenge, to ironize, to play with, and to subvert established meanings and modes of speech. The differend in politics does not just happen; only playful, resourceful and creative selves, who can also challenge and argue for principles from a hypothetical moral point of view, can operate in the public sphere and utilize its capacities.

The democratic public sphere and processes of deliberation and contestation which occur therein are doubly contingent: on the one hand, it is a historically contingent process of development which allows the formation of such a sphere in some polities and not in others; secondly, it is also contingent whether individuals in a polity will have the cultural and moral resources to become full participants of a discursive or deliberative public sphere. No matter how counterfactual and contingent these processes may be, without the institutionalization of some form of free public sphere, successful democracies are inconceivable. For in a world without metaphysics, identity-formation, constitutional sovereignty and democratic legitimacy require processes and channels of deliberation, contestation, argument and subversion which only the interlocking net of many public spheres can allow.

I agree with Jacques Derrida and Jean-François Lyotard that the task of philosophical politics today is the conceptualization of new forms of association which will let the 'differend' appear in their midst. For reasons which I have outlined in this article I consider the deliberative democracy[44] approach to be more suited for this task than the double gesture which affirms and deconstructs 'republican foundationalism'.

AFTERWORD

I first laid eyes on Jacques Derrida around 1976, when, as a graduate student in Yale University's Philosophy Department, I found myself one day waiting in line for lunch at Naple's Pizza, behind Derrida and Paul de Man. I recall Derrida's stunning suit, made of a grey-purple velvet, and his shock of grey-silver hair. He seemed totally out of place in a fast-food place, known for its greasy calzones and pizza slices, which you might fear would stain that marvelous suit! Yet Derrida seemed quite at home, talking to graduate students hovering around the two masters.

Although studying and writing on German philosophy – Hegel in particular – I had decided to keep my distance from Derrida's courses at Yale. Partly the snobbery of us philosophers against literature students motivated this; Derrida was not a visiting professor in the philosophy department but in comparative literature. Partly it was my own sense of 'gravitas', of wanting to save the world through philosophy which made me think that somehow Derrida was frivolous, too much of an aesthete in his impeccable velour suit. What philosopher dressed that well?

But Derrida was not so easily to be dismissed. We would hear from our best undergraduate students at the time – among them Judith Butler – that his courses were spectacular and magnificent, that something new was afoot – a new teacher, a new method of reading.

Margins of Philosophy was the first text of his which I encountered.[45] I still recall my respect and awe in reading the often undisciplined, but brilliant, disquisitions on commodification, Aristotle and Marx. I remember the compelling attention to levels of signification – to the 'trace', which left its mark not only upon the numeral value of the coin and in whose name it was issued, but also upon the very material which embodied the coin – nickel, silver, gold. The circulation of the commodities, like the circulation of meaning in language, operated at multiple levels at once – symbolic, material, semiotic.

Then came the English translation of *Of Grammatology* by Gayatri Spivak.[46] Suddenly, Derrida's discourse about the sign, the signature, and the text had a political face, one that left us breathless. What had seemed to me at its best a version of the American pragmatist Charles Sanders Peirce's semiotics, all of a sudden appeared as a philosophical methodology – deconstruction or *Destruktion* – situated at the epochal challenge posed to reason and the Enlightenment by the non-Western, non-Eurocentric world, by the 'Other'. Deconstruction was not frivolous but deadly serious. Claude Levi-Strauss was not a neutral translator of the hidden structure of the language of kinship of the others but was himself implicated in the act of deception through which the natives were seduced into disclosing their proper names in exchange for worthless glass beads. Knowledge is extracted through power; knowledge is power.

In the essay with the equivocal title 'The Ends of Man', – end in the sense of goal, *Zweck*, telos and end, in the sense of *finis, Ende* – Derrida makes clearer this interconnection between the critique of western metaphysics and the political follies of Eurocentrism. Throughout western metaphysics, there is a premature foreclosure of the being of man, of the being of the one who asks the question of being. Here Derrida follows Heidegger. The ends of man are always defined anthropomorphically – man as the *bios politikos*; as the *zoon legein echein*; as immaterial substance; as noumenon. There is an attempt at closure, a cordon sanitaire, which western metaphysics draws around this concept and in doing so, excludes, excises, ejects the 'other' – the one who is not rational, who is not capable of rational self-mastery, of being the thinking substance alone. These others are not only women and children but also the non–Western others, who never seemed capable of the degree of the rational mastery of nature accomplished by western modernity. The essay ends with a haunting invocation of the encirclement of the city, of the center of western metaphysics by the 'periphery' – allusions to Rousseau's 'sauvage noble', together with a Maoist invocation of the country against the city... Deconstruction now seemed as an ideology-critique of 'phallologocentric' male western imperialism – and so indeed it was received in wide sections of American Academia. Foucault, Edward Said and Gayatri Spivak, all contributed to that profound anti-Eurocentric and anti-imperialist critique of the late-1970s and 80s. This was also the context in which Derrida's work flowed so easily into the feminist and anti-colonialist critique of western discourse, so prevalent in the American Academy.

I remained unconvinced: first I found the anti-Eurocentrism of this discourse politically naïve and dangerous; second it was still unclear to me whether there was something in Derrida's philosophy of language over and beyond the best insights of Charles Sanders Peirce and John Searle. I disliked the concept of the 'performative', because it seemed to make linguistic utterances almost magically responsible for their own communicative effects; the concept of the 'performative' was such an easy way of not answering the question, how in fact we could do things with words. What made a listener accept the illocutionary force of the utterances of the speaker? The indeterminacy of the concept of the performative made any critique of the validity conditions of the speech act irrelevant.

Paradoxical as this may seem, Derrida became really interesting and compelling for me just as many of his erstwhile admirers abandoned him after the scandal concerning Paul de Man's crypto-fascist past and Derrida's apologia for his friend. Increasingly confronted with the question of ethics *and* deconstruction, and the ethics *of* deconstruction, in the late nineteen-eighties Derrida wrote a number of brilliant texts – 'The Force of Law', a subtle reading in Montaigne and Walter Benjamin which permitted him to dwell on deconstruction and justice;[47] the book translated into English as *Politics of Friendship*, which finally addressed Carl Schmitt and the political implications of deconstruction;[48] lastly, a short but marvelous essay, 'The Declarations of Independence', which Derrida delivered upon the bicentennial of the American Revolution, and which engaged him with the legacy of American liberalism.[49] The very pluralisation in the title – 'Declarations' of Independence – heralded the strategy with which Derrida would approach this foundational text.

In this period, my understanding of Derrida changed: far from seeing him as a naïve Maoist who may have thought that Pol-Pot would redeem the Enlightenment, I now began to see him as an ultra-liberal, whose purpose was to disclose the fragility of those foundational distinctions upon which all liberalism rested – law and custom; right and justice; natural law and positive law; the performative and the constative. Derrida's 'deconstruction' of the sentence from the American Declaration of Independence, 'We hold these truths to be self-evident, that all men are created equal and endowed by their creator with the rights to life, liberty and the pursuit of happiness', still astonishes my students. Are these truths really 'self-evident'? What evidence do we have that all men are created equal, when so many facts seem to attest to the contrary? Or are these truths self-evident because we posit them, we declare them to be so? But then, men are not created equal, we must say with Hannah Arendt, they become equal because they create a political order in which they guarantee one another's equality through promises and covenants. But if the equality proclaimed by the Declaration of Independence is itself a human construction, then why appeal to God as guaranteeing this equality in virtue of being our 'creator'? Or, perish the thought, do we also create our own God through this Declaration?

Furthermore, who is the 'we' who holds these truths to be self-evident? Is it the signatories of the Declaration alone? The representative of the thirteen colonies? Or Thomas Jefferson? May be the Declaration does not 'declare' in the name of an already constituted people, but constitutes this very people in the very process of acting in its name? The 'floating signifier', that which can never be pinned down through the act of signification, now reveals its subversive force: in questioning the constitution of the we, we can also question the exclusions which this act of creation posits. Who belongs among the people and who does not? Were African-American slaves, who were accorded three-fifths personhood by the Constitution in the counting of states' populations to apportion congressional seats, among the addressees of the 'we'? What about women? And who were the property holders? And who were the 'foreigners' among the sovereign people?

It is the Derrida of these later years which I have most come to appreciate. I now see how deconstruction can be so close to an ethos of radical democracy. Even before Derrida turned to cosmopolitanism and the predicament of 'les sans-papiers' in Europe, pleading for the revival of the old Judeo-Christian tradition of 'cities of refuge', a text with the impossible title – *Monolingualism of the Other; Or The Prosthesis of Origin* – stunned me.[50] I still do not understand the Prostheses in this title, but the agony of not being able to reach the ear of the other, of the inability to communicate – this agony made me understand Derrida better. Certainly, not in any essentialist sense of seeing the 'true Derrida' revealed. Nonetheless, I do believe that this autobiographical text throws light on that preoccupation with the treachery as well as the beauty of language which haunts Derrida. Here he recounts how, growing up as a middle-class Algerian Jew, he was equally 'tongueless' with respect to the two most important existential languages for him: he did not know Hebrew, beyond liturgical generalities; and he did not know Arabic – the language of the country in which he grew up. Equally removed from both, as an Algerian-Jew, he became one of the masters of the French language, that language which he loved so much as to become a world-wide philosopher through it. Yet at the same time, the sense of the fragility, equivocation, multivocity, and indeterminacy of language never left him. Like Albert Camus, another Algerian-born French intellectual, Jacques Derrida, was a stranger in his own land. He translated that sense of estrangement into the seminal discovery of the instability, indeterminacy and creative playfulness of all language. We understand one another may be because so often we fail to do so.

At a moment in world history, where intolerance toward as well as violent confrontation with 'otherness', ranges rampant, Derrida's work reminds of the indeterminacy, multivocity, and fragmentation at the heart of all claims to identity. The interior is what it is in virtue of excluding from itself the constitutive exterior. Being is always and fundamentally broken from within. This is not just an epistemological or metaphysical proposition, but also an ethico-political one to embrace heterogeneity and plurality through acts of playful, ironic, and at times frustratingly ambiguous acts of deconstruction.

December 2004

NOTES

1. A Note to the Reader. The following article originally appeared in *The Journal of Political Philosophy* as 'Democracy and Difference. Reflections on Rationality, Democracy and Postmodernism' (*Journal of Political Philosophy*, vol. 2, no. 1, March 1994, pp. 1–23). The invitation to include it in the present volume was a pleasant surprise, but one which I welcomed after the intellectual and spiritual loss that I, like many others, experienced in view of Jacques Derrida's untimely death.

   As I explain in the Afterword, Derrida's voice was present to me since the very beginnings of my philosophical career. More often than not, I engaged with this voice at certain crucial junctures in my own theoretical evolution. My article 'Feminism and the Question of Postmodernism' (first published in 1991 and reprinted in Benhabib, *Situating the Self. Gender, Community and Postmodernism in Contemporary Ethics* [New York and London: Routledge, 1992]) initiated a contentious dialogue with feminist theorists who had been influenced by Michel Foucault, Jacques Derrida and Jean-François Lyotard, perhaps rhetorically bringing them together under the contentious title of 'postmodernism'.

The present article belongs to the same period of the mid-1990s, when the paradigm struggle between French and German modes of theorizing, critical theory and postmodernisms of various sorts, appeared most intense. Rereading and revising this essay after many years, I am surprised by the extent to which certain themes announce themselves in it which proved decisive not only for the evolution of my own work but for the eventual redrawing of the theoretical and political lines between critical theory and Derrida's work as well. I have in mind the themes of the new post-1989 Europe; the tragedy of the civil war in the once unified Yugoslavia; the problem of refugees and asylum seekers; and, most importantly, the significance of democratic exclusions through acts of republican founding. It was truly surprising to find in this essay *in nuce* the problems which were to preoccupy me in the decade after the mid-1990s, such as European unification and citizenship; the rights of others – aliens, refugees and citizens –; and cosmopolitanism. It is around these issues as well that the eventual rapprochement between Habermas and Derrida, as documented in this volume, took place.

Thus it seemed appropriate even at this late date to offer this essay as a token of critical appreciation to an honorable and brilliant interlocutor without whose voice undoubtedly one's own is impoverished as well. The article has been revised and stylistically modified for this present publication.

2. Alexis de Tocqueville, *Democracy in America*, trans. George Lawrence and ed. J. P. Mayer (New York: Doubleday and Co., 1969), p. xiii.
3. Ibid., p. xiv.
4. The only research paradigm which was attuned to transformations taking place in these societies throughout the 1970s and the 80s was that of 'civil society'. Here too it is possible to distinguish between Alain Touraine's work on the 'self-organization of society', and a second civil society paradigm, inspired by East European dissidents, but developed within a framework indebted to the social theory of Jürgen Habermas. For the first see Alain Touraine et al., *Solidarity. Poland 1980–1981* (Cambridge, England: Cambridge University Press, 1983); for the second, Jean Cohen and Andrew Arato, *Civil Society and Political Theory* (Cambridge, Massachusetts: MIT Press, 1992). Andrew Arato gives a helpful and comprehensive overview of the general literature in 'Interpreting 1989' (unpublished ms., New York, 1991).
5. Ernst Bloch, *Erbschaft dieser Zeit* (Frankfurt: Suhrkamp, 1973; first published 1935), pp. 110ff.
6. See J. Habermas, 'Die nachholende Revolution,' *Die Nachholende Revolution* (Frankfurt/Main: Suhrkamp Verlag, 1990); an English version has appeared as 'The Rectifying Revolution,' *New Left Review*, no. 183 (September–October 1990).
7. Jacques Derrida, 'The Other Heading: Memories, Responses, and Responsibilities,' *The Other Heading: Reflections on Today's Europe*, trans. Pascale-Anne Brault and Michael B. Naas (Bloomington: Indiana University Press, 1992), p. 6.
8. In his thoughtful book, *Political Theory and Postmodernism* (Cambridge: Cambridge University Press, 1991), p. 133, Stephen K. White writes: 'No postmodern thinkers I know of would give blanket endorsement to the explosions of violence associated with, say, the resurgence of ethnic group nationalism in the Soviet Union or with the growth of street gangs in Los Angeles. And yet it is not at all clear that they have a normative discourse available to condemn such violence.' I think this statement expresses very well the sense of misgiving which some of us share about the 'meta-politics' of postmodernism, as distinguished from the personal political positions of the thinkers involved. On the whole, I think that White's

sensitive and subtle analysis also underplays the 'decisionistic' streak in postmodern political thought which I discuss below.

9. Thomas McCarthy explores some of the deeper conceptual reasons why Derrida's philosophy in particular does not permit a historically differentiated social theory of institutions in: 'The Politics of the Ineffable: Derrida's Deconstructionism,' *Ideals and Illusions: On Reconstruction and Deconstruction in Contemporary Critical Theory* (Cambridge, Mass.: MIT Press, 1991), pp. 97–120.
10. Of course, in the current climate of continuing and at times bitter debate about Martin Heidegger's involvement with National Socialism, the place of Heidegger's philosophy for contemporary French thought in general is being questioned, re-examined and re-analyzed. Jean-François Lyotard, *Heidegger and the 'Jews'*, trans. by Andreas Michel and Mark Roberts (Minneapolis: University of Minnesota Press, 1990) and Jacques Derrida, *Of Spirit: Heidegger and the Question* (Chicago: University of Chicago Press, 1989) have each addressed these issues. I address the relation of politics and philosophy in Martin Heidegger's work in a different context in *The Reluctant Modernism of Hannah Arendt* (Berkeley, Calif.: Sage, 1994; second edition with a new Preface by Lanham, MD: Rowman and Littlefield, 2003). My suggestion in section 4 that certain formulations of Derrida and Lyotard bring them into the company of 'decisionist' political theory does not mean that the political consequences of their philosophy would support reactionary, conservative thought. 'Decisionism', of which I see Carl Schmitt's political philosophy as the prime example, is not National Socialism; it is a political philosophy which says that true political sovereignty is only revealed in the moment of the 'emergency' (Ausnahmezustand), and that it is neither reason nor morality but the capacity of the sovereign to set itself through via its power that legitimizes all law and politics. See Schmitt, *Political Theology* and *The Concept of the Political.*

    There can be 'left' as well as 'right' wing variants of political decisionism. Walter Benjamin and Otto Kirchheimer, members of the Frankfurt School, were very influenced by Carl Schmitt's political philosophy in their critique of the Weimar Republic. Kirchheimer eventually developed a penetrating critique of Carl Schmitt himself; Walter Benjamin's life came to a sudden and tragic end before the entire political mischief which Carl Schmitt got involved in with the Third Reich could lie before his eyes. An excellent treatment of the influence of Carl Schmitt on early members of the Frankfurt School, and in particular on Otto Kirchheimer and Franz Neumann, is given by William E. Scheuerman, *Between the Norm and the Exception: The Frankfurt School and the Rule of Law* (Cambridge, Mass.: MIT Press, 1997). Cf. also, Ellen Kennedy, 'Carl Schmitt and the Frankfurt School: A Rejoinder,' *Telos*, 73 (Fall 1987), and the articles by Martin Jay, Ulrich Preuss and Alfons Soellner in 'Special Section on Carl Schmitt and the Frankfurt School,' *Telos*, 71 (Spring 1987).
11. See Richard Wolin, *The Politics of Being: The Political Thought of Martin Heidegger* (New York: Columbia University Press, 1990), p. 30. Richard Wolin is referring to the influence of Carl Schmitt and Ernst Jünger upon the political thought of Martin Heidegger. Just as there is a conservative, right wing variant of politics of the limit, there is a left-romantic, radical, variant of it as well. Thinkers like Walter Benjamin, Otto Kirchheimer, and Franz Neumann were all at some point in their lives very influenced by the meta-politics of the limit. Is it 'par hazard' then that the legal and political philosophy of Walter Benjamin occupies such a prominent place in Jacques Derrida's recent writings on the law as well?
12. Jean-François Lyotard, *The Differend: Phrases in Dispute*, trans. Georges Van Den Abbeele (University of Minnesota Press: Minneapolis, 1988). The French edition, *Le Differend*, appeared in 1983. All page numbers in parentheses in my text refer to this English edition.

13. Jacques Derrida, 'Declarations of Independence,' *New Political Science*, 15 (1986), pp. 7–15.
14. See Lyotard, *The Differend*, pp. 118ff., 145ff. See Jacques Derrida, 'Force of Law: The "Mystical Foundation of Authority",' *Cardozo Law Review* (Special Issue on 'Deconstruction and the Possibility of Justice'), 11 (July–August 1990), pp. 919–1047.
15. Lyotard, *The Differend*, p. 98.
16. In the Preface to *Le Differend* Lyotard states precisely the connection he is establishing between a certain view of language and a certain politics. 'By showing that the linking of one phrase onto another is problematic and that this problem is the problem of politics, to set up a philosophical politics apart from the politics of "intellectuals" and of politicians. To bear witness to the differend' (p. xiii). This puzzling claim tying together the status of linguistic phrases with politics is repeated even more forcefully in the following passage: 'Were politics a genre and were that genre to pretend to that supreme status, its vanity would be quickly revealed. Politics, however, is the threat of the differend. It is not a genre, it is the multiplicity of genres, the diversity of ends, and par excellence the question of linkage' (p.138).
17. Ibid., p. 138.
18. Yet there is something remarkably brief, impatient, almost staccato in these formulations. The premise of the absolute heterogeneity and incommensurability of regimens and discourses is never argued for; it is simply posited. It corresponds to what Richard Bernstein has called a 'pervasive amorphous mood'. 'It is a mood of deconstruction, destabilization, rupture and fracture – of resistance to all forms of *abstract* totality, universalism and rationalism.' See R. J. Bernstein, 'Incommensurability and Otherness Revisited,' *The New Constellation* (London: Polity Press, 1991), p. 57 (emphasis in original). Moods cannot replace arguments. Lyotard nowhere distinguishes between incommensurability, heterogeneity, incompatibility and untranslatability. Cf. the following remark: 'Incommensurability, in the sense of the heterogeneity of phrase regimens and the impossibility of subjecting them to a single law (except by neutralizing them), also marks the relation between either cognitives or prescriptives and interrogatives, performatives, exhaustives... For each of these regimens there corresponds a mode of presenting a universe, and one mode is not translateable into another' (p. 128). Incommensurability is the central epistemic premise of Lyotard's philosophy of language as well as politics, and also its weakest. Lyotard here assembles under one heading a range of meanings extending from radical untranslatability in language to the sense of unfairness or injustice experienced when the language of the victor is imposed to describe the wounds of the vanquished. The thesis of radical untranslatability of genres of discourse and phrase regimens is no more meaningful than the thesis of the radical incommensurability of conceptual frameworks. For, if frameworks, linguistic, conceptual or otherwise are so radically incommensurable with each other, then we would not be able to know this; for our ability to describe a framework as a framework in the first place rests upon the possibility of being able to identify, select and specify certain features of these conceptual networks as being sufficiently like ours such that they can be characterized as conceptual activities in the first place. This argument, which is usually deployed in the context of epistemic and cultural-relativism debates, is no less applicable in this case. See Donald Davidson, 'On the Very Idea of a Conceptual Scheme,' *Inquiries into Truth and Interpretation* (Oxford: Clarendon Press, 1985), pp. 183–99; W. V. Quine, 'Ontological Relativity' and 'Speaking of Objects,' *Ontological Relativity and Other Essays* (New York: Columbia University Press, 1966). Also, Hilary Putnam, 'Two Conceptions of Rationality,' *Reason, Truth and History* (Cambridge: Cambridge University Press, 1981), pp. 103–27. If phrase regimens and genres of discourse were so radically heterogeneous, disparate, untranslatable,

then indeed it would be impossible to account for one of the most usual competencies of language users: namely that in the course of the same conversation, we can move from teaching to advertising, from informing to seducing, from judging to ironizing. As competent users of a language we can negotiate these nuances of meaning, shifts of style, suggestions of innuendo, playfulness, and irony. But if ordinary language use and performance suggest that phrase regimens and genres of discourse are not insular and unbridgeable units, what becomes of the thesis of their absolute heterogeneity?

19. Jacques Derrida, 'Declarations of Independence,' p. 11.
20. See G. W. F. Hgel, *Phaenomenologie des Geistes*, Philosophische Bibliothek, Bd. 114, ed. J. Hoffmeister (Hamburg: Felix Meiner, 1952), 6th edition, pp. 413ff.; this appears in English as *Hegel's Phenomenology of Spirit*, trans. A. V. Miller (Oxford: Clarendon Press, 1977), pp. 355ff.
21. Hannah Arendt, *On Revolution* (New York: The Viking Press, 1969), 7th printing, pp. 153ff.
22. Ibid., p. 160.
23. Ibid., p. 162.
24. Ibid., pp. 165ff.
25. In her provocative piece, 'Declarations of Independence: Arendt and Derrida On the Problem of Founding a Republic,' *American Political Science Review*, 85 (1991), pp. 97–113, Bonnie Honig uses the distinction between 'constative' and 'performative' utterances to criticize Hannah Arendt and to defend Derrida's thesis of the ultimate arbitrariness of all power. She writes: 'Derrida's point, like Nietzsche's, is that in every system (every practice), whether linguistic, cultural, or political, there is a moment or place that the system cannot account for' (p. 106). Arendt is taken to task for not seeing that for the revolutionaries every performative was also a constative. Despite Honig's provocative reading, I feel that a linguistic distinction that originates in the context of ordinary language philosophy in J. L. Austin's thought is being used here to carry and enormous systematic burden, ultimately obfuscating questions of normative validity and justification. If problems of political legitimation, legal validity, the moral foundations of the law, and the justification of moral and social norms could be solved by declaring them to be simply performatives which we mistakenly think to be in need of validation by constatives and other normatives, then indeed much of moral and political theory would rest on a category mistake. Declarations of category mistakes, however, are always deceptive in their simplicity. Just as Prichard's article 'Does Moral Philosophy Rest on a Mistake?' did not prevent the flourishing and development of moral theory and normative thinking in the forty odd years after which it was published, I doubt that the Austinian distinction between 'constatives' and 'performatives' will help us solve problems of political legitimacy and questions concerning the moral foundations of the law.
26. Would Lyotard's and Derrida's critique be obviated and lose their object if they were to focus on the Constitution of the United States in place of the Declaration of Independence? Since the Constitution is remarkably silent on the seat of ultimate authority, would this be proof of its performativity? I think one has to see how anachronistic this mode of questioning is, distinguishing as it does sharply between constatives and performatives, for the Age of the Enlightenment. For Jefferson there was no contradiction between the formulation, 'We hold these truths to be self-evident,' and that it was 'the Laws of Nature' and 'Nature's God' that prescribed the inalienable rights of all men. One held these truths to be self-evident, because 'the opinions and beliefs of men [which] depend not on their own will, but follow involuntarily the evidence proposed to their minds' (Thomas Jefferson, Draft Preamble to the Virginia Bill for Establishing Religious Freedom as cited by Hannah Arendt, *On Revolution*, pp. 193, 314). Furthermore, in the case of the Constitution, the 'Union of the People of the United States' was presupposed as a

political and historical fact; it is in the name of this authority that the representatives act. By September 17 1787, when the Constitution was declared, the Union was not merely a 'fact to create', so to speak, but had historical reality, although it was an 'imperfect union'. For the text of the Declaration of Independence and the Constitution of the United States, I have consulted the editions contained in Edmund S. Morgan, *The Birth of the Republic 1763–89* (Chicago: University of Chicago Press, 1977), revised edition. I thank Alan Wolfe for bringing the problem of the disparity between the Declaration and the Constitution to my attention.

27. See Joan B. Landes, *Women and the Public Sphere in the Age of the French Revolution* (Ithaca, NY: Cornell University Press, 1988) and Linda Kerber, *Women of the Republic: Intellect and Ideology in Revolutionary America* (New York: Norton, 1986) for works dealing with the dialectic of revolutionary inclusion and exclusion in the case of women.
28. Contemporary theorists of democracy have been paying increasing attention to this issue, see Iris Marion Young, *Justice and the Politics of Difference* (Princeton, NJ: Princeton University Press, 1990).
29. See Jacques Derrida, 'White Mythologies,' *Margins of Philosophy*, trans. A. Bass (Chicago: University of Chicago Press, 1982) and Jacques Derrida, *Writing and Difference*, trans. and intro. by Alan Bass (Chicago: University of Chicago Press, 1978).
30. Jacques Derrida, 'Force of Law. The Mystical Foundation of Authority,' *Cardozo Law Review*, special issue on Deconstruction and the Possibility of Justice, 11 (July–August 1990), p. 961.
31. Ibid., p. 969.
32. Thomas Hobbes, *Leviathan*, ed. C. B. Macpherson (London: Penguin Books, 1980; originally published 1651), p. 223.
33. See H. Arendt, *On Revolution*, pp. 167ff. Richard Bernstein has pointed out to me in conversation that there may be more affinity between Lyotard and Derrida one the one hand and Hannah Arendt on the other, insofar as Arendt as well focuses on the 'new' and the 'unprecedented' as the hallmark of authentic political action. Of course it is possible to read Lyotard's concept of 'le differend' and Derrida's concept of 'irruptive violence' as kindred concepts to Arendt's emphasis upon natality in action. I think that an adequate discussion of this issue would involve a thorough analysis of the various concepts of action and interpretation in the work of these thinkers; however, on a more basic level, we should note that for Arendt the experience of the 'new' in politics is confined to action *within the city, once its walls have been established*. Acts of constitution-giving for her are more like acts of art, and thus fall under the concept of 'work', rather than of action. Law-giving is an art; Arendt often cites the Greek and Roman perspective of the legislator as a 'divine presence'. This sharp distinction between 'constitution-making' and political action in Arendt's work is to be understood in the light of her own profound sense of the potential arbitrariness and danger lurking in every beginning. Rather than revel in this 'danger', Arendt, like most political theorists of the tradition (Jean-Jacques Rousseau in particular comes to mind here with his call for a 'divine law-giver'), seeks to contain it by 'housing' it in the city. For the distinction between political action and constitution-making or law-giving, see Hannah Arendt, *On Revolution*, pp. 189ff. and *The Human Condition*, pp. 194ff., where she both explicates the distinction and criticizes the Greeks for trying to make all political action like law-giving, a craft.
34. The world-wide phenomena of emigrations and immigrations, ranging from economic and political migrations to the plight of refugees of civil wars and religious and ethnic persecution, is a pertinent example here. In many European countries, immigration and citizenship laws have become a battleground between the political will of the legislatures and democratic majorities on the one hand, and

Constitutional instances, such as the 'Bundesverfassungsgericht' and The European Court of Human Rights on the other. For further discussion, cf. Seyla Benhabib, *The Rights of Others. Aliens, Resident and Citizens. The John Seeley Memorial Lectures* (Cambridge: Cambridge University Press, 2004), ch. 5 on 'Democratic Iterations: the local, the national and the global,' for a redeployment of Derridean categories via the concept of democratic iterations.

35. See Carl Schmitt, *The Crisis of Parliamentary Democracy*, trans. Ellen Kennedy (Cambridge, Mass.: MIT Press, 1985; originally published 1923) and C. Schmitt, *Political Theology: Four Chapters on the Concept of Sovereignty*, trans. George Schwab (Cambridge, Mass.: MIT Press, 1988).
36. For an excellent and creative analysis of foundational politics and constitutional interpretation and the concept of 'jurisgenerative politics', see Frank Michelman, 'Law's Republic,' *Yale Law Journal*.
37. See Stanley Hoffman's thoughtful analysis which untangles some of the complex issues involved in quests for national self-determination and sovereignty. Stanley Hoffman, 'The Delusion of World Order,' *The New York Review of Books*, 39, no. 7 (April 4, 1992), pp. 37ff.
38. Kant, 'Idea for a Universal History From a Cosmopolitan Point of View' [1784] in *On History*, ed. Lewis White Beck (New York: The Bobbs-Merrill Company, 1963), pp. 11–27.
39. Jacques Derrida, 'The Other Heading,' p. 73.
40. I have explored this tension in subsequent writings. See Seyla Benhabib 'Kantian Questions, Arendtian Answers: Statelessness, Cosmopolitanism, and the Right to Have Rights,' in *Pragmatism, Critique, Judgment: Essays for Richard J. Bernstein*, ed. Seyla Benhabib and Nancy Fraser (Cambridge, Mass.: MIT Press, 2004), pp. 171–96; and Benhabib, *The Rights of Others*, ch. 2.
41. See Kenneth Baynes's cogent analysis of some of the problems of circularity and conversational constraints, *The Normative Grounds of Social Criticism: Kant, Rawls and Habermas* (New York: SUNY Press, 1992), pp. 167ff., and 'The Liberal/Communitarian Controversy and Communicative Ethics,' *Philosophy and Social Criticism*, 14 (1988), pp. 293–313.
42. See Claude Lefort, *Democracy and Political Theory*, trans. David Macey (Minneapolis: University of Minnesota Press, 1988), pp. 9ff.
43. In an illuminating analysis, Wolfgang Welsch has dealt in depth with Lyotard's philosophy of language and has named it Lyotard's 'Sprachobjektivismus' ('linguistic objectivism'), see W. Welsch, *Unsere postmoderne Moderne* (Weinheim: Acta Humaniora, 1988), pp. 250ff. This is the view that the linkage of phrases in language just happens; that genres of discourse occur; they fill the void. The source of multiplicity, plurality, the play of meaning in language are not language users – they are part of an anthropomorphic illusion. All this takes place beyond the exercise of spontaneity and phronesis by individual actors. The following passage from *The Differend* is remarkable in this respect: 'Our "intentions" are tensions (to link in a certain way) exerted by genres upon the addressors and addressees of phrases, upon their referents, and upon their sense . . . There is no reason to call these tensions intentions or wills, except for the vanity of ascribing to our account what is due to occurrence (das Ereignis) and to the differend it arouses between ways of linking unto it' (p. 136).

    It is hard to make sense of this self-effacing objectivism that attributes all creativity in language to a quasi-metaphysical category of happening (das Ereignis) while robbing language-in-use of that dimension of play, meaning creation, experimentation and cross-contextual signification. We may not want to reduce all that 'happens' in language to the intentions of the speakers; undoubtedly in language intentions are rediscovered, recovered and constituted. The intentional act of a rational agent does not stand behind every language act; for that speech act may be the very process through which the language user discovers, uncovers, recovers her intentionality in the first place. The dichotomy with which Lyotard confronts us is wrong: either the 'subjectless' Ereignis of language or the Cartesian myth of a perfectly self-transparent subject. But precisely if we want to account for those phenomena in language which Lyotard also focuses upon – the new creation of meaning; the forcing open of established idioms; the articulation of new modes of saying and doing things with words – we must move to a different view of subjectivity and of the subject and language user. Wolfgang Welsch puts this very well: 'Lyotard's linguistic objectivism and his anti-anthropological position ... prove to be untenable, as soon as we consider not static but dynamic phenomena, as soon as we try to decide not among available claims but we try to build new linguistic forms. Such phenomena are not to be grasped on the basis of any kind of objectivism. What we need here is a theory in which humans are not viewed merely as carrying out already assigned positions in a game; what we need is a theory that views humans as inventors of new games (which does not mean: as creators ex nihilo)' (W. Welsch, *Unsere postmoderne Moderne*, p. 251). Between Lyotard's metaphysics of power and his late Heideggerian objectivism an irresolvable conflict exists: either the thesis of the absolute heterogeneity of language games or the thesis of the absolute irrelevance of anthropocentrism to account for language must be sacrificed. If Lyotard wants so much as to retain the plurality, multiplicity and diversity of phrase regimens and genres of discourse, he will have to attribute to language users more spontaneity, imagination, and the creative exercise of judgment than he is wont to do; if he retains his thesis of 'Sprachobjektivismus' then he will have to give up the multiplicity, plurality, and irreducibility of language games which he also wants to hold onto.

44. I have pursued aspects of the deliberative democracy model in 'Deliberative Rationality and Models of Democratic Legitimacy,' in *Constellations*, vol. 1, no. 1, April 1994, pp. 25–53.
45. J. Derrida, *Margins of Philosophy*, trans. A. Bass (New York: Harvester Wheatsheaf, 1982).
46. J. Derrida, *Of Grammatology*, trans. G. C. Spivak, Corrected Version (Baltimore: Johns Hopkins University Press, 1997).
47. Derrida, 'The Force of Law'.
48. J. Derrida, *Politics of Friendship*, trans. G. Collins (London: Verso, 1997).
49. Derrida, 'Declarations of Independence'.
50. J. Derrida, *Monolingualism of the Other; Or The Prosthesis of Origin*, trans. P. Mensah (Stanford: Stanford University Press, 1998).

PART III
IDENTITY/DIFFERENCE: RIGHTS, TOLERANCE AND POLITICAL SPACE

INTRODUCTION

This Part includes chapters on Derrida's and Habermas's respective writings on contemporary issues such as identity politics and multiculturalism, constitutional rights, and tolerance. Like the issues covered in Part IV, these are issues central to Derrida and Habermas's later work.

Both Derrida and Habermas are concerned with multiculturalism and pluralism, even if they have different approaches to it. Broadly speaking, Habermas seeks to include difference through a distinction between the plurality of ethical conceptions of the good life and political integration at the level of a common political culture and political institutions, which are neutral vis-à-vis ethical conceptions of the good (see also Chapter 7). Habermas is often accused by deconstructionists and others of imposing a rationalistic model of subjectivity upon all constituencies thereby excluding those that are deemed irrational and stifling democracy. Derrida, on the other hand, is often accused of simply celebrating difference and particularism with no criteria for distinguishing legitimate from illegitimate differences (for instance, democratic from anti-democratic constituencies).

Constitutionalism and rights have been the focus of much of Habermas's work since the late 1980s. He has put forward the argument that if conceived as co-original, constitutionalism and democracy can be reconciled and mutually support one another. Derrida has not dealt with this explicitly, but in Chapters 9 and 10 and inspired by Derrida, Bonnie Honig and Lasse Thomassen argue that there are both political and conceptual problems with Habermas's co-originality thesis.

In light of multiculturalism and pluralism, tolerance is increasingly important, and both Derrida and Habermas have addressed it, albeit from different perspectives as reflected in Chapters 11 and 12. Whereas Habermas seeks to rationally reconstruct the normative content of tolerance, Derrida argues that it contains inherent and irresolvable aporias.

Finally, in Chapter 13, Martin Morris tries to take the best from Habermas and Derrida. While Habermas provides us with an account of the public sphere, Derrida points to the inherent contingent nature of identities and political spaces.

Further Reading

Matuštík (1995; 1998) discusses the relative merits of Habermas and Derrida in relation to multiculturalism. He argues for a combination for Habermas's procedural egalitarianism and Derrida's critique of stable and closed identities. On Derrida's and Habermas's responses to diversity, see also Shabani 2003.

For Habermas on constitutional democracy, see Habermas, 1996b, 1998b, 2001b, and 2003. While Derrida has not written explicitly about constitutional democracy, the argument informing Honig's and Thomassen's criticisms of Habermas can be found in Derrida 1986, see also Honig 1993.

For Habermas on tolerance, see 2004b, and his comments in Borradori 2003, pp. 40–2. For Derrida on tolerance and hospitality, see Derrida 2000, 2001b and his comments in Borradori 2003, pp. 124–30.

9

Bonnie Honig

DEAD RIGHTS, LIVE FUTURES: ON HABERMAS'S ATTEMPT TO RECONCILE CONSTITUTIONALISM AND DEMOCRACY[1]

Working within the general trajectory of Hannah Arendt and Jacques Derrida, Bonnie Honig responds to Habermas's thesis about the co-originality of constitutionalism and democracy, individual rights and popular sovereignty.

Habermas's argument is that in a deliberative democracy, constitutionalism and democracy are co-original. They mutually imply one another since both arise from – that is, originate in – the citizens' free and equal opinion and will formation. Hence, when democracy is conceived in deliberative terms, the citizens exercise popular sovereignty (democracy) under conditions that secure everyone's individual autonomy (constitutionalism). Democracy is mediated by constitutionalism, thereby securing individual autonomy against, for instance, majority rule. Likewise, the addressees of the laws, including the constitution, are simultaneously the authors of the laws, because constitutionalism is mediated by democracy and thereby not imposed on the citizens in a paternalistic fashion. This is an example of Habermas's method of rational reconstruction: he asks what are the conditions for the legitimate exercise of popular sovereignty (the answer being its mediation by constitutionalism), and what are the conditions for legitimate constitutional rules (the answer being their mediation by democracy).

Honig gives an account of Habermas's argument and finds that he gets the balance between constitutionalism and democracy wrong. She argues that he places too much emphasis on constitutionalism and too little on democracy, thereby stifling constitutional democracy.

The tense relationship between constitutionalism and democracy is built into the very heart of liberal democracies, which take as their ground and goal both the rule of law and the rule of the people. For centuries, democratic and liberal theorists as well as actual founders have argued about what should be the proper terms of cohabitation for the courts and the people. The stakes are high: whichever premise carries the day, champions of its alternative may lose confidence in the regime's legitimacy. This is not to suggest that such loss of confidence is, per se, a bad thing. A popular loss of confidence in a regime's legitimacy may be warranted and it may be a first necessary step toward a reinvigorated and democratized politics.

Given his longstanding preoccupation with the problem of democratic legitimation, it is unsurprising that Jürgen Habermas should seek to rescue law and democracy from their supposedly permanent tension (which is how liberals and republicans see it or set it up, on his account).[2] In an effort to end the longstanding quarrel about how to 'rank the two principles, human rights [law] and popular sovereignty [democracy]', Habermas develops his 'co-originality thesis', which puts the two principles into a harmonious, non – zero sum relation and unifies them into a single 'normative justification of constitutional democracy'.[3]

Co-originality means that from the perspective of the social contract, neither set of rights depends for its justification on the other or 'sets limits on the other' because private and public rights are created simultaneously.[4] But co-originality also means that law and democracy have an internal relation. Just as autonomy is not mere freedom, so popular sovereignty is not mere majoritarianism. It matters whether our willing, as individuals or as a people, meets the internal disciplining or enabling (but not constraining) requirements of the categorical imperative or the rule of law.[5] It also matters that we will. At his best, Habermas insists that if liberal democracy stands for anything, it stands for the notion that users and addressees of law should also be its authors.[6] And conversely, law's authors should also be its users and addressees.[7]

But as it turns out, the analogy of political autonomy with moral autonomy is incomplete or misleading on at least two counts: first, treating the rule of law as a categorical imperative leaves untouched the named issue of democracy versus constitutionalism.[8] Constitutions are not as abstract as the principle of the rule of law. They specify particular rights, procedures, and values as the rules of a regime's particular democratic game. These vary widely, and different procedures have significant impacts on substantive outcomes. Thus, democracies often revisit constitutive rules to consider alternatives such as proportional representation, term limits, and campaign

Bonnie Honig, 'Dead Rights, Live Futures: A Reply to Habermas's "Constitutional Democracy"', *Political Theory*, 29: 6, 2001, pp. 792–805.

finance reform, any of which, if adopted, could radically change substantive outcomes in the United States.

Second, as Kant pointed out in the *Metaphysical Elements of Justice*, positive law is unlike moral law in that positive law is susceptible to coercive enforcement. Thus, Habermas explains,

> the positivity of law necessitates an interesting split in autonomy to which there is nothing analogous in the moral sphere. The binding character of legal norms stems not just from the insight into what is equally good for all but from the collectively binding decisions of authorities who make and apply the law. This results in the conceptually necessary division of roles between authors . . . and addressees [of law].[9]

What should we make of this 'necessary division', of this split within life under law? Habermas does not remark it, but even under the best circumstances of legitimate, publicly authored law, we may lose sight of our authorship and become alienated from law once the law we pressed for (or some thing sort of like it; it goes through a potentially transforming set of sluices and processes; *Between Facts and Norms*, chapters 7 and 8) is created and becomes an enforceable thing. Moreover, once enforceable, the law in question also becomes a productive force, not just a regulative force but a power whereby subjects are interpellated into and by the very law they would like to be able to say they authored.[10]

Which is the better course for democracies? To see such perhaps necessary moments of alienation in life under law as welcome gaps that remind us of the insufficiencies of juridical efforts to institute justice or legitimacy without remainder?[11] Or to seek, as Kant and Rousseau did, as Habermas often does, to overcome the moments of alienation that interrupt our would-be affective or rational politics? Or both?

In his latest essay, Habermas takes on the authorship/interpellation problem, but he construes it in generational terms (the constitution was authored by historical founders, but we are ruled by it), and he responds to the problem by adding a new, third argument for co-originality. The people in the present are not just paradoxically constrained by a constitution authored by their forebears because the full development of constitutional democracy depends on the agency of the present generation, whose responsibility it is to 'tap the system of rights ever more fully'. In short, the tension between constitutionalism and democracy is one that gets worked out in the future, *if* the present generation fulfills its political responsibilities:

> The allegedly paradoxical relation between democracy and the rule of law resolves itself in the dimension of historical time, *provided one conceives of the constitution as a project that makes the founding act*

> *into an ongoing process of constitution-making that continues across generations.*[12]

In short, the people in the present are part of a constitutional democratic project that is larger than themselves, but they have a role to play in that project nonetheless.

That role must be played in certain ways, however, if the tension between democracy and constitutionalism is to be erased in the future. Claiming the constitution as one's own by 'tapping' it is a solution unlike the ward system recommended by Thomas Jefferson to address the same problem. Habermas's emphasis is not on localism or on infrastructure but on influence and agenda setting from a distance. The present generation may be politically active, but their activism takes the form of agitation for the expansion of rights. They have participation rights but they must exercise them in the *right* way. ('The entitlement to political participation is bound up with the expectation of a public use of reason: as democratic colegislators, citizens may not ignore the informal demand to orient themselves toward the common good.')[13] Their medium is law and so they agitate for change by way of constitution-oriented practices that require them 'to recognize the project [of constitutionalism] as *the same* throughout history and to judge it from *the same* perspective' as their forebears.[14] (But how could we know whether our perspective is the same as that of the founders?)

The problem is that these requirements merely reproduce at another level the very problem Habermas is trying to solve. In what sense can the people be said to have free authorship if they are required to approach the constitution as their forebears did, with the same standards and from the same perspective, even if also permittedly 'in a critical fashion?' If they are required to inhabit their forebears to exercise their political autonomy, surely it is a curious autonomy they are exercising? In what sense can they be said to be politically free if they understand themselves to be bound to a progressive temporality in and out of which constitutional democracy in its full, unconflicted expression is required to unfold? In what sense is Habermas's gesture to futurity meaningful if that future is always already known to be governed by progress? In what sense can the people be said to be learning from their experience if their learning process is said to be 'self-correcting?'

But perhaps Habermas means something a bit different. Perhaps he means merely to suggest that we will not experience our constitution as an alien thing if we adopt the attitudes and perspectives he recommends here. We should act *as if* the constitution is the same over time, *as if* our perspective is the same as that of our forebears.[15] (Then it would not matter whether or how we could know if our perspective was *really* the same as that of our forebears. Getting it right would not be the point. Perhaps this is why Habermas stresses the 'performative' character of this project.) If we do so, we might achieve a level of identification with our constitution such that we would never experience it as a constraint but rather always as the would-have-been-willed expression of our freedom under law.

Thus, Habermas closes the gaps of alienation that afflict our sense of autonomy by developing a fable of origins (*co*-origins) that we are to adopt as if it were true. In so doing, he repeats the move made by Kant in 'Speculative Beginnings of Human History'. There, Kant turns to reason in the 'company of the imagination' to tell an origin story that makes sense of man's felt alienation and is meant to help heal it. But reason is also the power that created the very alienations, 'the dissatisfactions', Kant wants to heal. Reason is what disrupted the original Edenic unity of man's existence and turned man from a happy natural animal into an appetitive, desiring, finite creature who fears death. (No such ambivalence troubles Habermas's account of reason or, perhaps better, Habermas tries to rid himself of such ambivalence by distinguishing varieties of reason, strategic, communicative, etc., and privileging some over others.) The Janus-like character of reason means that Kant must draw on another power, as well. The power of providence supplements that of reason (already supplemented by imagination) and gives us assurance that 'human things as a whole . . . do not progress from good to bad, but gradually develop from worse to better.' But providence cannot do our work for us. Kant appeals finally to a duty to hope, or rather a duty to act hopefully, an 'inborn duty of influencing posterity in such a way that it will make constant progress (and I must thus assume that progress is possible)' ('Speculative Beginnings', p. 59). Similarly, Habermas, who rejects providentialism in politics, also assures us that the gap between reason and will, law and democracy, can be closed if we take upon ourselves a (non-providential) duty to act hopefully in pursuit of the unfinished project of modern constitutionalism.[16]

Habermas means to reject providentialism, but the rejection is incomplete. In response to Frank Michelman's worry that 'the democratic process is caught in a circular self-constitution that leads to an infinite regress' (that is, the grounds of legitimation are always themselves in need of legitimation, all the way down),[17] Habermas refuses to appeal 'to a moral realism that would be hard to defend'. Instead, he claims that we should 'understand the regress itself as the understandable expression of the future-oriented character, or openness, of the democratic constitution.'[18] Here Habermas seems to agree with Hannah Arendt's observation that the problem of infinite regress is a foundationalist's problem, the product of an old providential model of authority that leads us to look for authorization prior to action rather than the other way around. He seems to think that we might recast legitimation as a *horizon* rather than a *ground*. These italicized terms are Judith Butler's, not Habermas's, however, and that is because, in fact, Habermas's position is different from Butler's and from Arendt's.[19] The future to which he looks is not Arendt's post-providentially contingent and open-ended future. Instead, it is a teleological process in which the co-originality of law and democracy emerges at last in and out of time, understood 'as a self-correcting learning process'. Nietzsche's warning comes to mind here: the fact that we have killed god does not mean we have stopped living in his old houses.

Why does this matter? It matters because when Habermas characterizes his hoped-for future in progressive terms, he turns that future into a ground. Its character as a future is undone by progress' guarantee. The agency of the present generation, on behalf of which Habermas lays out his argument, is now in the service of a set of forces quite beyond itself, which it may only fulfill or betray, speed up or slow down. It may not author or make or inaugurate its future. It may only reposition itself in relation to its past (affirmatively or critically). (Of course, all our actions position us in relation to a past, but action's meaning and effects also exceed such repositioning. Moreover, there is always the question of which of many possible pasts conditions our actions.) History moves on and our actions place us on the right or wrong side of it. Thus, Habermas legitimates constitutional democracy by way of a promised future reconciliation. But what if democratic agency is the price of this particular solution to the problem?

When Habermas says that we should *conceive of 'the constitution as a project that makes the founding act into an ongoing process of constitution-making that continues across generations'*,[20] where we understand generational time as a self-correcting learning process, he positions himself between two established poles: against those who insist on the a-temporality of the constitution (e.g., original intentionalists) and against those who insist on its *mere* temporality (realists as well as critical legal theorists). Habermas is right to want to find an alternative to both positions. Original intent is overly restrictive in insulating constitutionalism from varieties of active democratic politics favored by both Habermas and agonistic political theorists. And realists as well as critical legal theorists too easily allow constitutionalism to sink entirely into ordinary power politics. Some alternative is needed, but the assumption of progress has its own costs.

As Hannah Arendt put it in a 1973 interview, 'The law of progress holds that everything now must be better than what was before. Don't you see, if you want something better, and better, and better, you lose the good. The good is no longer even being measured.'[21] And neither, often enough, is the bad: when political philosophers like Rawls and Habermas celebrate the abolition of juridical slavery in the United States *as progress* (as opposed, say, to celebrating it as a contingent historical achievement that could have gone otherwise and may yet do so), they are less inclined to ask what might 'be analogous to slavery [juridically tolerated or secured] in today's advanced economies of low wages, coerced overtime, and a permanent underclass.'[22] Faith in progress and even advocacy on its behalf tends to encourage self-satisfaction and undermine practices much needed by democracies – self-examination, genealogy, and critique.

Progress gets us into other problems as well. Habermas's requirement that we be able to learn from past mistakes presses him to what seems to me an indefensible position. With regard to past constitutional battles such as those in the United States over the New Deal, he says,

> Once the interpretive battles have subsided, *all parties recognize that the reforms are achievements, although they were at first sharply contested. In retrospect they agree* that, with the inclusion of marginalized groups and with the empowerment of deprived classes, the hitherto poorly satisfied presuppositions for the legitimacy of existing democratic procedures are better realized.[23]

In short, the wave of progress sweeps us all up. But does it? Are dissenters always persuaded? Are they never minoritized, over and over, into silence or aggression?

Most constitutional battles are never finally won. Courts change, contexts change, popular perceptions and demands change, and power shifts. We can describe such changes, as Habermas does, as 'contingent interruptions and historical regressions' of an otherwise secure trajectory of progress, but doing so leaves us unprepared for the reemergence of old claims that were thought to be discredited; it leaves us unprepared for the appearance of ressentiment. And we become blind to our own ressentiment, which tends to manifest itself in a battle-fatigued triumphalism that does not want, understandably enough, to have to fight *that* battle yet again. We may even promote as political virtues 'stability, cooperation, duration and unified system' without realizing that these are, as Sheldon Wolin memorably puts it with regard to Rawls's liberalism, 'but the yearnings of an ideology seeking repose'.[24]

In the United States, almost 150 years after the Civil War, some fly the flag of the pre-Civil War South (although even calling it the pre-Civil War South participates in a Habermasian temporality, as if the flag is archaic, not still significant in the post-Civil War South [and North]). Others demand the end of affirmative action or declare the illegitimacy of a centralized national government and conduct war against it. Years after the disestablishment of the Church, a 'values question' on the exit polls of the 2004 US presidential election has helped give new life and resources to an already ongoing movement to put religion (read: Christianity) into a central role in American public and governmental life.[25] How should we think of the varieties of people who advocate on behalf of these very different agendas? A triumphalist attitude casts them as dinosaurs, curious remnants of a past age. We find it easy to see them as insane, strange, atavistic, but not agents. Do such attitudes make it easier for us to regard them with incredulity, see them as relics from another time (another temporality), discard them, kill them, lock them up and throw away the key? On the other sides, the same trick of time is used to cast unsavory elements of the present as always already past: Conservatives in the US treat progressives and dissenters today as 'throwbacks' to the 60's, calling them 'Woodstock weirdoes', as if their time has come . . . and gone. Certainly such triumphalist attitudes make it more likely that the 'we' formed around triumphalism will treat others as enemies or antagonists rather than as agonistic adversaries, to borrow a useful distinction from Chantal Mouffe.[26]

Whig histories, by telling the stories of winners and losers, invite their adherents to treat dissenters as nonminoritized remnants of earlier battles who are, as it were, always already dead. This is what Tocqueville does to Native Americans in his own account of democracy's emergence in *Democracy in America*.[27] How will his rendering appear if, in a couple of hundred years' time, a resurgent Native American population reclaims the land from its white and other settlers? Our judgments about winners and losers depend completely on what we take to be the ending of the story in question, but this ending is precisely always in question. One of the things at stake in cultural/symbolic politics is precisely the identification of a certain point in time as an *end* from which other points in time are to be judged.

Of the four modes of relation to a constitution – application, interpretation, amendment, and revolution – Habermas treats mostly the first two and reserves those for courts, which may, however, he says, be influenced by episodic political action. Amendment and revolution are more obviously modes of relation to a constitution that might introduce something new. Focusing also on these other modes of relation opens up room to see the truth in Sheldon Wolin's observation 'that democracy is inherently unstable, inclined toward anarchy, and identified with revolution' (p. 37). But democracy is not just anarchic in this sense; it also seeks stability and is a form of government; hence, 'cracy'. When Wolin presses for a different view of democracy as, per se, '*a*constitutional', he seems to set up a choice: between thinking of democratic constitutionalism as 'a teleologically completed form' versus a representation of a 'moment'.[28] Habermas rightly resists the choice and tries to strike a balance between the two. His constitutional democracy is fed (through discriminating sluices) by the publics and counter-publics of a decentered and dispersed popular sovereignty that he repeatedly characterizes as 'wild' and 'anarchic'. But Habermas fails to strike the right balance: on his account, democracy as constitutionalism and democracy as *a*constitutionalism exist side by side and worlds apart. Wild and anarchic social movement activity is on the periphery, he says (*BFN*, pp. 480–81, 485–86). By implication, law, which is at the center, appears always calm, never itself wild. (By the end of his life, Jefferson, by contrast, saw local political activity as calmly democratic and worried that the national constitutional center was wild, bound to usurp popular energies.) Moreover, the calm center of Habermasian constitutional democracy is never overtaken by the wild periphery. A spatialized metaphorics and a set of normative and juridical requirements guarantee that the two spheres meet but do not overcome each other: law should not overreach to normalize its subjects (*The Inclusion of the Other*, p. 263) and civil society is self-limiting (*BFN*, p. 372), Habermas says. But what democracy has ever conformed to these directives? In the context of the often long-tentacled reach of law, a self-limiting civil society is either impossible or suicidal from a democratic perspective.

The promise of constitutional politics is that worthwhile gains such as newly won human rights are taken out of political play for a period of time. Activists could use the respite. But the risks are several: Often, we rest on our laurels and are overtaken by new events. Or laws that once looked progressive acquire significations and have impacts in new contexts that no longer serve democratic political purposes. Another risk is that we think we have won more than we have. We forget that even entrenched rights depend for their meaning and power on their vulnerability, on the fact that we (or our forebears) took them and that we must take them again and again, sometimes even agitating against the very laws we once fought for in order to better secure old and new rights. Rights are not dead instruments, they are live practices. But they must be kept animate. The failure to keep them alive by continuing to use them, recraft them, and fight for them even (paradoxically) after they have been entrenched undoes the very power that we give them and they give us.[29] Dead rights require live futures – promisingly and dangerously unscripted futures – if they are to come back to life.

I think Habermas would want to agree with this emphasis on the importance of democratic activism (or *a*constitutionalism) to constitutionalism. But whether he could agree would depend partly on whether he was willing to concede that the structure of constitutional or textual maintenance itself produces what Jacques Derrida calls 'new textual bodies'. Agreement might be difficult since, against Habermas's commitment to progress, stands Derrida's claim that such maintenance, which he calls survivance, should be understood not 'in the sense of posterity . . . but of "more living" ' in the sense of 'plus de vie and plus que vie' [. . .].[30] The perpetual production of new textual bodies points to something that exceeds the economy of constitutional democracy and even haunts it: something that Derrida elsewhere calls an unconditional principle, expressed but also necessarily betrayed by the conditional economy of constitutional democracy.[31] The fact that we are haunted by a principle, a sentiment, an ideal that we can't fully specify does not mean that we are paralyzed politically, nor does it mean that we cannot distinguish between better and worse political efforts to show fidelity to the unconditional.[32] Quite the opposite. Sensitivity to the remainders of any particular order can lead us to prefer some sets of arrangements over others and it mobilizes political action, sometimes constitutional, sometimes a-constitutional.

All in all, my sense is that it is not unfair to say that Habermas's impulse is to emphasize the importance of constitutionalism to democracy while neglecting to stress *equally* the importance of democracy – of *a*constitutionalism and democratic agency (and not just as a nutritional source, but also as a dangerous, potentially unsettling supplement) – to constitutionalism. That neglect is costly: a constitutionalism that is uninhabited by a-constitutionalism is the dead letter of the law. A constitutionalism that seeks to secure itself against the radically risky tumult of a-constitutionalism becomes its own enemy: a narcissistic, necrophilic document. Is that what all constitutions necessarily are?

In recent years, diverse democratic theorists have studied the deadening effects of rights-centered constitutionalism on spontaneous political action: Ernesto Laclau, Chantal Mouffe, William Connolly, Jill Frank, Wendy Brown, James Tully, Jane Bennett, Judith Butler, Romand Coles, Linda Zerilli, Sheldon Wolin, Jacques Derrida, Michael Warner, Jeremy Waldron, Patchen Markell, Charles Taylor, Eric Clarke, Kirstie McClure, and Jacques Rancière investigate constitutional democracies' tendency to paper over moments of alienation they might otherwise engage and to translate the emergence of new world-building powers and agencies into (mostly individual) rights claims that can be adjudicated positively or negatively within an existing economy of rights and liberties. The content and significance of basic rights and liberties may change in time (for better and/or worse), but the basic economy that supports and is supported by them does not. Habermas's effort to establish co-originality is an admirable attempt to stem the translation tide of liberal constitutionalism and give participation its due. But he does not take up the challenge to think about how the rights-centered pressures of public reason may get in the way of a politics devoted to world-building.[33] He does not ask whether a rights-centered constitutionalism, in its effort to preserve the rule of existing constitutional norms and forms, might do unacknowledged violence to new forms of life, new textual bodies. He does not really acknowledge clashes between constitutionalism's promise and risks. Many of these clashes occur beneath the radar of official constitutionalism, where it is quietly suggested that a politics too focused on the realization or production of promised or implied rights cannot by itself operate as justly as Habermas would like.[34]

Sometimes justice may require that we heighten the *a*constitutionalism of a regime, sometimes it may lead us to defend the temporary stasis of constitutional settlement. Talk of a contradiction between constitutionalism and democracy, per se, prevents us from developing nuanced analyses of varying situations. Thinking in terms of a *constitutional/democracy spectrum rather than in terms of an abstract binary* might broaden our vision, permitting us to see that contexts and constitutions vary and that some are more hospitable than others to democratic agency or *a*constitutionalism. While all are haunted, as it were, by Derrida's unconditional, some constitutions are also more aware than others of their own limitations, some are more sensitive than others to the remainders they generate in their establishment of order.

For example: the Canadian constitution has a 'notwithstanding clause' that allows provinces to opt out of constitutionally binding decisions for five years, subject to local majority approval. The idea is that it is worth the risk of a time-limited bad majoritarianism to offset another risk: that of a legalistic constitution that has no ear for context or for its own injustices.[35] Like any institutional measure, this one too can be used for good or ill. What is admirable about it is its self-aware declaration of the possible shortcomings of constitutionalism and the nod given by the clause to democratic agency and popular sovereignty. Five years is time for local or federal activists to press for constitutional amendment, debate, or reform in light of a court's particular finding. Alternatively, five years gives social movements a chance to develop new strategies of covertness or to persuade opposing majorities to yield to a controversial court decision. As Habermas knows, such exercises of popular and legislative agency may in turn affect future directions of constitutional interpretation and policy making. The clause is just one of many possible ways to entrench the inhabitation of the constitutional by the *a*constitutional. And, of course, that entrenchment will have advantages and dangers of its own. Nonetheless, it is a measure of which Machiavelli, who understood the importance of allowing for the venting of humors, would be proud.

Notes

1. Thanks to Lasse Thomassen for providing me with the opportunity and prodding to modify and expand upon the earlier, published version of this essay, which first appeared as a response to Habermas in: Bonnie Honig, 'Dead Rights, Live Futures: A Reply to Habermas's "Constitutional Democracy",' *Political Theory* 29:6 (2001), pp. 792–805.
2. 'From both [liberal and republican] perspectives, human rights and popular sovereignty do not so much mutually complement as compete with each other' (Jürgen Habermas, *Between Facts and Norms* [hereafter, *BFN*] [Cambridge, MA: MIT Press, 1996], p. 99).
3. Jürgen Habermas, 'Constitutional Democracy: A Paradoxical Union of Contradictory Principles,' *Political Theory* 29:6 (December 2001), p. 767. Hereafter CD.
4. CD, p. 767. The claim of social contractual co-originality is belied by the fact that when Habermas turns to elucidate the basic rights of citizens, their private rights come first and their citizenship rights second. Habermas assures us that the first three categories of rights, which 'anticipate only that [the parties] will be future users and *addressees* of the law' (CD, p. 777), come first just 'in mente'. Thus far, the parties have only achieved 'clarity regarding the enterprise they have resolved upon with their entrance into a practice of constitution making' (CD, p. 777). They are not yet done. 'Because they want to ground an association of citizens who make their own laws, it next occurs to them that they need a fourth category of rights, so they can mutually recognize one another also as the *authors* of these rights as well as of law in general' (CD, p. 777). Once they have clarified the full list

of rights, private and public, all the rights are created simultaneously, 'in a single stroke'. Until that moment of simultaneity, Habermas insists, 'nothing has *actually* happened'. Hasn't it? The priority of private rights is repeatedly on display in *Between Facts and Norms*, where Habermas claims to be working from a position of co-originality but nonetheless repeatedly puts law at the center and participation at the margins of his account. Might not the order of our thinking have implications for our future practice of politics and the operation of our political imagination? As Charles Taylor points out, the starting point of our thinking about politics reflects a set of ontological commitments or assumptions that we ignore at our peril (Taylor, 'Cross-Purposes: The Liberal-Communitarian Debate,' in *Liberalism and the Moral Life*, ed. Nancy Rosenblum [Cambridge: Harvard University Press, 1989], 164 and passim).

5. Jürgen Habermas, *The Inclusion of the Other* (Cambridge, MA: MIT Press, 1998 [hereafter, *IO*]), p. 259. Here Habermas seems to echo Stephen Holmes: 'Constitutions may be usefully compared to the rules of a game and even to the rules of grammar. While *regulative* rules (for instance "no smoking") govern pre-existent activities, *constitutive* rules (for instance, 'bishops move diagonally') make a practice possible for the first time. . . . Constitutions do not merely limit power; they can create and organize power as well as give it direction. . . . When a constituent assembly establishes a decision procedure, rather than restrict a preexistent will, it actually creates a framework in which the nation can, for the first time, have a will' – hence: co-originality? (Stephen Holmes, *Passions and Constraints*, quoted in Jeremy Waldron, 'Precommitment and Disagreement,' *Constitutionalism: Philosophical Foundations*, ed. Larry Alexander [Cambridge, UK: Cambridge University Press, 1998], p. 290). As Waldron points out, however, the view of constitutional rules as constitutive does not, as such, remove them from the purview of democratic revision and review; that is, it does not secure co-originality as Habermas conceives of it, for it leaves the priority of democracy over constitutionalism intact. Indeed, Waldron points out, democracies often revise the rules of their games, often amid disagreement, as is evidenced by majority but not unanimous decisions in referenda, parliamentary votes, or judicial decisions (pp. 292–94). Constitutive rules require merely that a democracy not change the rules in the very middle of the games being played. That is, we cannot revise the rules of elections in the middle of the election, 'Bush v. Gore notwithstanding' (as Waldron said in a personal communication) – although if, as Dworkin argues in *Law's Empire* (Oxford, UK: Hart, 1998), all interpretation involves innovation, even such midstream rule changes are de facto probably unavoidable.
6. True, the authorship requirement is hypothetical not actual: 'a regulation may claim legitimacy only if all those possibly affected by it could consent to it after participating in rational discourses.' But sometimes the requirement has a more participatory cast, as when Habermas says in agreement with 'radical feminism' that 'the appropriate interpretation of needs and criteria [in gender politics] be a matter of public debate in the political public sphere' (*IO*, p. 263).
7. The problem with liberalism is that it is inadequately concerned with the authorship requirement. It is not uncomfortable with the idea of law as an external constraint on majoritarianism or, as Habermas puts it, as an 'external barrier to' (*IO*, p. 259) popular sovereignty. Republicanism, by contrast, does try to satisfy the authorship requirement, but it does so by way of recourse to an ethical commonality that violates the universalist aspirations of law, properly understood. (The republican reliance on the ethical also begs the question it is trying to answer: it makes 'legal coercion superfluous by replacing it with custom and moral self-control' [CD, p. 771]). Habermas's proceduralist conception of deliberative democracy makes law and democracy compatible by replacing the republican reliance on the ethical with a discursive commitment to the processural.

8. It also leaves untouched the experience of life under actual law. In the United States, for example, legislation, even if technically universalizable and constitutionally permissible, tends to apply to particular populations, many of which are marked as governed but not governing: pregnant women, the indigent, aliens, welfare recipients, users of drugs or alcohol, homosexuals, and so on. This condition is unaddressed by invocations of the rule of law.
9. CD, p. 779.
10. Even unenforced and unenforceable laws have certain interpellative effects. On the impact of seldom enforced antisodomy laws, for example, see Richard Mohr, *Gays/Justice: A Study of Ethics, Society and Law* (New York: Columbia University Press, 1988), p. 67 and passim.
11. Sometimes Habermas acknowledges this insufficiency, as when he insists on the fallibility of claims, on the permanent revisability of our settlements (as in his discussion of feminist critiques of welfare paternalism [*IO*, p. 263]), on the need for perpetual contributions to constitutional orders from the wild public spheres (*BFN*, chap. 9), and (in an apparently positive way) on the 'permanent risk of dissensus'(*BFN*, p. 462) – (but then why is it a *risk*?). On the other hand, all of these acknowledgments occur within the framework of constitutionalism, and no complaint ever rises to a level where it *might* make us ask after the (in)justice of constitutionalism itself.
12. CD, p. 768, emphasis added.
13. CD, p. 779.
14. CD, p. 775.
15. For a wonderful critique (which I do not take up here) of the conservative effects of Habermas's deployment of the subjunctive *as if* in his work, see Eric O. Clarke, *Virtuous Vice: Homoeroticism and the Public Sphere* (Durham, NC: Duke University Press, 2000).
16. Kant's faith in the future depends on an assumption. His fable of beginnings begins with a single human couple, 'only a single pair' so that 'war does not arise, as it would if men lived close to one another and were yet strangers.' This assumption rules out 'differences in lines of descent' and so secures the possibility of a future sociability, in accord with man's 'supreme end'. Habermas's faith in the future also depends on an assumption. He, too, turns to a single pair, to a co-original law and democracy, whose perfect union secures us against radical plurality, division, and irresolvable strife. The assumption of a single pair secures the supreme end of constitutional democracy, protecting it against paradox and contradiction. Why the singleness of the pair, in either case, should rule out conflict is, however, a mystery, especially given, in the case of Kant's single pair, the rift of sexual difference.
17. Frank I. Michelman, 'Constitutional Authorship,' *Constitutionalism: Philosophical Foundations*, ed. L. Alexander (Cambridge, UK: Cambridge University Press, 1998), pp. 64–98. This is a problem with a history, posed also by Sieyés, Rousseau, Hannah Arendt (*On Revolution* [New York: Penguin, 1970 (hereafter, *OR*)], pp. 183–84), and Jacques Derrida. It is the problem of authorization in the absence of foundational grounds, the problem of how to stop the cycle of revolution and stabilize political order, the problem, as Derrida puts it, of what to put 'in the place of the last instance' (Jacques Derrida, 'Declarations of Independence,' *New Political Science* 15 [1987]: pp. 7–15 at 10). Rousseau solved the problem by way of the lawgiver, a good man prior to good law, whose agency enables law's inauguration. But this was no solution, since the lawgiver merely deepens rather than resolves the tension between law and democracy. How can the people be free when they need the guidance of a lawgiver? (See Alan Keenan, *Democracy in Question: Rethinking Democratic Openness in a Time of Political Closure* [Stanford, CA: Stanford University Press, 2003], chap. 1 and Honig, *Democracy and the Foreigner*, chap. 2.) Michelman also responds to the law versus democracy problem by turning to a good

man prior to good law: Justice Brennan (Frank I. Michelman, *Brennan and Democracy* [Princeton, NJ: Princeton University Press, 1999]). Arendt argued that America never really faced the abyss of infinite regress because many local and state constitutions and compacts predated the new federal constitution and were able to funnel power to it and secure it, before being themselves undone by it (*OR*, chaps 4 and 6).

18. CD, p. 774. Of course, no modern constitution is as humble as Habermas claims. All reach for a 'moral realism that is hard to defend', filling their place of the last instance, as Derrida points out, with God, or nature's law. Arendt has a tendency, like Habermas, to underestimate the American founding documents' many references to natural law and divine will. Indeed, Arendt somewhat improbably insists that the good fortune of the American people was their capacity to regard as sacred something that they themselves had made: they had, she says, 'an extraordinary capacity to look upon yesterday with the eyes of centuries to come' (*OR*, p.198). For my reading of Arendt on this point, see chapter 4, *Political Theory and the Displacement of Politics*.
19. *OR* (chap. 5); Judith Butler, 'Contingent Foundations,' *Feminist Contentions*, ed. Seyla Benhabib, Judith Butler, Nancy Fraser, and Drucilla Cornell (New York: Routledge, 1995).
20. CD, p. 768.
21. Hannah Arendt, 'Hannah Arendt: From an Interview,' *New York Review of Books* 25, no. 16 (October 26, 1978): p. 18.
22. The wording is Sheldon Wolin's ('The Liberal/Democratic Divide: On Rawls' Political Liberalism,' *Political Theory* 24, no. 1 [1996]: pp. 97–142 at 117). The point is not that Rawls (or Habermas) would not object to these inequalities, he would, but he would not ask whether they might be remnants or traces of an earlier practice of slavery supposedly left behind by enlightened constitutionalism (*Political Liberalism* [New York: Columbia University Press, 1996], p. xxix).
23. CD, p. 775, emphasis added.
24. Wolin, 'Liberal/Democratic Divide,' p. 108.
25. On these developments, no one is a better commentator than Frank Rich, Arts columnist for the *New York Times*. See any of his Sunday columns from Jan. to Apr. 2005.
26. Chantal Mouffe, *The Democratic Paradox* (London: Verso, 2000), chap. 2.
27. For a reading of Tocqueville's Indians as always already dead, see William Connolly, *The Ethos of Pluralization* (Minneapolis: University of Minnesota Press, 1995), chap. 7; and Michael Shapiro, 'Bowling Blind: Post Liberal Civil Society and the Worlds of Neo-Tocquevillean Social Theory,' *Theory & Event* [online] 1, no. 1 (1997). Available from: http://muse.jhu.edu/journals/theory_&_event.
28. Sheldon Wolin, 'Norm and Form: The Constitutionalising of Democracy,' *Athenian Political Thought and the Reconstruction of American Democracy*, ed. J. Peter Euben, John R. Wallach, and Josiah Ober (Ithaca, NY: Cornell University Press, 1994).
29. See Richard Flathman, *The Practice of Rights* (Cambridge, UK: Cambridge University Press, 1976); and Michael Warner, *The Trouble with Normal* (New York: Free Press, 2000). Flathman emphasizes the practiced character of rights; Warner calls attention to (among other things) their normalizing power and the ways in which satisfaction with rights works against the generation of power as action in concert.
30. Jacques Derrida, 'Deconstruction in America: An Interview with Jacques Derrida,' *Critical Exchange* 17 (1985): pp. 24–25. See also my discussion of these issues by way of Derrida and Arendt in Bonnie Honig, *Political Theory and the Displacement of Politics* (Ithaca, NY: Cornell University Press, 1993), chap. 4.

31. Jacques Derrida, *Rogues: Two Essays on Reason*, trans. Pascale-Anne Brault and Michael Naas (Stanford: Stanford University Press, 2005). I discuss this argument of Derrida in more detail in my comment on Seyla Benhabib's Tanner Lectures, forthcoming from Cambridge University Press, 2006.
32. Contra Habermas's critique of Foucault in *Philosophical Discourses of Modernity* (trans. Frederick G. Lawrence) (Boston: The MIT Press, 1990).
33. Building on Cohen and Arato, Habermas uses the term 'dual orientation' to describe the democratic actor's coupling of her agitation on behalf of her own agenda with a reflexive concern to 'revitalize and enlarge civil society' (*BFN*, p. 370). It does not occur to him that the two parts of this orientation might conflict. What if care for the public sphere or the common good requires a commitment to practices of genealogy and critique that demand that we commit ourselves to forms of social upheaval that make it impossible to sustain practices of public reason? What if the rights-centered pressures of public reason get in the way of political efforts at world building? What if care for the world presses us to frame arguments in such a way that our immediate agenda may be lost (as when racial activists, seeking to enter 'racism' into liberal lexicons, refuse to translate all of their claims of harm into individual wrongs, even though that translation might be efficacious in the moment)?
34. As William Connolly points out, a politics that 'suggests that the most recent identities [rights, achievements, constitutional decisions] are also the most true, natural or advanced' is one that 'discourages proponents from cultivating that partial, comparative sense of contingency in their own identities from which responsiveness to new claims of difference might proceed' (*Why I Am Not a Secularist* [Minneapolis: University of Minnesota Press, 1999], p. 71).
35. Joseph Carens stresses the importance of contextualism to political theory and likes the Canadian 'notwithstanding clause' for its apparent sensitivity to context (*Culture, Citizenship, and Community: A Contextual Exploration of Justice As Evenhandedness* [Oxford, UK: Oxford University Press, 2000]). For a more ambivalent account of the notwithstanding clause than the one presented by me here or by Carens, see my review of Carens in *Polity* 33, no. 3 (Spring 2001): pp. 479–85.

10

Lasse Thomassen

'A BIZARRE, EVEN OPAQUE PRACTICE': HABERMAS ON CONSTITUTIONALISM AND DEMOCRACY

In this chapter, Lasse Thomassen deals with Habermas's thesis about the co-originality of constitutionalism and democracy and Honig's response to it. Thomassen does a Derridean deconstructive reading of Habermas's texts. He thereby puts Derrida to work on Habermas in order to show what a deconstructive reading can consist of, and in so doing, he develops an alternative, deconstructive position on constitutional democracy. Thomassen argues that the relationship between constitutionalism and democracy is undecidable, and that Habermas is unable to resolve this undecidability. As a result, the two elements of constitutional democracy – constitutionalism and democracy – cannot be reconciled, and constitutional democracy is destabilised. However, the undecidability at the heart of constitutional democracy is not necessarily negative, but instead creates a more vigorous constitutional democracy. Moreover, undecidability is, paradoxically, what makes constitutional democracy work, and Derridean deconstruction, not Habermasian rational reconstruction, thus provides a better explanation of how constitutional democracy works. In the final section of the chapter, Thomassen criticises Honig, arguing that she buys into Habermas's terms of the debate when she talks about a balance, rather than undecidability, between constitutionalism and democracy.

Introduction[1]

The 2004 US election again saw controversy over the election procedures. One of the most memorable images from the 2000 presidential election was that of election officials in the state of Florida examining ballot cards and looking for dimples and holes. What looked trivial and absurd to the onlooking world in fact turned upon an important political and philosophical problem. The election officials were engaged in the identification of the will of the American people. The election was supposed to be the expression of popular sovereignty, and the officials were trying to recognise the true will of the people in those holes and dimples.

The will of the people did not express itself in an unmediated fashion. It was mediated by those ballot cards and by election officials' interpretation of them. Moreover, there are rules in place concerning how to identify the will of the people: constitutional rules and election laws determining who can vote, how they can vote, how to count the votes, and so on. And there are institutional remedies in place for interpreting those rules, namely the courts and, in the last instance, the US Supreme Court. So, democracy – the popular sovereignty of the people – is mediated by the rule of law and constitutionalism, for instance by rules for the equal right to vote and, hence, for the equal right to be counted as partaking in the people. This mediation of democracy by constitutionalism secures equality and bestows legitimacy upon the former. Similarly, constitutionalism is mediated by democracy. Constitutional rules and human rights are not simply given, but put in place by elected representatives chosen by the people and interpreted by judges chosen by the people or their representatives. So, democracy mediates constitutionalism and thereby bestows legitimacy on it.

It is a widely held belief today among laypersons as well as experts that constitutional democracy is the best available form of government, and that it involves a 'balancing' or even 'interdependence' of its two key components: constitutionalism (human rights, the rule of law, and so on) and democracy (popular sovereignty, and so on). This idea has also been central to Jürgen Habermas's work in legal and political theory and to the development of his theory of deliberative democracy during the last fifteen years. In *Between Facts and Norms* and subsequent writings, Habermas has argued that his discourse theory of democracy can reconcile constitutionalism and democracy and, thereby, solve some of the problems with other approaches.[2] What he calls the co-originality thesis aims to show that constitutionalism and democracy simultaneously enable and require one another. There is, according to Habermas, a mutual mediation of constitutionalism and democracy, and only a political system that is both constitutional and democratic is legitimate. This thesis of the co-originality of constitutionalism and democracy is meant to solve a number of problems, among them the relationship between the legislative and the judiciary, the role of judiciary review, and interpretive constitutional disagreements. I will not be able to touch upon all these issues in this chapter, nor will I be able to address all the historical and contemporary literature on the relation between constitutionalism and democracy. Instead I wish to pursue a deconstructive reading of Habermas's co-originality thesis, showing its inherent aporias and how a different conception of constitutional democracy emerges from this reading. Before stating my thesis at more length, it is necessary, however, to say a few words about Habermas's project.

HABERMAS'S CO-ORIGINALITY THESIS

Habermas's co-originality thesis should be seen in the context of his discourse theory and his conception of autonomy. Habermas understands democratic autonomy to be in place when the 'citizens [are] able to understand themselves also as authors of the law to which they are subject as addressees' (*BFN*, p. 449). This notion of autonomy is closely linked to the discourse principle and the democratic principle. The thrust of these principles is that validity, including the validity of legal norms, can only be settled in public deliberations under certain idealised conditions of full information, equal access, symmetry, and so on.[3] Constitutional democracy is the concrete realisation of these principles. The addressees of the law must simultaneously be its authors, and this condition extends to the laws of lawmaking, that is, the constitution. In large and complex societies, the immediate identity of addressees and authors is possible neither in everyday lawmaking nor in constitutional lawmaking. Yet, the addressees of the law must at least be able to *understand* themselves as simultaneously the authors of the law. So, the constitution must be subject to democratic will-formation. At the same time, however, the latter must be constitutionally regulated in such a way as to protect the pluralism of modern societies and the singularity of each individual. The citizens can only understand themselves as the authors of the law if they are simultaneously constituted as free and equal subjects under the law (CD, p. 767). Hence, the thesis of co-originality – or 'co-implication' (CD, p. 779) – states that there is a relation of mutual implication and presupposition between constitutionalism and democracy. Their relationship is internal and enabling rather than external and constraining (*BFN*, p. 128; *IO*, pp. 259, 261).

In this way, Habermas seeks to reconcile constitutionalism and democracy. The aim of my deconstructive reading of Habermas's texts in the following is to show that the relationship between constitutionalism and democracy is ultimately undecidable, and that, *contra* Habermas, this undecidability is what accounts for how constitutional democracy works. In addition, I will show that Habermas is only able to reconcile constitutionalism and democracy by introducing a 'fiction'; yet this fiction does not solve the undecidability, but only displaces it. Bonnie Honig has put forward a similar critique of Habermas,[4] but in the last section of the chapter, I discuss the limitations of her critique. This also serves to show the implications of the deconstructive reading for the politics of constitutional democracy and for how one reads philosophical and political texts. The differences between a Habermasian rational reconstructive approach and a Derridean deconstructive approach to constitutional democracy have been noted by several commentators.[5] While there was some rapprochement between Derrida and Habermas during the last few years before Derrida's recent death, important differences remain over, among other things, the role of philosophy and how one should approach political concepts.

VICIOUS CIRCULARITY AND INFINITE REGRESS

How can the process of constitution-making itself be constitutional? The democratic process of making (and interpreting[6]) the constitution must not only be democratic, according to Habermas, it must simultaneously be constitutional so that the citizens exercise their democratic autonomy as free and equal legal persons. Were it not constitutional, it would not be democratic, because constitutionalism and democracy are not only mutually enabling but also *presuppose* one another. Without constitutionalism, democracy is lacking, and *vice versa*.

If democracy is not already constitutional, it cannot be democratic proper, according to Habermas. Likewise, if constitutionalism is not already mediated by democracy, it is not constitutional proper, but lacking. Here one need only think of the current situation in Iraq. One may argue that a new Iraqi constitution can only be legitimate if the Iraqis can view it as the result of their own exercise of democratic autonomy, rather than being imposed on them from the outside. However, in order for democratic constitution making to be legitimate, it must already be constitutional. So, one is caught in a vicious circle. Constitutionalism and democracy must *already* be co-original and mutually mediated; they cannot *become* so. If democracy is not already constitutional (and *vice versa*), it will not be able to properly mediate constitutionalism, which will then not be able to properly mediate democracy, and so on and so forth. Constitutionalism is precisely not only an enabling but also a necessary condition of democracy (and *vice versa*).

What should have been the solution to the problem of legitimate law and democratic autonomy – namely the co-originality of constitutionalism and democracy – turns out to be the problem, because you cannot have one without the other. Insofar as one of the two components – constitutionalism or democracy – is not fully in place, we are dealing with a vicious circularity. Only when both are fully in place, mediating and supporting one another, is the circularity positive. This is not only a problem arising at the beginning of the circle, as it were. There is a vicious circularity whenever one of the two necessary elements – constitutionalism or democracy – is not fully in place, because there is not only a relation of mutual implication between the two but also one of mutual presupposition. Thus, one cannot reject this kind of argument, as Seyla Benhabib does in her critique of Derrida, by saying that it only focuses on the origin of constitutional democracy and, hence, confuses the ordinary practice of constitutional democracy with the exception on which it relies.[7] The undecidable relation between constitutionalism and democracy that I propose to trace in Habermas's conception of constitutional democracy is not something marginal, but at the heart of constitutional democracy as it works on an 'everyday' level. It may be most visible at the moment of the foundation of constitutional democracy, but in fact it arises whenever the legitimacy of the law is at stake. When constitutionalism and democracy are not both fully in place, the co-originality thesis will need to be supplemented. As I shall argue below, for Habermas, this supplement is an idea of a constitutional interpretive tradition and a *telos* of future reconciliation.

The reverse side of the vicious circularity is a problem of infinite regress. The problem of infinite regress, which Frank I. Michelman has pointed out in relation to Habermas's work,[8] arises when we ask for the constitutionalism of democracy. Although this question can be answered, at least provisionally, with reference to the constitution or an interpretation of it, this answer only raises the further problem of the democraticness of the constitution. The regress of the chain of reasoning can only be stopped by arbitrarily cutting it off at some point, for instance, by asserting a certain constitutional content.[9] This is so at least if there is disagreement all the way down, that is, if, as Habermas says, there is 'a permanent risk of dissensus' (*BFN*, p. 462) and 'radical and enduring controversies on constitutional matters' (LD, p. 187). Constitutionalism is supposed to protect the singularity of each individual, but must itself be mediated by democracy. The chain of reasoning about the democraticness of the constitution (and the constitutionalism of democracy) cannot be closed with reference to an original constitutional text, because the latter is open to an infinite number of different interpretations irreducible to any essential core of the constitutional text. Nor can the regress be stopped with reference to the democratic process of constitutional interpretation, because disagreement, it would seem, also concerns the conditions of that process. Thus, the infinite regress prevents the reconciliation of constitutionalism and democracy as well as the stabilisation of any of the two elements and of their mutual relationship.

A 'STABLE POINT OF REFERENCE'? IN THE 'WHIRLPOOL OF TEMPORALITY'

As a solution to the circularity and regress problems, Habermas proposes that the relationship between constitutionalism and democracy 'can develop only in the dimension of time – as a self-correcting historical process' (LD, p. 768). He continues:

> the alleged paradoxical relation between democracy and the rule of law [i.e., constitutionalism] resolves itself in the dimension of historical time, provided one conceives the constitution as a project that makes the founding act into an ongoing process of constitution-making that continues across generations. (LD, p. 768)

For this learning process, it is not critical that the 'constitution that is democratic – not just in its content but also according to its source of legitimation – is a tradition-building project with a clearly marked beginning in time' (LD, p. 774). In other words, it is not critical that the project has an arbitrary genesis, one that is not simultaneously fully constitutional and democratic. However, for the project of constitutional democracy not to be contaminated by its particular and arbitrary historical genesis, the latter must be seen as part of a project 'understood in the long run as a self-correcting learning process' (LD, p. 774). Only in this way can the genesis of constitutional democracy be conceived as internal to constitutional democracy without contaminating it with its arbitrariness and its non-reconciliation of its two components – only in this way can constitutional democracy pull itself up by the hair, as it were.

One of the things at stake here is Habermas's conception of time and history. He writes:

> To be sure, this fallible continuation of the founding event can break out of the circle of a polity's groundless discursive self-constitution only if this process – *which is not immune to contingent interruptions and historical regressions* – can be understood in the long run as a self-correcting learning process. (LD, p. 774, my emphasis)

On the one hand, Habermas takes seriously the 'contingent interruptions and historical regressions' of time. The contingency of history makes a difference, and, as a result, the reconciliation of constitutionalism and democracy is in no way guaranteed, but merely a contingent possibility. On the other hand, as Honig has pointed out,[10] contingency and historicity are framed by and constrained within a quasi-teleological conception of history: 'in the long run', contingency is relative to the progress of the history of constitutional democracy. It is with reference to this history of progress that past and present mistakes can be recognised as just that: accidental mistakes from which we can learn and thereby progress. It is to the time of constitutional democracy that I now turn.

Habermas characterises the relationship between constitutionalism and democracy as a learning process along two lines, each taking his argument in slightly different directions: (1) in terms of a constitutional tradition, where later generations continue the project interpreting the normative content of the constitution embarked upon by earlier generations; and (2) in terms of the performativity and promise of reconciliation inherent in the democratic practice of constitution making.

(1) Habermas wants to steer clear of the Scylla of communitarianism and the Charybdis of non-cognitivism. The problem with the former is that it dissolves constitutional disagreement in the tradition of a given community. This guarantees the reconciliation of constitutionalism and democracy,

because they are both mediated by and internal to the content of the communitarian tradition. It simultaneously guarantees the identity of lawgivers and lawtakers because their identity is secured by the fact that they belong to the *same* tradition. However, Habermas argues that this limits the autonomy of the citizens in a paternalistic way, because the tradition is given to them from the outside, unmediated by their free and equal yes/no positioning. The tradition stops the regress in an arbitrary and illegitimate fashion by positing 'something given, something that is no longer in need of further justification'.[11] The non-cognitivist approach does not provide an adequate answer to the challenge of infinite regress either. For non-cognitivists, there can be no interpretation of the constitution that is both final and rational, and hence there can be no final and rational reconciliation of constitutionalism and democracy (LD, p. 189). On the contrary, Habermas wants to retain the promise of reconciliation and agreement while respecting 'the unavoidability of endemic disagreement' (LD, p. 194) among irrepresentable individuals.

Habermas's first line of argument is, then, the following:

> the interpretation of constitutional history as a learning process is predicated on the nontrivial assumption that later generations will start with the same standards as did the founders. . . . The descendants can learn from past mistakes only if they are 'in the same boat' as their forebears. . . . All participants must be able to recognize the project as *the same* throughout history and to judge it from *the same* perspective. (CD, p. 775)

However, this immediately raises the problem that present and future generations are constrained by something given and external to their democratic interpretation of the constitution, namely the 'standards' and 'perspective' of a constitutional tradition. This is so even when the democratic interpretation of the constitution is understood as 'the task of actualizing the still-untapped normative substance of the system of rights laid down in the original document of the constitution' (CD, p. 774). This presupposes that 'the original document of the constitution' really does contain as-yet unrealised sources of rights. The citizens are, then, as Honig has also argued, restricted to interpret in different ways the normative content of a document and a tradition handed down to them, which they cannot reject as not theirs.[12] The democratic interpretation of the constitution is framed by and takes place *within* a constitutional tradition, when this constitutional tradition is precisely what should also be at stake and should not limit, but only enable, democracy. The question whether this tradition is indeed *ours* cannot be raised, and the question of who 'we' are and whether we belong to the same 'we' is bracketed. In this way, a certain content of the constitution is posited as external to and beyond the practice of constitutional democracy – precisely what Habermas wanted to avoid.[13] The citizens will be able to pull themselves up by the hair, but only through the introduction of an unquestioned ground on which they can stand.

(2) There is another line of argument in Habermas that seeks to avoid recourse to a pre-given identity in any of the forms considered above. This second line of argument substitutes a focus on the future for the focus on the past, and it moves the focus from the constative content of the constitutional tradition to the performativity of constitution making.[14] According to this line of argument, the only 'constraint' on democratic constitution making and interpretation 'is that citizens must see themselves as heirs to a founding generation, carrying on with the common project' (LD, p. 193). This now has a different meaning because it refers to 'the intuitive meaning of [the] performance' of constitution making (LD, p. 193; see also *BFN*, p. 128). As such, it is supposedly an internal and enabling rather than an external and constraining condition. Habermas continues:

> The performance of those founding acts from which self-governing communities originate thus contains an implicit, intuitively available meaning that is the same for everybody, though it is spelled out and explicated in the wordings of so many different texts, interpretations, and implementations. The performative meaning remains the implicit but stable point of reference, though any attempt at its explication is only one among various possible versions. (LD, p. 193)

The focus is now on the process of constitution making and interpretation rather than on the constative content of a constitutional tradition. The intuitive performative meaning of democratic constitution making ultimately refers to 'the epistemic promise of an unrestricted exchange of a sufficiently wide range of relevant reasons' (LD, p. 193). That is, it refers to the idealised presuppositions of a process of constitution making and interpretation among citizens 'tacitly presupposing, albeit counterfactually, the possibility of an agreement that is worthwhile to aim at' (LD, p. 192). The promise of future agreement and reconciliation, rather than the agreements of the past, Habermas argues, simultaneously provides room for disagreement and a 'stable point of reference'. The constative content of the constitution refers to the performativity of democratic lawmaking; there is, thus, no tension between the two. Instead the process proceeds in a 'performatively self-referential manner' (*BFN*, p. 128).

In the final analysis, both the standards of the past and the brightness of the future guarantee the reconciliation of constitutionalism and democracy and the unity of the process of constitution making. Constitutional democracy is framed by the constitutional tradition orientating the interpretations so that they do not multiply indefinitely. Similarly, the idea of a future reconciliation of constitutionalism and democracy fills the gap that may exist at any time between the two. In both cases, Habermas's conception of history and temporality reduces the past, present and future to different internal moments of the same (quasi-teleological) space.[15] Habermas presupposes that the process of constitution making, understood as a learning process, is of one piece. For instance, the orientation towards agreement and consensus in the future is not at stake, and neither is the learning process as a *progressive* learning process nor the perspective of past constitution making as *our* perspective. For instance, in Habermas's model, will the citizens of a future Iraq be able to disagree that their constitution is in fact *theirs* and not something imposed upon them by a past occupational power? Whether Habermas would in fact exclude such a critical attitude on the part of the Iraqis is unlikely, but it is not clear that he would not be forced to do so as a result of his theoretical standpoint.

Whether the standards of the past or the brightness of the future, disagreements are framed by and internal to a given space. This is what, following Cornelius Castoriadis, I refer to as 'spatialisation':[16] difference, disagreement, contingency, and constitutional democratic practices are framed by and contained within a space whose boundaries are given in advance. This framing serves to fill out the gap between constitutionalism and democracy, thus reconciling them, and it serves as a way to master difference, disagreement, contingency, and so on – in short, all the risks of constitutional democracy. In a similar vein, the notion of the future in Habermas's texts is what Jacques Derrida referred to as a 'future present'.[17] It is temporality, historicity and futurity understood as presence, as a modality of the present. It is a future understood as the continuation of the same, for instance, as the unfolding of a system of rights in the constitution, or as the anticipation of a future agreement. In both cases, what will be, and what can come to be, are already there in some form. Hence, Habermas is only able to close the gap between constitutionalism and democracy, and thus reconcile them, by casting as secondary the contingency and historicity of constitutional democracy that he has otherwise insisted are constitutive.

If, however, one insists on the irreducibility of disagreement and difference and on the ineradicability of contingency – and Habermas *also* does that – then the reconciliation of constitutionalism and democracy retains, and must retain, the character of *to come*, Derrida's term for a future ultimately irreducible to and heterogeneous to any present.[18] A future *to come* is not only different from the present or the past, but also has a temporal character that cannot be reduced to any spatial difference. The future *to come* cannot be mapped, not because it lies in a beyond, but because it is simultaneously constituted and deferred through our contingent and imperfect action here and now. Thus, the reconciliation of constitutionalism and democracy is always deferred and never present. For Habermas, this deferral is one that both should and can be overcome. Without the *telos* of agreement, democratic interpretation of the constitution would be 'a bizarre, even opaque practice' (LD, p. 192). However, as I shall argue in more detail below, this temporal out of joint-ness is also what makes practices of constitutional democracy meaningful. If constitutionalism and democracy were reconciled, if the addressees of the constitution were identical to its authors, or if we had arrived at a final and rational consensus eliminating all disagreement, there would be neither need nor room for deliberation, constitutional interpretation, or other practices of constitutional democracy. Only in the 'whirlpool of temporality' (*IO*, p. 255) can constitutional democracy be understood as a project for the *future*. Disagreement and contingency, vicious circularity and infinite regress, and so on, are not things to be overcome, but part of what makes constitutional democracy a worthwhile enterprise.

UNDECIDABILITY AND FICTIONS

The thrust of Habermas's co-originality thesis is that constitutionalism and democracy both enable and require one another. Without constitutionalism, democracy is lacking, and *vice versa*. However, my argument is that there always remains a gap between constitutionalism and democracy, and that this offers a better account of how constitutional democracy works.

Democracy must posit – retroactively, as it were – constitutionalism as prior to itself in order to be constitutional, because it cannot be properly democratic and legitimate without being simultaneously constitutional. Democracy must posit itself as always and already fully constitutional. Although constitutionalism is mediated by democracy, it must be posited as if it *will already have been* fully in place, prior to democracy. The process of democratic constitution making can only be legitimate if it is already constitutionally regulated. And yet, this is not all. Democracy must be constitutional, but constitutionalism must also be mediated by democracy in order not simply to be given to democracy from the outside.

The moment when democracy posits itself – 'in a sort of fabulous retroactivity'[19] – as constitutional, for instance, cannot be complete. The retroactive suture must be successful in order for democracy to be constitutional. Yet, it cannot succeed if democracy is not simply to be the vehicle of constitutionalism; that is, if democracy is not simply to be the repetition of constitutionalism. There must, in other words, remain a role for democracy in putting into place and interpreting constitutionalism, so that the performative aspect of democracy exceeds the constative aspect of constitutionalism. Democracy must also give, and not simply be given, the conditions of democratic constitution making, which are set down in the constitution. In order to be legitimate (and, indeed, in order to be democratic), democracy must be the continuation of constitutionalism, yet it must also be able to break with the latter. Likewise, constitutionalism must be at once iterable by (because the ground of) and alterable by (because the product of) democracy. In Derridean terms, constitutional democracy is marked by iterability, that is, by the undecidable relationship between iteration and alteration.[20] But this iterability – and the gap between constitutionalism and democracy – is required for its functioning. In Derrida's words: 'It is not a question here of an obscurity or of a difficulty of interpretation, of a problematic on the way to its (re)solution. . . . This obscurity, this undecidability between, let us say, a performative structure and a constative structure is *required* to produce the sought-after effect.'[21]

This is not a matter of either repetition or alteration, either continuity or discontinuity, or of more or less of one or the other. Rather, the undecidability arises because what is the condition of possibility of constitutionalism (namely, democracy) is simultaneously its condition of impossibility and limit (and *vice versa* from the viewpoint of democracy). It is not a problem that can be solved by choosing one over the other or by adjusting the relative weight of the two terms. When prioritising constitutionalism over democracy, for instance, you *also* get less constitutionalism, because the relation between the two is one of mutual competition *and* mutual presupposition.

Constitutionalism is, thus, simultaneously the condition of possibility and the condition of impossibility of democracy (and *vice versa*). One requires, yet – *contra* Habermas – is also limited by the other. Their relationship is undecidable. This undecidability can be expressed in terms of iterability, but it can also, and following the argument of the previous section, be expressed in terms of Derrida's notion of *différance*.[22] The relationship between constitutionalism and democracy is marked by a simultaneous lack and lag, both of which undermine the co-presence of constitutionalism and democracy. It is marked by a lack insofar as one is never fully present for the other, insofar as they differ through the constitutive gap between them; and it is marked by a lag insofar as their co-presence is always deferred, thus making constitutional democracy constitutively out of joint.

The relationship between constitutionalism and democracy is not one of either internality or externality, either mutually enabling conditions or limits. You cannot have one without the other, yet they stand at a slight distance from one another. It is not a distance that can be measured, or a gap that can be closed, though. This lack (or lag), the slight but infinite distance between constitutionalism and democracy, cannot be recuperated; it is constitutive. This is what makes constitutional democracy go around. Without the undecidability, constitutional democracy would not work. Without democracy as its condition of possibility, constitutionalism would not be properly constitutional, yet democracy, at the very moment it makes constitutionalism possible, also limits it. But, if democracy needs constitutionalism (and *vice versa*), then democracy cannot repair a lack in constitutionalism, because democracy will itself be lacking as a result of this incompleteness in constitutionalism. We cannot escape vicious circularity and infinite regress. The irreconcilability of constitutionalism and democracy – and the undecidability of their relation – both makes constitutional democratic practices meaningful and means that we live in an imperfect world and will continue to do so. This undecidability is not something to be regretted or overcome. We are caught in the vicious circularity and infinite regress resulting from this undecidability, but the overcoming of these would be the end to constitutional democracy. The undecidability not only explains better how constitutional democracy is in fact possible, because the reconciliation of the two components of constitutional democracy would be the end to it; the undecidability also provides a different view of the politics of constitutional democracy, which I shall return to in the two final sections of this chapter.

Habermas, of course, attempts to reconcile constitutionalism and democracy. As I argued above, he does so in two different ways: first, by situating the relationship between constitutionalism and democracy within a constitutional tradition; and, second, by situating the relationship within a quasi-teleological movement towards agreement and reconciliation. In both cases, they provide the frame for and stabilise the relationship between constitutionalism and democracy. They 'hold the place of the last instance'[23] so that we avoid vicious circularity and infinite regress. In either case

> discourse theory *simulates* an original condition: an arbitrary number of persons freely enter into a constitution making practice. The *fiction* of freedom *satisfies* the important condition of an original equality of the participating parties, whose 'yes' and 'no' count equally. . . . a series of constructive tasks that must be completed before the work of constitution making can actually begin. (CD, p. 776, my emphases)[24]

The fiction of constitution making under conditions of freedom and equality, posited outside and prior to the whirlpool of constitutionalism and democracy, frames the latter. It thereby secures their reconciliation and solves the vicious circularity and infinite regress. This fiction opens up a space and a time for constitutional democracy, but simultaneously closes them. For instance, the fiction frames the politics of constitutional democracy as a question of the reconciliation of constitutionalism and democracy. The fiction – the simulation, 'as if'[25] – serves to master undecidability by putting in place the conditions for the reconciliation of constitutionalism and democracy even before the politics of constitutional democracy have begun. '[I]n a sort of fabulous retroactivity',[26] the fiction asserts that equality and freedom have already been in place. The 'work of constitution making' only begins after these conditions are in place, according to Habermas, and so the political struggles over constitutionalism and democracy are relative to these conditions. But this means that 'the work of constitution making' only begins when it is already too late, when it would seem that there is no longer any point in it because constitutional democracy, and freedom and equality have already been put in place.

'A BIZARRE, EVEN OPAQUE PRACTICE': PHILOSOPHICAL AND POLITICAL STRATEGIES

This argument not only has implications for constitutional democracy, but also for how one reads and philosophises. The reading of Habermas's texts must proceed by locating the undecidability in his texts as well as those elements that make him able to reconcile constitutionalism and democracy. The conceptual unity of constitutional democracy in Habermas's texts is marked by the undecidability of presence and absence (*différance*) and continuity and discontinuity (iterability). This undecidability is displaced by the fictions; they serve as the conditions of possibility of reconciling constitutionalism and democracy. However, while these elements may well serve this purpose, they do no eradicate undecidability from the texts. The fiction of 'an original condition: an arbitrary number of persons freely enter into a constitution making practice' merely displaces the undecidability, because 'the work of constitution making can' then only 'actually begin' when it is already too late, when there is no longer any point to it.

Thus, rather than re-establishing the unity of the text, the deconstructive reading identifies the condition of possibility of its unity as simultaneously the limit of closure of the text. This does not mean that the deconstructive reading simply dissolves or negates constitutional democracy. Rather, as I have argued above, the textual undecidability in fact explains the possibility of constitutional democracy. As opposed to this, Habermas believes that '[b]y simply clarifying the concepts [of constitutionalism and democracy], the alleged paradox disappears: enabling conditions should not be confused with constraining conditions' (CD, p. 770). Habermas, like Seyla Benhabib[27] and David Ingram[28] conceive of the relationship between constitutionalism and democracy as a self-correcting learning process in which an inherent rationality is extracted through a process of immanent critique. At the level of philosophy and reading, this implies a hermeneutic circle of clarification. This difference over the role of philosophy is another way of expressing the difference between Habermasian rational reconstruction and Derridean deconstruction. So, despite the rapprochement between Derrida and Habermas prior to Derrida's death, important differences between their philosophical approaches nonetheless remain.

Constitutional democracy, then, does not work in spite of, but because of undecidability. Habermas's texts should be read as ultimately failed attempts to reconcile constitutionalism and democracy, and this failure is not accidental but structural. This is not a question of simply being true to or betraying Habermas's texts. A deconstructive reading cannot simply make the text transparent or neutralise whatever contradictions there may be in the text. For instance, one cannot neutralise the undecidability by referring to it as 'mistakes' on the part of the author. Instead, a deconstructive reading is an intervention into the text. The deconstructive reading will be caught in a double bind when, following the conceptual scheme governing the text, it comes upon something which is undecidable according to that scheme. At this point, the reading must *both* be 'true' to the text *and* displace and, as such, 'betray' the text (although not in the sense of betraying it in order to be true to it at another and higher level of rationality). These are competing injunctions, each excluding the other, and cannot be reconciled under a single rule for the reading of the text. As a consequence, every deconstructive reading is not only an intervention but also singular.

The constitutivity of undecidability does not mean that nihilism or conservative resignation are our only options. Just as the deconstructive strategy of reading is not guided by a *telos* of the unity of the text, so a deconstructive politics is not guided by a *telos* of reconciliation of constitutionalism and democracy. However, appeals to the fiction of democratic constitution making among free and equal individuals may serve as the starting point for critique.[29] While aporetic, the appeal to a fiction is also unavoidable, even if not necessarily in this or that particular form. It is important to be clear about the way in which I am using the term 'fiction', though. I borrow it from Habermas's texts, as one must always borrow the resources of deconstruction from what one is deconstructing, even if only in a strategic way.[30] Moreover, one should not understand 'fiction' in a simple opposition to 'real'. Although the fiction does involve the illusion of the co-presence of constitutionalism and democracy, its effects are real enough insofar as it secures their reconciliation. So, the argument here does not reject the use of fictions, only that we should be aware of their aporetic status; in the case of Habermas's constitutional democracy, if his fiction were true, it would render constitutional democracy meaningless as an ongoing practice. Nor does it mean that we have to give up on the big normative questions – how is equality possible? how is freedom possible? – to which the fictions are answers. These questions are unavoidable, even if there are no non-aporetic answers to them. The politics of constitutional democracy, then, becomes a question of how constitutionalism and democracy are articulated together and of what 'constitutionalism' and 'democracy' respectively should mean. This politics introduces a temporality that cannot be spatially mediated, one marked by *différance*; for instance, it cannot be viewed as a progressive learning process.

HONIG'S (DERRIDEAN?) ALTERNATIVE

Despite her deconstructive critique of attempts to spatialise and objectify politics, Bonnie Honig, in a recent critique of Habermas's co-originality thesis, partially succumbs to the temptation of spatialising the relationship between constitutionalism and democracy. Honig argues that we need constitutionalism because it can be an important political instrument.[31] Yet, constitutional '[r]ights are not dead instruments, they are live practices'.[32]

Constitutional rights must remain open to future contestation that cannot be understood in teleological terms, and, according to Honig, the correct relationship between constitutionalism and democracy will depend on the concrete circumstances.[33] However, Honig accepts Habermas's terms of the debate: 'Habermas,' she writes, 'rightly resists the choice [between constitutionalism and democracy] and tries to strike the right balance between the two . . . But he fails to strike the right balance'.[34] And, she continues,

> my sense is that it is not unfair to say that his impulse is to emphasize the importance of constitutionalism to democracy while neglecting to stress *equally* the importance of democracy – of *a*constitutionalism and democratic agency (and not just as a nutritional source, but also as a dangerous supplement) – to constitutionalism.[35]

Honig criticises the relative weight given by Habermas to the two principles of constitutionalism and democracy, but the appeal to 'the right balance' between the two principles implies a mediating ground between them, and she suggests that we think of the relationship in terms of a spectrum of more or less: 'Talk of a contradiction between constitutionalism and democracy, per se, prevents us from developing nuanced analyses of varying situations. Thinking in terms of a *constitutional/democracy spectrum rather than in terms of an abstract binary* might broaden our vision'.[36]

The problem is that the different ways of understanding the relationship between constitutionalism and democracy that Honig mentions (and some of which she endorses) all leave intact the concepts of constitutionalism and democracy and presuppose that they are constituted within an objective space: a contradiction presupposes that the two poles of the contradiction are fully constituted; a spectrum and a balance presuppose a mediating third to which both principles can be referred; and so on. In each case, the objectification – and, ultimately, the potential reconciliation at a higher level – of the relation between constitutionalism and democracy is still possible. Honig rightly criticises Habermas for his attempt to reconcile constitutionalism and democracy within a spatial conception of history.[37] However, she substitutes the balancing of constitutionalism and democracy for their reconciliation. The attempt to balance is itself spatial because it presupposes a third mediating point from which to balance constitutionalism and democracy, for instance a complete description of the relevant context.[38]

The relationship between constitutionalism and democracy is undecidable. There is a constitutive gap between constitutionalism and democracy, a slight but infinite distance that cannot be objectified, and, as a result, the two cannot be reconciled. But one must also avoid the opposite conclusion – equally spatialising – that constitutionalism and democracy can be kept apart or opposed. Their undecidability means that they are not only external but also, and at the same time, internal to one another. As Honig notes, Habermas is wrong to '[put] the two principles into a harmonious, non-zero sum relation'.[39] Here one need only add that it would be equally mistaken to put them into a simple zero sum relation. This is also why it does not make sense to speak of more or less, balancing or a spectrum: this presupposes what constitutional democracy is not, namely one-dimensional. Constitutionalism and democracy cannot be symmetrically opposed, and neither can depoliticisation and politicisation, closure and openness.

In an earlier work, Honig rightly criticised Hannah Arendt for depoliticising the constatives supporting her performatives. Yet, Honig also associated, on the one hand, constitutionalism (and the constative) with depoliticisation and, on the other hand, democracy (and the performative) with contestation and politicisation.[40] As Alan Keenan has rightly argued Honig oscillates between Arendt and Derrida.[41] This is also reflected in her critique of Habermas, when she argues that constitutionalism and the courts limit democracy and the will of the people. During the 2000 presidential election, 'the tension became an all-out fight over who would decide the outcome of the American presidential election: the Supreme Court or the people'.[42] This leads her to argue that what was needed with regard to the 2000 election was more democracy and less constitutionalism.[43] This misses the point, because it overlooks the mutually and simultaneously limiting and enabling relationship between constitutionalism and democracy. One may, of course, argue that the rules for counting the votes were too restrictive and, like the majority of the judges on the Supreme Court, biased in favour of one of the candidates. But it is not enough to demand that the votes be counted, because counting the votes (that is, identifying the will of the people) is mediated by rules stipulating how to count. Even if relatively fixed, these rules are highly political; in fact, part of what is political about them is the way they have been constructed as given and natural. Similarly, although political issues may be depoliticised by referring them to the courts (as has happened, for instance, in the cases of abortion and race relations), the courts are at the same time, and especially in the US, politicised. Hence, the relationship between constatives and performatives, constitutionalism and democracy, depoliticisation and politicisation, and so on, is not a straightforward competition or a relationship of mutual enablement only.

Any politics is partly spatial, asserting a ground and taking something as given, even if only temporarily. Yet, spatialisation not only limits openness and temporality, it also makes them possible. The politics of constitutional democracy cannot proceed as either closure or openness, as either depoliticisation or politicisation, or as either constitutionalism or democracy. We therefore need a site of contestation, but paradoxically it must at the same time be a non-site, a site that does not spatialise and frame contestation. The site must also itself be at stake. The ambition is to think this site as a point where constitutionalism and democracy are articulated; a site or space whose identity is at once different from itself and deferred, deterritorialised and temporalised. Honig provides an example of such a site with her reference to the clause in the Canadian constitution 'that allows provinces to opt out of constitutionally binding decisions for five years'.[44] It is not a site that would stop the vicious circularity or infinite regress of constitutional democracy. On the contrary, without these there would be no constitutional democracy for the future. If there is a motto for this deconstructive constitutional democratic politics it is this: keep open the gap between constitutionalism and democracy.[45]

One must, of course, resist the fetishisation of undecidability; it cannot become a new ground. Likewise, the names I have given to the aporias in Habermas's texts – undecidability, iterability, *différance* – are ways of accounting for the aporias, but they do not claim to be the last word, nor could they be. Like reading and philosophising, constitutional democracy is 'a bizarre, even opaque practice' (LD, p. 192).

NOTES

1. I would like to thank Lars Tønder, Paulina Ochoa-Espejo, Lars Ethelberg Nielsen, Ian O'Flynn and the participants at the conferences where I first presented this paper for their comments on earlier versions of the chapter. The research for the paper was supported financially by the ESRC and the Danish Research Academy.
2. Jürgen Habermas, *Between Facts and Norms: Contributions to a Discourse Theory of Law and Democracy*, trans. William Rehg (Cambridge, MA: MIT Press, 1996) [in the following: *BFN*], pp. 104, 127f.; Jürgen Habermas, *The Inclusion of the Other: Studies in Political Theory*, trans. Ciaran Cronin (Cambridge: Polity Press, 1998) [in the following: *IO*], chapter 10; Jürgen Habermas, 'Constitutional Democracy: A Paradoxical Union of Contradictory Principles?', trans. William Rehg, *Political Theory* 29: pp. 766–81 [in the following: *CD*]; and Jürgen Habermas, 'On Law and Disagreement. Some Comments on "Interpretative Pluralism"', *Ratio Juris* 16: pp. 187–94 [in the following: LD].

   Habermas uses a number of different sets of terms to refer to approximately the same: private and public (or civic) autonomy, individual (or human) rights and popular sovereignty, the rule of law and democracy, and constitutionalism and democracy. He uses these sets of terms more or less interchangeably, and I will not go into a deeper discussion of the differences among them.

   The relationship between constitutionalism and democracy is of course not a new problem or a problem confined to Habermas's work. For instance, Habermas himself traces it back to a discussion of Rousseau and Kant (*BFN*, pp. 100ff.; *IO*, chapter 10), and he engages in discussions with contemporaries such as Frank I. Michelman and Jeremy Waldron on just this question (*BFN*, pp. 100, 267ff.; CD; LD). Moreover, the relationship between constitutionalism and democracy is closely related to the paradoxical relationship between the constituting and the constituted powers. The most obvious points of reference here are Sieyès and Rousseau and, in a contemporary context, Paul Ricoeur, 'The Political Paradox', in W. E. Connolly (ed.), *Legitimacy and the State* (Oxford: Basil Blackwell, 1984).
3. The democratic principle states that 'only those [legal] statutes may claim legitimacy that can meet with the assent (*Zustimmung*) of all citizens in a discursive process of legislation that in turn has been legally constituted' (*BFN*, p. 110). The discourse

principle stipulates that 'Just those action norms are valid to which all possibly affected persons could agree as participants in rational discourses' (*BFN*, p. 107) This is also expressed in the 'system of rights' that Habermas reconstructs as the basis of legitimate law and of constitutional democracy (*BFN*, pp. 121ff.).

4. Bonnie Honig, 'Dead Rights, Live Futures: A Reply to Habermas's "Constitutional Democracy"', *Political Theory* 29:6 (2001), pp. 792–805. For a revised version of this paper, see Chapter 10 in the present volume; I will continue to refer to the original text.
5. Honig, 'Dead Rights, Live Futures'; Seyla Benhabib, 'Democracy and Difference: Reflections on the Metapolitics of Lyotard and Derrida', Chapter 8 in this volume; David Ingram, 'Novus Ordo Seclorum: The Trial of (Post)Modernity or the Tale of Two Revolutions', in L. May and J. Kohn (eds), *Hannah Arendt Twenty Years Later* (Cambridge, MA: MIT Press, 1996), pp. 221–50; and Sofia Näsström, 'What Globalization Overshadows', *Political Theory* 31:6 (2003), pp. 808–34. See also Peter Lassman, 'Political theory as utopia', *History of the Human Sciences* 16:1 (2003), pp. 49–62.
6. Given Habermas's view that the constitution is not given once and for all, the distinction between constitution making and interpretation of the constitution is blurred.
7. Benhabib, 'Democracy and Difference', pp. 131, 139, 140–1.
8. Frank I. Michelman, 'Constitutional Authorship', in L. Alexander (ed.), *Constitutionalism: Philosophical Foundations* (Cambridge: Cambridge University Press, 1998), pp. 64–98.
9. Habermas is facing a Münchhausen trilemma: he must avoid vicious circularity, infinite regress, and arbitrary decisionism.
10. Honig, 'Dead Rights, Live Futures'.
11. LD, p. 192. For an example of the kind of position that Habermas criticises, see Alessandro Ferrara's communitarian-republican critique of Habermas: 'Of Boats and Principles: Reflections on Habermas's "Constitutional Democracy"', *Political Theory* 29:6 (2001), pp. 782–91.
12. Honig, 'Dead Rights, Live Futures', p. 795.
13. Indeed, if progress is possible and the past and present therefore imperfect, the past and present must be open to improvement and even rejection, cf. Ingram, 'Novus Ordo Seclorum', pp. 238ff.
14. It is not clear to what extent Habermas sees the two lines of argument as distinct or the second line as a correction to the first. The focus on the performativity and the promise of agreement of the process of constitution making is most pronounced in his most recent work, cf. LD.
15. Honig, 'Dead Rights, Live Futures', pp. 796f.
16. Cornelius Castoriadis, *The Imaginary Institution of Society*, trans K. Blamey (Cambridge, MA: MIT Press, 1987), pp. 187–96.
17. Jacques Derrida, *Specters of Marx: The State of the Debt, the Work of Mourning, and the New International*, trans. P. Kamuf (London: Routledge, 1994), pp. 64f.
18. Ibid., pp. 28, 64f.
19. Jacques Derrida, 'Declarations of Independence', in Jacques Derrida, *Negotiations: Interventions and Interviews, 1971–2001*, ed. Elizabeth Rottenberg, trans. Tom Keenan and Tom Pepper (Stanford: Stanford University Press, 2002), pp. 46–54, at p. 50. Derrida is writing about the foundation of a republic, not about constitutionalism and democracy, but his argument is analogous to the one I am making here. See also Jacques Derrida, 'The Laws of Reflection: Nelson Mandela, in Admiration', trans. Mary Ann Caws and Isabelle Lorenz, in J. Derrida and M. Tlili (eds), *For Nelson Mandela* (New York: Seaver Books, 1987), pp. 11–42; and, for a succinct summary of Derrida, Noah Horwitz, 'Derrida and the Aporia of the Political, or The Theologico-Political Dimension of Deconstruction', *Research in Phenomenology* 32 (2002), pp. 156–76.

20. Jacques Derrida, *Margins of Philosophy*, trans. A. Bass (London: Harvester Wheatsheaf, 1982), pp. 315–30.
21. Derrida, 'Declarations of Independence', p. 49.
22. Derrida, *Margins of Philosophy*, pp. 1–27.
23. Bonnie Honig, *Political Theory and the Displacement of Politics* (Ithaca: Cornell University Press, 1993), p. 106.
24. For a similar formulation in a different context, see *IO*, p. 116. For Derrida on the use of 'fictions' in a related context, see Derrida, 'The Laws of Reflection', p. 18. Similarly, with reference to Habermas among others, Näsström, argues that democracy needs to supplement its factual history with a normative fiction in order to work (Näsström, 'What Globalization Overshadows', pp. 819–21. Here I would only add, that the fiction does not need to be normative (if we by that understand something as opposed to factual), but can also be a certain description of history. See for instance Habermas's rendition of US constitutional history (CD, pp. 774f.). For Habermas, it is important to show how the fiction of freedom and equality is inherent to certain historical structures, including modern constitutional democracy so that there is an inherent relation 'between facts and norms' (*BFN*).
25. Honig, 'Dead Rights, Live Futures', p. 795.
26. Derrida, 'Declarations of Independence', p. 50.
27. Benhabib, 'Democracy and Difference', p. 140.
28. Ingram, 'Novus Ordo Seclorum', p. 245.
29. Derrida, 'The Laws of Reflection'; and Horwitz, 'Derrida and the Aporia of the Political', pp. 166–70.
30. Jacques Derrida, *Positions*, 2nd edition, trans. Alan Bass (London: Continuum, 2002), p. 10.
31. Honig, 'Dead Rights, Live Futures', p. 799.
32. Ibid., p. 800.
33. Ibid., p. 801.
34. Ibid., p. 799.
35. Ibid., p. 800.
36. Ibid., p. 801.
37. Ibid., p. 799.
38. Compare CD, p. 801. In Derrida's words, there is a 'structural nonsaturation' of the context, cf. Derrida, *Margins of Philosophy*, p. 310. Hence, constitutionalism and democracy are articulated anew in each context, but the contingency of this articulation cannot be dissolved in an objectification of the context.
39. Honig, 'Dead Rights, Live Futures', p. 793.
40. Honig, *Political Theory and the Displacement of Politics*, pp. 120–25.
41. Alan Keenan, *Democracy in Question: Democratic Openness in a Time of Political Closure* (Stanford: Stanford University Press, 2003), pp. 212f.
42. Honig, 'Dead Rights, Live Futures', p. 792.
43. Ibid., pp. 792f., 801.
44. Honig, 'Dead Rights, Live Futures', p. 801. Compare Derrida's deconstruction of the *khôra* in Jacques Derrida, '*Khôra*', trans. Ian McLeod, in Jacques Derrida, *On the Name* (Stanford: Stanford University Press, 1995).
45. Näsström, 'What Globalization Overshadows', p. 829; and Chantal Mouffe, *The Democratic Paradox* (London: Verso, 2000).

11

Jürgen Habermas

RELIGIOUS TOLERANCE – THE PACEMAKER FOR CULTURAL RIGHTS*

In much of his later work, Habermas has addressed the irreducible fact of pluralism in contemporary societies. He argues that although societies are ethically divided – for instance, along religious lines – it is possible to integrate them through a shared political culture crystallised around a constitutional patriotism. Tolerance is an important part of this, and it is the topic of this chapter.

The problem with traditional accounts of tolerance, according to Habermas, is that they conceive of tolerance as an asymmetrical and one-sided relationship where the tolerated depends on the tolerating bestowing tolerance upon her as an act of grace. As a consequence, tolerance is paternalistic and does not involve the equal respect of persons. While Habermas is critical of this notion of tolerance, his rational reconstruction of the concept of tolerance is meant to save what he sees as its inherent normative content. He argues that, in a pluralist society where no particular conception of the good can be privileged over another, an intersubjectivist notion of tolerance avoids the paternalistic attitude. Thus conceived, tolerance emerges from the parties' mutual recognition as equal partners in a dialogue over the norms that should govern society.

This chapter also gives a good sense of Habermas's method of rational reconstruction. Although critical of many contemporary practices, including tolerance, Habermas nevertheless believes that these practices, along with the tradition of modernity itself, contain a normative content that can be critically appropriated. What is more, Habermas is not only interested in concepts but also social practice, reflecting his view that philosophy and the social sciences are intrinsically linked and inform one another.

---

(1) It was not until the 16th century that the German language borrowed the word 'Toleranz' – or tolerance – from the Latin and French, which is why in the context of the Reformation the concept immediately assumed the narrow meaning of toleration of other religious confessions.[1] In the course of the 16th and 17th centuries, religious toleration becomes a legal concept. Governments issued toleration edicts that compelled state officials and the population to be tolerant in their behaviour toward religious minorities, such as Lutherans, Huguenots, and Papists.[2] Legal acts of toleration by state authorities led the expectation that people (as a rule the majority of the population[3]) behave tolerantly toward members of religious communities that had until then been oppressed or persecuted.

With greater precision than in German, in English, the word 'tolerance' as a form of behaviour is distinguished from 'toleration', the legal act with which a government grants more or less unrestricted permission to practice one's own particular religion. In German, the predicate 'tolerant' refers to both, to a legal order that guarantees toleration and to the political virtue of tolerant behaviour. Montesquieu emphasizes the constitutive link between toleration and tolerance: 'As soon as the laws of a land have come to terms with permitting several religions, they must oblige these to show tolerance also to one another.'[4] Through to the French Revolution the concept not only retains its link to religious addressees, but also the authoritarian connotation of *mere* toleration. That said, ever since the days of Spinoza and Locke the philosophical justifications given for religious tolerance point the absolutist state in a direction away from *unilaterally* declared religious toleration, the limits of which are defined by the authorities, and towards a conception of tolerance based on the *mutual* recognition of everybody's religious freedom. Rainer Forst contrasts the 'concept of permission' issued by the authorities who grant religious freedoms to the 'concept of respect' that concurs with our understanding of religious freedom as a civil right.[5]

Pierre Bayle already dreamed up various examples in order to force his intolerant opponents to adopt also the perspective of the other persons and to apply their own principles to their opponents, too: 'If it should thus suddenly cross the Mufti's mind to send some missionaries to the Christians, just as the Pope sends such to India, and someone were to surprise these Turkish missionaries in the process of forcing their way into our houses to

---

Jürgen Habermas, 'Religious Tolerance – The Pacemaker for Cultural Rights', *Philosophy*, 79, 2004, pp. 5–18.

fulfill their duties converting us, then I do not believe we would have the authority to punish them. For if they were to give the same answers as the Christian missionaries in Japan, namely that they had arrived to zealously familiarize those with the true religion who were not yet acquainted with it, and to care for the salvation of their fellow men – now if we were to string up these Turks, would it not then actually be ridiculous to find it bad if the Japanese did the same thing?'[6] Bayle, who in this respect was the forerunner of Kant, practices mutual perspective-taking. He insists on the *universalization of* those 'ideas' in the light of which we judge 'the nature of human action'.[7]

On this basis of a *reciprocal* recognition of the rules of tolerant behaviour we can find a solution to the paradox which prompted Goethe to reject toleration as insulting and patronizing benevolence. The ostensible paradox is that each act of toleration must circumscribe the range of behaviour everybody must accept, thereby drawing a line for what can*not* be tolerated. There can be no inclusion without exclusion. And as long as this line is drawn in an authoritarian manner, i.e., unilaterally, the stigma of arbitrary exclusion remains inscribed in toleration. Only with a *universally convincing* delineation of the borderline, and this requires that all those involved *reciprocally* take the perspectives of the others, can toleration blunt the thorn of intolerance. Everyone who could be affected by the future practice must first voluntarily agree on those conditions under which they wish to exercise mutual toleration.

The usual conditions for liberal co-existence between different religious communities stand this test of reciprocity. They refer in the first place to prohibiting the use of political power for missionary purposes, and to the freedom of association that also prevents religious authorities being able to influence their members' conscience compulsorily. Only if they find intersubjective recognition across confessional boundaries can such specifying norms provide justifications that *out-trump* those personally maintained reasons for rejecting alien religious convictions and practices. Even if there is no historical substantiation for Jellinek's suggestion that all human rights are rooted in religious freedom, there is certainly a conceptual link between the universalistic justification for religious tolerance, on the one hand, and democracy as the basis for legitimation for a secular state, on the other.

The purported paradox dissolves if we conceive of religious freedom – covering both, the right to free expression of one's own religion and the corresponding negative freedom to remain undisturbed by the others' practicing their respective religions – as part of a democratic constitution. Religious tolerance can be practiced in a tolerant manner precisely under those conditions which the citizens of a democratic community mutually accord one another. From the viewpoint of the democratic lawmaker who makes the addressees of such a law likewise the authors thereof, the legal act of mutual toleration melds with the virtuous self-obligation to behave tolerantly.

(2) However, the paradox does not seem to be fully resolved by the reciprocal generalization of religious freedom, since it appears to reemerge, in secular terms, at the very core of the constitutional state. A democratic order that guarantees tolerance also in terms of political freedoms, such as free speech, must take preventive protection against the enemies of that very core of the constitution. At latest since the 'legal' transition from the Weimar Republic to the Nazi régime we in Germany have become aware of the necessity of selfassertion – but equally of that strange dialectic of the self-assertion of a 'militant' democracy that is 'prepared to defend itself'.[8] Courts can on a case-by-case basis pass judgment on the limits of religious freedom, basing their conclusions on the law. However, if the constitution faces the opposition of enemies who make use of their political freedom in order to abolish the constitution that grants it, then the question arises as to the limits of political freedom in a selfreferential form. How tolerantly may a democracy treat the enemies of democracy?

If the democratic state does not wish to give itself up, then it must resort to intolerance toward the enemy of the constitution, either bringing to bear the means afforded by political criminal law or by decreeing the prohibition of particular political parties (Article 21.2 of the German Constitution) and the forfeiture of basic rights (Article 18 and Article 9.2 of the same). The 'enemy of the state', a concept originally with religious connotations, resurfaces in the guise of the enemy of the constitution: be it in the secularized figure of the political ideologist who combats the liberal state, or in the religious shape of the fundamentalist who violently attacks the modern way of life *per se*. Today's terrorists seem to embody a combination of both. Yet it is precisely the agencies of the constitutional state itself who define what or who shall be classified as an enemy of the constitution. A constitutional state must perform a twofold act here: it must repel the animosity of existential enemies while avoiding any betrayal of its own principles – in other words, it is exposed in this situation to the constantly lurking danger of itself being guilty of retrogressively resorting to an authoritarian practice of *unilaterally* deciding the limits of tolerance. Those who are suspicious of being 'enemies of the state' might well turn out to be radical defenders of democracy. This is the problem: Whereas the task of a seemingly paradoxical self-limitation of religious tolerance can be ceded to democracy, the latter must process the conundrum of constitutional tolerance through the medium of its own laws.

A self-defensive democracy can sidestep the danger of paternalism only by allowing the self-referentiality of the self-establishing democratic process to be brought to bear on controversial interpretations of constitutional principles. In this regard, it is something like a litmus test, how a constitutional state treats the issue of civil disobedience. Needless to say, the constitution itself decides what the procedure should be in the case of conflicts over the correct interpretation of the constitution. With a legal recognition of '*civil disobedience*' (which does not mean it does not punish such acts), the tolerant spirit of a liberal constitution extends even beyond the ensemble of those existing institutions and practices in which its normative contents have become actually embodied so far. A democratic constitution that is understood as the project of realizing equal civil rights tolerates the resistance shown by dissidents who, even after all the legal channels have been exhausted, still insist on combating decisions that came about legitimately. Under the proviso, of course, that the 'disobedient' citizens plausibly justify their resistance by citing constitutional principles and express it by nonviolent, i.e., symbolic means.[9] These two conditions again specify the limits of political tolerance in a constitutional democracy that defends itself against its enemies by non-paternalist means – and they are limits that are acceptable for its democratically minded opponents, too.

By recognizing civil disobedience, the democratic state copes with the paradox of tolerance that reoccurs at the level of constitutional law in a tolerant manner. It draws a line between a tolerant and a self-destructive handling of ambivalent dissidents in such a way as to ensure that these persons (who could in the final analysis transpire to be enemies of the constitution) nevertheless have the opportunity contrary to their image to prove themselves to actually be the true patriotic champions of a constitution that is dynamically understood as an ongoing *project* – the project to exhaust and implement basic rights in changing historical contexts.

(3) Now, pluralism and the struggle for religious tolerance were not only driving forces behind the emergence of the democratic state, but continue to stimulate its further evolution up to now. Before addressing religious tolerance as the pacemaker for multiculturalism, in the correct sense of the term, allow me to analyse the concept of tolerance a bit further (a) and to explain the specific burden imposed on citizens by the expectation to behave tolerantly (b). For the purpose of conceptual analysis it is useful to distinguish the two kinds of reasons that are involved: reasons to reject the convictions of others and reasons to accept nevertheless common membership of essentially disagreeing people within the same political community. From the latter reasons – political reasons for civic inclusion – the third kind of reasons, I have already mentioned, can be derived – reasons for the limits of tolerance and the repression of intolerant behaviour. These legal reasons then open the door to the justification of cultural rights.

(a) The religious context of discovering tolerance brings first to mind the key component of a 'rejection based on existentially relevant conviction'. That rejection is a condition necessary for all kinds of tolerant behaviour. We can only exercise tolerance towards other people's beliefs if we reject them for subjectively *good* reasons. We do not need to be tolerant if we are indifferent to other opinions and attitudes anyway or even appreciate the value of such 'otherness'. The expectation of tolerance assumes that we can endure a form of ongoing non-concurrence at the level of social interaction, while we accept the persistence of mutually exclusive validity claims at the cognitive level of existentially relevant beliefs. We are expected to neutralize the practical impact of a cognitive dissonance that nevertheless calls for further attempts to resolve it within its own domain. In other words, we must be able to socially accept mutual cognitive dissonances that will remain unresolved for the time being. Yet such a cognitive difference must prove to be 'reasonable' if tolerance is to be a meaningful response here. Tolerance can only come to bear if there are legitimate justifications for the rejection of competing validity claims: 'If someone rejects people whose skin is black we should not call on him to be "tolerant toward people who look different" . . . For then we would accept his prejudice as an ethical judgment similar to the rejection of a different religion. A racist should not be tolerant, he should quite simply overcome his racism.'[10] In this and similar cases, we consider a critique of the *prejudices* and the struggle against *discrimination* to be the appropriate response – and not 'more tolerance'.

The issue of tolerance only arises after those prejudices have been eliminated that led to discrimination in the first place. But what gives us the right to call those descriptions 'prejudices' that a religious fundamentalist, a racist, the sexual chauvinist, the radical nationalist or the xenophobic ethnocentric have of their respective 'other'? This points to the second kind of reasons. We allow ourselves those stigmatizing expressions in light of the egalitarian and universalistic standards of democratic citizenship, something that calls for the equal treatment of the 'other' and mutual recognition of all as 'full' members of the political community. The norm of complete inclusion of all citizens as members with equal rights must be accepted before all of us, members of a democratic community, can mutually expect one another to be tolerant. It is the standard of non-discrimination that first provides this expectation with moral and legal reasons that can *out-trump* the epistemic reasons for the persisting rejection of those convictions and attitudes, we merely tolerate. On the base of that normative agreement, the potential for conflict in the cognitive dimension of ongoing contradictions between competing worldviews can be defused in the social dimension of shared citizenship. Thus, tolerance only begins where discrimination ends.

(b) Keeping in mind both kinds of reasons, reasons for rejection at the cognitive, and for acceptance on the social level, we can better answer the question of which sort of burden the tolerant person is expected to carry. What exactly must this person 'endure'? As we have seen, it is not the contradiction between premises and perspectives of different worldviews that has to be 'accepted' as such: there is no contradiction in one's own head. An unresolved contradiction remains only in the interpersonal dimension of the encounter of different persons who are aware that they hold contradictory beliefs. The crux is rather the neutralization or containment of specific practical consequences of unresolved contradictions. To tolerate that pragmatic contradiction means a twofold burden: She who is tolerant may only realize the ethos inscribed in her own worldview within the limits of what everyone is accorded. The way of life prescribed by a particular religion or worldview may be realized only under conditions of equal rights for everybody. And, within these limits she must also respect the ethos of the others.

This burden is of a cognitive kind to the extent that those beliefs in which each person's ethos is rooted must be brought into harmony with the liberal norms of state and society. What this requires can be seen from the accommodation of religion in modern Europe. Every religion is originally a '*worldview*' or, as John Rawls would say, a 'comprehensive doctrine' – also in the sense that it lays claim to the authority to structure a form of life in its entirety. A religion has to relinquish this claim to an encompassing definition of life as soon as the life of the religious community is differentiated from the life of the larger society. A hitherto prevailing religion forfeits its political impact on society at large if the political regime can no longer obey just one universal ethos. Emancipated minority religions face a similar challenge. By having to deal with the fact of pluralism, religious doctrines are forced to reflect on their own relations to the environments of the liberal state and a secularized society. This results, among other things, in the renunciation of violence and the acceptance of the voluntary character of religious association. Violence may not be used to advance religious beliefs, both inside and outside the community.[11] However, the major religions must appropriate the normative foundations of the liberal state under conditions of *their own premises* even if (as in the European case of the Judaeo-Christian legacy) both evolved from the same historical context.

John Rawls has chosen the image of a module in order to describe the 'embedding' of the political morality of equal respect for everybody in different religious world views. The normative frame of the liberal state is a module that, because it is constructed by means of neutral or secular reasons, fits into different orthodox chains of justifications.[12] Compared with the idea of a rational religion that absorbs the moral substance shared by all religious doctrines, that image of a module has the advantage of not denying that those mutually exclusive belief-systems raise absolute claims to truth. It therefore does not need to downplay the radical thrust of a cognitively challenging tolerance. Depending on the context of the doctrine, a respectively different dogmatic solution will be found to the problem of finding justifications for human rights from within. In functional terms, religious tolerance should absorb the social destructiveness of irreconcilably persistent dissent. The latter may not tear the social bond that ties believers to those who believe in other faiths or are unbelievers. However, the functional solution requires the solving of a cognitive problem.

If conflicts of loyalty are not to simmer, the necessary role differentiation between members of one's own religious community and co-citizens of the larger society needs to be justified convincingly from one's internal viewpoint. Religious membership is in tune with its secular counterpart only if (from the internal point of view of each) the corresponding norms and values are not only different *from each other*, but if the one set of norms can consistently be derived *from the other*. If differentiation of both memberships is to go beyond a mere *modus vivendi*, then the modernization of religious consciousness must not be limited to some cognitively undiscerning attempt to ensure that the religious ethos conforms to externally *imposed* laws of the secular society. It calls instead for developing the normative principles of the secular order from within the view of a respective religious tradition and community. In many cases this makes it necessary to revise attitudes and prescriptions that (as with the dogmatic prejudice against homosexuality for example) claim support from a long-standing traditions of interpretations of holy scriptures.

(4) Thus, the cognitive demand we make of someone in expectation of tolerance is the following: he shall develop from his own worldview reasons that tell him why he may realize the ethos inscribed in that view only within the limits of what everyone is allowed to do and to pursue. Of course, these limits themselves are often up for discussion, at which point the courts decide who must accept whose ethos – the majority that of a minority, or vice versa.[13] This brings me, following the reasons for rejection and acceptance, on to the third kind of reasons. The legal *reasons for excluding intolerant behaviour* provide the yardstick for measuring whether the state adheres to the imperative of remaining neutral and whether legislature and jurisdiction have institutionalized tolerance in the right way. Let me first discuss some familiar examples (a) and then introduce the notion of a cultural right (b).

(a) Sikhs in Great Britain and the United States gained exceptions from generally binding safety regulations and are permitted to wear turbans (rather than crash helmets) and daggers (kirpans). In Germany Jehovah's Witnesses successfully fought for being recognized as a public-law entity ('Anstalt öffentlichen Rechts') and thereby gained the same legal privileges our large churches enjoy. In these cases when minorities call for equal standing, for exceptions from established laws, or for special subsidies (e.g. for curricula transmitting the language and tradition of a minority culture), in many cases the courts must decide who has to accept whose ethos or form of life: Must the Christian inhabitants of the village accept the call of the muezzin? Must the local majority for strict animal protection accept the ritual slaughter of poultry and cattle by Jewish butchers? Must the non-confessional pupils, or those of different confessions, accept the Islamic teacher's head scarf? Must the owner of the grocery shop accept the decision of his employee to wear what to the customers appear conspicuously strange symbols or clothes? Must the Turkish father accept coeducational sports for his daughters at public schools?

In all these cases religious freedom tests the neutrality of the state. Frequently neutrality is threatened by the predominance of a majority culture, which abuses its historically acquired influence and definitional power to decide according to its own standards what shall be considered the norms and values of the political culture which is expected to be equally shared by all.[14] This implicit fusion of the common political culture with a divisive majority culture leads to the infiltration of the manifest legal form by inconspicuous cultural substance, thus distorting the very procedural nature of a democratic order. After all, the moral *substance* of democratic principles is spelled out in terms of legal *procedures* that can only build up legitimacy because they enjoy a reputation of granting impartiality by focusing consideration on all interests equally. Legal procedures thus stand to lose the force to found legitimacy if notions of a substantial ethical life slowly creep into the interpretation and practice of formal requirements. In this regard, political neutrality can be violated just as easily by the secular or laical side as by the religious camp.

For the one side, the paramount example is the *affaire foulard*, for the other, the response of the Bavarian State government to the German Supreme Court's judgment on whether crucifixes should be mandatory for classrooms in elementary schools. In the former case, the headmaster of a French school prohibited Muslim girls to wear their traditional head scarves; in the other, the German Supreme Court agreed with the complaint brought by anthroposophical parents that there should be no crucifix in the classroom in which their daughter had to sit for lessons. In the French case, positive religious freedom is called into question; in the German case, it is the negative version which is cast into doubt. The Catholic opponents of the crucifix verdict of our Supreme Court defend the religious symbol of the crucified Christ as an expression of 'Occidental values' and thus as part of a political culture which all citizens may be expected to share. This is the classical case of a political over-generalization of a regionally dominant religious practice, as it was reflected in the Bavarian Public Primary School Order of 1983. By contrast, in France the Muslim pupils were forbidden from wearing head scarves – the laical argument given was that religion is a private matter that has to be kept out of the public domain. This is the case of a secularist interpretation of the constitution that must face the challenge whether the republican interpretation of constitutional principles that prevails in France is not too 'strong' and is thus not able to avoid violating due neutrality of the state vis-à-vis legitimate claims of a religious minority to enjoy the right of self-expression and to receive public recognition.

These legal conflicts show why the spread of religious tolerance – and we have seen that it was already a driving force for the emergence of democracies – has now become also a stimulus for developing further cultural rights. The inclusion of religious minorities in the political community kindles and fosters sensitivity to the claims of other discriminated groups. The recognition of religious pluralism can fulfil the role of a pacemaker in legal development, as it makes us aware in an exemplary fashion of the *claims of minorities to civic inclusion*. One might object that the debate on multiculturalism hinges less on neglecting religious minorities than on other issues such as defining national holidays, specifying official language(s), promoting instruction for ethnic and national minorities, set quotas for women, colored people, indigenous populations at the working place, in schools or politics. From the viewpoint of equal inclusion of all citizens, however, religious discrimination takes its place in the long list of forms of cultural and linguistic, ethnic and racial, sexual and physical discrimination, and thus function as a pacemaker of 'cultural rights'. Let me explain what I mean by this term.

Inclusion refers to one of two aspects of the equal standing of citizens, or civic equality. Although the discrimination of minorities is usually associated with social under-privileging, it is well worth keeping these two categories of unequal treatment separate. The one is measured against the yardstick of *distributive justice*, the other against that of *full membership*.[15] From the viewpoint of distributive justice, the principle of equal treatment of everybody requires that all citizens have the same opportunities to make actual use of equally distributed rights and liberties in order to realize their own particular life plans. Political struggles and social movements opposing status deprivation and fighting for redistribution are fuelled by the experiences of injustice at the level of distributive justice. By contrast, the struggles that relate to the *recognition of a specific collective identity* are based on a different kind of experience of injustice – not status deprivation but disregard, marginalization or exclusion depending on membership in a group, considered as 'inferior' according to prevailing standards.[16] From this aspect of incomplete inclusion, overcoming religious discrimination is the pacemaker for a new kind of cultural rights.

Cultural rights serve, as does the freedom to practice one's religion, the purpose of guaranteeing all citizens equal access to those associations, communication patterns, traditions and practices, which they respectively deem important in order to develop and maintain their personal identities. Cultural rights need not in each case refer to the ascribed group of origin; the personal identity in need of protection can just as well be based on a chosen and achieved environment. Religious convictions and practices have a decisive influence on the ethical conception of believers in all cultures. Linguistic and cultural traditions are similarly relevant for the formation and maintenance of one's own personal identity. In light of this insight we need to revise the traditional conception of the 'legal person'. The individuation of natural persons occurs through socialization. Individuals socialized in this manner can form and stabilize their identity only within a network of relationships of reciprocal recognition. This should have consequences for the protection of the integrity of the legal person – and for an intersubjectivist expansion of a person concept that has to date been tailored to the narrow lens of the tradition of possessive individualism.

All rights protecting the integrity of an individual define the legal status of that person. These rights must now extend to the access to that community's matrix of experience, communication and recognition, within which people can articulate their self-understanding and maintain their identity. From this angle, cultural rights are introduced as individual rights in the first place. In line with the model of religious freedom, they are what German lawyers call 'subjective rights', designed for the purpose of granting full inclusion.[17] The point of cultural rights is to guarantee all citizens equal access to cultural environments, interpersonal relations and traditions as far as these are essential for them to form and secure their personal identity.

Yet cultural rights do not just mean 'more difference' and 'more independence' for cultural groups and their leaders. Members of discriminated groups do not enjoy equal cultural rights 'free of charge'. They cannot benefit from a morality of equal inclusion without themselves making this morality their own. The cognitive demand the liberal state makes of religious communities is all the same for 'strong' secular communities (such as national or ethnic minorities, immigrant or indigenous populations, descendants of slave cultures, etc.).[18] The traditions they continue open up 'world perspectives' that, *like* religious world views, can come into conflict with one another.[19] Therefore, cultural groups are equally expected to adapt their internal ethos to the egalitarian standards of the community at large. Some of them may find this even tougher than do those communities who are able to resort to the highly developed conceptual resources of one or the other of the great world religion.

Anyway, the leap in reflexivity that has come to characterize the modernization of religious consciousness within liberal societies provides a model for the mind-set of secular groups in multicultural societies as well. A multiculturalism that does not misunderstand itself does not constitute a *one-way street* to cultural self-assertion by groups with their own collective identities. The coexistence of different life forms as equals must not be allowed to prompt segmentation. Instead, it requires the integration of all citizens – and their mutual recognition across cultural divisions as citizens – within the framework of a shared political culture. Citizens are equally empowered to develop what is for them their cultural identity and might appear to others as cultural idiosyncrasies, but only under the condition that all of them (across boundaries) understand themselves to be citizens of one and the same political community. From this point of view, the very same normative base of the constitution that justifies cultural rights and entitlements likewise limits a kind of aggressive self-assertion that leads to fragmenting the larger community.

NOTES

* Royal Institute of Philosophy Annual Lecture, 2003.

1. See the *Allgemeine Handwörterbuch der philosophischen Wissenschaften nebst ihrer Literatur und Geschichte*, ed. Wilhelm Traugott Krug (2nd edn., 1832): 'Toleranz (von tolerare, dulden, ertragen) ist Duldsamkeit . . . Doch wird jenes Wort

meist im engeren Sinne von religiöser Duldsamkeit gebraucht, wie das entgegengesetzte Intoleranz von der religiösen Unduldsamkeit'.

2. In 1598, Henri IV of France issued the *Edict of Nantes*, see also the *Act Concerning Religion* passed by the Government of Maryland in 1649, the *Toleration Act* issued by the King of England in 1689 or – as one of the last instances in this chain of sovereign 'authorizations' – the 'Patent of Toleration' proclaimed by Joseph II in 1781.
3. The case was different in Maryland, where a Catholic minority ruled over a Protestant majority.
4. Quoted from C. Herdtle, Th. Leeb (eds), *Toleranz, Texte zur Theorie und politischen Praxis* (Stuttgart, 1987), p. 49.
5. See note 10.
6. P. Bayle, quoted from Herdtle & Leeb (1987), p. 42.
7. Ibid., p. 38.
8. K. Loewenstein, 'Militant Democracy and Fundamental Rights', *American Political Science Review* (31), 1937; see also his *Verfassungslehre*, 3rd edition, 1975, pp. 348ff.
9. On the problematic issue of civil disobedience see my two essays in: J. Habermas, *Die Neue Unübersichtlichkeit*, Frankfurt/Main, 1985, 79–117.
10. R. Forst, 'Der schmale Grat zwischen Ablehnung und Akzeptanz', *Frankfurter Rundschau* (Dec. 28, 2001).
11. J. Rawls, *Political Liberalism* (New York: Columbia UP), 1993, pp. 58ff.
12. J. Rawls, loc. cit. pp. 11ff.
13. See the list offered by D. Grimm in the *Frankfurter Allgemeine Zeitung*, of June 21, 2002, p. 49: 'Can a Sikh riding a motorcycle be excused from obeying the general law to wear a helmet on grounds of his religious duty to wear a turban? Must a Jewish prisoner be offered kosher food? Does a Muslim employee have the right to briefly interrupt his work time in order to pray? Can an employee be fired because he did not appear for work on the High holy days? Does an employee dismissed for this reason forfeit his entitlement to unemployment benefits? Must Jewish entrepreneurs be permitted to open their businesses on Sundays simply because for religious reasons they had to keep them shut on Saturday? Does a Muslim pupil have the right to be exempted from PE classes because she is not allowed to show herself to other pupils wearing sports clothes? May Muslim pupils wear headscarves in class? What is the case if the woman concerned is a teacher at a government-owned school? Should the law be different for nuns than it is for a Muslim teacher? . . . Must muezzins be allowed to broadcast their call to prayer by loudspeaker in German cities just as churches are allowed to ring their bells? Must foreigners be allowed to ritually slaughter animals although it contravenes the local animal protection regulations? . . . Must Mormons be permitted to practise polygamy here because it is allowed them in their country of origin?'
14. On the unity of political culture in the diversity of sub-cultures see. J. Habermas, *The Inclusion of the Other* (Cambridge, Mass: MIT Press), pp. 117ff.
15. On this distinction see N. Fraser, 'From Redistribution to Recognition?', in C. Willett (ed.), *Theorizing Multiculturalism*, Oxford, 1998, pp. 19–49.
16. A. Honneth, *Das Andere der Gerechtigkeit* (Frankfurt/Main: Suhrkamp, 2000) focuses specifically on these pathologies of refused recognition.
17. Charles Taylor, *Multiculturalism and 'The Politics of Recognition'*, with commentary by Amy Gutmann (ed.), Steven C. Rockefeller, Michael Walzer, and Susan Wolf (Princeton University Press, 1992). See in the German edition my critique of the communitarian conception of cultural rights as collective rights (pp. 117–46).
18. On the concept of such 'encompassing groups' see A. Margalit, J. Raz, 'National Self-Determination', in W. Kymlicka (ed.), *The Rights of Minority Cultures* (Oxford UP, 1995), pp. 79–92, esp. pp. 81ff.

19. The more comprehensive the cultural life form is, the stronger its cognitive content, the more it resembles a way of life structured by religious worldviews: 'The inescapable problem is that cultures have propositional content. It is an inevitable aspect of any culture that it will include ideas to the effect that some beliefs are true and some are false, and that some things are right and others wrong.' T. B. Barry, *Culture and Equality* (Cambridge, UK: Polity Press, 2001), p. 270.

12

Jacques Derrida

HOSTIPITALITY[1]

Some of Derrida's latest work is concerned with tolerance and, more broadly, inclusion and hospitality. Like Habermas, he starts from the philosophical tradition, especially the Enlightenment and Kant. He critically engages with the tradition, and, like Habermas, is critical of the one-sided exercise of tolerance, inclusion or hospitality. However, unlike Habermas, he does not aim at retrieving a rational kernel from the concept of tolerance. Instead, Derrida shows that the concept of tolerance (and hospitality) is marked by undecidability and aporias simultaneously making it possible and impossible. His argument is that tolerance involves the assertion of the sovereignty of the tolerating party without which the exercise of tolerance would be impossible. Likewise, hospitality involves the assertion of a home into which the other can be welcomed, and inclusion involves exclusion, opening closure, and so on. What makes tolerance possible also limits it, because it is made conditional on the assertion of sovereignty. This makes tolerance a matter of political negotiation – a negotiation that could not end simply with the displacement of the undecidability and aporia at the heart of tolerance. This undecidability is reflected in the title of the chapter: 'Hostipitality', which combines, on the one hand, hospitality towards and welcoming of the other and, on the other hand, the host and home and even hostility towards the other.

This chapter serves as a good example of Derrida's method of deconstruction and of the way he works. Deconstruction serves not to reconcile or resolve undecidability, but to show how it both makes possible and impossible a concept like tolerance. As in other places, Derrida here combines etymology, conceptual analysis, and references to the philosophical tradition and contemporary practices.

Before even beginning, I will read, I will reread with you by way of an epigraph, a long and celebrated passage from Kant.

To begin with, I will read it almost without commentary. But in each of its words, it will preside over the whole of this lecture and all questions of hospitality, the historical questions – those questions at once timeless, archaic, modern, current, and future [*à venir*] that the single word 'hospitality' magnetizes – the historical, ethical, juridical, political, and economic questions of hospitality.

As you have no doubt already guessed, it is a question in *Perpetual Peace* of the famous 'Third Definitive Article of a Perpetual Peace [*Dritter Definitivartikel zum ewigen Frieden*]',[2] the title of which is: '*Das* ***Weltbürgerrecht*** *soll auf Bedingungen der allgemeinen* ***Hospitalität*** *eingeschränkt sein*': '**Cosmopolitan Right** shall be limited to Conditions of Universal **Hospitality**'. <Already the question of conditionality, of conditional or unconditional hospitality, presents itself.>[3]

Two words are underlined by Kant in this title: 'cosmopolitan right' [***Weltbürgerrecht***: the right of world citizens] – we are thus in the space of right, not of morality and politics or anything else but of a right determined in its relation to citizenship, the state, the subject of the state, even if it is a world state – it is a question therefore of an international right; the other underlined word is 'hospitality' [*der Allgemeinen* ***Hospitalität***, universal hospitality]. It is a question therefore of defining the conditions of a cosmopolitan right, of a right the terms of which would be established by a treaty between states, by a kind of UN charter before the fact, and one of these conditions would be what Kant calls universal hospitality, *die Allgemeine Hospitalität*.

I quote this title in German to indicate that the word for 'hospitality' is a Latin word (*Hospitalität*, a word of Latin origin, of a troubled and troubling origin, a word which carries its own contradiction incorporated into it, a Latin word which allows itself to be parasitized by its opposite, 'hostility', the undesirable guest [*hôte*][4] which it harbors as the self-contradiction in its own body, and which we will speak of again later).

Kant will find a German equivalent, *Wirtbarkeit* (which he will put in parentheses as the equivalent of *Hospitalität*), for this Latin word, *Hospitalität*, from the first sentence which I am now going to read.

The equivalent Kant recalls is *Wirtbarkeit*. Kant writes: 'As in the foregoing articles, we are concerned here not with philanthropy, but with right [*Es ist hier . . . nicht von Philanthropie, sondern vom Recht die Rede*]' (in specifying that it is a question here of right and not philanthropy, Kant, of course, does not want to show that this right must be misanthropic, or

Jacques Derrida, 'Hostipitality', trans. Barry Stocker and Forbes Morlock, *Angelaki: Journal of the Theoretical Humanities*, 5: 3, 2000, pp. 3–18.

even ananthropic; it is a human right, this right to hospitality – and for us it already broaches an important question, that of the anthropological dimension of hospitality or the right to hospitality: what can be said of, indeed can one speak of, hospitality toward the non-human, the divine, for example, or the animal or vegetable; does one owe hospitality, and is that the right word when it is a question of welcoming – or being made welcome by – the other or the stranger [*l'étranger*[5]] as god, animal or plant, to use those conventional categories?). In underlining that it is a question here of right and not philanthropy, Kant does not mean that the right of hospitality is a-human or inhuman, but rather that, as a right, it does not arise [*relève*] from 'the love of man as a sentimental motive'. Universal hospitality arises [*relève*] from an obligation, a right, and a duty all regulated by law; elsewhere, in the 'Elements of Ethics' which concludes his 'Doctrine of Virtue',[6] Kant distinguishes the philanthropist from what he calls 'the friend of man' (allow me to refer those whom this distinction may interest to what I say in *The Politics of Friendship* in the passage devoted to the 'black swan'[7]). I return, then, to this first sentence and to the German word which accompanies *Hospitalität* in parentheses: 'As in the foregoing articles, we are here concerned not with philanthropy, but with right. In this context hospitality [*Hospitalität* (*Wirtbarkeit*)] means the right of a stranger [*bedeutet das Recht eines Fremdlings*] not to be treated with hostility [*en ennemi*] when he arrives on someone else's territory [*seiner Ankunft auf der Boden eines andern wegen von diesem nicht feindselig behandelt zu werden*].'

Already hospitality is opposed to what is nothing other than opposition itself, namely, hostility [*Feindseligkeit*]. The welcomed guest [*hôte*] is a stranger treated as a friend or ally, as opposed to the stranger treated as an enemy (friend/enemy, hospitality/hostility). The pair we will continue to speak of, hospitality/hostility, is in place. Before pursuing my simple reading or quotation, I would like to underline the German word *Wirtbarkeit* which Kant adds in parentheses, as the equivalent of the Latin *Hospitalität*. *Wirt* (*Wirtin* in the feminine) is at the same time the *patron*[8] and the host [*hôte*], the host*[9] who receives the *Gast*, the *Gastgeber*, the *patron* of a hotel or restaurant. *Wirtlich*, like *gastlich*, means 'hospitable', 'welcoming'. *Wirtshaus* is the café, the cabaret, the inn, the place that accommodates. And *Wirt* governs the whole lexicon of *Wirtschaft*, which is to say, economy and, thus, *oikonomia*, law of the household <where it is precisely the *patron* of the house – he who receives, who is master in his house, in his household, in his state, in his nation, in his city, in his town, who remains master in his house – who defines the conditions of hospitality or welcome; where consequently there can be no unconditional welcome, no unconditional passage through the door>. Here the *Wirt*, the *Gast*, is just as much the one who as host [*hôte*] (as host* and not as guest*) receives, welcomes, offers hospitality in his house or *hôtel*, as he is, in the first instance and with reason, the master of the household, the *patron*, the master *in his own home*. At bottom, before even beginning, we could end our reflections here in the formalization of a law of hospitality which violently imposes a contradiction on the very concept of hospitality in fixing a limit to it, in de-termining it: hospitality is certainly, necessarily, a right, a duty, an obligation, the *greeting* of the foreign other [*l'autre étranger*] as a friend but on the condition that the host*, the *Wirt*, the one who receives, lodges or *gives asylum* remains the *patron*, the master of the household, on the condition that he maintains his own authority *in his own home*, that he looks after himself and sees to and considers all that concerns him [*qu'il se garde et garde et regarde ce qui le regarde*] and thereby affirms the law of hospitality as the law of the household, *oikonomia*, the law of his household, the law of a place (house, hotel, hospital, hospice, family, city, nation, language, etc.), the law of identity which de-limits the *very* place of proffered hospitality and maintains authority over it, maintains the truth of authority, remains the place of this maintaining, which is to say, of truth, thus limiting the gift proffered and making of this limitation, namely, the *being-oneself in one's own home*, the condition of the gift and of hospitality. This is the principle, <one could say, the aporia,> of both the constitution and the implosion of the concept of hospitality, the effects of which – it is my hypothesis – we will only continue to confirm. This implosion or, if you prefer, this self-deconstruction having already taken place, we could, I was saying, end here <the reflection on this aporia>. Hospitality is a self-contradictory concept and experience which can only self-destruct <put otherwise, produce itself as impossible, only be possible on the condition of its impossibility> or protect itself from itself, auto-immunize itself in some way, which is to say, deconstruct itself – precisely – in being put into practice.

But in order not to stop here before even having started, I will go on as if we had not yet said anything and we will continue for a little longer.

Still by way of an epigraph, I will continue reading Kant's text to the end, this time without stopping. It would be possible to come to a stop before each word, but as it is an epigraph, I won't do that, I will press on. We will have plenty of opportunities to come back to it later.

> As in the foregoing articles, we are concerned here not with philanthropy, but with *right*. In this context, *hospitality* [l'hospitalité (hospitalitas)] means the right of a stranger not to be treated with hostility when he arrives on someone else's territory. He can indeed be turned away, if this is done without causing his death,[10] but he must not be treated with hostility so long as he behaves in a peaceable manner in the place he happens to be. The stranger cannot claim the *right of a guest* to be entertained [*un* droit de résidence], for this would require a

special friendly agreement whereby he might become a member of the native household for a certain time. He may only claim a *right of resort* [*un* droit de visite],[11] for all men are entitled to present themselves in the society of others by virtue of their right to communal possession of the earth's surface. Since the earth is a globe, they cannot disperse over an infinite area, but must tolerate one another's company. And no one originally has any greater right than anyone else to occupy any particular portion of the earth.[12] The community of man is divided by uninhabitable parts of the earth's surface such as oceans and deserts, but even then the *ship* or the *camel* (the ship of the desert) makes it possible for them to approach their fellows over these ownerless tracts, and to utilize as a means of social intercourse that *right to the earth's surface* which the human race shares in common. The inhospitable behavior of coastal dwellers (as on the Barbary coast) in plundering ships on the adjoining seas or enslaving stranded seafarers, or that of inhabitants of the desert (as with the Arab Bedouins), who regard their proximity to nomadic tribes as a justification for plundering them, is contrary to natural right.[13] But this natural right of hospitality, i.e. the right of strangers, does not extend beyond those conditions which make it possible for them to *attempt* to enter into relations with the native inhabitants. In this way, continents distant from each other can enter into peaceful mutual relations which may eventually be regulated by public laws, thus bringing the human race nearer and nearer to a cosmopolitan constitution.

If we compare with this ultimate end the *inhospitable* conduct of the civilized states of our continent, especially the commercial states, the injustice which they display in *visiting* foreign countries and peoples (which in their case is the same as *conquering* them) seems appallingly great. America, the negro countries, the Spice Islands, the Cape, etc. were looked upon at the time of their discovery as ownerless territories; for the native inhabitants were counted as nothing. In East India (Hindustan), foreign troops were brought in under the pretext of merely setting up trading posts. This led to the oppression of the natives, incitement of the various Indian states to widespread wars, famine, insurrection, treachery and the whole litany of evils which afflict the human race.

. . . The peoples of the earth have thus entered in varying degrees into a universal community, and it has developed to the point where a violation of rights in *one* part of the world is felt *everywhere*. The idea of a cosmopolitan right is therefore not fantastic and overstrained; it is a necessary complement to the unwritten code of political and international right, transforming it into a universal right of humanity. Only under this condition can we flatter ourselves that we are continually advancing towards a perpetual peace. (pp. 105–08)

<Perpetual peace for Kant is not simply a utopian concept projected to infinity. As soon as one thinks the concept of peace in all strictness, one must be thinking of perpetual peace. A peace that would simply be an armistice would not be a peace. Peace implies within its concept of peace the promise of eternity. Otherwise it is not a peace. Kant here is only laying out the very structure of the concept of peace, which implies a promise of indefinite, and therefore eternal, renewal.>

Now we are beginning or pretending to open the door <that impossible door, sublime or not>. We are on the threshold.

We do not know what hospitality is [*Nous ne savons pas ce que c'est que l'hospitalité*]. Not yet.

Not yet, but will we ever know? Is it a question of knowledge and of time?

Here, in any case, is the sentence which I address to you, which I have already addressed to you, and which I now put in quotation marks. 'We do not know what hospitality is.' It is a sentence which I address to you in French, in my language, in my home, in order to begin and to bid you welcome <where I am received in your home> when I begin to speak in my language, which seems to suppose that I am here <at home> master in my own home, that I am receiving, inviting, accepting or welcoming you, allowing you to come across the threshold, by saying '*bienvenu*', '*welcome*',* to you.

I repeat: **'We do not know what hospitality is.'**

Already, as you have heard, I have used, and even used up, the most used words in the code of hospitality, the lexicon of which consists of the words 'invite', 'welcome', receive 'at home' while one is 'master of one's own home' and of the threshold.

Consequently, to address the first sentence with which I began, **'We do not know what hospitality is'**, as a host to a guest [*comme un hôte à un hôte* (a host to a guest)] seems to contradict, in a self-contradiction, <an aporia, if you like,> a performative contradiction, everything I have just recalled, namely, that we comprehend all these words well enough, and that they belong to the current lexicon or the common semantics of hospitality, of all precomprehension of what 'hospitality' is and means, namely, to 'welcome', 'accept', 'invite', 'receive', 'bid' someone welcome 'to one's home', where, in one's own home, one is master of the household, master of the city, or master of the nation, the language, or the state, places from which one bids the other welcome (but what is a 'welcome'?) and grants him a kind of *right of asylum* by authorizing him to cross a threshold that would be a threshold, <a door that would be a door,> a threshold that is determinable because it is self-identical and indivisible, a threshold the line of which can be traced (the door of a house, human household, family or house of god, temple or general hospital [*hôteldieu*], hospice [*hospice*], hospital or poor-house [*hôpital ou hôtel hospitalier*], frontier of a city, or a country, or a language, etc.). We think we comprehend all these ordinary words in French – in which I am *at home* – and the French language itself in all that it translates (translation also being, as we noted earlier, an enigmatic phenomenon or experience of hospitality, if not the condition of all hospitality in general).

And yet, even though, I am assuming, we understand each other rather well over the meaning or pre-comprehension of all this vocabulary of hospitality and the said laws of hospitality, I dared to begin by putting to you, in the way of a welcome: **'We do not know what hospitality is.'** In appearance, a performative contradiction which bids welcome by acknowledging that we do not know what 'welcome' means and that perhaps no one welcomed is ever completely welcome <in a welcome which is not justifiably hypocritical or conditional,> a performative contradiction which is as unusual and confusing as an apostrophe of the sort, 'O my friends, there is no friend',[14] <a sentence attributed to Aristotle,> the meaning and consequences of which are doubtless not completely foreign, assuming we know what 'foreign [*étranger*]' means; the whole question of hospitality is focused here, too.

Thus, I owe you as my hosts an explanation. This short sentence, **'We do not know what hospitality is'**, which implicates us, which has already authoritatively and in advance implicated you in a we that speaks French, <a sentence we comprehend without comprehending,> can have several acceptations. **At least three and doubtless more than four.**

Before beginning to unfold them, note in passing that the word 'acceptation [*acception*]', from *accipere* or *acceptio* and which in French means 'the meaning given to a word' (and which many people make the easy mistake of confusing with 'acception [*acceptation*]'),[15] this word 'acceptation' also belongs quite specifically to the discourse of hospitality; it lives at the heart of the discourse of hospitality; acceptation in Latin is the same as acception, the action of receiving, the welcome given, the way one receives. <Obviously, a reflection on hospitality is a reflection on what the word 'receive' means. What does 'receive' mean?> It is like a postscript to Plato's *Timaeus*, where <Khôra,[16]> the place is spoken of as that which receives (*endekhomai*, *endekhomenon*), the receptacle (*dekhomenon* – which can also mean 'it is acceptable, permitted, possible'); in Latin, *acceptio* is the action of receiving, reception, welcome ('reception' and 'welcome [*accueil*]' are words you also often see at the entrances to hotels and hospitals, what were once known as hospices, places of public hospitality). The 'acceptor' is the one who receives, makes welcome, has – as is also said – a welcome in store, or who approves, who accepts, the other and what the other says or does. When I said I am at home here speaking my language, French, that also means I am more welcoming to Latin and Latinate languages than to others, and you see how violently I am behaving as master in my own home at the very moment of welcoming. *Accepto* – the frequentative of *accipio* (that is, of the verb that matters most here, *accipio*) which means 'to take' [*prendre*] (*capere* or comprehend in order to make come to one, in order to receive, welcome) – *accepto*, that is, the frequentative of *accipio*, means 'being in the habit of receiving'. *Accepto*: I am in the habit of receiving, of making welcome; in this sense, from this point of view, it is almost synonymous with *recipio*, which means both 'take in return, again' and 'receive', 'welcome', 'accept', the *re-* often having the sense of return or repetition, the new of 'anew' [*du nouveau de 'de nouveau', à nouveau*], and, when the *re-* disappears from 'receive' in the sense of 'welcome', 'accept', even if for the first time. Already you see that, besides the idea of necessary repetition and thus of law, iterability, and the law of iterability at the heart of every law of hospitality, we have – with the semantics of acceptation or acception, reception – the double postulation of giving and taking (*capere*), of giving and comprehending in itself and at home with itself [*en soi et chez soi*], <in its language,> not just on one occasion but in its readiness from the outset to repeat, to renew, to continue. Yes, yes, you are welcome. Hospitality gives and takes more than once in its own home. It gives, it offers, it holds out, but what it gives, offers, holds out, is the greeting which comprehends and makes or lets come into one's home, folding the foreign other into the internal law of the host [*hôte* (host, *Wirt*, etc.)] which tends to begin by dictating the law of its language and its own acceptation of the sense of words, which is to say, its own concepts as well. The acceptation of words is also the concept, the *Begriff*, the manner in which one takes hold of or comprehends, takes, apprehends [*comprend*, *prend*, *appréhende*] the meaning of a word in giving it a meaning.

I was saying that the sentence that I addressed to you, which is, **'We do not know what hospitality is'**, can have several acceptations. **At least three and doubtless more than four.**

1. The first acceptation is the one that would rely on stressing the word 'know': we do not *know*, we do not *know* what hospitality is. This not-knowing is not necessarily a deficiency, an infirmity, a lack. Its apparent negativity, this grammatical negativity (the not-knowing) would not signify ignorance, but rather indicate or recall only that hospitality is not a concept which lends itself to objective knowledge. Of course, there is a concept of hospitality, of the meaning of this word 'hospitality', and we already have some pre-comprehension of it. Otherwise we could not speak of it, to suppose that in speaking of it we know what 'speaking' means. On the one hand, what we pre-comprehend in this way – we will verify this – rebels against any self-identity or any consistent, stable, and objectifiable conceptual determination. On the other hand, what this concept is the concept of *is not* [n'est pas], is not a being, is not something which as a being,

thing, or object can belong [*relever*] to knowledge. Hospitality, if there is such a thing, is not only an experience in the most enigmatic sense of the word, which appeals to an act and an intention beyond the thing, object, or present being, but is also an intentional experience which proceeds beyond knowledge toward the other as absolute stranger, as unknown, where I know that I know nothing of him (we will return sooner or later to the difficult and necessary distinction between these two nevertheless indissociable concepts, the other and the stranger, an indispensable distinction if we are to delimit any specificity to hospitality). <Hospitality is owed to the other as stranger. But if one determines the other as stranger, one is already introducing the circles of conditionality that are family, nation, state, and citizenship. Perhaps there is an other who is still more foreign than the one whose foreignness cannot be restricted to foreignness in relation to language, family, or citizenship. Naturally, I am trying to determine the dimension of not-knowing that is essential in hospitality.> It is doubtless necessary to know all that can be known of hospitality, and there is much to know; it is certainly necessary to bring this knowledge to the highest and fullest consciousness possible; but it is also necessary to know that hospitality gives itself, and gives itself to thought beyond knowledge [*se donne à penser au-delà du savoir*].

2. The second acceptation of this apparently negative sentence, **'We do not know what hospitality is'**, could seem wrapped up in the first. If we do not know what hospitality is, it is because it is not [*n'est pas*], it is not a present being. This intentional act, this address or invitation,[17] this experience which calls and addresses itself to the other as a stranger in order to say 'Welcome' to him, is not [*n'est pas*] in several senses of not-being [*du non-être*], by which I do not mean nothingness. First of all, it is not [*n'est pas*] because it often proclaims itself (that will be one of our major problems) as a law, a duty or right, an obligation, that is, as a should-be [*un devoir-être*] rather than as being or a being [*un être ou un étant*]. Without referring to Kant's text with which we opened this session (the juridical text that defines the right of the stranger, which is reciprocally the duty or obligation of the host* who is master in his house, who is *what he is* in his house), we could invoke all those texts inscribable under the title 'The Laws of Hospitality' – in particular Klossowski's *Roberte Ce Soir*,[18] a text which we will definitely return to and which analyzes an internal and essential contradiction in hospitality, one foreshadowed in the sort of preface or protocol entitled 'Difficulties', where the temporal contradiction of hospitality is such that the experience cannot last; it can only pre-form itself in the imminence of what is 'about to happen [*sur le point d'arriver*]' and can only last an instant, precisely because a contradiction cannot last without being dialectized (a Kierkegaardian paradox), or, as the text puts it, one cannot 'at the same time take and not take' (p. 11). I will read these

'Difficulties' very quickly, underlining this temporal contradiction and the position of these 'Difficulties' as a preface or protocol to the text or charter entitled 'The Laws of Hospitality':

> When my Uncle Octave took my Aunt Roberte in his arms, one must not suppose that in taking her he was alone. An invited guest [*un invité*] would enter while Roberte, entirely given over to my uncle's presence, was not expecting him, and while she was in fear lest the guest would arrive – for with irresistible resolution Roberte awaited the arrival of some guest – the guest would already be looming up behind her as my uncle made his entry just in time to surprise my aunt's satisfied fright at being surprised by the guest. But in my uncle's mind it would last only an instant, and once again my uncle would be on the point of taking my aunt in his arms. It would last only an instant . . . for, after all, one cannot at the same time take and not take, be there and not be there, enter a room when one is already in it. My Uncle Octave would have been asking too much had he wished to prolong the instant of the opened door, he was already doing exceedingly well in getting the guest to appear in the doorway at the precise instant he did, getting the guest to loom up behind Roberte so that he, Octave, might be able to sense that he himself was the guest as, borrowing from the guest his door-opening gesture, he could behold from the threshold and have the impression it was he, Octave, who was taking my aunt in surprise.
>
> Nothing could give a better idea of my uncle's mentality than these hand-written pages he had framed under glass and then hung on the wall of the guest room, just above the bed, a spray of fading wildflowers drooping over the old-fashioned frame. (pp. 11–12)

The laws of hospitality properly speaking will be marked by this contradiction inscribed in the essence of the hostess – since the interest, one of the interests, of Klossowski's book is having treated the problem of hospitality by taking the sharpest and most painful but also the most ecstatic account of sexual difference in the couple and in the couple's relation to a third (to the *terstis* who is both witness and guest here) – a contradiction inscribed in the essence of the hostess which Klossowski analyzes, as so often, in the theologico-scholastic language of essence and existence, and which must lead, according to a necessity we will often put to the test, to the reversal in which the master of this house, the master in his own home, the host*, can only accomplish his task as host, that is, hospitality, in becoming invited by the other into his home, in being welcomed by him whom he welcomes, in receiving the hospitality he gives. Expecting to return to them later, I will content myself with reading two passages from 'The Laws of Hospitality', one which describes the contradiction in the essence of the hostess, the other, a conclusion, which tells of the final reversal of the roles of host and guest [*de l'hôte et de l'hôte*], of the inviting *hôte* as host* (the master in his own home) and the invited *hôte* as guest*, of the inviting and the invited,[19] of the becoming-invited, if you like, of the one inviting. The one inviting becomes almost the hostage of the one invited, of the guest [*hôte*], the hostage of the one he receives, the one who keeps him at home. We need, we would need, to set about a lengthy examination of the hostage, the logic, economy, and politics of the hostage. The *Littré* disputes that the word "*otage* [hostage]" in its current usage comes from *ostage*, itself coming from *hoste*, *oste*, which could signify in certain thirteenth-century texts what we now call a hostage; for the *Littré* "*otage*" would come from the contraction *hostaticum* for *obsidaticum*, from *obsudatus*, which means 'guarantee', from *obses*, *obsiditis*, hostage, hostage of war (beyond question), from *obsidere*, to occupy, possess, indeed besiege, obsess; the *Robert* does not make as much of a fuss in deriving "*otage*" from *hostage*, which means 'lodgings', 'residence', 'place where guests [*hôtes*] are lodged', hostages being in the first instance guarantees, security, surety for the enemy lodged with the sovereign. I have not engaged in more serious etymological research, but it cannot be disputed that *obsess* means 'hostage of war' in Latin; the two etymologies ally themselves with one another easily; in both cases, the hostage is security for a possession: the hostage is a guarantee for the other, held in a place and taking its place [*tenu dans un lieu et tenant lieu*].

We would also need to pursue this terrifying and unsurpassable strategy of the hostage in the direction of a modernity and a techno-political specificity of hostage-taking (which is not what it was only a few decades ago), in the direction (the inverse, so to speak) of what Levinas calls 'the hostage' when he says that the exercise of ethical responsibility begins where I am and must be the hostage of the other, delivered passively to the other before being delivered to myself.[20] (The theme of obsession, obsidionality, persecution also playing an essential role and one indissociable from that of the hostage in Levinas' discourse on responsibility before the other, which assumes that I am, in a non-negative sense of that term, from the outset, me: myself, in as much as I say 'Here I am', the subjugated, substitutable subject, the other's hostage.) 'It is through the condition of being a hostage', says Levinas in 'Substitution', 'that there can be pity, compassion, pardon and proximity in the world',[21] or further, and here the word 'ipseity' will be of the utmost importance: 'Ipseity, in the passivity without arche characteristic of identity, is a hostage. The word "I" would answer for everything and everyone.'[22]

> The master of the house, having no greater nor more pressing concern than to shed the warmth of his joy at evening upon whomever comes to dine at his table and to rest under his roof from a day's wearying travel, waits anxiously on the threshold for the stranger he will see appear

> like a liberator upon the horizon. And catching a first glimpse of him in the distance, though he be still far off, the master will call out to him, 'Come quickly, my happiness is at stake.' (Klossowski, p. 12)

<He waits for anyone, anyone who arrives [*n'importe quel arrivant*], and welcomes the one who arrives [*l'arrivant*] by urging him to enter as a liberator.[23] Every word of this passage could be underlined. If there is a horizon, it is not what phenomenologists call the horizon of expectation, since it could be anyone. He waits without waiting. He waits without knowing whom he awaits. He waits for the Messiah. He waits for anyone who might come. And he will have him eat at his table. And he urges him to come, even though he has no way of making him come more quickly. He waits impatiently for him as a liberator. This is certainly a kind of Messiah.>

> Now it seems that the essence of the hostess, such as the host visualizes it, would in this sense be undetermined and contradictory. For either the essence of the hostess is constituted by her fidelity to the host, and in this case she eludes him the more he wishes to know her in the opposite state of betrayal, for she would be unable to betray him in order to be faithful to him; or else the essence of the hostess is really constituted by infidelity and then the host would cease to have any part in the essence of the hostess who would be susceptible of belonging, accidentally, as mistress of the house, to some one or other of the guests [*invités*]. The notion of mistress of the house reposes upon an existential basis: she is a hostess only upon an essential basis: this essence is therefore subjected to restraint by her actual existence as mistress of the house. And here the sole function of betrayal, we see, is to lift this restraint. If the essence of the hostess lies in fidelity to the host, this authorizes the host to cause the hostess, essential in the existent mistress of the house, to manifest herself before the eyes of the guest; for the host in playing host must accept the risks of the game and these include the consequences of his wife's strict application of the laws of hospitality and of the fact that she dare not be unmindful of her essence, composed of fidelity to the host, for fear that in the arms of the inactual guest come here to actualize her *qua* hostess, the mistress of the household exist only traitorously. (Klossowski, pp. 13–14)

If we do not know what hospitality is, it is because this thing which is not something is not an object of knowledge, nor in the mode of being-present, unless it is that of the law of the should-be or obligation, the law of hospitality, the imperative of which seems moreover contradictory or paradoxical.

3. But there is still a third acceptation or a third intonation, a third accentuation of the same sentence. This third accentuation seems also to relate to time and achrony or essential anachrony,[24] indeed to the paradoxical instant we were speaking of, but is in truth a question of another experience, another dimension of time and space. **'We do not know what hospitality is'** would imply 'we do **not yet** know what hospitality is', in a sense of 'not yet' which remains to be thought: <it is not only the 'not yet' of the threshold. The threshold, that is the 'not yet'. The threshold is what has not yet been crossed,> not 'not yet' because we will know better tomorrow in the future tense, in the present future, but 'not yet' for two other kinds of reason.

A. On the one hand, the system of right, national or international right, the political <or state> system which determines the obligations and limits of hospitality, the system of European right of which Kant's text, read at the beginning, gives us at least an idea, a regulative Idea, and a very high ideal, this system of right and concept of politics, indeed cosmopolitics, which he inscribes and prescribes, has a history, even if it is the history of the concept of history, of teleology and the regulative Idea which it brings into play. This history and this history of history call up questions and delimitations (which we will, of course, be speaking of) which justify the thought that the determination and experience of hospitality hold a future beyond this history and this thought of history – and that therefore we do not yet know what hospitality beyond this European, universally European, right is.

B. And, above all, on the other hand, the 'not yet' can define the very dimension of what, still in the future, still to come, comes from hospitality, what is called and called by [*s'appelle et reste appelé par*] hospitality. What we call hospitality maintains an essential relation with the opening of what is called to come [*à venir*]. When we say that **'We do not yet know what hospitality is'**, we also imply that we do not yet know who or what will come, nor what is called hospitality and what is called in hospitality, knowing that hospitality, in the first place, is called [*ça s'appelle*], even if this call does not take shape in human language. Calling the other, calling the one the other, inviting, inviting oneself, ingratiating oneself, having or letting oneself come, coming well, welcoming [*se faire ou se laisser venir, bien venir*], greeting, greeting one another as a sign of welcome – these are so many experiences which come from the future, which come from seeing come or from allowing to come without seeing come, no less than the 'not [*pas*]', and hence the 'not yet', the past 'not yet' of the step [*pas*] that crosses the threshold. What is called hospitality, which we do not yet know, is what is called. Although '*s'appeler* [to be called]' is an untranslatable French grammatical form (and the question of translation is always the question of hospitality), although '*s'appeler*' – that is, its untranslatable privilege in the French idiom – can be reflexive and not reflexive (on the one hand, I call myself such and such, he or she calls himself or herself by such and such a name; on the other hand, let's call one another [*on s'appelle l'un l'autre, l'une l'autre*]), although this is all very French, I would nevertheless refer to a celebrated text by Heidegger, *Was heisst Denken?*

Heidegger speaks there of at least two things that are of the utmost importance to us here and which I highlight too quickly.

On the one hand, in the opening pages which I am letting you read, he insists at length on this: 'Most thought-provoking is that we are not yet thinking', still 'not yet', the most disturbing, serious, important, unusual, and shady, '*das Bedenklichste*, is what we are not yet thinking; still not yet... [*Das Bedenklichste ist, dass wir noch nicht denken; immer noch nicht...*]' (p. 4).[25] And further on, after noting that '*Das Bedenklichste in unserer bedenkliche Zeit ist, dass wir noch nicht denken* [Most thought-provoking [*Le plus bizarre et inquiétant*] in our thought-provoking time is that we are not yet thinking],' he determines the noun '*das Bedenkliche*' as '*was uns zu denken gibt* [what gives us to think]' (p. 6), which doubtless legitimates the standard French translation that Granel rather artificially chooses for *das Bedenkliche*, '*ce qui donne à penser* [what gives to think]'; *das Bedenklichste*, '*ce qui donne le plus à penser* [what gives most to think].'[26]

But what I wanted above all to recall from this book, still too quickly, alas, is the play in it on 'to be called', precisely the '*heissen*' which means 'meaning', without a doubt, to be called, calling [*s'appeler*, *appeler*] (*was heisst Denken?*: what is called thinking? what does thinking mean? For *das heisst* means 'it means', 'that is to say'; but *heissen* also, or first of all, means 'calls', 'invites', 'names': *jenen willkommen heissen* is 'to bid someone welcome', 'address a word of welcome to someone'). And when he analyzes the four meanings of the expression '*was heisst Denken?*' (I refer you to the beginning of Part Two, lectures from the summer semester 1952, page 79 of the original), he notes in fourth place that it also means: 'what is it that calls us, as it were, commands us to think? What is it that calls us into thinking? [*was ist es, das uns heisst, uns gleichsam befiehlt, zu denken? Was ist es, das uns in das Denken ruft?*]' (p. 114). What calls us to thought, toward the thinking of thought, in giving us the order to do it, the call also being the call to reply 'Present, here I am'?

Heidegger underlines that this is no simple play on words, and I invite you to read all these pages (as I have tried to do elsewhere), in particular what relates the call or invitation in *heissen* to the promise (*Verheissung*), to the alliance and the 'yes' of acquiescence before the question (*Zusage*, *ein Zugesagtes*), to what is promised (*ein Versprochenes*). <Heidegger devotes himself much later, in the end fairly late in his itinerary, to the value of *Zusage* which means 'acquiescence', the 'yes' that would come before the question. For a long time Heidegger presented the act of questioning as the essential act of philosophy, of thought, that is to say, the piety of thinking

(*Frömmlichkeit des Denkens*). But before the question, if one can speak of a before that is neither chronological nor logical, in order for there to be a question there must first of all be an acquiescence, a 'yes'. In order to ask, there must first be a certain 'yes'. This is what Heidegger called *Zusage*, which is more originary than the question. And here it is a question in this passage of *Zusage*, *ein Zugesagtes*, of what is promised, of a 'yes' to a promise.>

But, as I am coming back from Freiburg-im-Brisgau where for the first time as a visitor I stepped across the threshold of Heidegger's hut in the mountains, I have chosen to quote another passage from *Was heisst Denken?* which at the same time names Freiburg-im-Brisgau, as the town is called, Freiburg where this course was given, alludes to a certain hut in the mountains, and says something essential about the call and hospitality.

Here then is what Heidegger says at the end of the lecture, in the recapping of the 'Summary and Transition' between the first and second lectures (I will read straight from the text, pointing out German words here and there):

> The ambiguity of the question: 'What is called thinking' lies in the ambiguity of the verb which is in itself a question: 'to call [*heissen*].' The town where we are is called Freiburg-im-Brisgau; it has this name.
>
> The frequent idiom 'to be called' or 'what we call [*das heisst*]' signifies: what we have just said has in reality this or that meaning, is to be understood this way or that. Instead of 'what we call [*das heisst*],' we also use the idiom 'that is to say [*das will sagen*].'
>
> On a day of changeable weather, someone might leave a mountain lodge alone to climb a peak. He soon loses his way in the fog that has suddenly descended. He has no notion of what we call [*was es heisst*] mountaineering. He does not know any of the things it calls for, all the things that must be taken into account and mastered.
>
> A voice calls us to have hope [*heisst uns hoffen*]. It beckons us to hope, invites us, commends us, directs us to hope.
>
> The town where we are is called [*heissen*] Freiburg. It is so named because that is what it has been called. This means: the town has been called to assume this name. Henceforth it is at the call of this name [*sous la Renommée de ce nom*] to which it has been commended. To call is not originally to name, but the other way round: naming is a kind of calling, in the original sense of demanding and commending. It is not that the call [*le 'Geheiss'*] has its being in the name; rather every name is a kind of call [*Geheiss*]. Every call [*Geheiss*] implies an approach, and thus, of course, the possibility of giving a name. We might call [*heissen*] a guest [*hôte*] welcome [*Geheiss*]. This does not mean that we attach to him the name 'Welcome [*Geheiss*],' but that

> we call him to come in and complete his arrival as a welcome friend. In that way, the welcome[*Geheiss*]-call of the invitation to come in is nonetheless also an act of naming, a calling which makes the newcomer what we call a guest [*hôte*] whom we are glad to see.
>
> "*Heissen*" – in gothic "*haitan*" – is to call; but calling is something other than merely making a sound. Something else again, essentially different from mere sound and noise, is the cry. (pp. 123–24)[27]

After which Heidegger insists on a classical distinction, necessary in his eyes, a bit more problematic in mine, between noise, the cry, and the call [*Schall und Schrei und Ruf*], but let us leave it here for the moment.

4. Finally, the fourth possible acceptation of my initial address (**'We do not know what hospitality is'**) would place us at both a critical crossroads of semantic (or, if you prefer, etymologico-institutional) filiations and an aporetic crossroads, which is to say, a crossroads or a sort of double postulation, contradictory double movement, double constraint or double bind* (I prefer 'double bind'* because this English expression retains the link to 'link' and thus to 'obligation', 'ligament', and 'alliance'). What may appear paradoxical is the meeting of the experience of hospitality and aporia, especially where we think that the host [*hôte*] offers the guest [*hôte*] passage across the threshold or the frontier in order to receive him into his home. Is aporia not, as its name indicates, the non-road, the barred way, the non-passage? My hypothesis or thesis would be that this necessary aporia is not negative; and that without the repeated enduring of this paralysis in contradiction, the responsibility of hospitality, hospitality *tout court* – when we do not yet know and will never know what it is – would have no chance of coming to pass, of coming, of making or letting welcome [*d'advenir, de venir, de faire ou de laisser bienvenir*].

For the moment, in the name of the critical crossroads of semantics or etymology and institutions, I will pass quickly and without transition from the welcome [*la bienvenue*] to Benveniste. Welcome to the welcomed [*Bienvenue au bienvenu*] who in this case is Benveniste.

As always in what is a vocabulary of Indo-European institutions, *Indo-European Language and Society*, Benveniste starts with an institution, that is to say, with what he calls a 'well-established social phenomenon'; and it is from this 'well-established social phenomenon', as he puts it, that he goes on to study a lexicon, what he calls a 'group of words' which he relates to 'hospitality'.[28] The name of the social phenomenon in this case is 'hospitality' – the title of chapter 7 of Book I (Economy). The 'basic term' is, thus, the Latin *hospes*, which, Benveniste recalls, is divided into two, two distinct elements which he says 'finally link up': **hosti-pet-s** (p. 72). *Pet-* alternates with *pot-* which means 'master' so clearly, Benveniste notes, that *hospes* would mean 'guest-master [*maître de l'hôte*]' (p. 72). As he rightly finds this 'a rather singular designation' (these are his words), he proposes to study these two terms, *potis* and *hostis*, separately and analyze their 'etymological connections' (p. 72). *Hostis* is going to effect this strange crossing between enemy and host which we will speak of later. But let us begin with *potis*, which unites the semantics of power, mastery, and despotic sovereignty.

Before returning to this notion of mastery <which conditions hospitality, and> which we have said so much about, let us follow Benveniste for a moment while he explicates '*potis*' in its proper meaning [*au sens propre*], 'in its own right [*en propre*]', as he says (p. 72). He goes back to Sanskrit where two meanings, 'master' and 'husband' (this is why I began with *Roberte Ce Soir* where the master is truly the master of this house, thus the master of the woman, that is, the husband), are the subject of the same stem in two different inflections. This is a phenomenon proper to the evolution of Sanskrit: one inflection signifies 'master', the other 'husband'. When Klossowski describes the laws of hospitality in speaking of a master of the house, a master of places like the family and a master of the wife, husband of the wife who becomes the stake and essence of hospitality, he is well within the domestic or *oikonomic* (law of the household, domestic lineage, family) logic which seems to govern this Indo-European history of hospitality. Benveniste passes from Sanskrit to the Greek *posis*, a poetic term for husband, spouse (which also means, although Benveniste does not note this, 'fiancé', 'lover', and, in Euripides, 'the secret spouse'; in Latin this will yield *potens*, *potentis*, master, sovereign, potentate). Benveniste specifies that *posis* be distanced from *despotes*, which according to him only signifies power or mastery without the domestic reference to the 'master of the house' (a remark which, I must say, greatly surprises me, for, although my proficiency is very limited, I see references elsewhere to Aeschylus who notes that *despotes* means 'master of the house', and to Plato's *Laws* or *Republic* in which *despotes* means 'master of the house', a synonym of *oikonomos* (the steward [*économe*] is the one who makes the law in the *oikos*, the household or the family, the master of the family also being the master of the slaves; we are here in the transition between the family and the state)). Benveniste then recalls that the Greek *despotes* and its Sanskrit equivalent *dam patih* enter into the composition of ancient expressions which relate to social unities the extension of which can vary: the master of the house, *dam patih*, the master of the clan, *vis patih*, the master of the lineage, *jas patih*. One could follow all the variations he cites in Iranian, Lithuanian, Hittite, etc. He does not cite, but could have, the word *hospodar*, prince, lord, which passed into French and was used even by Voltaire, just like the *hospodarat* (office or dignity of the *hospodar*), a word of Slavic origin (*hospodin* in Bohemian, *gospodar* in Russian, *gospoda* in Polish, whence *gospodarz*, hotelier, master of the house, host, innkeeper, etc.).

Let us leave Benveniste and his semantico-institutional filiations for a moment in order to underline very generally and structurally a paradoxical trait, namely, that the host, he who offers hospitality, must be the master in his house, he (male in the first instance) must be assured of his sovereignty over the space and goods he offers or opens to the other as stranger. This seems both the law of laws of hospitality and common sense in our culture. It does not seem to me that I am able to open up or offer hospitality, however generous, even in order to be generous, without reaffirming: this is mine, I am at home, you are welcome in my home, without any implication of 'make yourself at home' but on condition that you observe the rules of hospitality by respecting the being-at-home of my home, the being-itself of what I am. There is almost an axiom of self-limitation or self-contradiction in the law of hospitality. As a reaffirmation of mastery and being oneself in one's own home, from the outset hospitality limits itself at its very beginning, it remains forever on the threshold of itself [*l'hospitalité se limite dès le seuil sur le seuil d'elle-même, elle reste toujours au seuil d'elle-même*], it governs the threshold – and hence it forbids in some way even what it seems to allow to cross the threshold to pass across it. It becomes the threshold. This is why we do not know what it is, and why we cannot know. Once we know it, we no longer know it, what it properly is, what the threshold of its identity is.

<To take up the figure of the door, for there to be hospitality, there must be a door. But if there is a door, there is no longer hospitality. There is no hospitable house. There is no house without doors and windows. But as soon as there are a door and windows, it means that someone has the key to them and consequently controls the conditions of hospitality. There must be a threshold. But if there is a threshold, there is no longer hospitality. This is the difference, the gap, between the hospitality of invitation and the hospitality of visitation. In visitation there is no door. Anyone can come at any time and can come in without needing a key for the door. There are no customs checks with a visitation. But there are customs and police checks with an invitation. Hospitality thus becomes the threshold or the door.>

In saying that hospitality always in some way does the opposite of what it pretends to do and immobilizes itself on the threshold of itself, on the threshold which it re-marks and constitutes, on *itself* in short, on both its phenomenon and its essence, I am not claiming that hospitality is this double bind* or this aporetic contradiction and that therefore wherever hospitality is, there is no hospitality. No, I am saying that this apparently aporetic paralysis on the threshold 'is' (I put 'is' in quotation marks or, if you prefer, under erasure [*je le rature*]) what must be overcome <it is the impossibility which must be overcome where it is possible to become impossible. It is necessary to do the impossible. If there is hospitality, the impossible must be done>, this 'is' being in order that, beyond hospitality, hospitality may come to pass. Hospitality can only take place beyond hospitality, in deciding to let it come, overcoming the hospitality that paralyzes itself on the threshold which it is. It is perhaps in this sense that 'we do not know (not yet, but always not yet) what hospitality is', and that hospitality awaits [*attend*] its chance, that it holds itself out to [*se tend vers*] its chance beyond what it is, namely, the paralysis on the threshold which it is. In this sense hospitality is always to come [*à venir*], but a 'to come' that does not and will never present itself as such, in the present <and a future [*avenir*] that does not have a horizon, a futurity – a future without horizon>. To think hospitality from the future – this future that does not present itself or will only present itself when it is not awaited as a present or presentable – is to think hospitality from death no less than from birth. In general, it is the birthplace which will always have underpinned the definition of the stranger (the stranger as non-autochthonous, non-indigenous, we will say more of this) and the place of death. <The stranger is, first of all, he who is born elsewhere. The stranger is defined from birth rather than death.> The 'dying elsewhere' or the 'dying at home'. Perhaps we can read together a passage from Montaigne on this subject, on dying while travelling, in a text in which, having enumerated what he calls the 'forms of dying', notably away from home, he asks the question of what he calls in a sublime, but perhaps only sublime, word, *commourans* [comrades-in-death], those who die together, at the same time – as if that were possible – if not in the same place. Rightly, he does not speak of Romeo and Juliet, who illustrate in this regard an irreducible bad timing [*contretemps*], but he does wonder, I quote, 'Might we not even make death luxurious, like Antony and Cleopatra, those comrades-in-death?'[29]

What would be needed would be to pursue this analysis of the *critical* crossroads of semantic (or, if you prefer, etymologico-institutional) filiations and the *aporetic* crossroads, that is to say, a crossroads where a sort of double bifurcation, double postulation, contradictory double movement, double constraint or double bind* paralyzes and opens hospitality, holding it over itself in holding it out to the other, depriving it of and bestowing on it its chance; we will see how power (despotic sovereignty and the virile mastery of the master of the house) is nothing other than ipseity itself, the same of the selfsame, to say nothing of the subject which is a stabilizing and despotic escalation of ipseity, the being oneself or the *Selbst*. The question of hospitality is also the question of ipseity. In his own way, Benveniste too will help us to confirm this from language, the *utpote* and what he calls the 'mysterious *-pse* of ipse'; we should stop at this phrase in Benveniste and its context, the phrase being both luminous and philosophically a bit ingenuous in its form as a question and in the astonishment it reveals (p. 74). Thus Benveniste writes: 'While it is difficult to see how a word meaning "the master", could become so weakened in force as to signify "himself", it is easy to understand how an adjective denoting the identity of a person, signifying "himself", could acquire the proper meaning of "'master"' (p. 74). (Benveniste likes 'proper meaning [*sens propre*]' a lot and quietly makes use of the expression on every page, as I have already and often noted, as if the request for the proper meaning were exactly the *same* as the request for the proper, for what is the *same* as itself, for the selfsame, for the essence itself, for the word 'same', ipseity never being separable from properness [*propriété*] and the self-identity of whatever or whomever.) Thus we would need to attempt a difficult distinction – subtle but necessary – between the *other* and the *stranger*; and we would need to venture into what is both the implication and the consequence of this double bind*, this impossibility as condition of possibility, namely, the troubling analogy in their common origin between *hostis* as host and *hostis* as enemy, between hospitality and hostility.

Translated by Barry Stocker and Forbes Morlock

NOTES

This text is based on a paper Derrida delivered in Istanbul (at the workshop Pera Peras Poros, Bosphorus University, 9–10 May 1997). The published text includes the paper Derrida spoke from and additional remarks he made during the symposium. It retains the informal syntax of an oral presentation which the translators have tried to preserve. Some English translations of texts Derrida quotes have been silently modified. The translators would like to thank Cathérine Pingeot for her comments on a first draft of this translation.

1. Originally published as 'Hostipitalité', *Cogito* 85 (1999, special issue *Pera Peras Poros*, ed. Ferda Keskin and Önay Sözer): pp. 17–44. [Tr.]
2. Immanuel Kant, *Kant's Political Writings*, ed. Hans Reiss (Cambridge: Cambridge UP, 1970). German interpolations in square brackets are Derrida's. Those in French and English have been added by the translators. [Tr.]
3. Angular brackets < > indicate comments made by Derrida during the symposium and added to the text by its original editors. [Tr.]
4. 'Host' and 'guest' can both translate '*hôte*'. The ambivalence of the French is of course important for Derrida. Occasionally, he resorts to English to specify the sense of '*hôte*' as either 'host' or 'guest'. Many such questions and passages – including some of those from Kant, Klossowski, Levinas, and Benveniste – are also and differently broached in 'A Word of Welcome', *Adieu: To Emmanuel Levinas*, trans. Pascale-Anne Brault and Michael Naas (Stanford: Stanford UP, 1999). See pages 15–123, 135–52. A number of the same topics are extended in *Of Hospitality: Anne Dufourmantelle Invites Jacques Derrida to Respond*, trans. Rachel Bowlby (Stanford: Stanford UP, 2000). [Tr.]
5. '*Étranger*' has been translated variously as 'stranger', 'foreigner', and 'foreign', depending on the context. [Tr.]
6. Derrida is referring to Immanuel Kant, *The Metaphysics of Morals*, trans. Mary Gregor (Cambridge: Cambridge UP, 1991) pp. 261–64. [Tr.]
7. *The Politics of Friendship*, trans. George Collins (London: Verso, 1997) p. 257. The black swan appears in the middle of a discussion of Kant on friendship. Kant's own

discussion can be found in the section of *The Metaphysics of Morals* cited above. [Tr.]

8. The French '*patron*' does not have the same range as the English 'patron', suggesting 'boss' or 'owner' but not 'client' as well. The ambiguity of the English 'patron' might suit Derrida's point nicely, but would also transform it significantly. [Tr.]
9. An asterisk after a word or phrase indicates that it appears in English in the original. [Tr.]
10. <Already you will see many of the conditions of hospitality appear. One can turn the person who arrives away on condition that this does not lead to his death. Today we all have (in France in particular – I will allow myself to speak only of France) plenty of experience of the expulsion of foreigners when we know that expulsion will lead to their deaths for either political reasons in their countries of origin or pathological reasons. This raises the whole grave question of AIDS. We know, for example, when foreigners are turned away from France, that they will face conditions in the countries they return to where the treatment of AIDS is not as successful as it is in France. We are doing what Kant says we must not do. That is to say, we are turning people away even when this implies their death. If the stranger behaves himself, however, we cannot turn him away. But this also means there is conditionality. What are the limits? What is the content of these conditions?>
11. <The stranger can pass through but cannot stay. He is not given the rights of a resident. In order for there to be a right of residence, there must be an agreement between states. Everything – and this is what cosmopolitanism means – is subject to an inter-state conditionality. Hence, there is no hospitality for people who are not citizens. Behind this thought are the enormous problems on which Hannah Arendt reflected regarding what had happened in Europe. With the decline of the nation-state we were dealing with millions of people who were no longer even exiles or émigrés but displaced persons, that is, people who did not even have the guarantee of a citizenship, the political guarantee of a citizenship, with all the consequences that entails. This is the challenge today, too: a hospitality which would be more than cosmopolitical, which would go beyond strictly cosmopolitical conditions, those which imply state authority and state legislation. The foreigner cannot claim a right of residence (that would require a special friendly agreement which would make him the member of a native household for a certain period of time), but can claim a right to visit, a right of resort.>
12. <So what is Kant saying to us here? He is saying that this universal right, this political right implying states, this is what he is calling the common possession of the earth's surface. He insists on this common surface for two reasons which are clear but perhaps not underlined. One is that because the earth is spherical, circular, and thus finite, men must learn to live together. And the surface is at the same time space, naturally, the surface area, but it is also superficiality, that is, what is common, what is a priori shared by all men, what is neither above nor below. What is above is culture, institutions, construction. Everything men construct is not common property: foundations, institutions, architecture, hence culture, are not naturally common property. What is common is the natural surface. And, as we will see later, it is a natural right which grounds universal hospitality.>
13. <What Kant does not know here is that the Muslim right which we were speaking of earlier, the right of hospitality, is first founded on a nomadic right. The right of hospitality is, first of all, a nomadic right precisely linked to a sum of differences [*écarts*] which form the pre-Islamic right in which Islamic right and hospitality are rooted.>
14. The opening and organizing line of *Politics of Friendship*. [Tr.]
15. In English 'acceptation' has the same meaning as '*acception*' in French. '*Acception*' has thus been translated as 'acceptation' and '*acceptation*' as 'acception'. The

different evolutions of the Latin word in French and English in fact illustrate Derrida's points about the 'easy mistake' and how these questions are always questions of translation. [Tr.]

16. See 'Khôra', trans. Ian McLeod, *On the Name*, ed. Thomas Dutoit (Stanford: Stanford UP, 1995) pp. 87–127, 146–50. [Tr.]
17. <I say 'invitation' – allow me to mark in a parenthesis the site of a development which I will not have time to enter into today. I think that precisely the invitation defines conditional hospitality. When I invite someone to come into my home, it is on condition that I receive him. Everything is conditioned by the fact that I remain at home and foresee his coming. We must distinguish the invitation from what we would have to call the visitation. The visitor is not necessarily an invited guest [*un invité*]. The visitor is someone who could come at any moment, without any horizon of expectation, who could like the Messiah come by surprise. Anyone could come at any moment. So it is in religious language, in Levinas' language, and elsewhere in the Christian language in which one speaks of the visitation that is the arrival of the other, of God, when no one is waiting for Him. And no one is there to impose conditions on His coming. Thus, the distinction between invitation and visitation may be the distinction between conditional hospitality (invitation) and unconditional hospitality, if I accept the coming of the other, the arriving [*arrivance*] of the other who could come at any moment without asking my opinion and who could come with the best or worst of intentions: a visitation could be an invasion by the worst. Unconditional hospitality must remain open without horizon of expectation, without anticipation, to any surprise visitation. I close this parenthesis, but obviously it should count for a lot.>
18. Pierre Klossowski, *Roberte Ce Soir* and *The Revocation of the Edict of Nantes*, trans. Austryn Wainhouse (London: Calder and Boyars, 1971). [Tr.]
19. "*Invité*" can, of course, also be translated by 'guest'. [Tr.]
20. <I am the hostage of the other insofar as I welcome the face of the other, insofar as I welcome infinity. For Levinas the welcoming of the other is the welcoming of an other who is infinitely other and who consequently extends beyond me infinitely, when I consequently welcome beyond my capacity to welcome. In hospitality I welcome an other greater than myself who can consequently overwhelm the space of my house.>
21. Emmanuel Levinas, *Otherwise than Being or Beyond Essence*, trans. Alphonso Lingis (The Hague: Martinus Nijhoff, 1981) p. 117. [Tr.]
22. 'La substitution', *Revue Philosophique de Louvain* 66 (août 1968): p. 500, rpt in *Autrement qu'être ou au-delà de l'essence* (The Hague: Martinus Nijhoff, 1974) p. 145 [*Otherwise than Being or Beyond Essence*, p. 114], where the sentence 'The word "I" would answer for everything and everyone' becomes 'The word "I" means "here I am", answering for everything and for everyone'. A formula resounds two pages earlier which we clearly must analyze in its context and in the logic of what Levinas calls 'substitution', the subject as the subject of substitution: 'A subject is a hostage' (p. 112). Then there is Sygne de Coufontaine in Claudel's *L'Otage* [The Hostage], which we should read together, as we should *L'Échange* [The Exchange].
23. On *l'arrivant*, see also *Aporias*, trans. Thomas Dutoit (Stanford: Stanford UP, 1993) pp. 33–35. [Tr.]
24. <In Levinas this notion of anachrony is essential to the definition of the subject as host and as hostage; hence the anachrony of this paradoxical instant.>
25. Martin Heidegger, *What Is Called Thinking?*, trans. Fred D. Wieck and J. Glenn Gray (New York: Harper & Row, 1968) p. 4. [Tr.]
26. [The French translation to which Derrida refers is:] *Qu'appelle-t-on penser*, trans. J. Granel (Paris: PUF, 1959) pp. 228–30.
27. The texts which serve as the bases of the French and English translations of this passage differ slightly. [Tr.]

28. Émile Benveniste, *Indo-European Language and Society*, trans. Elizabeth Palmer (London: Faber, 1973) p. 72.
Here Derrida begins to redeem his promise elsewhere to return to this 'magnificent chapter' in Benveniste 'in a more problematic and troubled way': *Monolingualism of the Other; or, The Prosthesis of Origin*, trans. Patrick Mensah (Stanford: Stanford UP, 1998) p. 77. [Tr.]
29. Michel de Montaigne, *The Essays of Michel de Montaigne*, trans. M. A. Screech (London: Penguin, 1991) Book III, chapter 9, p. 1113.

13

Martin Morris

BETWEEN DELIBERATION AND DECONSTRUCTION: THE CONDITION OF POST-NATIONAL DEMOCRACY[1]

Martin Morris is interested in political spaces and, in particular, in Derrida's and Habermas's critiques of the political space of the nation-state. Both are critical of nationalism, xenophobia, ethnocentrism, and so on – in short, of discourses that lay claim to given and natural identities, whether cultural, religious, or whatever. Morris holds that political spaces – including civil society and the public sphere – must be inclusive of diversity and must not take identities as given, for instance the identity of a particular nation. Political spaces must therefore facilitate both the contestation of identities and of the political spaces themselves. Morris argues that, while Habermas provides an account of postnational public spheres and political spaces, Derrida provides important qualifications on two accounts: first, he emphasises the constructed and open character of identities; and, second, he points to the difficulties of creating a political space free from relations of power.

Democracy is not about where the political is located but how it is experienced.[2]

The Problem of Democratic Political Space and its Importance

Within a democratic polity, the form, quality and abundance of the right kind of spaces are essential to the citizen's ability to exercise rights, respond

---

Martin Morris, 'Deliberation and Deconstruction: Two Views on the Space of a Post-National Democracy', *Canadian Journal of Political Science*, 34: 4, 2001, pp. 763–90.

to the duties of citizenship and act politically. This is the case even if no general agreement is possible on what constitutes the proper desirable political virtues or identities that citizens should actualise through such rights and duties. The space necessary for democratic freedom is, however, disfigured and limited if political questions are assimilated to those of technical administration (rationalisation), the interests of disciplinary power, or if public space is commodified in the interests of capital.[3]

The manifest dangers to the integrity and operation of a free public sphere presented by the distortions or limitations of 'unofficial' social power are described by Jürgen Habermas, following a Marxist-inspired model, as 'internal colonisations' by the imperatives specific to relatively autonomous economic and bureaucratic systems.[4] Habermas has argued that the public sphere is a key vehicle for public opinion and public will-formation – if by no means the most influential or powerful – in a modern liberal democracy that must be defended against such encroachments.[5] A democratic polity, one might then say, requires for its normative content and its reproduction open, non-institutionalised, public spaces on many levels and in many domains ranging from the open distribution of ideas in the mass media to the simple freedom of movement, assembly and interaction offered by the public street, grand thoroughfare, *Platz*, university, church, community centre or voluntary association. Such public spheres, large or small, highly organised and structured or relatively loose and diffuse, incorporate diverse and multiple publics and can encompass a variety of sites, media and levels of influence. They are necessary complements to the more formally constituted and instituted public spheres such as the law courts, Parliament or the insular spheres of bureaucracy. In contrast to the formally organised sites, the non-institutionalised public spheres are more flexible and open to radical challenges, more sensitive to problems and crises and uniquely able to articulate existentially grounded perspectives on issues relevant to political decision making.

A difficulty occurs, however, when we try to specify more concretely the indefinite object of the notion of political space as encompassing an openness appropriate to democracy. Unlike the street, mall, neighbourhood, or columns of a newspaper, political space cannot be physically measured, added up, depicted or surveyed; one cannot indicate political openness in the way that broad boulevards, unrestrained access and bustling motion might indicate an open city. Moreover, our sense of physical or geographic space is itself a product of the intellectually and socially mediated relations between objects. Political space, in contrast to concrete space, seems metaphorical, like the 'social space' referred to by sociologists, for it lacks identifiable dimensions or shape and is not even abstract in the sense that geometric spaces are abstract. It cannot be described or delineated easily in terms outside those governing its own existence, which are obscure, yet one seems to need recourse to topographical or especially architectural descriptors and metaphors (for example, the political arena, stage or forum). That said, it nevertheless seems impossible – or at least severely misguided – to think that one can adequately map the world of politics, or more deeply, political culture, with tools developed for the physical world. Rather, this observation on the intangible interiority yet intended 'sharedness' of political space draws attention to the apparent paradox of *how* we are to understand the openness attributed to the shared political space that the idea of democracy intends we should inhabit.

Habermas emphasises relations of intersubjectivity, but seeks to allow and indeed, encourage awareness of critical social issues and problems that require political solutions. He seeks a free and open context of public communication and interaction that might bring diverse and contesting interests together in a co-operative process of problem solving and consensus production in the public sphere. Far more than mere interest group pluralism, Habermas's model relies on a theory of communicatively achieved social bonding and a sociology of situated knowledges, perspectives and locations sensitive to social difference and inequality without collapsing distinctively political space. His position claims to establish a democratic political space of appearance and identity formation without relying on a phenomenological essentialism of proper political capacities or tasks that are distinguished from the social.

THE DELIBERATIVE PUBLIC SPHERE AND THE LIFEWORLD

In contrast to republican thinkers, Habermas regards the possibility of a united agreement on the common good unrealistic given our highly differentiated, complex and pluralistic societies. But he believes that participation is crucial if questions of social justice and the public good are to be addressed adequately. Instead of expecting collective participation and general agreement on values – a strong republican or nationalist politics – Habermas emphasises the conditions and procedures for discussion, argument and deliberation in the public sphere. This is the way in which the reality of plural competition can meet the democratic requirement of inclusive individual and group need-interpretation and identity formation.

> The success of deliberative politics depends not on a collectively acting citizenry but on the institutionalization of the corresponding procedures and conditions of communication, as well as on the interplay of institutionalized deliberative processes with informally developed public opinions.[6]

If the citizenry cannot deliberate, act or rule as a collective *subject* because 'the people' are always plural, there is no need to identify the collectivity in any substantive sense. For the republican, however, such embodiment is just what gives meaning to the participatory acts of all. Indeed, popular sovereignty cannot be *embodied* in this way at all, but is instead, according to Habermas, 'found in those subjectless forms of communication that regulate the flow of discursive opinion- and will-formation in such a way that their fallible outcomes have the presumption of practical reason on their side.' Sovereignty is thus located in 'the power of public discourses'.[7]

The presumption of practical reason, for Habermas, is not substantive but procedural. Yet it entails definitive contours. It presumes a '*co-operative* competition for the better argument' where 'the goal of a communicatively reached agreement unites the participants from the outset'.[8] If one takes *rational* argument seriously, then one wishes to convince using good reasons, and not by using rhetoric, lies, deception or coercion. The kind of agreement aimed for is not mere accord or de facto consensus but an agreement based on rational conviction. It is not simply the agreement one feels with like-minded souls, but rather enjoins participants actively. Thus Habermas can reconstruct the pragmatic presuppositions of the process of argumentation on which a statement's rational acceptability depends. The most important features of this process are:

> (i) that nobody who could make a relevant contribution may be excluded; (ii) that all participants are granted an equal opportunity to make contributions; (iii) that the participants must mean what they say; and (iv) that communication must be freed from external and internal coercion so that . . . participants . . . are motivated solely by the rational force of the better reasons.[9]

This reconstruction informs the concept of deliberative democracy that emphasises people's opportunities to have access to sufficient information and relevant reasons, and to participate in the informal and formal processes and institutions of public opinion formation and will-formation. All affected by the outcome of any particular decision should have equal opportunities to make their interests and the reasons for them known publicly. Such inclusion is implied by the very meaning of the process of argumentation, which aims at reaching agreement.

However, the inclusiveness of deliberative democracy does not *demand* that all interested representatives or parties be involved in particular decisions. This would place excessive burdens on citizens and institutions alike. The institutionalisation of communicative processes of public opinion formation and will-formation would instead establish the *presumption* of rational and democratic outcomes (at the very least) without the need for every citizen actually to participate. Such a position thus avoids, for Habermas, difficulties associated with the republican's requirement of shared public virtues of participation or respect for constitutive traditions, and makes his proposal amenable to practical-political decision making in large, complex, differentiated and pluralistic societies.

Yet Habermas also admits that the consolidation of 'the sociopolitical culture' is necessary so that 'forms of communication adequate to practical reason' do in fact emerge. The dispersal and diffusion of public discourses require 'a background political culture that is egalitarian, divested of all educational privileges and thoroughly intellectual'.[10] If the rise of fundamentalist defences of tradition are to be discouraged, then a robust civil society 'can blossom only in an already rationalized lifeworld'.[11] But rather than the specific assumptions of a Western liberal democratic political culture that, for example, Rawls relies on,[12] Habermas's 'already rationalized lifeworld' depends on the more clearly universal presuppositions behind identity formation that is achieved through intersubjective relations mediated by speech itself. These presuppositions of linguistically mediated communication guide communicative rationality and feed the communicative power that democracy should encourage. It is worth considering in some detail Habermas's idea of a rationalised lifeworld and how all modern subjects share in it.

At the heart of Habermas's democratic conception of identity-formation and political discourse lies the dynamics of linguistically-mediated intersubjectivity, a conception drawn especially from Schutz's (and Luckmann's) phenomenology and adapted via G. H. Mead and Anglo-American speech pragmatics. Habermas accounts for the 'space in-between' by locating it, so to speak, on the phenomenological ground provided by his concept of the lifeworld. The lifeworld, for Habermas, refers not only to the world of cultural meanings and identities in which we communicate, but also to the stock of interpretive knowledge, know-how and learning capacities that compose vast domains and reservoirs of communicative resources in society. Actors draw upon these resources and develop them in their action coordinated by communicative rationality, which is for Habermas sharply distinguished from strategic or instrumental rational action. Lifeworld structures and mechanisms govern the social reproduction of interpretive schemes and legitimate authority and instil life aspirations; they are constitutive of obligations and the social integration of diverse identities, behaviour and social memberships; and they enable socialisation via successful interpretations, motivations for action and personality formation.[13]

Despite this highly functional view, Habermas conceives of the lifeworld as a 'social space inhabited in common that emerges in the course of dialogue'.[14] But the lifeworld reveals only a portion of itself in any dialogue because it exists as a phenomenological 'background' of pre-theoretical, pre-interpreted contexts of meaning or relevance (*Verweisungszusammenhänge*). In the same way that 'language' itself, while in use, seems to remain 'at the backs' of participants, the lifeworld provides a substrate that is 'always already' familiar, a continual and substantively preinterpreted domain. Consequently, topographical-spatial metaphors abound when describing the lifeworld: Everyday communicative practice is 'embedded' in a lifeworld context; the lifeworld is a transcendental 'site' where speaker and hearer meet, in which a 'segment' (a 'situation') is 'thrown into relief'; such situational definitions need not be identical but must 'overlap'. A 'situation' occurs when the assumptions necessary for action co-ordination become uncertain. When this uncertainty is pursued, a specific aspect of the lifeworld background is 'thematised', that is, questioned and subjected to argument seeking to restore an agreement on the situational definition. Situations have boundaries but are never thereby finally delimited, for these limits shift with the requirements of action co-ordination. Following Husserl's image of the *horizon*, the boundaries of lifeworld situations in a discussion can be overstepped at any time similar to the way in which the horizon expands and shrinks as one moves through rough terrain.[15] However, the vast proportion of lifeworld convictions always remain in the background during any discussion.

What is of interest here about this idea of the lifeworld is its quasi-transcendental nature. The 'lifeworld' itself cannot be the proper theme of communicative utterances, for as a totality it provides the space in or ground upon which such utterances occur, even those that name it explicitly. It is, hence, 'at once unquestionable and shadowy . . . it remains indeterminate'[16]; its opacity and taken-for-grantedness endures even for theory, which hence cannot adopt a transcendental approach to the lifeworld's structures themselves. At best, theory 'can only hope to be equal to the *ratio essendi* of its object when there are grounds for assuming that the objective context of life in which the theoretician finds himself is opening up to him its *ratio cognoscendi*.'[17] One might conclude, as Habermas does here in reference to Marx, that such opening up only becomes possible when whole lifeworlds become threatened, as ours has become, on his reading, under colonisation by systems of instrumental and strategic reason. This effort to historicise his own position via a materialist theory of modernity and its potentials is often overlooked by those who too hastily criticise Habermas as a transcendentalist. It is important in understanding Habermas not to equate him with the more traditional Kant-inspired transcendentalism of, say, the Rawls of *A Theory of Justice* or Habermas's colleague K. O. Apel.[18]

Nevertheless for Habermas, the indeterminacy of the lifeworld does not consequently become decisive in a profound sense, as it does for postmodernists and other critical theorists who would challenge the idea that (some kind of) universal structures lie behind, or are constitutive for, identities. He still recognises a 'happy' dialectic operating in the linguistically-mediated lifeworld structures of modernity. That is, for Habermas, the shadowy background existence of the lifeworld does not entail that the operation of language as a totality is mystified with respect to the everyday practice of the linguistic medium itself. Indeed, modern learning processes are dependent on differentiated *claims to validity* that bind speakers and hearers in a co-operative search for truth. Rational motivation, in contrast to empirical motivation, relies on this special force of validity. The condition for claiming validity, Habermas argues, is that reasons must always be able to be given that *demonstrate* the validity of a claim to the satisfaction of all concerned. Acceptance of a validity claim is thus an acceptance that valid reasons *can* be given and, further, that both speaker and hearer *can* and *will* agree that these conditions for a claim's validity have been satisfied. This is how communicative action can be said to *bind* speakers and hearers rationally. The operation of the claim to validity functions rationally according to the communicative bonding needs of the species: reason as logos is reinscribed in this way by Habermas as an intersubjective communicative process of sociation.

Meaning, as distinguished from validity, finds explicit expression in language, in lifeworld situations, in the tacit knowledges and abilities sedimented in the background of the lifeworld. Linguistically mediated life exists, in turn, by virtue of a dialectical process between meaning and validity whereby world-disclosure becomes possible on condition of communicative-rational actions, and every claim to validity (mutual recognition) requires the enactment of some shared world even when the recognition of validity is not achieved. Habermas sees an intrinsic connection and reciprocal causality between meaning and validity, which nevertheless does not eliminate the difference between the two.[19] This distinction is central to his theory and is definitive for his rejection of competing positions such as poststructuralism and deconstruction.

This dynamic view of social reproduction corresponds for Habermas to a political theory of citizenship based on the recognition and respect of the democratic constitutional state. Regarding questions of 'struggles for recognition' and issues of 'the nation' in democratic states, he draws a sharp distinction between the ethical substance of groups and communities to which individuals belong as *members* and the legal content of the political state to which *citizens* belong.[20] This difference coincides with the two levels of social and political integration through which respective identities are formed and which cannot, and should not, be confused.

I would like to underline the connection between the sociological and phenomenological dimensions of Habermas's notion of the lifeworld and his concept of the citizen in democracy. The dialectical process of mutual determinacy between meaning and validity requires that the (speaking) self be involved with another (speaking self) in a *dialogical* process of identity formation and world-disclosure. This is a process distinguished paradigmatically from the *mono-logic* of subject-object relations or the contemplative thought experiments of the social contract tradition. The valid consensuses reached through this linguistically mediated intersubjective interaction must *in fact* occur; they cannot be validated by rational reflection alone. Thus identities and traditions are practically established and reproduced. But in order for *this* fact to be recognised and respected – a recognition and respect that undergirds the principles and ethos of liberal autonomy and plurality – a more general *political* consensus must be reached. This political consensus has its focal point in the constitutional arrangements of a democratic society. For it is the case in modern, post-conventional and complex societies, Habermas argues, that 'the citizenry as a whole can no longer be held together by a substantive consensus on values but only by a consensus on the procedures for the legitimate enactment of laws and the legitimate exercise of power.'[21] Substantive ethical life is only established *within* the open-ended and constantly shifting space of the lifeworld which, precisely by virtue of its open-endedness and variance, endows all substantive identities with a dynamic that must consequently be recognised politically. What makes such a dynamic of identity formation possible is the necessary recognition that democratic citizenship is of a higher order than cultural or group memberships.[22] This recognition is *formally* embodied in constitutional arrangements, but from the Habermasian perspective, it is a presupposition of the liberal democratic way of life. Cultural or group membership in and of themselves are thus not strictly forms of political citizenship at all on this view, despite all the contributions to the public good or displays of civic virtue such members may produce on account of their collective activities.

The ethical content of democracy is found at this conditioning level, formalised in the operation of the constitution. Hence Habermas concludes that politically relevant loyalty in a democratic state takes the form of a 'constitutional patriotism'. Any such constitution worthy of this kind of loyalty must approximate or aspire to the procedural norms of a discursive democracy. Such a set of norms guarantees the broad and open operation of reflective public opinion formation and will-formation based on raising and redeeming validity claims. Only then, one might add, can the democratic polity recognise difference safely – that is, without inviting domination of political space by a hegemonic identity or, conversely, allowing the fragmentation, deterioration, or stagnation of the political as a result of withdrawal, refusal, apathy, or inefficacy. Or, worse, without risking the destruction or usurpation of political space under assault from mere power politics, technological and administrative imperatives or, more subtly, from dominations inherent in consumerist culture. All these dangers may be seen as present to some degree in the contemporary political sphere. Deliberative democracy thus becomes the desired general model for political decision making and the ideal of effective, responsive and legitimate democracy. Constitutional patriotism in the democratic state represents a universality that values a legal and political idea of the citizen over all forms of particular belonging.[23]

My reading of Habermas stresses here the relationship between the level of identity formation and that of its conditions, which is deepened by the discussion of the philosophical importance attributed to Habermas's concept of the lifeworld. The lifeworld is ungraspable as a totality only so far as it is understood to present just one aspect or segment of itself to speakers in any particular situation. Its totality is beyond specific thought, for what would be the 'transcendental ground' for thinking the lifeworld as a whole? There cannot be one, since the boundaries of lifeworld situations are porous while the vast proportion of the lifeworld itself remains overwhelmingly at the backs of actors. 'Communicative actors are always moving *within* the horizon of their lifeworld; they cannot step outside of it.'[24] On this conception there is only this 'horizontality' to actors' relations; such actors relate to each other and to something *in* the lifeworld as context or theme of an utterance without being able to relate to the thing or the lifeworld *themselves*. To maintain that one may take up a relationship to a thing directly is to step back behind Kant and to invoke a metaphysics of the thing-in-itself; to do the same for the lifeworld would be to invoke a cosmology. These latter kinds of relations would, for Habermas, imply treating objects as subjects and project a literal voice of Nature – that is, communicative relations with something other than another human speaking subject yet an other who can recognise and respond to claims to validity. Such mystical or theological visions, for Habermas, would hold little promise for a democratic theory in disenchanted modern society.

The intersubjective dynamics of meaning and validity, which are said to be crucial for reasonable life, including democratic life, can only function successfully if both the phenomenal ground of the lifeworld and the regulative set of presuppositions of communicative rationality are invoked to steady the process of identity formation. If speakers and hearers cannot meet in the space created by a neutral (in the sense of unproblematic) but always potentially changeable lifeworld background, then the very operation of the validity claim could not occur. Turning our attention to the dynamics of intersubjective agreement frees us from the aporias associated with the reification of language – the aporias of trying to determine the 'true consciousness' of self and things[25] – *and* prevents a fall into mere relativism or nihilism.

What Habermas denies in this respect is a radical indeterminacy imputed to the lifeworld, because such radical indeterminacy would seem to blur the distinctions between validity and power, validity and meaning and thus threaten democracy, and perhaps even ethical life itself. But is this denial as necessary as he believes? I suggest that his solution to the problem of the indeterminacy of this space is unsatisfactory for the reason that the spatial conditions of speaking, thinking, naming, bringing forth, of opening onto and appearing in the world – in short, of *communication* and *understanding* – ought not to be considered only in terms of the horizontal or two dimensional metaphor offered by his notion of the lifeworld or based solely on the dynamics of reaching agreement in language. With reference to an ethical-political perspective on deconstruction, the remainder of this work explains why.

Radical Indeterminacy of the Lifeworld

If the space we occupy when we seek to communicate or understand has boundaries, they are not *simply* 'always already' there, even if their givenness is initially thrust upon us. Against what, precisely, the boundaries of the lifeworld stand remains obscure, mysterious; but this obscurity and mystery can be productive. Borders, frontiers, boundaries, are always seemingly also divisions, identities and oppositions, even if they are conceived as absolute limits. While an absolute limit cannot be crossed no matter what, its sense of limit always implies an opposite or further space beyond. For Habermas, this space beyond is never radically indeterminate in a non-foundational sense, which would destabilise the lifeworld, given the horizontal metaphor which informs his notion. It is only indeterminate to the extent that the 'space beyond' that is implied by current limits represents the future – and our expectations of what future generations might find true, good or beautiful are fallible. Within our activities of communicative understanding, there can be nothing beyond the horizontality of the lifeworld except more horizons. Speakers might move the horizon themselves through the dynamic performance of their conversation, but moving beyond the horizontality of intersubjective relations is allegedly impossible. Hence, there is, for Habermas, no 'extramundane' position available for communicative speakers. Outside the *communicative* horizons of reaching understanding lies only deception, violence, brute force and coercion. When lifeworld processes are colonised by system imperatives, they are subjected to a certain violence. One can of course walk away from reaching understanding and agreement (if there is room to do so), in which case no action co-ordination (social participation) occurs.

For a thinker like Derrida, on the contrary, it is extremely important to probe the difficulty presented by this aporia of horizontality. For Derrida, it is by no means necessary that the ontological limit of language forces us back to a dialectic between logos and its structure. Derrida's initial approach is, like Habermas's, a product of the crisis of representation and action associated with the exhaustion of the philosophy of consciousness. The subject of thought faces a paradox of self-referentiality imposed by the impossible grounds of subjectivity itself. Probing this dilemma, Derrida questions the distinction or opposition between logos and mythos, the 'paradigm' and its copy, that informs so much of the history of philosophical thought. Such oppositions, which might also include the critical opposition between truth and ideology, remain simulacra of language – inevitable abstraction. Derrida is interested in what might lie beyond them, as their conditions of possibility, but somehow, nevertheless, not opposed to another point or site, which would then produce just another representational model. But such conditions of possibility would seem to be in principle unnameable, untheorisable. Derrida, however, does not, like Habermas, follow a Kantian lead and develop the dynamics of intersubjective agreement. Instead, he turns to a kind of negative ontology in order to pursue this problematic.

In a discussion of the phenomenon of naming, Derrida refers to Plato's notion of (the) khôra, which is discussed in the *Timaeus*. Khôra is the space that 'gives place', which in Plato's dialogue is compared to a mother or a nurse. Derrida refers to khôra by playing on the French pronoun '*elle*' (she/it) and by using it as a proper name without the definite article, which would imply a thing. Derrida writes:

> Khôra marks a place apart, the spacing which keeps a dissymetrical relation to all that which, 'in herself,' beside or in addition to herself, seems to make couple with her... She/it eludes all anthropo-theological schemes, all history, all revelation and all truth. Preoriginary, before and outside of all generation, she no longer even has the meaning of a past, of a present that is past. *Before* signifies no temporal anteriority. The relation of independence, the non-relation, looks more like the relation of the interval or the spacing to what is lodged in it to be received by it.[26]

Here we return to an articulation of the 'space in-between'. This is a desert place, however, a wilderness, if one were to invoke a geographic metaphor to contrast with Habermas's rich and verdant geography of the lifeworld. But khôra is a concept at once non-identical with itself in its very intention 'as if they were two, the one and its double', for it opens 'an apparently empty space' but is not '*emptiness*'.[27] It is thus that which is in this sense indeconstructible, since 'the place that gives rise and place to Babel would be indeconstructible, not as a construction sheltered from every internal or external deconstruction, but as the very spacing of de-construction.'[28] Perhaps then it is '*place itself*, the irreplaceable place', that which 'gives place to all the stories, ontologic or mythic' without itself becoming the object of any discourse whatsoever. If khôra 'figures the place of inscription of *all that is marked in the world*', then one cannot, without further ado, 'call by the name *program* or *logic* the form which dictates... the law of such a composition: program and logic are apprehended in it, *as such*, though it be in a dream and put *en abyme*.'[29] One is reminded of the image of the vast, impenetrable and mysterious ocean on which sits the space station in Tarkovsky's adaptation of S. Lem's *Solaris*, an ocean that creates a reality for the space station occupants by reconstructing it from fragments of their memories, but which itself remains utterly 'beyond'. Khôra itself cannot be another language, even the metaphoric language of geographic space, as in Habermas's lifeworld or Tarkovsky's alien ocean, for the referent of this reference, Derrida contends, does not exist: 'there is khôra, but khôra does not exist'.[30]

For Habermas, the lifeworld, along with the formal structures of meaning and validity which give it its shape and content, remain insulated, immune from the indeterminacy (or deconstructive readiness) that resides in all identities. This immunity is guaranteed philosophically by the very condition of language itself: that every speaker always already assumes the rational presuppositions of communicative rationality with every utterance. Besides this philosophical argument, Habermas's main political reason for such immunisation is a conviction that the formal structure of reason must be protected otherwise the co-ordinating power of democracy itself is threatened with serious compromise or outright destruction. Openness, for Habermas, requires the substantial and stable boundaries established by multiple consensuses, which thereby seem to exhaust the scope of rational public discussion oriented toward politically relevant co-ordination. It cannot permit an openness to what might lie beyond consensus itself as a mode of useful co-ordination. Indeed, as I indicated, what lies beyond legitimate consensus-formation, for Habermas, is simply deception and violence. For Derrida, by contrast, what is indeconstructible is rather the formless, structureless space in-between, the abyss or chasm 'in' which the cleavages between sensible and intelligible, body and soul, can have a place and take place.[31] It is this shuddering spacing without end and without bottom which gives rise and receives – gives form by receiving imprint and inscription or by containing, without being either surface or receptacle, mother or nurse. It would only be this level, the spacing of deconstruction itself, that could be beyond the operation of the latter. This is not difference or *différance*, nor is it God, but it might be the condition of all, the condition for the very existence of politics and of God.[32]

In his ongoing explorations of the relationship between hegemony and democracy, Laclau understands the formless, structureless space in-between that I have been discussing as a 'signified without a signifier', that is, as an 'empty signifier'.[33] For Laclau, the social is essentially differentiated and uneven and not simply a diversification, which would imply some sort of original and positive unity or identity from which the diversity has sprung and to which a theory of politics can then refer. Given this condition, there is no natural identity among differentiated social identities that can claim the right to represent the wholeness of all and thereby mark the limits of what Laclau calls the chains of equivalence that are articulated in particular social struggles of opposition among them. But some identities do claim this right and achieve hegemony. Such an identity can do so only by signifying itself as that which takes the place of the 'empty signifier', the absent and impossible fullness of identity that I have analysed as the paradoxical presence of absence seemingly required for identity itself. The universal is for Laclau, like Derrida, 'an empty but ineradicable place'.[34] But, according to Laclau, given also the fact that not any position, not any particular social struggle is *equally* capable of transforming itself into the identity that takes the place of the absent universal, the operation of hegemonic identities depends on successfully taking the place of, and representing, this constitutive absence. This explains the very possibility of politics, which is essentially an historical activity of struggle to achieve hegemony in this fashion. For example, in a situation of radical Hobbesian disorder, '"order" is present as that which is absent; it becomes an empty signifier, as the signifier of that absence'. Political forces then compete to present their programmes as fulfilling that lack: 'To hegemonize something is exactly to carry out this filling function.'[35]

The widespread consciousness of such radical openness in the social is rare and perhaps has only occurred at unique historical moments when social struggle coincides with the breakdown of existing hegemonic projects. Žižek provides a striking example:

> The most sublime image that emerged in the political upheavals of the last years ... was undoubtedly the unique picture from the time of the violent overthrow of Ceausescu in Romania: the rebels waving the national flag with the red star, the Communist symbol, cut out, so that instead of the symbol standing for the organizing principle of the national life, there was nothing but a hole in its centre. It is difficult to imagine a more salient index of the 'open' character of a historical situation 'in its becoming' ... [T]he masses who poured into the streets of Bucharest 'experienced' the situation as 'open,' ... they participated in the unique intermediate state of passage from one discourse (social link) to another, when, for a brief, passing moment, the hole in the big Other, the symbolic order, became visible.[36]

It seems impossible for Habermas to account for this kind of space in-between, this khôra as Derrida calls it, without undermining the very structure which supports his theory of human communication and understanding. This phenomenological difference in accounting for 'spacing' – for the background or 'placing' of language and all its productions – thus identifies one of the profound differences between Habermasian critical theory and deconstruction. What needs to be clarified, then, are the implications of a deconstructive reading of this spacing for thinking about democratic identity and citizenship.

The Danger of Aesthetic Reduction and the Importance of Non-identity for Shared Political Space

For a thinker like Habermas, this paradoxical, aporetic situation seems to suggest a situation at best precarious and at worst highly dangerous to democracy and to critical thinking. 'Whoever transposes the radical critique of reason into the domain of rhetoric in order to blunt the paradox of self-referentiality', Habermas writes, 'also dulls the sword of the critique of reason itself.'[37] It is a most serious issue, for if linguistic efforts at world disclosure (representation) cannot be regarded as separable from what would amount to an aesthetic operation to bridge the space between referent and reality (meaning) as well as the intersubjective distance between speaker and hearer (in the dynamics of communication), then Habermas's view of the distinctive importance of communicative action is substantially undermined. This bridging need not require the simple re-enchantment of the world, where subjective or ethical relations are reintroduced with creatures, plants, and minerals and which would completely negate modern science. But it does require, at minimum, that positivist science lose its unquestioned superiority as the only genuine instrumental or purposive knowledge of the world – an aim that critical social theory has long held central. However, if the modern orientation of equating valid knowledge with what could be counted as universal knowledge ceases to inform how the parameters of the political are defined, even ideally, then the motivation for the criticism of injustice – for critical engagement with others – and the envisioning of social change may become unclear.

Consequently, charges of epistemological relativism and moral indifference are often levelled at the postmodern implications of a turn away from universality. Does the abandonment of universal pretensions mean that theory must affirm that all identities are somehow valid, where the mere assertion of unique identity is the only relevant truth required for recognition? Does it mean that the de facto preservation and flourishing of a global multiplicity and diversity of cultures and identities is all that is required to celebrate democracy against hegemony? If such weak and inadequate conclusions are to be avoided, then a political theory seems to be required through which self- and identity-formation can be somehow critically understood without relying on a universal that comes to it from outside.[38] The problem is that an insistence on radical indeterminacy seems to introduce a well nigh ontological constraint on the motivation for establishing the truth or the validity of knowledge, which science and philosophy in general have taken as fundamental missions and whose pursuit has generally been taken as crucial for effective liberatory democratic politics.

Thus Habermas criticises deconstruction for levelling the distinction between philosophy and literature because it does not recognise that 'language games only work because they presuppose idealizations that transcend any particular language game', namely, those that 'give rise to the perspective of an agreement that is open to criticism on the basis of validity claims'.[39] For deconstruction, the language of philosophy and science cannot be cleansed of metaphorical and rhetorical elements, of literary admixtures, which means that the 'qualities of texts in general' (the concern of *rhetoric*) have priority over any 'system of rules to which only certain types of discourse are subjected in an exclusive manner' (as in argumentation, or *logic*).[40]

One may readily see how the radical indeterminacy of meaning, which is established by the basic deconstructive position that all texts are already and indissolubly products of uncontrollable contexts and which is elaborated in the gestures toward khôra, can expand the world-disclosive capacity of language to cover *all* discourses. Among other things, this has the dual effect of denying the autonomous existence of art and aesthetic production as an object for a (pseudo) science of art criticism, and, conversely, showing that scientific discourses, including philosophy, contain ineradicable aesthetic features that belie their ostensible autonomy from the objects and processes they reveal. Deconstruction thus proceeds as a 'critique of style' – not thereby exempting itself from its critique of specialist discourses, but keeping faith with it by abandoning any claim to be revealing truth like philosophy and science and operating paradoxically as literature deconstructing literature. I have highlighted the ineffable khôra as all that is indeconstructable because it indicates what deconstruction is finally governed by: no thing or text at all, but the paradoxical absence of things as the condition for their appearance in space. From the deconstructive perspective, however, this unrevealable presence is just what calls us to democracy, to the passion for critique and engagement. For in the historical world, the identities of things and people are by no means equal in their power to represent themselves to the world or to reveal new worlds for themselves.

Habermas does not regard either the venerable hermeneutic insight that all meaning is contextual or the deconstructive verity that no discourse can be purified of rhetorical elements as entailing relativist or pan-aesthetic conclusions. On the contrary, he argues that poetic discourse can derive its meaning – and its language can assert the primacy of a world-disclosive function – only to the degree to which language, as fiction, *escapes* the structural constraints and communicative functions of everyday life. In other words, the fact that the space of fiction can be opened up *at all* is precisely due to the suspension of the binding forces and idealisations that make possible a use of language oriented to mutual understanding and agreement.[41] Perhaps nevertheless paralleling Arendt's phenomenological essentialism, Habermas accords each specialist discourse such as art criticism or philosophy its own form of argumentation appropriate to its object, notwithstanding that all such discourses contain indelible rhetorical features. For each performs unique *bridging functions*, connecting esoteric meaning with everyday life that rely on special claims to validity.

> The rhetorical element occurs in its pure form only in the self-referentiality of the poetic expression, that is, in the language of fiction specialized for world-disclosure. Even the normal language of everyday life is ineradicably rhetorical; but within the matrix of different linguistic functions, the rhetorical elements recede here. The world-disclosive linguistic framework is almost at a standstill in the routines

> of everyday practice. The same holds true of the specialized languages of science and technology, law and morality, economics, political science, etc. They, too, live off of the illuminating power of metaphorical tropes; but the rhetorical elements, which are by no means expunged, are tamed, as it were and enlisted for the special purposes of problem-solving.[42]

The most promising challenge to Habermas's position is, thus, not to re-assert a new version of the arguments affirming indeterminacy and the entwinement of rhetoric with reason as though he had somehow missed the point. A more successful route might be to historicise the allegedly necessary idealisations that are assumed in all 'normal' (as opposed to fictional) discourse. A great deal of work is done in Habermas's argument by concepts evoking functional relations and roles – indeed, much of his argument turns on the need to account for successful social co-ordination, which is, accordingly, achieved through communicative and systemic media. Successful social co-ordination is contrasted with breakdowns in rational co-ordination, which manifest in conflict and violence, among other things. To historicise communicative action as social co-ordination might be to ask, for example, whether there is only one, essentially benign and necessary sense in which the rhetorical elements mentioned in the quote above are 'tamed' and 'enlisted' for the specific purposes of 'problem-solving'. Can the orientation toward 'problem-solving' itself that has been so refined in modernity be historicised in a profound way that might then challenge the universality of language's communicative idealisations that are tied to it?

Instead of pursuing this line of criticism, which I have done elsewhere,[43] I want to suggest that introducing an openness to aesthetic relations and representation in the present public sphere, though risking dangers, offers a crucial mode of democratic inclusion of the other and of acknowledgement of difference. It cannot be the only mode, but it is essential to complement any reformation of institutions according to principles of free and open rational discourse. Habermas's warning to democratic thought against 'an analysis of an expressivist, somehow aesthetic, need for self-representation in public space'[44] should be taken seriously. Clear dangers to democracy would emerge in an utterly unconstrained desublimation of aesthetic energy, such as the possibility of sacrificing the interests of the weak to the aesthetic glory of the powerful (and the regressive totalitarian political aesthetic of Nazism clearly stands at the background of Habermas's fears concerning the power of the aesthetic within the political). It might be countered, however, that we already experience a powerfully conservative (if not totalitarian) political aesthetic operating through the mass media, especially in the spectacles achieved by televisual politics. Moreover, the mass culture produced by the culture industry can operate in the service of social power by the very ways it delivers aesthetic gratification to its consumers.[45] Hence there is, at the very least, a need for a strong counter-cultural or counter-hegemonic presence in the mass media to offset the distortions and domination of existing social interests and the culture industries.

The key to the dilemmas of culturalistic abridgement and aesthetic reduction is to draw out the aesthetic-ethical and political implications presented by the non-identical condition of all identities. Every identity is non-identical *in itself* because it depends on difference with and to an other; no identity exists a priori or can be constituted in a singularly original way. This is not quite an assertion of the unavoidability of intersubjectivity but rather that of the radical incompleteness of any identity or subject, for non-identity is required to complete any recognition at all. As such, social history is crucial to understanding all identities because historical processes of inclusion and exclusion always condition identity and recognition in contexts that involve relations of power and domination. The histories of internal and external colonialism are good examples. The best social history, therefore, is social history that recalls the misrecognitions immanent to the dominant identities that prevail (and have prevailed). The self and its other are always already implicated in processes of articulation that in turn comprise the non-identical existence of each. That these also involve histories of power and domination is central to any democratic response for coming to terms with present identities, which are revealed as intimately interrelated through such relations and not simply exogenous before they encounter each other. The misrecognised projection of the non-identical content of oneself or one's culture onto the other has consistently structured histories of intercultural relations and has permitted much domination.[46] It is also important for the democratic position to be clear that this is a *historical* argument and not an *ontological* claim about the nature of society as such.

To recognise that a cultural identity is simultaneously a product of its *own* non-identity with itself as well as a product of relations with and to an *other* culture is to take a first step toward recalling the shared political space that all identities occupy in communicative encounter. The hope is that such recollection will have a positive democratising effect on exclusive, hegemonising or egocentric individuals and groups who privilege their 'capital' or 'heading' and disregard or dominate 'the other *of* the heading' itself.[47] To counter, for example, repetitions of racism, xenophobia, sexism and the numerous forms of colonisation, Derrida calls us to start by recognising that we ourselves come from 'the other' in the sense that difference is the very condition of identity, since '*what is proper to a culture is to not be identical to itself*'. All identity and identification conforms to this:

> there is no self-relation, no relation to oneself, no identification with oneself, without culture, but the culture *of* one's self *as* a culture of the other, a culture of the double genitive and of the *difference to oneself*... signals that a culture never has a single origin.'[48]

Derrida believes that a profound responsibility is brought forth and required by this insight, a responsibility for the other as for oneself, which precedes and affects all ethical and political discourses.

A democratic vision consistent with these unsettling and critical conditions must promote the recognition and exploration of the non-identical 'grounds' of identity. 'No cultural identity presents itself as the opaque body of an untranslatable idiom, but always . . . as . . . the *unique testimony* to the human essence and to what is proper to man.' Every unique identity has 'the responsibility of testifying for universality'.[49] What is interesting and important about this conception of identity formation and mediation is that its shared experience implies a universality of communication from which we may draw an ethical constraint that seeks to limit certain kinds of behaviour and motivations only by denying limits of another sort. The result is a 'philosophy of the limit'[50] whose quasi-transcendental universal call denies the possibility of any metalanguage while trying to achieve 'the effects of metalanguage'.[51] The political communication that is required – and communication is always required, for the experience of language is 'irreducible' – need not, however, produce *consensus* or be oriented only toward *agreement* as its result, but, rather, primarily intends *understanding* and an opening up to the other. While a strict Habermasian may counter that no mutual understanding can occur without some level of agreement, it does not follow that agreement must then be the telos of all political communication. The meaning of *understanding* far exceeds the moment of agreement or identification, since thought, like language, is always in motion, always moving under one heading or another. The moment of decision is required for politics, the moment of agreement likewise; but the call of profound understanding that arises from the irreplaceable place in which identities gather themselves is a call for an openness to the new, to the unique other: 'it should be anticipated *as* the unforeseeable, the *unanticipatable*, the non-masterable, non-identifiable, in short, as that of which one does not yet have a memory'.[52]

Loosening the requirement of strong identification by contemplating the non-identical brings this truth of the self and its (particular) collectivity closer to the surface. This is why all insights into *radical* indeterminacy should not lead to utterly relativist or merely 'social constructionist' conclusions: identity *is and is not* identical (with itself). There is no having one without the other. One deconstructs down to *nothing* (for no referent exists, finally), but the fact that there is no true origin or reliable stability to any identity does not mean that what identity names historically is not *material* and that its existence is not important for the political response to questions of recognition and understanding. On the contrary, it is to this existential experience that the truth of democracy must testify by bearing witness to the unacknowledged suffering that accompanies identity formation.

More than this, however, the stress on the *dynamic* relations of identity and non-identity is also key if the positive effects of a deconstructive universal are to be realised. Speaking of the idea of 'Europe', Derrida argues against the reconstitution of Europe's 'centralising hegemony' but also against a mere anti-hegemony of particularist assertions. One must not simply 'multiply the borders, i.e., the movements [*marches*] and margins [*marges*]. It is necessary not to cultivate for their own sake minority differences, untranslatable idiolects, national antagonisms, or the chauvinisms of idiom.' But, he continues, responsibility consists

> in renouncing neither of these two contradictory imperatives. One must therefore try to *invent* gestures, discourses, politico-institutional practices that inscribe the alliance of these two imperatives, of these two promises or contracts: the capital and the a-capital. That is not easy. It is even impossible to conceive of a responsibility that consists in being responsible *for* two laws, or that consists in responding *to* two contradictory injunctions. No doubt. But there is no responsibility that is not the experience and experiment of the impossible.... European cultural identity, like identity or identification in general, if it must be equal *to itself and to the other*, up to the measure of its own and immeasurable difference with 'itself,' belongs, therefore *must* belong, to this *experience and experiment of the impossible.*[53]

The paradoxical and impossible holding together of these two contradictory injunctions of identity formation and interaction call forth for Derrida a radical 'experience and experiment' – radical because it has never been tried at an institutional level and because it challenges all presently existing imperialist identities to relinquish power. Indeed, it is unclear just what such experience and experiment would look like institutionally. Derrida himself is reluctant to delineate precise institutional implications beyond his call to '*invent*', to come together in an aesthetic, creative process of self-formation that involves most centrally the opening up to and welcoming of the other.[54] But the thrust of the deconstructive critique is to transform the experience of the encounter between self and other such that new institutions appropriate to such experience can emerge. If, as Tully argues, 'the failure mutually to recognize and live with cultural diversity is a failure of imagination'[55] – a failure to see the impossibility and manifest dangers of stable, unified, safe and sure identities – then Derrida contributes a philosophical analysis that supports the new constitutionalism appropriate to the 'strange multiplicity' that Tully wishes to protect and cultivate. The important question for our purposes is whether such *experience and experiment of the impossible* can in principle establish and foster a democratic culture worthy of the name under contemporary conditions that demand new ways of accepting and learning from human diversity, while criticizing oppression and exclusion. I think it does contain a promise in this respect.

Whether such a vision has the *power* to progressively affect the cultural 'capital' or capitalisation of, say, those with manifest interests in cultural hegemony or the pervasive commitments to commodification in our phase of techno-capitalism remains beyond the scope of theory alone. Yet the weakness of Derrida's deconstructive project may lie here in its capacity to motivate people and social movements to challenge the structures of social power that are served by the dominating identities and misrecognitions. Thus West finds that Derrida's 'sophisticated ironic consciousness tends to preclude and foreclose analyses that guide action with purpose.'[56] The implications of deconstruction in the political field have, nevertheless, more potential in this respect than many critics allow. Deconstruction does not blunt the sword of critique or level all discourses to rhetorical effects, as Habermas contends. Neither can Derrida's theory be dismissed, as Charles Taylor does from a perspective centred on the importance of the good, as merely subjectivist, as centred instead on 'power and counterpower' in a way that abandons the need for democratic recognition in favour of the political solidarity of merely 'taking sides'.[57] Derrida wants to get beyond 'all the exhausted programs of *Eurocentrism* and *anti-Eurocentrism*'[58] by bringing forth a new space of political encounter and engagement that relies on responsibility and respect for the other and the otherness of the other.[59] Such an encounter is best achieved if the parties are willing and able to understand each other in a rather demanding way – understanding not under the terms of a master code or a universalism that governs acceptable speech, but through an awareness that can convey historical experience and unique perspective in language and speech. This is much closer to the spirit if not the substance of the Gadamerian fusion of horizons that those such as Taylor favour for democratic political education and culture.[60]

Such understanding allows the world-disclosive element of language to act in a politically orienting and co-ordinating manner, a manner that cannot be assimilated to the consensual orientation given primacy by Habermas nor to a mere affirmation of concrete identities. Derrida declares that there is 'no democracy without literature; no literature without democracy' because only democratic freedom secures literature's '*right to say anything*'.[61] Aesthetic expression is a key element of such communication, even if its text can always be deconstructed. The responsibility of democracy may be impassioned by the very experience of its impossible ground, which Derrida conceives as the call of the 'secret' of the text, but its co-ordinating power will still depend on embodiment and hence representation. This at least suggests that the theory of democracy will benefit by including something of Habermas's commitment to the acting subject of discursive critical exchange as well as deconstruction's responsibility to the other.

NOTES

1. An earlier version of this article was presented at the Midwest Political Science Association Meeting, Chicago, 2000. I thank the anonymous reviewer of the *Canadian Journal of Political Science*, Nadine Changfoot, Bonnie Honig, Russ Janzen and Graham Todd for helpful comments on earlier elements and drafts. I benefited from participation in Romand Coles' seminar 'Derrida and His Critics' at Duke University, 1998, and I gratefully acknowledge the SSHRC postdoctoral fellowship that took me to Duke University.
2. Sheldon S. Wolin, 'Fugitive Democracy', in Seyla Benhabib (ed.), *Democracy and Difference: Contesting the Boundaries of the Political* (Princeton: Princeton University Press, 1996), p. 38.
3. Frankfurt School critical theory centre-staged new forms of domination in the 'scientisation' of politics and the commodification of 'democratic' power; see Douglas Kellner, *Critical Theory, Marxism, and Modernity* (Baltimore: Johns Hopkins University Press, 1989), and Jürgen Habermas, *Toward a Rational Society: Student Protest, Science, and Politics* (Boston: Beacon Press, 1970).
4. Jürgen Habermas, *The Theory of Communicative Action: Lifeworld and System: A Critique of Functionalist Reason Vol. 2*, trans. Thomas McCarthy (Boston: Beacon Press, 1987), pp. 332ff.
5. Jürgen Habermas, *The Structural Transformation of the Public Sphere: An Inquiry into a Category of Bourgeois Society*, trans. Thomas Burger (Cambridge: MIT Press, 1989); *Between Facts and Norms: Contributions to a Discourse Theory of Law and Democracy*, trans. William Rehg (Cambridge, Mass.: MIT Press, 1996).
6. Habermas, *Between Facts and Norms*, p. 298.
7. Ibid., p. 486.
8. Jürgen Habermas, *The Inclusion of the Other: Studies in Political Theory*, trans. Ciaran Cronin (Cambridge, Mass.: MIT, 1998), p. 44. The emphasis here and in subsequent quotations are in the original.
9. Ibid.
10. Habermas, *Between Facts and Norms*, pp. 489f.
11. Ibid., p. 371.
12. John Rawls, *Political Liberalism* (New York: Columbia University Press, 1993), pp. 40–43, 320–23.
13. Habermas, *Theory of Communicative Action*, pp. 140–45.
14. Jürgen Habermas, 'A Reply', in Axel Honneth and Hans Joas (eds), *Communicative Action: Essays on Jürgen Habermas's The Theory of Communicative Action* (Cambridge: MIT Press, 1991), p. 218.
15. Habermas, *Theory of Communicative Action*, pp. 121–26, 182.
16. Ibid., p. 132.
17. Ibid., p. 401.
18. Habermas is nevertheless clearly close to both thinkers. He acknowledges Apel's role in developing the transcendental pragmatics that substantially influenced his own position. He has declared in reference to Rawls' work: 'I admire this project, share its intentions and regard its essential results as correct', and that his own disagreements with Rawls are 'within the bounds of a family quarrel' (Habermas, *The Inclusion of the Other*, p. 50).
19. Jürgen Habermas, *The Philosophical Discourse of Modernity: Twelve Lectures*, trans. Frederick G. Lawrence (Cambridge: MIT Press, 1987), pp. 311, 319f.
20. See Habermas, *The Inclusion of the Other*, chapter 4.
21. Jürgen Habermas, 'Struggles for Recognition in the Democratic Constitutional State', trans. Shierry Weber Nicholson, in Amy Gutmann (ed.), *Multiculturalism: Examining the Politics of Recognition*, 2nd ed. (Princeton: Princeton University Press, 1994), pp. 107–48.

22. These dynamics of identity are specific to the broad notion of the lifeworld and do not properly extend to the identities necessary for systemic functioning. Since Habermas regards instrumental relations with nature or within the economic and bureaucratic spheres to be indispensable not only in order to undergird a correctly functioning democracy, but more generally as the conditions for survival of human society itself, these 'survival imperatives' cannot themselves be regarded as open to ethical self-formation in the same manner.
23. We may note that Habermas's concept of the citizen constituted by (morally well-grounded) legal liberties and protective rights can also apply to the international context in the call for the institutionalisation of basic rights existing only in relatively weak form in international law. For Habermas's discussion of the newly emerging cosmopolitan order of human rights in the context of a revision of Kant's idea of perpetual peace, see *The Inclusion of the Other*, pp. 165–201. See also David Held, *Democracy and the Global Order: From the Modern State to Cosmopolitan Governance* (Cambridge: Polity Press, 1995).
24. Habermas, *Theory of Communicative Action*, p. 126.
25. The reifications attending language, including the problems of grounding *representation* and *acting* for the philosophy of consciousness, are insoluble under the model of subject-object relations. The problems related to the epistemological fixation of the philosophy of consciousness fall away for Habermas, however, once identity formation is revealed as an intersubjectively achieved process of communicative action and thus primarily as a practical-political, not an epistemological, affair.
26. Jacques Derrida, *On the Name*, trans. John P. Leavey, David Wood, Jr. and Ian McLeod (Stanford: Stanford University Press, 1995), pp. 124f., emphasis in original.
27. Ibid., pp. 80, 103.
28. Ibid., p. 80.
29. Ibid., pp. 111, 117, 106.
30. Ibid., p. 97.
31. Ibid., p. 103.
32. It is a radical openness, the yawning chasm opened by radical indeterminacy. But it should not lead automatically or ultimately to the fear aroused by utter chaos and disorder. As fractal theory and chaos theory show, utter chaos does not exist, since there remain patterns even in what appears to be the most random configurations and events. To gaze into the abyss is not necessarily to succumb to the urge to jump. But it might be. Instead, this experience ought to cultivate a sensitivity to and for the other, for otherness itself. But this sensibility would seem to demand more than what can be expected from the consciousness of utter finitude. It may be that death is a 'gift' to which we should be far more ethically responsive and grateful, as Derrida, following Heidegger, has argued elsewhere (Jacques Derrida, *The Gift of Death*, trans. David Wills [Chicago: University of Chicago Press, 1995]), but the inevitability of death can also debilitate our need to criticize that which is responsible for so much death. For that, a far more developed critical social theory is required (though Derrida has made some efforts in this direction (*Specters of Marx: The State of the Debt, the Work of Mourning and the New International*, trans. Peggy Kamuf [New York: Routledge, 1994]).
33. Ernesto Laclau, *Emancipation(s)* (London: Verso, 1996), p. 36.
34. Ibid., p. 58.
35. Ibid., pp. 42–44.
36. Slavoj Žižek, *Tarrying with the Negative: Kant, Hegel and the Critique of Ideology* (Durham: Duke University Press, 1993), p. 1.
37. Habermas, *The Philosophical Discourse of Modernity*, p. 210.
38. Honig's deconstruction of the significance of 'foreignness' in democratic thought, especially the foreign 'founder', is useful for revealing how central the relationship

to otherness 'outside' has been for democratic theory (*Democracy and the Foreigner* [Princeton: Princeton University Press, 2001]).

39. Habermas, *The Philosophical Discourse of Modernity*, p. 199. For a good discussion of the Habermas-Derrida debate that focuses on the philosophical context and its historical dimensions, see Christopher Norris, 'Deconstruction, Postmodernism and Philosophy: Habermas and Derrida', in Passerin d'Entrèves and Benhabib, *Habermas and the Unfinished Project of Modernity*, pp. 97–123.
40. Habermas, *The Philosophical Discourse of Modernity*, p. 190.
41. Ibid., p. 204.
42. Ibid., pp. 208, 209.
43. Martin Morris, *Rethinking the Communicative Turn: Adorno, Habermas, and the Problem of Communicative Freedom* (Albany: State University of New York Press, 2001), chapters 4 and 5. However, I do not pose this question in quite the same way in this text.
44. Jürgen Habermas, 'Concluding Remarks', in Craig Calhoun (ed.), *Habermas and the Public Sphere* (Cambridge, Mass.: MIT Press, 1992), p. 466.
45. For a recent assessment of this critique, see Martin Morris, 'Contradictions of Postmodern Consumerism, Resistance and Democracy', *Studies in Political Economy* 64 (2001), pp. 7–32.
46. See, for example, the account of the American conquest in Tzvetan Todorov, *The Conquest of America: The Question of the Other* (New York: Harper & Row, 1984).
47. Jacques Derrida, *The Other Heading: Reflections on Today's Europe*, trans. Pascale-Anne Brault and Michael B. Naas (Bloomington: Indiana University Press, 1992), pp. 14–16.
48. Ibid., pp. 9f.
49. Ibid., p. 73.
50. Drucilla Cornell, *The Philosophy of the Limit* (London: Routledge, 1992).
51. Derrida, *The Other Heading*, p. 60.
52. Ibid., p. 18.
53. Ibid., pp. 44f.
54. Bonnie Honig extends Derrida's call when she considers the educative and political possibilities for democracy presented by encounters with foreignness in 'immigrant America' ('Immigrant America: How Foreignness 'Solves' Democracy's Problems', *Social Text* 56 [1998], pp. 1–27).
55. James Tully, *Strange Multiplicity: Constitutionalism in an Age of Diversity* (Cambridge: Cambridge University Press, 1995), p. 201.
56. Cornel West, *Keeping Faith: Philosophy and Race in America* (New York: Routledge, 1993), p. 22.
57. Charles Taylor, 'The Politics of Recognition', in Gutmann, *Multiculturalism*, p. 70.
58. Derrida, *The Other Heading*, pp. 12f.
59. The work of Emmanuel Levinas is clearly relevant here and Levinas's influence on Derrida is essential to fully understand the latter. Asher Horowitz offers a useful critical perspective on the Habermas-Levinas axis that raises important questions relevant to this study (' "How Can Anyone Be Called Guilty"? Speech, Responsibility and the Social Relation in Habermas and Levinas', *Philosophy Today* 44:3 [2000], pp. 295–317.
60. See the collected exchanges in Diane P. Michelfelder and Richard E. Palmer, *Dialogue and Deconstruction: The Gadamer-Derrida Encounter* (Albany: State University of New York Press, 1989).
61. Derrida, *On the Name*, pp. 28f.

PART IV
BEYOND THE NATION-STATE: EUROPE, COSMOPOLITANISM AND INTERNATIONAL LAW

INTRODUCTION

In their later works, Jacques Derrida and Jürgen Habermas have been preoccupied with the role of the nation-state and, beyond it, international law and the role of Europe. They have both argued that it is necessary to look beyond the nation-state, because nation-states often rely on nationalist ideology and because the nation-state is impotent in the face of global capitalism. These are the reasons why they have turned their attention to globalisation, international law, sovereignty, Europe, and the cosmopolitanism of Immanuel Kant.

Both Derrida and Habermas argue for increasing international cooperation, whether though a regime of international law or through institutions like the United Nations. They are also both critical of nationalism and Eurocentrism, and although in Chapter 15 they argue for an increasingly important role for Europe, they do so from a certain European tradition of international cooperation and institutions like the European Union. Despite these similarities, there are differences between Derrida and Habermas. Habermas is generally more positive of cosmopolitanism and of the prospects of getting rid of (nation-state) sovereignty. Derrida, on the contrary, sees not just practical difficulties, but also inherent limits to the realisation of a cosmopolitan order. He refers to a 'cosmo*politics*' instead of cosmopolitanism, thus highlighting his belief that, although we can work towards less exclusion and sovereignty, we can never get entirely rid of them (Chapter 14). Matuštík discusses the affinities and differences between Derrida and Habermas, and he points towards new areas of possible debate between Derrideans and Habermasians.

FURTHER READING

For Derrida on globalisation, see Derrida 2002a, and, on cosmopolitanism, Derrida 2000, 2001b, 2005, and Chapter 12 in this volume. See also his comments in Borradori 2003. For an interesting use of Derrida in the context of sovereignty, nation-states and cosmopolitanism, see Näsström 2003, which also deals with Habermas's cosmopolitanism.

For Habermas on cosmopolitanism and what he calls the 'postnational constellation', see Habermas 1998a, 2001a, 2005, and his comments in Borradori 2003. The articles published as part of Habermas's Europe project and responses to Derrida and Habermas's article (Chapter 15) are published in Levy, Pensky and Torpey 2005.

14

Jacques Derrida and Lieven De Cauter

FOR A JUSTICE TO COME: AN INTERVIEW WITH JACQUES DERRIDA

Derrida's later work paid increasing attention to questions of international law, cosmopolitanism, sovereignty and terrorism. In 2004, he was invited to take part in The BRussells Tribunal, a project echoing The Russell Tribunal organised by Bertrand Russell during the Vietnam War as a response to US military atrocities. The task of The BRussells Tribunal was to investigate the government of George W. Bush and, in particular, the Project for A New American Century (PNAC), one of the ideological forces behind it. Due to illness, Derrida could not take part in the Tribunal itself but granted this interview to one of the Tribunal's founders, Lieven de Cauter.

Derrida is critical of (nation-)state sovereignty and of rogue states, arguing for the extension of international law and the increased cooperation through multilateral institutions such as the United Nations. These are ways of moving beyond the sovereignty of (nation-)states, even if it may be ultimately impossible to get rid of sovereignty as such.

The 'justice to come' (justice à venir) *in the title is neither a utopia nor a realisable future society, but a continuously deferred horizon of existing law and democracy. This is what Derrida refers to in the interview as a 'messianicity without messianism'.*

The BRussells Tribunal is a commission of inquiry into the 'New Imperial Order', particularly the 'Project for A New American Century' (PNAC), the neo-conservative think tank that has inspired the Bush government's

Jacques Derrida and Lieven De Cauter, 'For a Justice to Come' (The BRussells Tribunal, 2004).

war logic. The co-signatories of the PNAC 'mission statement' include Dick Cheney, Donald Rumsfeld and Paul Wolfowitz. The programme of the think tank is to promote planetary hegemony on the basis of a super-technological army, to prevent the emergence of a rival super-power and to take pre-emptive action against all those who threaten American interests. The BRussells Tribunal was held in Brussels from 14 to 17 April 2004. One of the greatest living philosophers, Jacques Derrida, who suffered from cancer and was unable to attend the tribunal, invited the project's initiator, Lieven De Cauter, to his house for an interview.[1]

Lieven De Cauter: Thank you for your generosity – why have you decided to grant us this interview on our initiative, the 'BRussells Tribunal'?

Jacques Derrida: First of all I wanted to salute your initiative in its principle: to resuscitate the tradition of a Russell Tribunal is symbolically an important and necessary thing to do today.[2] I believe that, in its principle, it is a good thing for the world, even if only in that it feeds the geopolitical reflection of all citizens of the world. I am even more convinced of this necessity in light of the fact that, for a number of years now, we have witnessed an increased interest in the working, in the constitution of international institutions, institutions of international law, which, beyond the sovereignty of States, judge heads of State, generals. Not yet States as such, precisely, but persons responsible for, or suspected of being responsible for, war crimes, crimes against humanity – one could mention the case of Pinochet, despite its ambiguity, or of Milosevic. At any rate, heads of State have to appear as such before an International Criminal Court, for instance, which has a recognised status in international law, despite all the difficulties you know: the American, French, Israeli reservations. Nonetheless this tribunal exists, and even if it is still faltering, weak and problematic in the execution of its sanctions, it exists as a recognised phenomenon of international law.

Your project, if I understand it correctly, is not of the same type, even if it is inspired by the same spirit. It does not have a juridical or judicial status recognised by any State, and it consequently remains a private initiative. Citizens of different countries have agreed among each other to conduct, as honestly as possible, an inquiry into a policy, into a political project and its execution. The point is not to reach a verdict resulting in sanctions but to raise or to sharpen the vigilance of the citizens of the world, in the first place that of the responsible parties you propose to judge. That can have a symbolic weight in which I believe, an exemplary symbolic weight.

That is why, even though I do not feel involved in the actual experience you intend to set up, I think it is very important to underscore that the case you are about to examine – which is evidently a massive and extremely serious case – is only one case among many. In the logic of your project, other policies, other political or military staff, other countries, other statesmen can also be brought to be judged in the same manner, or to be associated with this case. Personally, I have a critical attitude towards the Bush administration and its project, its attack on Iraq, and the conditions in which this has come about in a unilateral fashion in spite of official protestations from European countries including France, in violation of the rules of the United Nations and the Security Council... But notwithstanding this criticism – which I have expressed in public, by the way – I would not wish for the United States in general to have to appear before such a tribunal. I would want to distinguish a number of forces within the United States that have opposed the policy on Iraq as firmly as in Europe. This policy does not involve the American people in general, nor even the American State, but a phase in American politics which, for that matter, is about to be questioned again in the run-up to the presidential elections. Perhaps there will be a change, at least partially, in the United States itself, so I would encourage you to be prudent as regards the target of the accusation.

Lieven De Cauter: That is why we have directed our attention not to the government in general but more particularly to the Project for the New American Century, the think tank which has issued all these extreme ideas of unilateralism, hegemony, militarisation of the world etc....

Jacques Derrida: Where there is an explicit political project which declares its hegemonic intent and proposes to put everything into place to accomplish this, there one can, in effect, level accusations, protest in the name of international law and existing institutions, in their spirit and in their letter. I am thinking as much of the United Nations as of the Security Council, which are respectable institutions, but whose structure, charter, procedures need to be reformed, especially the Security Council. The crisis that has been unfolding confirms this: these international institutions really need to be reformed. And here I would naturally plead for a radical transformation – I don't know whether this will come about in the short run – which would call into question even the Charter, that is to say the respect for the sovereignties of the nation-states and the non-divisibility of sovereignties. There is a contradiction between the respect for human rights in general, also part of the Charter, and the respect for the sovereignty of the nation-state. The States are in effect represented as States in the United Nations and a fortiori in the Security Council, which gathers together the victors of the last war. All this calls for a profound transformation. I would insist that it should be a transformation and not a destruction, for I believe in the spirit of the United Nations...

Lieven De Cauter: So you still remain within the vision of Kant...

Jacques Derrida: At least in the spirit of Kant, for I also have some questions concerning the Kantian concept of cosmopolitanism.[3] It is in this perspective that I believe initiatives such as yours (or analogous initiatives) are symbolically very important to raise consciousness about these necessary transformations. This will have – at least that is what I hope – the symbolic value of a call to reflection we are in need of, and which the States are not taking care of, which not even institutions like the International Criminal Court are taking care of . . .

Lieven De Cauter: If I may allow myself one specification: we are part of a whole network called 'World Tribunal on Iraq'. There will be sessions in Hiroshima, Tokyo, Mexico, New York, London, and Istanbul . . . In London, and there the link between the International Criminal Court and the moral tribunal is very strong. Those in charge of the Tribunal on Iraq have, together with specialists, assembled a dossier to investigate whether Blair (who has recognised the International Criminal Court) has broken international law. By all evidence, there is a considerable consensus among specialists to say that this war is a transgression, it is an 'aggressive war' in the technical sense of the term as used in the charter of the UN, since there was no imminent threat to the territory of the countries involved. The upshot of this inquiry is that they have submitted a dossier to the International Criminal Court in The Hague. Similarly in Copenhagen, since Denmark is part of the coalition. So it is possible that our moral initiative may be transformed, in some of its components, into a juridical procedure strictly speaking.

Jacques Derrida: That would be desirable, evidently! But the probability that this would come about seems low, for there would be too many States who would oppose your initiative becoming institutional and generally judicial, and not just the United States. Yet if this doesn't come about, that does not mean your project is destined to ineffectiveness. On the contrary. I believe in its considerable symbolic effectiveness in the public domain. The fact that it is said, published, even if it is not followed by a judgement in the strictly judicial sense, let alone actual sanctions, can have considerable symbolical impact on the political consciousness of the citizens, a relayed, deferred effect, but one that raises high expectations. I would hope that you would treat those you accuse justly, that yours would be an undertaking of true integrity, devoid of preliminary positioning, without preconditions, that everything would be done in serenity and justice, that the responsible parties would be accurately identified, that you would not go over the top and that you would not exclude other procedures of the same type in the future. I would not want this procedure to serve as an excuse for not conducting other procedures that are just as necessary concerning other countries, other policies, whether they be European or not. I would even wish that the exemplary character of your initiative would lead to a lasting, if not a permanent instance.

I believe that it would be perceived as being more just if you did not commit yourself to this target as if it were the only possible target, notably because, as you are aware, in this aggression against Iraq, American responsibility was naturally decisive but it didn't come about without complex complicities from many other quarters. We are dealing with a knot of nearly inextricable co-responsibilities. I would hope that this would be clearly taken into account and that it wouldn't be the accusation of one man only. Even if he is an ideologue, someone who has given the hegemony project a particularly readable form, he has not done it on his own, he cannot have imposed it on non-consenting people. So the contours of the accused, of the suspect or the suspects, are very hard to determine.

Lieven De Cauter: Yes, that is one of the reasons why we have abandoned the strictly juridical format. One of the disadvantages of the juridical format is that you can only target persons. Whereas we want to take aim at a system, a systemic logic. We name the accused (Cheney, Wolfowitz, Rumsfeld) to show people that we are not talking about phantoms, but we take aim at the PNAC as a set of performative discourses, that is to say, plans to achieve something, intentions to be translated into action. Our difficulty is also one of communication: communicating to people that PNAC exists and that it is important to spread this knowledge, is already a job in itself.

Jacques Derrida: Of course. And for that reason, it is important that matters are partly personalised and partly developed at the level of the system, of the principles, the concept, where this system, these principles, these concepts violate international laws which must be both respected and perhaps also changed. This is where you will not be able to avoid talking about sovereignty, about the crisis of sovereignty, about the necessary division or delimitation of sovereignty. Personally, when I have to take a position on this vast issue of sovereignty, of what I call its necessary deconstruction, I am very cautious. I believe it is necessary, by way of a philosophical, historical analysis, to deconstruct the political theology of sovereignty. It's an enormous philosophical task, requiring the re-reading of everything, from Kant to Bodin, from Hobbes to Schmitt. But at the same time you should not think that you must fight for the dissolution pure and simple of all sovereignty: that is neither realistic nor desirable. There are effects of sovereignty which in my view are still politically useful in the fight against certain forces or international concentrations of forces that sneer at sovereignty.

In the present case, we have precisely the convergence of the arrogant and hegemonic assertion of a sovereign Nation-State with a gathering of global economic forces, involving all kinds of transactions and complications in which China, Russia and many countries of the Middle East are equally mixed up. This is where matters become very hard to disentangle. I believe that sometimes the reclamation of sovereignty should not necessarily be denounced or criticised, it depends on the situation.

Lieven De Cauter: As you have clearly demonstrated in *Rogues*, in deconstructing the term, there is no democracy without 'cracy': a certain power, and even force, is required.

Jacques Derrida: Absolutely. You can also talk of the sovereignty of the citizen, who votes in a sovereign fashion, so you need to be very cautious. In my view, the interesting thing about your project is in taking up or pursuing this reflection starting from an actual case which takes a specific form: military, strategic, economic, and so on. It is very important to develop such reflection on a case, but this reflection requires considerable time and must accompany the entire geopolitical process in decades to come. It is not just as a Frenchman, European or citizen of the world but also as a philosopher concerned to see these questions developed that I find your attempt interesting and necessary. It will provide an opportunity for others, many others I hope, to adopt a position with regard to your efforts, to reflect, possibly to oppose you, or to join you, but this can only be beneficial for the political reflection we are in need of.

Lieven De Cauter: I was amazed by the definition you give in 'Autoimmunity':[4] a philosopher, you say, is someone who deals with this transition towards political and international institutions to come. That is a very political definition of the philosopher.

Jacques Derrida: What I wanted to convey is that it won't necessarily be the professional philosophers who will deal with this. The lawyer or the politician who takes charge of these questions will be the philosopher of tomorrow. Sometimes, politicians or lawyers are more able to philosophically think these questions through than professional academic philosophers, even though there are a few within the University dealing with this. At any rate, philosophy today, or the duty of philosophy, is to think this in action, by doing something.

Lieven De Cauter: I would like to return to this notion of sovereignty. Is not the New Imperial Order which names 'Rogue States' a State of exception (or state of emergency)? You speak in *Rogues* about the concept of the autoimmunity of democracy: democracy, at certain critical moments, believes it must suspend itself to defend democracy. This is what is happening in the United States now, both in its domestic policy and in its foreign policy. The ideology of the PNAC, and therefore of the Bush administration, is exactly that.

Jacques Derrida: The exception is the translation, the criterion of sovereignty, as was noted by Carl Schmitt (whom I have also criticised, one must be very cautious when one talks about Carl Schmitt, I have written some chapters on Carl Schmitt in *Politics of Friendship* where I take him seriously and where I criticise him and I would not want my reflection on Schmitt to be seen as an endorsement of either his theses or his history).[5] Sovereign is he who decides on the exception. Exception and sovereignty go hand in hand here. In the same way that democracy, at times, threatens or suspends itself, so sovereignty consists in giving oneself the right to suspend the law. That is the definition of the sovereign: he makes the law, he is above the law, he can suspend the law. That is what the United States has done, on the one hand when they trespassed against their own commitments with regard to the UN and the Security Council, and on the other hand, within the country itself, by threatening American democracy to a certain extent, that is to say by introducing exceptional police and judicial procedures. I am not only thinking of the Guantanamo prisoners but also of the Patriot Act: from its introduction, the FBI has carried out inquisitorial procedures of intimidation which have been denounced by the Americans themselves, notably by lawyers, as being in breach of the Constitution and of democracy.

Having said that, to be fair, we must recall that the United States is after all a democracy. Bush, who was elected with the narrowest of margins, risks losing the next elections: he is only sovereign for four years. It is a very legalistic country rich in displays of political liberty that would not be tolerated in a good many other countries. I am not only thinking of countries known to be non-democratic but also of our own Western European democracies. In the United States, when I saw those massive marches against the imminent war in Iraq, in front of the White House, right by Bush's offices, I said to myself that if in France protesters assembled in their thousands and marched in front of the Elysée in a similar situation, that would not be tolerated. To be fair, we must take into account this contradiction within American democracy – on the one hand, auto-immunity: democracy destroys itself in protecting itself; but on the other hand, we must take into account the fact that this hegemonic tendency is also a crisis of hegemony. The United States, to my mind, convulses upon its hegemony at a time when it is in crisis, precarious. There is no contradiction between the hegemonic drive and crisis. The United States realises all too well that within the next few years, both China and Russia will have begun to weigh in. The oil stories which have naturally determined the Iraq episode are linked to long-term forecasts notably concerning China: China's oil supply, control over oil in the Middle East . . . all of this indicates that hegemony is as much under threat as it is manifest and arrogant.

It is an extremely complex situation, which is why I am bound to say it should not be a matter of blanket accusations or denunciations levelled against the United States, but that we should take stock of all that is critical in American political life. There are forces in the United States that fight the Bush administration, alliances should be formed with these forces, their existence recognised. At times they express their criticism in ways much more radical than in Europe. But there is evidently – and I suppose you will discuss this in your commission of inquiry – the enormous problem of the media, of control of the media, of the media power which has accompanied this entire history in a decisive manner, from September 11 to the invasion of Iraq, an invasion which, by the way, in my opinion was already scheduled well before September 11.

Lieven De Cauter: Yes, as a matter of fact that is one of the things that need to be proven. The PNAC, in 2000, writes: 'the United States has for decades sought to play a more permanent role in Gulf regional security. While the unresolved conflict with Iraq provides the immediate justification, the need for a substantial American force presence in the Gulf transcends the issue of the regime of Saddam Hussein.'[6] They write this in September 2000: it was already decided, all the rest was just an alibi.

Jacques Derrida: I have had this debate in public with Baudrillard,[7] who said that the aggression against Iraq – which was then being prepared – was a direct consequence of September 11. I opposed that thesis, I said that I thought it would take place anyway, that the premises had been in place for a long time already, and that the two sequences can be dissociated, to a certain extent. The day when this history will be written, when the documents are made public, it will become clear that September 11 was preceded by highly complicated underhand negotiations, often in Europe, on the subject of petrol pipe-line passage, at a time when the petrol clan was in power. There were intrigues and threats, and it is not impossible to think that one day it will be discovered that it was really the Bush clan that was targeted rather than the country, the America of Clinton. But we shouldn't stop at petrol: there are numerous other strategic geopolitical stakes, among them the tensions with China, Europe, Russia. Alliances with the United States, variable as ever, since it has attacked those who they have supported for a very long time. Iraq was an ally of the United States as of France: all of this is part of diplomatic inconstancy, hypocritical from end to end, and not only on the part of the United States. There are many more stakes than petrol alone, especially since petrol is a matter of only a few more decades: there will not be any oil left in 50 years! We must take the petrol question into account, but we should not devote all our attention and analysis to it. There are military questions, passing through territorial questions of occupation and control. But military power is not only a territorial power, we know that now, it also passes through non-territorialised controls, techno-communicational channels, and so on. All of this has to be taken into account.

Lieven De Cauter: And Israel?

Jacques Derrida: Many have said that the American-Israeli alliance or the support the United States give to Israel is not unrelated to this intervention in Iraq. I believe this is true to some extent. But here too matters are very complicated, because even if the current Israeli government – and here I would take the same precautions as for the United States: there are Israelis in Israel who fight Sharon – has indeed congratulated itself officially and in public on the aggression against Iraq, the freedom this may have apparently given Israel in its offensive initiatives of colonisation and repression is very ambiguous. Here too we could speak of auto-immunity: it is very contradictory, because at the same time this has aggravated Palestinian terrorism, intensified or reawakened symptoms of anti-Semitism across Europe . . . It is very complicated, for if it is true that the Americans support Israel – just like the majority of European countries, with different political modulations –, the best American allies of Sharon's policy, that is to say the most offensive policy of all Israeli governments, are not only the American Jewish community but also the Christian fundamentalists. These are often the most pro-Israeli of all Americans, at times even more so than certain American Jews. I am not sure it will turn out to have been in Israel's best interest that this form of aggression against Iraq has come about. The future will tell. Even Sharon meets with opposition in his own government nowadays, in his own majority, because he claims to withdraw from the Gaza colonies. The difficulty of a project such as yours, however just and magnificent it may be in its principle, is that it must cautiously take this complexity into account, that it must try not to be unfair to any of the parties. That is one of the reasons why I insist in confirming my solidarity in principle. Unable to participate effectively in the inquiry and in the development of the judgement because of my illness, I prefer to restrict myself for now to this agreement in principle, but I will not hesitate to applaud you afterwards, if I find you have conducted matters well!

Lieven De Cauter: Your statements are limpid and will serve as drink for many who are thirsty (for justice, for instance). Thank you very much. By way of post-script: let us speak of messianism for a minute or so. That is to say of 'the weak force', which refers to Walter Benjamin and which you evoke in the 'Preface: Veni', the preface to *Rogues*. Allow me to quote from it: 'This vulnerable force, this force without power opens up unconditionality to what or who *comes* and comes to affect it. [. . .] The common affirmation of these two lectures [of *Rogues*] resembles yet again an act of messianic faith – irreligious and without messianism. [. . .]

On it, perhaps, on what here receives the name *khōra*, a call might thus be taken up and take hold: the call for a thinking of the event *to come*, of the democracy *to come*, of the reason *to come*. This call bears every hope, to be sure, although it remains, in itself, without hope. Not hopeless, in despair, but foreign to the teleology, the hopefulness, and the *salut* of salvation. Not foreign to the *salut* as the greeting or salutation of the other, not foreign to the *adieu* ("come" or "go" in peace), not foreign to justice, but nonetheless heterogeneous and rebellious, irreducible, to law, to power, and to the economy of redemption.'[8]. . . I thought this very beautiful. Almost a prayer to insert – into the everyday, into our project. What is it, this messianism without religion?

Jacques Derrida: The weak force indeed refers to the interpretation of Benjamin, but it is not exactly mine. It is what I call 'messianicity without messianism': I would say that today, one of the incarnations, one of the implementations of this messianicity, of this messianism without religion, may be found in the alter-globalisation movements. Movements that are still heterogeneous, still somewhat unformed, full of contradictions, but that gather together the weak of the earth, all those who feel themselves crushed by the economic hegemonies, by the liberal market, by sovereignism, and so on. I believe it is these weak who will prove to be strongest in the end and who represent the future. Even though I am not a militant involved in these movements, I place my bet on the weak force of those alter-globalisation movements, who will have to explain themselves, to unravel their contradictions, but who march against all the hegemonic organisations of the world. Not just the United States, also the International Monetary Fund, the G8, all those organised hegemonies of the rich countries, the strong and powerful countries, of which Europe is part. It is these alter-globalisation movements that offer one of the best figures of what I would call messianicity without messianism, that is to say a messianicity that does not belong to any determined religion. The conflict with Iraq involved numerous religious elements, from all sides – from the Christian side as well as from the Muslim side. What I call messianicity without messianism is a call, a promise of an independent future for what is to come, and which comes like every messiah in the shape of peace and justice, a promise independent of religion, that is to say universal. A promise independent of the three religions when they oppose each other, since in fact it is a war between three Abrahamic religions. A promise beyond the Abrahamic religions, universal, without relation to revelations or to the history of religions. My intent here is not anti-religious, it is not a matter of waging war on the religious messianisms properly speaking, that is to say Judaic, Christian, Islamic. But it is a matter of marking a place where these messianisms are exceeded by messianicity, that is to say by that waiting without waiting, without horizon for the event to come, the democracy to come with all its contradictions. And I believe we must seek today, very cautiously, to give force and form to this messianicity, without giving in to the old concepts of politics (sovereignism, territorialised nation-state), without giving in to the Churches or to the religious powers, theologico-political or theocratic of all orders, whether they be the theocracies of the Islamic Middle East, or whether they be, disguised, the theocracies of the West. (In spite of everything, Europe, France especially, but also the United States are secular in principle in their Constitutions. I recently heard a journalist say to an American: 'how do you explain that Bush always says "God bless America", that the President swears on the Bible, and so on?', and the American replied: 'do not lecture us on secularity for we put the separation of Church and State into our Constitution long before you did', that the State was not under the control of any religion whatsoever, which does not stop the Christian domination from asserting itself, but there too it is imperative to be very cautious.) Messianicity without messianism, that is: independence in respect of religion in general. In a sense, a faith without religion of some sort.

NOTES

1. The interview was conducted in Ris Orangis, Paris, 19 February 2004. It was transcribed by Maïwenn Furic and translated by Ortwin de Graef. For further information on the BRussells Tribunal, see www.brusselstribunal.org.
2. The Russell Tribunal was an international tribunal organised by Bertrand Russell as a response to American atrocities during the Vietnam War.
3. Derrida is alluding to his reflections on Kant and his idea of an alliance of peoples (*Völkerbund*) in Jacques Derrida, *Rogues: Two Essays on Reason*, trans. Pascale-Anne Brault and Michael Naas (Stanford: Stanford University Press, 2005), pp. 80–86.
4. Jacques Derrida, 'Autoimmunity: Real and Symbolic Suicides – A Dialogue with Jacques Derrida', trans. Pascale-Anne Brault and Michael Naas, in G. Borradori, *Philosophy In a Time of Terror: Dialogues with Jürgen Habermas and Jacques Derrida* (Chicago: The University of Chicago Press, 2003), pp. 85–136, at p. 106.
5. Jacques Derrida, *Politics of Friendship*, trans. George Collins (London: Verso, 1997).
6. The Project for a New American Century, 'Rebuilding America's Defenses. Strategy, Forces and Resources For a New Century', September 2000, available at http://www.newamericancentury.org/publicationsreports.htm.
7. 'Pourquoi la guerre?', Maison des Cultures du Monde, Paris, 19 February 2003. Conference organised by Institut des Hautes Études en Psychanalyse and *Le Monde diplomatique*.
8. Derrida, *Rogues*, pp. xiv–xv.

15

Jürgen Habermas and Jacques Derrida

FEBRUARY 15, OR WHAT BINDS EUROPEANS TOGETHER: A PLEA FOR A COMMON FOREIGN POLICY, BEGINNING IN THE CORE OF EUROPE

On 30 January 2003, eight European heads of government published a public letter in newspapers across Europe calling for European unity with the United States. On 15 February 2003, millions went to the streets across the world, protesting against the imminent US attack on Iraq. On 31 May 2003, six European philosophers, Jürgen Habermas, Jacques Derrida, Adolf Muschg, Fernando Salvater, Umberto Eco and Gianni Vattimo, along with the US philosopher Richard Rorty, published individual articles in seven European newspapers.

One of the articles published on 31 May 2003 was this piece by Derrida and Habermas, initially published simultaneously in German (in the Frankfurter Allgemeine Zeitung*) and French (in* Libération*). It was written by Habermas, but co-signed by Derrida, who was unable to write a piece of his own due to illness. As Derrida wrote in the German version of it, 'despite all obvious differences in [Habermas's and my] approaches and arguments, our aspirations converge regarding the future of the institutions of international law and the new challenges for Europe'.*

Habermas and Derrida argue that Europe must assert itself against the current US government and its unilateral policies. In this way, Europe should become the vehicle for increased international cooperation and the spread of international law. For this purpose, it is necessary to have a European polity and especially a common European foreign policy, initially spearheaded by a core of European states (France and Germany) acting as a locomotive for further integration. This in turn requires a European public sphere to feed into and as a check on the European polity. Habermas originated the idea of the simultaneous publication of articles on 31 May 2003. He saw it as an attempt to speak in the name of and to, thereby invoking, a common European public sphere; thus, he saw the project as a continuation of the events of 31 January and 15 February 2003.

It is the wish of Jacques Derrida and Jürgen Habermas to be co-signatories of what is both an analysis and an appeal. They regard it as necessary and urgent that French and German philosophers lift their voices together, whatever disagreements may have separated them in the past. The following text was composed by Jürgen Habermas, as will be readily apparent. Though he would have liked to very much, due to personal circumstances Jacques Derrida was unable to compose his own text. Nevertheless, he suggested to Jürgen Habermas that he be the co-signatory of this appeal, and shares its definitive premises and perspectives: the determination of new European political responsibilities beyond any Eurocentrism; the call for a renewed confirmation and effective transformation of international law and its institutions, in particular the UN; a new conception and a new praxis for the distribution of state authority, etc., according to the spirit, if not the precise sense, that refers back to the Kantian tradition.

We should not forget two dates: not the day the newspapers reported to their astonished readers the Spanish prime minister's invitation to the other European nations willing to support the Iraq war to swear an oath of loyalty to George W. Bush, an invitation issued behind the back of the other countries of the European Union. But we should also remember February 15, 2003, as mass demonstrations in London and Rome, Madrid and Barcelona, Berlin and Paris reacted to this sneak attack. The simultaneity of these overwhelming demonstrations – the largest since the end of the Second World War – may well, in hindsight, go down in history as a sign of the birth of a European public sphere.

During the leaden months prior to the outbreak of the war in Iraq, a morally obscene division of labor provoked strong emotions. The large-scale logistical operation of ceaseless military preparation and the frenetic activity of humanitarian aid organizations meshed together as precisely as the teeth of a gear. Moreover, the spectacle took place undisturbed before the eyes of the very population which – robbed of their own initiative – was to be its victim. The precautionary mustering of relief workers, relief services, and relief goods dressed itself in the rash rhetoric of alleviation of suffering yet to be inflicted; the planned reconstruction of cities and administrations yet to be ruined. Like searchlights, they picked out the civilized barbarism of coolly

Jacques Derrida and Jürgen Habermas, 'February 15, or What Binds Europeans Together: A Plea for a Common Foreign Policy, Beginning in the Heart of Europe', *Constellations*, 10, 2003, pp. 291–7.

planned death (of how many victims?), of torments long since totted up (of how many injured and mutilated, how many thirsty and hungry?), of the long-planned destruction (of how many residential districts and hospitals, how many houses, museums, and markets?). As the war finally began, the Ernst Jünger aesthetic of the skyline of the nighttime Baghdad, illuminated by countless explosions, seemed almost harmless.

A Common European Foreign Policy: Who First?

There is no doubt that the power of emotions has brought European citizens jointly to their feet. Yet at the same time, the war made Europeans conscious of the failure of their common foreign policy, a failure that has been a long time in the making. As in the rest of the world, the impetuous break with international law has ignited a debate over the future of the international order in Europe as well. But here, the divisive arguments have cut deeper, and have caused familiar faultlines to emerge even more sharply. Controversies over the role of the American superpower, over a future world order, over the relevance of international law and the United Nations – all have caused latent contradictions to break into the open. The gap between continental and Anglo-American countries on the one side, and 'the old Europe' and the Central and East European candidates for entry into the European Union on the other side, has grown deeper.

In Great Britain, while the special relationship with the United States is by no means uncontested, the priorities of Downing Street are still quite clear. And the central and eastern European countries, while certainly working hard for their admission into the EU, are nevertheless not yet ready to place limits on the sovereignty that they have so recently regained. The Iraq crisis was only a catalyst. In the Brussels constitutional convention, there is now a visible contrast between the nations that really want a stronger EU, and those with an *understandable* interest in freezing, or at best cosmetically changing, the existing mode of intergovernmental governance. This contradiction can no longer be finessed. The future constitution will grant us a European foreign minister. But what good is a new political office if governments don't unify in a common policy? A Fischer with a changed job description would remain as powerless as Solana.

For the moment, only the core European nations are ready to endow the EU with certain qualities of a state. But what happens if these countries can only find agreement on the definition of 'self-interest'? If Europe is not to fall apart, these countries will have to make use of the mechanisms for 'strengthened cooperation' created in Nice as a way of taking a first step toward a common foreign policy, a common security policy, and a common defense policy. Only such a step will succeed in generating the momentum that other member states – initially in the Euro zone – will not be able to resist in the long run. In the framework of the future European constitution, there can and must be no separatism. Taking a leading role does not mean excluding. The avant-gardist core of Europe must not wall itself off into a new Small Europe. It must – as it has so often – be the locomotive. It is from their own self-interest, to be sure, that the more closely-cooperating member states of the EU will hold the door open. And the probability that the invited states will pass through that door will increase the more capable the core of Europe becomes of effective action externally, and the sooner it can prove that in a complex global society, it is not just divisions that count, but also the soft power of negotiating agendas, relations, and economic advantages.

In this world, the reduction of politics to the stupid and costly alternative of war or peace simply doesn't pay. At the international level and in the framework of the UN, Europe has to throw its weight on the scale to counterbalance the hegemonic unilateralism of the United States. At global economic summits and in the institutions of the WTO, the World Bank, and the IMF, it should exert its influence in shaping the design for a coming global domestic policy.

Political projects that aim at the further development of the EU are now colliding with the limits of the medium of administrative steering. Until now, the functional imperatives for the construction of a common market and the Euro-zone have driven reforms. These driving forces are now exhausted. A *transformative* politics, which would demand that member states not just overcome obstacles for competitiveness but form a common will, must take recourse to the motives and the attitudes of *the citizens themselves*. Majority decisions on highly consequential foreign policies can only expect acceptance assuming the solidarity of outnumbered minorities. But this presupposes a feeling of common political belonging on both sides. The population must so to speak 'build up' their national identities, and add to them a European dimension. What is already a fairly abstract form of civic solidarity, still largely confined to members of nation-states, must be extended to include the European citizens of other nations as well.

This raises the question of 'European identity'. Only the consciousness of a shared political fate, and the prospect of a common future, can halt outvoted minorities from the obstruction of a majority will. The citizens of one nation must regard the citizens of another nation as fundamentally 'one of us'. This desideratum leads to the question that so many skeptics have called attention to: are there historical experiences, traditions, and achievements offering European citizens the consciousness of a political fate that has been shared together, and *that can be shaped together*? An attractive, indeed an infectious 'vision' for a future Europe will not emerge from thin air. At present it can arise only from the disquieting perception of perplexity. But it well can emerge from the difficulties of a situation into which we Europeans have been cast. And it must articulate itself from out of the wild cacophony of a multi-vocal public sphere. If this theme has so far not even gotten on to the agenda, it is we intellectuals who have failed.

The Treacheries of a European Identity

It is easy to find unity without commitment. The image of a peaceful, cooperative Europe, open toward other cultures and capable of dialogue, floats like a mirage before us all. We welcome the Europe that found exemplary solutions for two problems during the second half of the twentieth century. The EU already offers itself as a form of 'governance beyond the nation-state', which could set a pre in the postnational constellation. And for decades, European social welfare systems served as a model. Certainly, they have now been thrown on the defensive at the level of the national state. Yet future political efforts at the domestication of global capitalism must not fall below the standards of social justice that they established. If Europe has solved two problems of this magnitude, why shouldn't it issue a further challenge: to defend and promote a cosmopolitan order on the basis of international law against competing visions?

Such a Europe-wide discourse, of course, would have to match up with existing dispositions, which are waiting, so to speak, for the stimulation of a process of self-understanding. Two facts would seem to contradict this bold assumption. Haven't the most significant historical achievements of Europe forfeited their identity-forming power precisely through the fact of their worldwide success? And what could hold together a region characterized more than any other by the ongoing rivalries between self-conscious nations?

Insofar as Christianity and capitalism, natural science and technology, Roman law and the Code Napoleon, the bourgeois-urban form of life, democracy and human rights, the secularization of state and society have spread across other continents, these legacies no longer constitute a *proprium*. The Western form of spirit, rooted in the Judeo-Christian tradition, certainly has its characteristic features. But the nations of Europe also share this mental habitus, characterized by individualism, rationalism, and activism, with the United States, Canada, and Australia. The 'West' encompasses more than just Europe. Moreover, Europe is composed of nation-states that delimit one another polemically. National consciousness, formed by national languages, national literatures, and national histories, has long operated as an explosive force.

However, in response to the destructive power of this nationalism, values and habits have also developed which have given contemporary Europe, in its incomparably rich cultural diversity, its own face. This is how Europe at large presents itself to of non-Europeans. A culture which for centuries has been beset more than any other by conflicts between town and country, sacred and secular authorities, by the competition between faith and knowledge, the struggle between states and antagonistic classes, has had to painfully learn how differences can be communicated, contradictions institutionalized, and tensions stabilized. The acknowledgement of differences – the reciprocal acknowledgement of the Other in his otherness – can also become a feature of a common identity.

The pacification of class conflicts within the welfare state, and the self-limitation of state sovereignty within the framework of the EU, are only the most recent examples of this. In the third quarter of the twentieth century, Europe on this side of the Iron Curtain experienced its 'golden age', as Eric Hobsbawm has called it. Since then, features of a common political mentality have taken shape, so that others often recognize us as Europeans rather than as Germans or French – and that happens not just in Hong Kong, but even in Tel Aviv. And isn't it true? In European societies, secularization is relatively far advanced. Citizens here regard transgressions of the border between politics and religion with suspicion. Europeans have a relatively large amount of trust in the organizational and steering capacities of the state, while remaining skeptical toward the achievements of markets. They possess a keen sense of the 'dialectic of enlightenment'; they have no naïvely optimistic expectations about technological progress. They maintain a preference for the welfare state's guarantees of social security and for regulations on the basis of solidarity. The threshold of tolerance for the use of force against persons lies relatively low. The desire for a multilateral and legally regulated international order is connected with the hope for an effective global domestic policy, within the framework of a reformed United Nations.

The fortunate historical constellation in which West Europeans developed this kind of mentality in the shadow of the Cold War has changed since 1989–90. But February 15 shows that the mentality has survived the context from which it sprang. This also explains why 'old Europe' sees itself challenged by the blunt hegemonic politics of its ally. And why so many in Europe who welcome the fall of Saddam as an act of liberation also reject the illegality of the unilateral, pre-emptive, and deceptively justified invasion. But how stable is this mentality? Does it have roots in deeper historical experiences and traditions?

Today we know that many political traditions that command their authority through the illusion of 'naturalness' have in fact been 'invented'. By contrast, a European identity born in the daylight of the public sphere would have something constructed about it from the very beginning. But only what is constructed through an arbitrary choice carries the stigma of randomness. The political-ethical will that drives the hermeneutics of processes of self-understanding is not arbitrary. Distinguishing between the legacy we appropriate and the one we want to refuse demands just as much circumspection as the decision over the interpretation through which we appropriate it for ourselves. Historical experiences are only *candidates* for self-conscious appropriation; without such a self-conscious act they cannot attain the power to shape our identity. To conclude, a few notes on such 'candidates', in light of which the European postwar consciousness can win a sharper profile.

HISTORICAL ROOTS OF A POLITICAL PROFILE

In modern Europe, the relation between church and state developed differently on either side of the Pyrenees, differently north and south of the Alps, west and east of the Rhine. In different European countries, the idea of the state's neutrality in relation to different worldviews has assumed different legal forms. And yet within civil society, religion overall assumes a comparably unpolitical position. We may have cause to regret this social *privatization of faith* in other respects, but it has desirable consequences for our political culture. For us, a president who opens his daily business with open prayer, and associates his significant political decisions with a divine mission, is hard to imagine.

Civil society's emancipation from the protection of an absolutist regime was not connected with the democratic appropriation and transformation of the modern administrative state everywhere in Europe. But the spread of the ideals of the French Revolution throughout Europe explains, among other things, why politics in both of its forms – as the organization of power and as a medium for the institutionalization of political liberty – has been welcomed in Europe. By contrast, the triumph of capitalism was bound up with sharp class conflicts, and this fact has prevented an equally unprejudiced appraisal of the market. That different evaluation of *politics and market* may back Europeans' trust in the civilizing power of the state, and their expectations for its capacity to correct 'market failures'.

The party system that emerged from the French Revolution has often been copied. But only in Europe does this system also serve an ideological competition that subjects the socio-pathological results of capitalist modernization to an ongoing political evaluation. This fosters the *sensitivity of citizens to the paradoxes of progress*. The contest between conservative, liberal, and socialist agendas comes down to the weighing of two aspects: Do the benefits of a chimerical progress outweigh the losses that come with the disintegration of protective, traditional forms of life? Or do the benefits that today's processes of 'creative destruction' promise for tomorrow outweigh the pain of modernization losers?

In Europe, those who have been affected by class distinctions and their enduring consequences understood these burdens as a fate that could be averted only through collective action. In the context of workers' movements and the Christian socialist traditions, an ethics of solidarity, *the struggle for 'more social justice'*, with the goal of equal provision for all, asserted itself against the individualistic ethos of market justice that accepts glaring social inequalities as part of the bargain.

Contemporary Europe has been shaped by the experience of the totalitarian regimes of the twentieth century and through the Holocaust – the persecution and the annihilation of European Jews in which the National Socialist regime made the societies of the conquered countries complicit as well.

Self-critical controversies about this past remind us of the moral basis of politics. A heightened *sensitivity to injuries to personal and bodily integrity* is reflected, among other ways, in the fact that both the Council of Europe and the EU made the ban on capital punishment a condition for entrance.

A bellicose past once entangled all European nations in bloody conflicts. They drew a conclusion from that military and spiritual mobilization against one another: the imperative of developing new, supranational forms of cooperation after the Second World War. The successful history of the European Union may have confirmed Europeans in their belief that the *domestication of state power* demands a *mutual* limitation of sovereignty, on the global as well as the national-state level.

Each of the great European nations has experienced the bloom of its imperial power. And, what in our context is more important still, each has had to work through the experience of the loss of its empire. In many cases this experience of decline was associated with the loss of colonial territories. With the growing distance of imperial domination and the history of colonialism, the European powers also got the chance to *assume a reflexive distance from themselves*. They could learn from the perspective of the defeated to perceive themselves in the dubious role of victors who are called to account for the violence of a forcible and uprooting process of modernization. This could support the rejection of Eurocentrism, and inspire the Kantian hope for a global domestic policy.

Translated by Max Pensky

NOTE

This article originally appeared in the *Frankfurter Allgemeine Zeitung*, 31 May 2003.

16

Martin Beck Matuštík

BETWEEN HOPE AND TERROR: HABERMAS AND DERRIDA PLEAD FOR THE IM/POSSIBLE

Martin Beck Matuštík has written extensively on Continental philosophy, covering both sides of the modern/postmodern divide and linking philosophical concerns to ethics, politics and religion in contemporary multicultural societies. This chapter takes off where his earlier writings end. At that time his response to multiculturalism and identity politics was radical democracy combined with a critique of capitalism. Matuštík wanted to combine Habermas's fallibilist appropriation of the Enlightenment tradition with Derrida's questioning of identitarian logics, egalitarian procedures with resistance to the formation of closed identities, and an egalitarian politics with resistance to totalisation in all possible forms. With this, Matuštík sought to move beyond the oppositions between modernity and postmodernity and between identity and difference.

The present chapter places these earlier arguments in the context of Derrida's and Habermas's most recent writings. Two issues are especially important. First, as their co-signed newspaper article shows (Chapter 15), they are both critical of the (nation-)state and of Eurocentrism. Second, both are interested in the role of religion and faith in pluralist and secular societies, and both allow a place for religion, albeit in different ways. This, Matuštík argues, is one of the most interesting areas for future debate between Derrideans and Habermasians.

Martin Beck Matuštík, 'Between Hope and Terror: Habermas and Derrida Plead for the Im/Possible' *Epoché*, 9: 1, 2004, pp. 1–18.

To Jacques Derrida in memoriam (1930–2004)

His Paulskirche speech on October 14, 2001, marked Habermas's turn to public criticism of the unilateral politics of global hegemony as he promoted a global domestic and human rights policy. Two years later he joined ranks with the consistently pro-human rights and internationally responsible European voices, a motley crew ranging from Umberto Eco and Gianni Vattimo to Jacques Derrida and Pope John Paul II. Against the eight 'new' Europeans who lent signatures to the second Gulf War and against Donald Rumsfeld, Habermas and Derrida mobilized the 'old' European values, thus meriting an ironic title of 'new conservatives'.

Oddly, the most vocal of Europe's humanists and human rights activists, Václav Havel, joined the eight 'new' Europeans, although, in a conspicuously underreported speech to the NATO summit in Prague (2002), he indirectly taunted the Atlantic alliance: Is there not some danger that they could return to the world historical stage in a farcical echo of the Soviet 'brotherly' internationalist help to Czechoslovakia in 1968?[1] With his pro-war signature, Havel either lost existential bearings or political nerve and ended his dissident journey as Rumsfeld's, rather than Derrida's, 'new' European. But it was just as odd for market conservative Václav Klaus, who replaced his nemesis, Havel, at the Prague Castle in the spring of 2003, to land on the side of the vocal war critics (cf. Matuštík 2004).

Lest we misjudge the joint letter by Habermas and Derrida as peculiarly Eurocentric and even oblivious to the worldwide nature of the antiwar protest on February 15, 2003, we must read their new alliance in the context of its emergence. It is the calls for a 'beginning in the core of Europe' and 'the birth of a European public sphere' that concern the critics of this letter (PWE, p. 291). Critics of Derrida and Habermas rightly demand the provincializing rather than recentering of Europe. What shocks 'new' Europeans is that when the core of Europe left Prague, as with Havel's military humanism, the European heart was transplanted westward, where Heidegger once situated Central Europe between the pincers of the East and West. In this geographical shift of Europe's heart, Czechs must hear the echoes of the Munich and Yalta betrayals. As true as such echoes are, they also mislead. Derrida and Habermas introduce a corrective margin of sobriety against the eight European pro-war renegades. The corrective neither invokes the *geographical* heart of Europe nor the cosmopolitan *Westernization* of the world. Speaking *to* the emerging European public sphere, rather than *for* the world, does not implicate them in ignoring the global character of the mass demonstrations. Rather, the pro-war Europe became at once falsely self-centered and provincial. The context for understanding the new alliance between Derrida and Habermas must be the *gulash postcommunism*[2] with its Faustian potions of populist ethnocentrism and warrior cosmopolitanism.

First, I want to revisit the imaginary conversation between Habermas and Derrida from 1995. Second, I will highlight the persisting differences in their post-2001 thinking, pairing up key political concepts that illustrate how each thinker hopes for that which is to come after the death of God. Third, I press ahead to a new critical theory that not only articulates postsecular hope *after* the death of God but also meditates earnestly on the *impossible*.

1. Which Europe? Whose Enlightenment?

I imagined in 1995 an improbable encounter between 'Habermas's fallibilist self-limitation of the Western Enlightenment project (its revolutionary promise of social equality)' and 'Derrida's multicultural-democratic intensification of this same project (refusing identity-logic in culture and capital-logic in the economy)'. I dreamed that 'critical post/modern social theorists and activists' forge one day 'new political coalitions'. I named this imaginary project a 'multicultural enlightenment' or 'radical multicultural democracy'. In the first round of my imagined encounter, I solicited from Habermas the procedural conditions for the possibility of dialogic reciprocity, as these are required by deliberative democracy. Derrida's deconstructive critique found home in Habermas's procedural institutions, thereby curbing the dangers of idealist unreality and political ineffectiveness. Intensifying the promise of democracy, deconstruction assisted Habermas to bring the exiled otherness back to the very ideal of communication community. By letting *political capital* (the regulative idea of communicative pluralism and deliberative democracy) tremble, Derrida flung open the shutters of the European club to its other. In the second round of my imagined encounter, I noted how in the post-1989 landscape the post-Heideggerian Derrida took the wind from the post-Marxian Habermas. Derrida turned to Marx with the kerygma of an unbelieving centurion proclaiming the dying god's promise of redemption. Derrida chastised *economic capital* at the moment when one became tired of Marx just as much as Europeans once were wearied of *all* religion after the Thirty Years War. I argued that Derrida's deconstruction of the market gospel required Habermas's permanent democratic revolution to become firmly lodged in the institutions of procedural justice. From the opposite side, 'by joining a post/modern Marxian hope with a Kierkegaardian fear and trembling, . . . [Derrida] stands a double guard against the new world order cynicism and revolutionary fanaticism' (Matuštík 1998: pp. 51, 60–2). September 11 outran any 'imagined encounter between Derrida and Habermas'(p. 60). The global war on terror threw them together against transatlantic globalism. What 'hope, fear, and trembling' (p. 50) about 1989 materialized in their post-2001 alliance? Drawing on their post-2001 texts, I wish to address the Eurocentric charge by focusing on Habermas's hope for Europe's second chance and Derrida's 'new figure of Europe' (A, p. 116).

First, in a letter to the editor, Habermas (NWE) brings down Rumsfeld's blasphemy of 'new Europe' as quickly as it is uttered. Habermas defends the 'old Europe' that has learned through secularization, defeat, and reflective self-limitation how to vanquish its own ambitions for empire and colonial domination. The old imperial 'Europe' becomes retrogressively new: 'It is a remarkable change of front lines.' Here Habermas ironizes vintage Orwellian doublespeak: 'when Rumsfeld – the politician of the externally enforced "regime change" and the theoretician of "preemptive strike" – calls this new Europe the "old" one.'

Second, it is Rumsfeld who shifts the European center of gravity to the East just when the one-time captive nations partly fearfully, partly eagerly replace the vassal relation to the Soviet empire with the one across the Atlantic. This is the context in which Derrida (A) and Habermas (PWE, FT) plead for a rebirth of Europe from its core. What does it mean to begin from the *core* or *heart* of Europe against the moving center of its gravity? In the first place, Habermas explains in an interview (IEM), 'the core of Europe is at first a technical expression coined in the 1990s by German experts on foreign affairs, Schäuble and Lamers, . . . at the time the integration process again started to take place, in order to recall the leading role of the six grounding members of the European Union.' Second, 'the core of Europe', by defining the final form of the integration process in a unified foreign policy, responds to the divisive pressure of US unilateralism. Third, and this is my more philosophical reading, at 'the core' lies the care for the soul and polis in at once a Socratic and a democratic sense. To constitute oneself and the city in justice cannot geographically privilege nation (France/Germany), continent (Europe), industrial hemisphere (North), world axis (Occident). A post-Eurocentric Europe requires minimally five *core subjects* in the curriculum of just constitution:

- Multicultural and postcolonial world without imperial ambitions
- Receptivity to the radical otherness of the other
- Decisive opposition to the violence of terror
- Secularized politics
- Ancillary role of critical theorists, philosophers, deconstructors

The first two core subjects should deflect any easy condemnation of the alliance between Habermas and Derrida as just another recentering exercise.[3] Responsibility for one's history of exclusion, violence, and promise can be read charitably as accounting for oneself in humility before one can say anything to anybody else. Derrida's 'new figure of Europe' relinquishes all *terra*, territory, or terror as part of its figure. Decisions on the future of Europe's traditions inevitably involve the struggle against its own demons of exclusion, assimilation, and murder. The idea of Europe must draw on its dangerous memory of failed empires, colonialism, religious intolerance, and the Holocaust. Such dangerous remembrance of its own victims both deconstructs the gestures of hegemony waived from the other side of the Atlantic and invites hope (A, p. 116). The heart of *this* 'Europe' hurries the incomplete transatlantic Enlightenment against its imperial temptations (A, p. 117). Only in this sense may Derrida and Habermas (PWE, p. 292) prompt 'the avant-gardist core of Europe' to become a 'locomotive' of the greater inclusion of the other. Against this backdrop, a provincialized Europe must not become a closed fortress of affluence nor sleep with military humanism. The shared experience of struggle produces a 'post-national constellation' that lends life to a new mentality, but with the following anti-imperial centers of gravity: self-limitation of state sovereignty, care for social welfare to resolve class conflict, and trust in the achievement of international law (PWE, p. 294). The new multicultural enlightenment acts as an imperative of learning: 'Europe' ought to become other than its imperial heading (OH), as this new mentality alone can allow the formation of the common European identity that would be in solidarity with worldwide anti-war demonstrations:

> A culture which for centuries has been beset more than any other by conflicts between town and country, sacred and secular authorities, by the competition between faith and knowledge, the struggle between states and antagonistic classes, has had to painfully learn how differences can be communicated, contradictions institutionalized, and tensions stabilized. The acknowledgments of differences – the reciprocal acknowledgment of the other as Other in his otherness – can also become a feature of a common identity. (PWE, p. 294)

Each European nation underwent its history of bloody empire striving and 'the loss of its empire' and colonies. With that loss, most Europeans, Derrida and Habermas conclude, are able to 'assume a reflexive distance from themselves'. This is elusive for the North American experience because of its young history and incomplete secularization. The European mentality is borne of witnessing its uprooting violence in modernity, apprehending victories 'from the perspective of the defeated' (PWE, p. 297). The plea is a vanishing point of self-corrective, 'old' European learning for a new figure of Europe. 'This could support the rejection of Eurocentrism and inspire the Kantian hope for a global domestic policy' (PWE, p. 297).

In the third core subject of their plea and new alliance, Derrida and Habermas's opposition to terror emerges as more consistent than the hegemonic war on terror they oppose. Habermas drives home that there is no moral excuse for terror; since terrorism is neither a war nor a private criminal act, it should be treated more like a political deed (FT, p. 34). Communicative action can have essentially (in the *telos* of speech oriented to an understanding with another) no truck with violence. Communicative ideality requires that we can overcome the structural violence issuing from material inequalities and distortions by power politics. Habermas argues that there are no alternatives to the uses of violence except developing 'world citizenry' and strengthening its requisite institutions like the United Nations and World Court (FT, pp. 35–9). He offers no kind words for the 'self-centered course of a callous superpower' with its strategy of unilateral war. Habermas (PWE, p. 296) and Derrida (A, p. 117) not only refuse all normative bases for the death penalty, viewing it as a covert survival of religious fundamentalism in politics, but also show how the core curriculum inscribes 'the ban on capital punishment as a condition for entrance' into the ideal polis. Should decentered Europe ever require accepting the retributive and fundamentalist virus back into the core? The US death penalty and the language of crusades that accompanied the US declaration of the war on terror were snubbed by most commonsense Europeans as at best medieval and at worst barbaric, and yet these critical attitudes are normative rather than anti-American.

Derrida notes that terror brings 'semantic instability' to concepts, borders, as it is itself 'self-escalating' (A, pp. 102, 107). Terror uses the worst of 'technocapitalist modernity for the purposes of religious fanaticism.' He judges that terror carries 'no future . . . for the "world" itself' (A, p. 113). Bracketing all theoretical undecidability, Derrida decisively enters into the post/modern binary and in so doing joins Habermas on the side of democratic institutions:

> If I had to take one of two sides and choose in a binary situation, well, I would . . . take the side of the camp that, in principle, by right of law, leaves a perspective open to perfectibility in the name of the 'political,' democracy, international law, international institutions, and so on. . . . Even in its most cynical mode, such an assertion still lets resonate within it an invincible promise. (A, p. 114)

In the fourth core subject of their plea and new alliance, Derrida and Habermas detect the key issue between terror and hope in one-sided, incomplete secularization. Derrida defends

> 'Europe,' even if in quotation marks, because, in the long and patient deconstruction required for the transformation to-come, the experience Europe inaugurated at the time of the Enlightenment . . . in the relationship between the political and the theological or, rather, religious, . . . will have left in European political space absolutely original marks with regard to religious doctrine . . . over the political. (A, pp. 116f.)

In this instance (Matuštík 1993, 2001), Derrida (A, p. 135, GD) distinguishes with Kierkegaard religious doctrines or belief systems from faith. Derrida shoots a Socratic torpedo shock[4] into the permanent terror alerts by claiming that the demarcation between belief and faith exists neither in Arab, Muslim, or Far East nations, nor in North America and Israel. The 'post–September 11' division comes down for him to 'two political theologies' of the terrorists and the US war on terror at one end, and 'Europe' that has opted out of the 'double theologico-political program' at the other end. In place of the intolerant, provincial, and dangerously global US discourse on evildoers, axis of evil, infinite justice, and the civic religious pledges of allegiance and appeals to 'God bless America', the core subjects of secularization inaugurated a discourse beyond the empire centrism of the theological politics (A, pp. 117f.).

Derrida and Habermas (PWE, p. 296) do not cover over the sense in which they behold the 'old' European politics as more sober than the 'new' regime changes exported by the United States, whose values they consider Eurocentric in the pregnant sense: 'For us [Europeans], a president who opens his daily business with open prayer, and associates his significant political decisions with a divine mission, is hard to imagine.' Europeans 'possess a keen sense of the "dialectic of enlightenment"', they no longer believe naively the gospel of technological progress and unregulated markets to deliver the world to justice (PWE, p. 295). Habermas judges universalism sought by all empires as a transfigured, depraved political way of recapturing the singular cosmologies of world religions. Fundamentalism, as well as the unilateral global policy that opposes it, can be defined by the very same claim as 'a stubborn attitude that insists on the political imposition of its own convictions and reasons.' Fundamentalism and hegemonic politics are postmodern phenomena that repress 'cognitive dissonance' of the plural world through a 'holy' or nationalist intolerance. Secularization can stabilize a 'nonexclusive place within a universal discourse shared with other religions' (FT, p. 31, cf. FK, p. 102).

In the fifth core subject of their plea and new alliance, Derrida's philosopher aspires to be neither a king nor an idealistically aloof adviser to the king nor a materially pedestrian consumer of the myth of the given. A deconstructor inhabits the discipline of responsible self-reflection, demands accountability from the powers that be, and contributes critical reflection to the life of the polis (A, p. 106). A deconstructor is thus akin to a critical theorist who acts as witness (Matuštík 2001, pp. 139–56). The new alliance between deconstructor and critical theorist ushers to no philosophical or party vanguard. Derrida and Habermas begin where my imaginary dialogue set up for them concluded:

> What emerges from this encounter is neither a rejection of Derrida or Habermas, nor a simple recipe or eclecticism. Perhaps, *we* receive an invitation to renew critical social theory with the existential pathos and material concretion of the young Marcuse. . . . I cannot know what shape political coalitions among critical post/modern social theorists

> and activists will take. One has learned already that not to make steps in concrete hope, fear, and trembling is to evade the task. Assuming its challenge in this fashion raises new specters of deconstructive and critical theory. (Matuštík 1998, p. 64)

2. What Is To Come?

A more than superficial difference between Derrida and Habermas turns on the nuance of how each invokes hope after Nietzsche's death of God. Habermas hopes with Kant's Enlightenment for the possibility of discursive democracy. When Derrida denudes even this disenchanted and linguistified hope, he hopes against hope for the *impossible*. While such hope, even as it comes *after* secularization, is postsecular, Derrida's *impossibility* does not oppose Habermas's possibility. I clarify this nuance under three umbrellas: secularization, radical democracy, and postsecular hope (cf. RR, p. 152; Matuštík 1998, pp. 40, 49–64, 135–41, 228, 247).

Secularization. What the two thinkers secularize is an already secular exile of God – the God who was first sent out from the monastic enclosure to attend the world of needs and then, along with church property, was handed over to the secular affairs of the state. Secularization of cultural and social modernity completes the exile of God from the public sphere. Habermas (RR, p. 159, cf. FK, pp. 103–5, 109ff.), always-already irritated with Heidegger for gesturing toward that God who alone can save us now, proposes a cooperative, translatable relationship between the claims of knowledge and those of faith. Habermas values religion as a semantic reservoir of meanings. The boundaries, at once porous and treacherous (FK, pp. 109, 113), between secular and religious claims – like the tracks in the sand left by the desert wanderings of the exiled God – require mutual perspective taking and from it issuing mutual recognition between faith and knowledge. The secularizing reflection supplants the exiled God (FK, p. 104). Reflection evinces the capacity to raise and defend unconditioned validity claims to truth, rightness, and sincerity. This linguistified God becomes but the placeholder of the vanishing point traversed by reflection. Into the empty space vacated by transcendent divinity, Habermas projects the ideal communication community. The ideal exists neither within the world (God has been gradually exiled from it) nor in some beyond (the vanishing point of secularizing reflection closed the gap between this world and transcendence beyond it). The ideal of this exiled, secularized, dead God undergoes, however, repeated social resurrection of what is to come *after*: the ideal comes to life in actual discourses when the formal-pragmatic placeholder acts as the final court of appeal to which speakers and hearers offer reasons for their claims. Perhaps Habermasian transcendence on this side of the world betrays the neurotic compulsion-repetition of Freud, who would be suspicious, even in

Habermas's linguistified ideality, of the surviving phantom limb of religious longing (FK, p. 111).

When he confesses the disconsolate character of communicative reason, Habermas closes ranks with the secular theologians of the death of God. That a translation relationship ought to be possible between such different modes of existence as faith and reason, is something the secularizing reflection optimistically assumes. Reflection gradually strips religions of their self-enclosed claims to be the comprehensive worldview: 'religious consciousness itself undergoes a learning process . . . [and becomes] modernized by a way of cognitive adaptation to the individualistic and egalitarian nature of the laws of the secular community.' This learning ought to accomplish the 'renunciation of violence' that used 'to push forward religious beliefs inside or outside the community.' We replace violence with the 'acceptance of the voluntary character of religious association' (Habermas, ID, p. 6). Reflection coexists side by side with the absolutizing imaginary of belief systems. Beliefs continue to raise absolute claims to truth, rightness, and sincerity. Secularization demands that the belief claims learn mutual tolerance. Tolerance also demands its price: the abdication of missionary zeal towards infidels or heretics (ID, p. 7).

Derrida depicts September 11 as an incomprehensible, unpresentable 'event' of 'nonknowledge' and 'pure singularity' that we can neither name, date, nor utter (A, pp. 90–4). He shows how this radical 'limit' on experience and knowledge completes the death of God. It likewise limits what may be hoped for as possible. Terror's wounding is 'infinite' because it cannot be mourned or redeemed by any known or possible future to come. While secularization yielded reflection on the possibility of the Enlightenment hope to come, terror inflicts a threefold suicidal destruction of reflection's autoimmunity.

The first moment aggressively attacks the 'symbolic head' of modern economy and power from within its own ground and with its own means (A, pp. 95f.). The second moment wounds without granting a future, ushering the present age into trauma without the possibility of earthly consolation at least through mourning. The third moment moves in the vicious circle of terror renewed with every attempt to fight it. All three moments arrive at the unnameable and 'im-presentable to come' (A, pp. 97–100). For the lack of better words, I borrow from Kant the concept of radical evil: This possibility *is* of 'the worst' to come. Its terror, rather than hope, lies in 'the repetition to come – though worse' (A, p. 97). Acts of terror/war on terror deliberately move in the circle of a 'suicidal autoimmunity' (A, p. 95). The death of God has self-escalated. I borrow from Kant the concept of radical evil, while with Derrida I want to think against Kant and Habermas of the 'diabolical' acts as something humans are willing to do freely. Derrida pleads for the impossible against the grain of the human failure to be God and its irreversible wound.

Radical democracy. Whereas Habermas (DIL) presents democracy as a disconsolate regulative ideal of deliberative and procedural justice, Derrida says that democracy-to-come requires faith and hope (A, p. 119). Habermas reforms national sovereignty in the direction of popular procedural sovereignty. Derrida's waiting for democracy does not envision an arrival of a political regime. Democracy-to-come is a contested space, an event without history or visible horizon. Habermas redresses the violent effects of one-sided secularization (FK) by enlarging the sphere of public tolerance (FT, pp. 37–41, ID, DIL). Derrida insists on 'gift, forgiveness, hospitality' in the public sphere (A, pp. 120f.). I want to pair Habermas's concepts of democracy with Derrida's:

- Habermas's regulative ideal with Derrida's event
- Habermas's tolerance with Derrida's hospitality
- Habermas's world citizenship with Derrida's democracy-to-come
- Habermas's self-limited sovereignty with Derrida's alliance beyond sovereignty
- Habermas's Enlightenment's possibility with Derrida's gift's impossibility
- Habermas's procedural justice with Derrida's forgiveness

The key nuance in each pair pivots between Habermas's world cosmopolitanism, which assumes shared, divisible, and self-limiting sovereignty, and Derrida's deconstruction of the state form itself for the sake of 'an alliance . . . beyond the "political."' In Derrida, democracy-to-come gathers singular beings beyond the limits of cosmopolitanism and citizenship (A, p. 130, cf. SM). Habermas's democracy radicalizes the Stoic, Pauline, and Kantian ideals of human sociality under the regulative limits of secular globalization. Derrida secularizes the horizon of sovereignty those same ideals still assume. For him the Greco-Roman, Pauline, and Kantian imaginaries of world citizenship (along with Carl Schmitt who so worries Habermas) transmit the legacy of the political onto-theology (A, pp. 121ff.). Democracy-to-come after the death of God for Derrida sheds even the popular aspirations to sovereignty and strives for 'a universal alliance or solidarity that extends beyond the internationality of nation-states and thus beyond citizenship' (A, p. 124).[5]

Derrida is neither an antidemocratic prophet of the death of God nor a cynical power politician advising the elites how use the pseudoreligiosity of the Grand Inquisitor to induce intoxication in conservative moralists and pliable masses (cf. Postel 2003). Derrida's alliance with Habermas guards against the new political onto-theology of sovereignty. Derrida cautions Habermas that 'tolerance' can become but 'a conditioned, circumspect, careful hospitality' of the religiousness of those in power. He invites into community 'whomever arrives as an absolutely foreign *visitor*, as a new *arrival*, nonidentifiable and unforeseeable, in short wholly other.' This is hardly an abstract otherness. A new figure of Europe, more than an 'invitation' into the regulative-ideal club of the possible, is a 'visitation' of the unexpected and uninvited (A, p. 129) and a task to welcome strangers beyond duty and law (A, pp. 132f.).

Postsecular hope. The coming of the im/possible turns on the margin between what was secularized without violent reminder of onto-theological-political programs and what is left over after acts of terror/war on terror. The slash stands for the invisible margin, not undecidability between Habermas and Derrida. That margin is faith purified of imaginary's belief in its own power. If Derridean visitations conjure up angels, if hospitality echoes the biblical prophets, then the plea must be more than a spiritless prayer. I recognize in this uncanny, post-Nietzschean guest the postsecular return of the religious without religion (Caputo 2001, pp. 109–12, 132–41), hope given for the sake of those without hope (Benjamin in Marcuse 1991, p. 257).

Habermas's impassioned plea for a fallible Enlightenment harkens back to a nondestructive secularization that *invited* reason and faith to coexist in tolerance and freedom from terror (FK, pp. 108–11). Now that the terror of the twenty-first century revealed the fundamentalist abyss of Nietzsche's death of God, coming to terms with hope becomes our difficult task. After too many genocides, we grasp with greater acuity what Nietzsche's madman meant by saying that we were not yet up to our own deed. Fundamentalism marks a disconsolate return of this abysmal God in the form of a punishing superego and a longing imaginary that together demand adherence to power, doctrine, and discipline. Habermas calls 'fundamentalist'

> those religious movements which, given the cognitive limits of *modern* life, nevertheless persist in practicing or promoting a return to the exclusivity of premodern religious attitudes. Fundamentalism lacks the epistemic innocence of those long-ago realms in which world religions first flourished, and which could somehow still be experienced as limitless (RR, p. 151, cf. FK, p. 102).

For Derrida, fundamentalism responds to the death of God in acts of terror/the war on terror, and this is why terror has no *terra* and no future (A, p. 118).

Derrida and Habermas venture into the postsecular desert of religion without religion. How they venture defines their difference. Habermas's religious discourse is but a phantom limb – a "musically tone-deaf" (FK, p. 114) and unredeemable absence of the impossible. What alone can be redeemed for him lies in human solidarity – the profanized religious ideal of communication community. Nondestructive secularization must translate religious and rational claims into the language of communicative freedom.

Equal freedoms shared among humans require, more than the death of God, that the divine throne remains empty. Not a psychoanalytically vacuumed desire for oneself as *causa sui*, Habermas's communicatively responsible atheism resists both terror and fundamentalism that try to appropriate the place of God (FK, pp. 113ff.). After depth psychology revealed that our desire to be God died on the analyst's couch in at once transferred and disappointed desire, that dying divinity can still save by absence. Habermas's communicative ideal of community is disconsolate but not inherently predestined to celebrate the human failure (see n. 5 below, cf. Žižek 2003, pp. 145–71).

Can Heidegger's own postsecular absencing of God come to a truce with Habermas's disconsolate ideal? Or must we interpret even *this* dimension of Heidegger's silence – humans not speaking with the mandate of the God whom they exiled, killed, and psychoanalytically amputated – as an evasion of responsibility for our disasters (nights without stars)? Or are not those who proclaim the past closed, as if this modernist, critical claim could be more than a belief (FK, pp. 110f.), imposing mythical hopelessness on the victims of history? Is not speaking of what one should be silent about another evasion of responsibility?

Questions like these allow Habermas to make a political alliance *with* Derrida. He concedes that what binds him with Derrida philosophically is a certain reading of Kant. What continues to divide them is Derrida's late Heideggerian inspiration, which Habermas finds, even when viewed through Derrida's Lévinasian angle of vision, betraying both the Judaic prophetic and the Socratic enlightenment legacies of the West (IEM). Questions like these prompt Derrida to hold reservations about regulative ideals (A, pp. 134f.): Hope is not impossible because of some counterfactually deferred or imaginary ideality. Hope's urgency cannot be ideally projected onto abstract otherness. Hope 'precedes me – and seizes me *here now*', or I have never been infused with hope. Political theorists and activists, even Habermas, assume hope when they set up truth commissions to deal with war crimes and unforgivable human disasters. Yet their assumption is wrong, as hope is never available as a regulative ideal. Camus declared in the opening pages of his *Myth of Sisyphus* that he has never seen anyone die for the ontological argument, in the same way one could reiterate that to hope in regulative ideals would be odd rather than impossible. If Habermas does not want any truck even with Derrida's Jewish transformation of Heidegger, then the same angle of vision can be had with Marcuse's appeal to Benjamin at the end of *One-Dimensional Man*, indicating hope as a granting, a gift, not an ideal or pragmatic presupposition. The visitation of hope arrives as 'what is most undeniably real'. Responsibility (spoken of or not) cannot be settled by a norm or rule. What comes after the death of the God of onto-theology may never be a regulative ideal but must always remain concrete, albeit aporetic, reality (A, p. 115).

Derrida saves his most playfully irreverent reading of Nietzsche's death of God against the grain of Heidegger's saving God for a footnote (A, p. 190, n. 14; cf. n.16). Derrida's postsecular God names 'an ultimate form of sovereignty that would reconcile absolute justice with absolute law and thus, like all sovereignty and all law, with absolute force, with an absolute saving power.' This impossible God names 'a new international' without institution or party. Such 'improbable institution' requires 'faith' rather than a zealot, St. Paul, or vanguard, Lenin. The impossible is the gift of 'messianicity without messianism', 'democracy-to-come', and 'the untenable promise of *just international institution*'. Neither Heidegger, in his critique of technological age, nor Nietzsche, lamenting the nihilism of all value positing, held hope for radical democracy; but Derrida does. Echoing Benjamin's theological materialism, Derrida's democracy-to-come solicits 'faith in the possibility of this impossible and, in truth, undecidable thing from the point of view of knowledge, science, and conscience', and such faith 'must govern all our decisions' (A, p. 115). Hardly even noticed, two years before issuing their joint plea, Habermas writes approvingly of Derrida: 'Today, Jacques Derrida, from different premises, comes to a similar position [of the early Frankfurt school] – a worthy winner of the Adorno Award.... All he wants to retain of Messianism is "messianicity, stripped of everything"' (FK, p. 113, cf. Derrida GD, FaK, p. 18).

3. 'Unhappy the Land that Is in Need of Heroes'

Michal Zantovsky, former Czech ambassador to the United States, commented on the end of Havel's presidency (Remnick 2003) by citing Bertolt Brecht. The same Brechtian Jeremiad concluded Habermas's (FT, p. 43) philosophizing in a time of terror: 'Pity the land that needs heroes.' Zantovsky, Havel's long-term associate, gave a diplomatic toast to the outgoing Czech president at the Prague Castle farewell party by adding a wish to Brecht's lament, 'I hope we don't need another.' That US culture and politics are not up to Brecht's secular sobriety motivated Habermas's recourse to the citation. Yet is either Havel's or Habermas's Europe more up to it? I used to think that Kierkegaard acted for them as a passageway to political sobriety (1993). But it seems that Derrida alone among the three of them speaks with a sober voice that hope-to-come is *impossible* because it can have no truck with human heroic projects.

I conclude with *untimely postsecular meditations* on the impossible. Such meditations begin to breathe life and grant a crucial edge to a redemptive critical theory suited for our present age, but they remain untimely until they take root in a new postsecular sensibility of hope-to-come. As untimely redemptive critical theory, the first meditation names the return of radical evil by its name. In the second meditation, new critical theory comes to terms with the realization that even its ideal and hope cannot heal all wounds of history. In the third, it learns from the secular masters of suspicion to expose the false prophets who blaspheme by speaking about vanquishing evil and delivering hope as heroic acts. As a new postsecular sensibility, the first meditation detects that evil can be called radical only as one acts deliberately to suspend goodwill; the second begins by mourning the trauma of the human condition for which hope is always-already impossible; and the third ventures with risky faith against all personal and social heroic projects and belief systems.

First Meditation: Radical Evil Is Diabolical. We need no devil to personify the diabolical in deliberate acts of destruction that intend no future. The truly problematic for the present age is Kant's harnessing of evil, not that of religion, within the bounds of mere reason. The beliefs of rational religion(s) can be easily translated into secular terms to yield the moral point of view, and Habermas completes Kant's task brilliantly. By translating and assimilating radical evil within the bounds of mere reason – a secularizing project that Habermas (FK, p. 110, ORSR) also inherits from Kant – we rob ourselves of naming critically the coming of the worst. Derrida's (A) three moments of suicidal autoimmunity restore the postsecular edge to critical theory. Moreover, learning from Kierkegaard, yet for him unlike for Habermas in his secular translations, Derrida names the post-Kantian willed ignorance by its true name as stupidity. Radical evil presents the existential (untranslatable either/or) boundary that 'both destroys and institutes the religious' (FaK, p. 100). This nuance makes me meditate on what Derrida, like Kierkegaard yet unlike Kant and Habermas, finds in radical evil – the demarcation between the religious and ethical spheres of existence. Habermas (FK, p. 110) translates sin into guilt, and hence forgiveness into ethical repentance or righting of social injustice. Would there be need for forgiveness if it were in our power to repent evil ethically and undo all wrongs socially? This meditation on the sources of forgiveness – a capacity that does not lie in human power alone – intimates the most offensive though nonetheless spiritual logic. In another telling footnote, Derrida (GT, pp. 165–6, n. 31; cf. SP) shows that the weakness of Kant's watered-down definition of evil is a reduction of forgiveness to repentance. Unforgivable cruelty and willed stupidity are called radical evil because by bursting rational bounds of guilt, they cannot be repented ethically.

The human possibility of diabolical evil revisits us with the religious phenomenon after the death of God. This human phenomenon of evil invokes the religious phenomenon of forgiveness. If need for forgiveness did not arise, would any evil ever be 'radical'? Without the uncanny phenomena of evil and forgiveness there could be no phenomenology of the 'religious' after the death of the God of onto-theology. If such evil never arose, would there be philosopher's need for its rational translation? Kant and Habermas cannot have it both ways, and Nietzsche does not live up to this task.

Second Meditation: Hope Is Impossible. Truths lie beyond our rational horizon of what is known or not yet conscious; from this ignorance humans can be delivered by a self-corrective process of learning. What is not known, that rational enlightenment can cure. Rational criticism, learning, and communication are the greatest possible hope for the continual progress of the human race. If some wounds cannot be healed by progress or learning projected under the regulative ideal of communication community, then hope that appears as a phenomenon of what could still deliver us carries the name of the *impossible*. The sheer lack of human possibility can be ignored or repressed, or one can despair of the impossible. Yet all second-degree ignorance, repression, and despair are willed by us, and in that willing act we acknowledge the appearance of the *impossible* itself. To go on pretending that all wounds of history can be healed rationally is to deliberately ignore, repress, or despair of the impossible. The ultimate pretense reactively defies all healing by placing deliberate accents on the *im*possibility of hope, celebrating the human failure or trauma. The convex mirror of theism is then atheism held dogmatically as a belief in the *im*possibility of hope. But *impossible* hope is not an objectifiable phenomenon of *belief* and hence not a rational validity claim against what is humanly possible. To stop pretending altogether, one must complete the death of that God who survives not just in our grammar, as Nietzsche once thought, but in all atheistic beliefs we imbue with false reverence.

The religious phenomenon returns after the completed death of God under the figures of impossible hope. No amount of talking or learning or force can break the boundary that protects unmourned trauma from what rational enlightenment or possible hope can deliver. The unmourned, to be accessible, requires self-acceptance and forgiveness. Negatively, redemptive critical theory calls evil by its name and shows how rational enlightenment fails to heal all wounds of history or forgive. Positively, now without despair's defiance of the *impossible*, the new sensibility of self-forgiveness opens to the cosmos and oneself with uncanny hope.

Third Meditation: Heroism Is Idol Worship. Heroism is the other face of the human terror of possibility or its loss. Self in terror of its freedom either searches for and imposes fundamental(ist) certainties or puffs up with war on its terror externalized. The idols of broken emptiness on either side usher the terror-stricken self into heroic projects. There one bolts and takes a last stance. Heroism – whether religious or secular – is idolatrous precisely because its worship of self lies opposite of faith. Derrida drives this point home with his Benjaminian-Lévinasian view of Kierkegaard (A, p. 135): 'I always make *as if* I subscribed to the *as if*'s of Kant . . . or *as if* Kierkegaard helped me to think beyond his own Christianity, *as if* in the end he did not want to know that he was not Christian or refused to admit that he did not know what being Christian means.' Habermas learns from Kierkegaard's existential ethics how to adopt the either/or decision of EuroAmerican traditions that would foster the democratic political culture and identity (PWE, p. 295). But his public either/or does not help us to unmask the sacral language of heroism emerging anew in postsecular political culture. Derrida resists all conflation of the ethical-political sphere with the religious because he grasps religion without religion as contrary to heroism.

We know better why we should take heed from Brecht's profane lament. *Hero worship is the most spiritless not because it is godless but because in its appearing pseudo-religious phenomenon we recognize an idolatrous divinization of human projects.* Heroism emerges in the anxiety of freedom's possibility. Ripened anxiety masks the despair of the weak will as it embraces the heroic crowd. Ultimately the hero's will to power manifests the full-blown despair of religious-cum-political defiance. The defiant self feeds the life of empires that in turn celebrate the hero's deeds. To grasp the nature of terror we need to supplant the death of God by the category of spiritlessness. In this way we deliver the requisite blow to heroic religiousness – whether couched in a fundamentalist or patriotic mission – as the most dangerously desperate of all in its spiritlessness. Any religiosity can become spiritless when it worships itself. The role of critical theory with a postsecular edge suited to our desperate times must expose not only secular but most of all the religious false prophets. They are false who speak the language of vanquishing evil and delivering hope through heroic projects.

This meditation is needed most when divine blessings on a country are counted by the deeds of its heroes. Intoned in hymnals or as religious and national flags, along with civic prayers for national victories, are raised side by side, to pity all lands that need heroes – this prayer would become the most devastating public performance in any international forum (Matuštík 2004).

> *Baruch Atah Adonai Elohenu Melech haOlam ... Sanctus, Sanctus, Sanctus Dominus Deus Sabaoth ... Allah Akbar ... Pity the land that needs heroes.*

We should chant in synagogues and at the Wailing Wall, in churches and at the bully pulpits, and from the loudspeakers of great mosques, in all places where humans call God's name great but dress it in the heroic caricature of greatness.

The meditation that could breathe life into a new redemptive critical theory inhabits the self that rests transparently in the work of mourning and recovery, knowing all along that the human race cannot heal all wounds of history yet, freed from all pretensions to heroism, yields to visitations of impossible hope.[6]

Bibliography

Works cited by abbreviation (where they exist, listed English translations are used).

Jacques Derrida:

A: 2003. 'Autoimmunity: Real and Symbolic Suicides.' In Borradori, Derrida, and Habermas (2003), pp. 85–136.

FaK: 2002. 'Faith and Knowledge: The Two Sources of "Religion" at the Limit of Reason Alone.' In Gil Anidjar, ed. *Acts of Religion* (New York: Routledge), pp. 42–101.

GD: 1955. *The Gift of Death*. Trans. David Willis (Chicago: University of Chicago Press).

GT: 1994. *Given Time/Counterfeit Money*. Trans. Peggy Kamuf (Chicago: University of Chicago Press).

OH: 1992. *The Other Heading: Reflections On Today's Europe*. Trans. Pascale-Anne Brault and Michael B. Naas (Bloomington: Indiana University Press).

SM: 1994. *Specters of Marx: The State of the Debt, the Work of Mourning, and the New International*. Trans. Peggy Kamuf (New York: Routledge).

SP: 1999. 'Le Siècle et le Pardon.' (Conversation with Michel Wieviorka). *Monde des débats*. Published together with FaK in: *Foi et Savoir suivi de Le Siècle et le Pardon* (Paris: Édition du Seuil [2000]).

Jürgen Habermas:

AS: 1992. *Autonomy and Solidarity: Interviews with Jürgen Habermas*. Ed. Peter Dews (London: Verso, revised and enlarged ed., 1992).

DIL: 2003. 'Dispute on the Past and Future of International Law: Transition from a National to a Postnational Constellation.' Unpublished presentation at the World Congress of Philosophy, Istanbul (August 10).

FHN: 2003. *The Future of Human Nature* (Cambridge, Mass.: Polity Press).

FK: 2001. 'Glauben und Wissen. Zum Friedenspreis des deutschen Buchhandels: Eine Dankrede.' The speech, 'Faith and Knowledge' (October 14), Frankfurt's Paulskirche, the Peace Award of the German Publishers. *Süddeutsche Zeitung* (October 15)./FHN, pp. 101–15, 126–7 trans. Hella Beister and Max Pensky.

FT: 2003. 'Fundamentalism and Terror.' In Borradori, Derrida, and Habermas (2003), pp. 25–43.

ID: 2003. 'Intolerance and Discrimination.' *International Journal of Constitutional Law* 1:1 (January): pp. 2–12.

IEM: 2004. 'America and the World: Interview with Eduardo Mendieta.' English translation forthcoming in *Logos* [Editor's note: 'America and the World: A Conversation with Jürgen Habermas', trans. Jeffrey Craig Miller, *Logos*, 3:3 (Summer 2004)].

IFM: 2003. 'Was bedeutet das Denkmalsturz?' *Frankfurter Allgemeine Zeitung* (April 17)/'Interpreting the Fall of a Monument.' Trans. and ed. Max Pensky. *Globalizing Critical Theory* (Lanham, Md.: Rowman and Littlefield, forthcoming 2005).

LA: 2002. 'Letter to America.' Interview by Danny Postel. *The Nation* (December 16).

NWE: 2003. 'Neue Welt Europa.' *Frankfurter Allgemeine Zeitung* (January 24).

ORSR: 2004. 'On the Relation between the Secular Liberal State and Religion.' Ed. Eduardo Mendieta. *The Frankfurt School on Religion* (New York: Routledge).

RR: 2002. *Religion and Rationality: Essays on Reason, God, and Modernity*. Ed. and with an introduction by Eduardo Mendieta (Cambridge, Mass.: MIT Press).

Jürgen Habermas and Jacques Derrida

PWE: 2003. 'Plädoyer zu einer Wiedergeburt Europas.' *Frankfurter Allgemeine Zeitung* (May 31)./'February 15, or, What Binds Europeans Together: A Plea for a Common

Foreign Policy, Beginning in the Core of Europe.' Trans. and ed. Max Pensky. *Globalizing Critical Theory* (Lanham, Md.: Rowman and Littlefield, forthcoming 2005).

Other Works Cited:

Adorno, Theodor W. 1986 (1959). 'What Does Coming to Terms with the Past Mean?' in Geoffrey H. Hartman, *Bitburg in Moral and Political Perspective* (Indianapolis: Indiana University Press), 114–29.

Caputo, Jack. 2001. *On Religion* (New York: Routledge).

Borradori, Giovanna, Jacques Derrida, and Jürgen Habermas. 2003. *Philosophy in a Time of Terror* (Chicago: University of Chicago Press).

Havel, Václav. 2002. 'The Transformation of NATO' (Prague: Sovovy mlýny) (speech at the conference organized by Host Committee and Aspen Institute of Berlin [November 20]).

Marcuse, Herbert. 1991. *One-Dimensional Man* (Boston: Beacon Press).

Matuštík, Martin J. Beck. 1993. *Postnational Identity: Critical Theory and Existential Philosophy in Habermas, Kierkegaard, and Havel* (New York: Guilford).

Matuštík, Martin J. Beck. 1995. 'Derrida and Habermas on the Aporia of the Politics of Identity and Difference: Towards Radical Democratic Multiculturalism.' *Constellations* 1:3 (January): pp. 383–98.

Matuštík, Martin J. Beck. 1998. *Specters of Liberation: Great Refusals in the New World Order* (Albany: State University of New York Press).

Matuštík, Martin J. Beck. 2001. *Jürgen Habermas: A Philosophical-Political Profile* (Lanham, Md.: Rowman and Littlefield).

Matuštík, Martin J. Beck. 2003. Letter in response to Alan Ryan review article ('The Power of Positive Thinking,' *The New York Review of Books* [January 16, 2003], pp. 43–6) on Matuštík (2001), *The New York Review of Books* (February 27), p. 49.

Matuštík, Martin J. Beck. 2004. 'America's Prayer.' *Open Democracy* (online issue, http://www.opendemocracy.com/, June 3). In Czech as 'Modlitba pro Ameriku.' *Literární noviny* (May 17), pp. 1, 4.

Postel, Danny. 2003. 'Noble Lies and Perpetual War: Leo Strauss, the Neocons, and Iraq.' *Open Democracy* (online issue, http://www.opendemocracy.com/, October 16).

Remnick, David. 2003. 'Letter from Prague: Exit Havel.' *The New Yorker* (February 17, 24).

Žižek, Slavoj. 2003. *The Puppet and the Dwarf: The Perverse Core of Christianity* Cambridge, Mass.: MIT Press).

NOTES

1. The second half of the fifth comment on NATO is vintage Kafkaesque Havel (2002) who should have been in the foreground rather than ultimately subordinated to power politics: 'We have also had another experience: the occupation by the Warsaw Pact States in 1968. At that time the entire nation reiterated the word "sovereignty," cursing the official Soviet interpretation that the intervention was an act of "brotherly help" offered in the name of a value that ranked higher than national sovereignty in the name of socialism that was allegedly endangered in our country, which allegedly meant a danger to the prospects for a better life for the human race. Almost everyone in our country knew that the sole objective was to preserve Soviet domination and economic exploitation but millions of people in the Soviet Union probably believed that the sovereignty of our State was being suppressed in the name of a higher human value. This second experience makes me very cautious. It seems to me that whenever we think of intervening against a State in the name of protection of human life we

should always ask ourselves even if only for a moment, or in our innermost thoughts the question of whether this would not be some kind of a "brotherly help" again.'

2. 'Gulash communism' was the name given to the models of social and political accommodation by the communist regimes to consumers in the late 1970s and 1980s.
3. This view has been voiced by Iris Marion Young on Habermas and Derrida (PWE) at the World Congress of Philosophy (Istanbul 2003) and by Eduardo Mendieta at the Critical Theory Roundtable (SUNY Stony Brook, October 2003).
4. Socrates' gadfly posture was like the stingray, which emits electric torpedo shocks.
5. A contrast with Žižek (2003: pp. 90, 140ff.) helps us fine-tune the nuance between Habermas and Derrida. Žižek locates suicidal autoimmunity in the human imaginary with its desire for absolute otherness. Žižek (2003: pp. 66–70, 86–91) *perverts* but unabashedly recenters Pauline-cum-Leninist (i.e., atheistically and materialistically inflected) Christianity against messianic Judaism. Human empathy with the divine failure of the crucified God mirrors the emptiness inscribed into our failure to possess an absolute, transcendent reality. As if anticipating and caricaturing Mel Gibson's *The Passion of the Christ*, Žižek welcomes the failure of Jesus who, abandoned by the Father, gets himself killed and thus inaugurates a this-worldly passion for justice. Against Derrida's Benjaminian-Lévinasian Judaic transcendence, the *perverse* in Christianity is the epiphany of the disconsolate 'divine Fool'. The Messiah has come to reveal the infinite failure of the imaginary to bridge the human and divine reality. We must not wait for the messianic promise of the wholly other world than this unjust one. Žižek frowns on all appeals to Other as abstract or imaginary projections. We must accept trauma without the possibility of mourning. His post-Hegelian materialist theology – Holy Spirit as the life of community – would be an outcome of successful Lacanian therapy. Wounding continues to define the human condition after the coming of Christ. Enter Žižek's Lacanian-Calvinist rendition of original sin. Repelled by unredeemable terror, yet attracted by a dying God, 'in our very failure, we identify with the divine failure', confessing universal human failure. Žižek promotes against Derrida-Lévinas's and Habermas's appeals to the wholly other than this unjust world, the Pauline-Leninist vision of community. The atheist lamentation of Christ who finds himself alone on the cross helps Žižek give up the imaginary longing for the absolute Thing. How St. Paul of Habermas's Peircean community ideal lines up with Žižek's Pauline materialist theology is a good question; or whether, on Derrida's account, both these Pauline versions of community (Habermas's communication ideal and Žižek's Leninist materialism) still involve onto-theology exposed by Kant as transcendental illusion and thoroughly discredited by late Heidegger's move beyond it.
6. In response to my correspondence to him regarding my recent work, and this article in particular, Derrida wrote the following words: 'Dear friend, Forgive me for having taken so long to thank you for your very friendly letter, book about Habermas, and especially your two manuscript articles that you devote to Habermas and me. Today I lack the strength to enter into a rigorous and detailed discussion of those two texts, but be assured that I have read them with passion and gratitude. The lucidity and vigilant attention that you direct at the last episodes of this history (I mean between Habermas and me) impressed me and for this you have my heartfelt thanks. You evoke with moving fidelity our last encounters. I hope other encounters will follow...' (Paris, February 17, 2004). Habermas confirms these sentiments in his obituary for Derrida, 'Ein letzer Gruss', *Frankfurter Rundschau* (October 9, 2004) [Editor's note: reprinted as Chapter 18 in this volume].

AFTERWORDS

INTRODUCTION

As evidenced in Chapters 1 and 2, the initial exchanges between Jacques Derrida and Jürgen Habermas were polemical to say the least. From the late 1990s onwards, there was a certain rapprochement between the two, however. In Chapter 17, Derrida recounts how, at a 'party' at Northwestern University, where they were both teaching at the end of the 1990s, Habermas 'approached me [Derrida], laughing in a friendly manner, and suggested that we have a "discussion"'. As is clear from the two afterwords, the tone between Derrida and Habermas was conciliatory during the last years prior to Derrida's death in 2004. This is also reflected in other places (Derrida 1998; Habermas 2004a; and Chapter 6 in this volume). Furthermore, they agreed to have their interviews on the international situation after 9/11 published in the same volume (Borradori 2003), they co-signed a piece on the future of Europe (Chapter 15), and they held several seminars together (Chapters 5, 6 and 7). This is not to say that Derrida and Habermas agree on everything (see Derrida 1998; Habermas 2004a). However, as is evident from the chapters in Part IV, what brings them together are common political concerns such as economic, social and political inequalities, international law, terrorism, migration and Europe.

17

Jacques Derrida

HONESTY OF THOUGHT

When originally published in the German newspaper Frankfurter Rundschau *on 18 June 2004, this chapter was subtitled 'Each in his country, but both in Europe: the history of a friendship with obstacles – on Jürgen Habermas's 75th birthday'.*

Derrida's tone is conciliatory. The title is a play on Friedrich Nietzsche's Daybreak *(§370), and it alludes to what Derrida sees as Habermas's honesty as a thinker and person. The chapter recounts the history of Derrida and Habermas's relationship, from the 1980s until shortly before Derrida's death in 2004. Thus, it recounts the initial polemical exchanges as well as the rapprochement during the last years of Derrida's life. Derrida stresses in particular his and Habermas's shared concerns about the future of Europe, the United Nations, international law, and Kant.*

Each in his own country, but both in Europe: The history of a friendship with obstacles – on Jürgen Habermas's 75th birthday

First of all, a word of reassurance. To my way of thinking, this title, borrowed from Nietzsche, does not claim to refer to an 'honesty' (*Redlichkeit*) that was shared by Jürgen Habermas and me. My greeting applies to his honesty – Habermas's honesty – as I believe I have experienced it.

Jacques Derrida, 'Unsere Redlichteit!', trans. Ulrich Müller Schöll, *Frankfurter Rundschau*, 18 June 2004.

Why is it that I first remember the wonderful lines devoted to Nietzsche's use of the word *Redlichkeit* by my friend Jean-Luc Nancy in his book *L'impératif catégorique*?[1] Because, among many other reasons, Nancy proposes a surprising, yet convincing reconciliation of a certain Nietzsche with a certain Kant, who means a great deal to Habermas and me. Here is just one quotation from Nancy's lengthy and ingenious analysis (I would have liked to give more space to his illustration as well as that of Nietzsche): 'And while something's worth as such is always that which Kant calls its price, that is, its relative value, the truth of honesty – this imperative honesty – does not possess a relative value, but instead, in the words of Kant, an "intrinsic worth, that is, dignity".'

Incidentally, some years ago in *Die Zukunft der menschlichen Natur*,[2] Habermas reminded us that the German Basic Law of 1949 was the first constitution in which the 'dignity of man' was expressly included ('The dignity of man shall be inviolable. To respect and protect it shall be the duty of all state authority.')[3]

I should like to date my admiration and best wishes for Jürgen Habermas. In doing so I recall more than one date, and the first is not the unique and happy 'occasion' of his 75th birthday today. I will be forgiven if I choose rather those dates that, in my view, mark our unusual shared history. I love this history, I am learning to love it. It is not only the altogether quite recent birth of a friendship or personal affection; the philosophical and political significance of this history already towers over both of us. It makes me discharge my duties, and I hope that in the order of philosophy (the 'ethics of discussion') it demands more than just two different things: a political engagement of philosophers – to reflect on the meaning of responsibility, beyond life's usual passions – and the honesty, the probity, the *Redlichkeit* of thought. Thought about the other, the event, politics and history, and the future. In Germany, in France, in Europe, and in the world to come.

For those who cannot be expected to know about them, I would like briefly to recall the 'encounters' between Habermas and myself. The first of these occurred, I think, on his invitation in 1984, at a lecture I gave at the University of Frankfurt on 'The eyes of the university: The principle of reason and the idea of the university'. (And this may or may not be a significant coincidence: it was renewed at the second lecture I gave in Frankfurt in 2000 on the political problem of the university, 'The absolute university'. That was on the invitation of Axel Honneth, but again it was initiated by Habermas.)

A year after my first visit to Frankfurt, Habermas published *Der philosophische Diskurs der Moderne*.[4] I read the book with the greatest interest; and was not alone in finding the two chapters that were largely intended for me, shall we say, unjust or overhasty. In 1989 (*Memoires for Paul de Man*) and in 1988 (*Limited Inc*)[5] I responded to these chapters in two lengthy comments on behalf of the 'ethics of discussion' – as far as possible with arguments, but admittedly a little polemical. After this, although we both kept silent, 'parties' came into being in many countries. They conducted a kind of 'war', in which we ourselves never took part, either personally or directly. This typically academic war probably made people think, as I hope. However, I can testify to the fact that it also harmed the students who had to form alliances and were then sometimes handicapped in making progress.

THE GHOST OF NIETZSCHE

At the end of the 1990s – and the first token of my gratitude to Habermas is for this – we met at a 'party' after a lecture I gave in Evanston in the United States. With a friendly smile, he came up to me and proposed that we have a 'discussion'. Without hesitation I agreed. 'It's about time,' I said, 'let's not wait until it is too late.' Our next meeting took place in Paris shortly afterwards. In the course of a particularly amicable meal, Habermas, with exemplary decency, for which I will always be grateful to him, did his utmost to get rid of all traces of the former polemics. Again the ghost of Nietzsche reappeared and murmured in my ear: Honesty! 'How greatly the thinker loves his enemy. – Never to hold something back or conceal from you that which can be thought against your thoughts! Promise yourself! It is essential to the highest level of the honesty of thought. And every day you must also conduct your campaign against yourself.' (*Morgenröte*, §370)[6]

Since then we have jointly signed a number of petitions and political manifestos (on Algeria, for example, and sometimes on the initiative of our mutual friend Pierre Bourdieu). Incidentally, the political positions on Germany's historical problems that Habermas took in Germany, with great courage and at numerous opportunities, always met with more than my sympathy, they had my full consent and admiration. That too was for both of us a sign of agreement and a kind of closeness.

In the course of the meal mentioned above our political closeness was confirmed on more than one point. On that occasion it concerned primarily Europe and its future. We reached an agreement to organise a joint seminar on problems of philosophy, right, ethics, and politics. Axel Honneth helped us by inviting me to Frankfurt in 2000. After my lecture we spent a whole day with several colleagues and students. At last it was possible to have a discussion – and for me that was vital. The discussion was sustained politely, honestly – *redlich* – in a labyrinth in which our philosophical or ethical-philosophical paths crossed now and again, coincided sometimes, and sometimes were in opposite directions. At the end of that year Habermas delighted me with a wonderful lecture in Paris at a colloquium dedicated to me ('*Judéités, Questions pour Jacques Derrida*').[7] The discussion continued, and we promised to go on...

In the following year, 2001, we met again shortly after '9-11' at the Adorno Prize. Then, as chance would have it, we met at the home of a mutual friend, Richard Bernstein, in New York at the beginning of October. In a conversation in passing we shared absolutely the same sympathy for the victims of the attack and the same outrage over that sort of aggression. Above all, however, we felt the same critical concern over the reaction of the Bush administration and the opinions of the majority of Americans under the shock of the two attacks. We felt the same uneasiness and shared the same disapproval of what was already beginning to develop: the worst, that is proving to be true every day.

We both took up the suggestion of giving two long interviews on the subject (in a very broad philosophical sense). These were published as a book, first in the United States (*Philosophy in a Time of Terror*),[8] then in Italy, and finally in France (*Le 'concept' du 11 septembre*). And now also in Germany (*Philosophie in Zeiten des Terrors*, Philo-Verlag, 2004). We were also co-signatories of a text for which, fortunately, Habermas had taken the initiative and had written. It circulated widely, calling for a new European public, as well as a common foreign policy (cf. *FAZ*, 31 May 2003).[9]

The book and this sort of manifesto, as well as a number of similar works, puzzled our respective friends. Some were worried, others annoyed. Numerous publications have appeared about them since then, and out of exemplary politeness Habermas informs me each time of the answers he has given in interviews to questions on them. But nothing should, nothing must – I make this wish today – discourage us from continuing on such a path.

A Common Political Culture

Which path? That of 'discussion' direct or indirect, certainly, because much remains to be done. At this point I cannot say anything in the form of a brief message about the reasons and the historical-philosophical background on which we are, or are not, in agreement. I have neither the strength, nor the authority, nor the right. Today, now that it is urgent, I am tempted by a path that allows us to seize on our agreement more tightly and take joint responsibility, each in his own country, but both in Europe. I would like today to fix this path with Habermas's words precisely there, where others of my texts, that in the *Gestus* of the writing, arguments, and premises, are certainly very different, overlap Habermas's approach, are strangely close to it, or show parallels to it.

For instance, I find informative and exemplary all his writings on what ought to come 'after the nation-state', particularly what concerns the necessity of a 'common political culture' that contrasts with the different 'national cultures'. Following an illuminating analysis, Habermas, in an appendix to *Faktizität und Geltung*, defines the conditions of this new political culture, distinguishes it from what has happened in the United States, and then concludes on the now legendary formula that 'a European constitutional patriotism' ought to come into being.[10]

The next European elections (I am writing this on 4 June 2004) will perhaps lead to decisions on the direction of the European constitution and the socio-political shape of Europe. On these I share the same hope and apprehension as Habermas. I believe in the necessity of a new European political culture, and, so that it can be carried effectively into the body and soul and concrete existence of the European citizens, in the necessity of a new political *Affekt*, a feeling of belonging – as it were a rational feeling which, however, is not that of a new European nationalism. When I say 'feeling', I am thinking of something analogous to Kantian *Achtung* (respect): a physical *Affekt*, an individual feeling, as Kant says, but which is not comparable to any 'pathological feeling'. This feeling 'is of such a peculiar type that it seems simply to be at the command of reason, and, to be precise, of pure practical reason'. As it is a question of respect for the laws of a European constitution, I would perhaps hesitate to call this feeling 'patriotism', because of this word's far too many worrying connotations. But beyond the word or the letter, Habermas's discourse on this theme remains, in my eyes, of fundamental significance for today and for the future.

In *Die postnationale Konstellation* Habermas specifies his aims, always with the same honesty in his answers to counter-arguments.[11] He replies that he accepts the argument, and as always he draws from it the impetus to go further. 'Here we seize on the reservations that the neo-Aristotelians are already bringing forth against a national, and even more against a European, constitutional patriotism. For this reason a cosmopolitan community of world citizens offers an insufficient basis for a world domestic policy. The institutionalisation of the process of voting on a world-wide interest, the generalisation of interests, and imaginative construction of common interests cannot occur in the organisational structure of a world-state. Designs for a 'cosmopolitan democracy' must follow another model.' (In parentheses it must be added that, as I totally agree with such a thesis, in particular in *Spectres de Marx* and *Cosmopolites de tous les pays, encore un effort!*,[12] I believed that there should be a proposal for a new *Internationale* which, because it goes beyond the borders of the state (*polis*) as world-state, as well as beyond the borders of the nation, implies more than the concepts of world citizens or cosmopolitanism – despite all the sympathy I have retained for the letter and spirit of cosmopolitanism).

ANOTHER EUROPE

Can one hope, as I do today, though without being convinced of it, that 'those responsible' in the Europe of tomorrow will hear the perceptive Habermas messages? 'A Europe that commits itself to subduing power in every form, including social and cultural, would be protected against the postcolonial return to Eurocentrism'. Or: The political parties that show courage about the future 'must develop the European scope for action in their programmes, with the dual objective of creating a social Europe that brings its weight to bear in the cosmopolitan scales.'

In these lines of Habermas (I would like to comment on many more) I read the best political philosophy. Not only for the Europe of tomorrow. According to him, all parties, even those that do not desire it, would certainly agree to the project of a 'social Europe'. There the true debate will take place, the real fight to determine what 'social' will mean tomorrow. It will not be resolved in Europe alone. For this reason it is necessary for Europe to bring all 'its weight to bear in the cosmopolitan scales' without laying claim to a new hegemonic superpower.

Such a debate is spreading already in a world which Europe was supposed to help and force to change its international law, improve its institutions, and in particular to give the UN a new form. Yes, re-establish this respectable but so weak, reformable, and perfectible UN, whose headquarters should be moved and whose executive powers should be strengthened and made autonomous. A new UN should, with the help of European forces, be able to implement just solutions in the Middle East, both in Iraq and in a process that brings the Israeli-Palestinian conflict harmoniously to an end. It should be able to halt the extremely barbaric violence and make a new voice heard, that from its past and future legacies would clear a new way against the hegemony of the American administration.

This way would be, for example, that of a feasible democratic sovereignty in Iraq and a new Palestinian state. The present one is being cruelly ruined, although its legitimacy has been recognised by the international community as a whole, even – at least verbally – by the Israeli government, which, all the same, pays so little heed to UN 'resolutions'. In short, a different Europe, an old-new Europe, which finds the power for other world-wide (*altermondial*) politics that can fight the official channels and accomplish new things from the ambiguous process of globalisation or *mondialisation* today. Change namely the disastrous, merciless, and impracticable ideology of the all-embracing free market, the G8, World Bank, IWF, OECD, WHO and many other bodies or 'interests' that endanger the planet far into its 'ecological' future.

I would like to provide, with the help of other texts of Habermas, still more signs of the recognition he deserves. But I lack the space and the strength. Nevertheless, from my heart, I wish that the voice, the writings, and the person of Jürgen Habermas will continue to brighten our hopes for a long time to come in this period of powerlessness and in the face of the dark threats that are appearing.

Translated by Marian Hill

NOTES

1. [Editor's note: Jean-Luc Nancy, *L'impératif catégorique* (Paris: Flammarion, 1983).]
2. [Editor's note: Jürgen Habermas, *The Future of Human Nature* (Cambridge: Polity, 2003).]
3. [Translator's note: Art. 1 (1) of the Basic Law, in Carl-Christoph Schweitzer, Detlev Karsten, Robert Spencer, R. Taylor Cole, Donald Kommers, Anthony Nicholls (eds), *Politics and Government in the Federal Republic of Germany, Basic Documents* (Oxford: Berg Publishers Limited, 1984), p. 116.]
4. [Editor's note: Jürgen Habermas, *The Philosophical Discourse of Modernity: Twelve Lectures*, trans. Frederick G. Lawrence, Cambridge: Polity, 1987). See Chapter 1 in this volume.]
5. [Editor's note: Jacques Derrida, *Memoires for Paul de Man*, trans. Peggy Kamuf, 2nd and revised edition (New York: Columbia University Press), pp. 255–61 (note 44). (Also in Jacques Derrida, 'Like the Sound of the Sea Deep Within a Shell: Paul de Man's Flemish Writings', in Werner Hamacher, Neil Hertz and Thomas Keenan (eds), *Responses: On Paul de Man's Wartime Journalism* (Lincoln: University of Nebraska Press, 1989), pp. 160–4 (note 44)); and Jacques Derrida, 'Afterword: Toward An Ethic of Discussion', trans. Samuel Weber, in Jacques Derrida, *Limited Inc* (Evanston: Northwestern University Press, 1988), pp. 156–8 (note 9).]
6. [Editor's note: Friedrich Nietzsche, *Daybreak: Thoughts on the Prejudices of Morality*, trans. R. J. Hollingdale (Cambridge: Cambridge University Press, 1982).]
7. [Editor's note: included here as Chapter 7.]
8. [Editor's note: Giovanna Borradori, *Philosophy In a Time of Terror: Dialogues with Jürgen Habermas and Jacques Derrida* (Chicago: The University of Chicago Press, 2003).]
9. [Editor's note: included here as Chapter 15.]
10. [Editor's note: Jürgen Habermas, 'Citizenship and National Identity', in Jürgen Habermas, *Between Facts and Norms: Contributions to a Discourse Theory of Law and Democracy*, trans. William Rehg (Cambridge, MA: MIT Press, 1996), pp. 491–515.]
11. [Editor's note: Jürgen Habermas, *The Postnational Constellation: Political Essays*, trans. Max Pensky (Cambridge: Polity, 2001).]
12. [Editor's note: Jacques Derrida, *Specters of Marx: The State of the Debt, the Work of Mourning, and the New International*, trans. Peggy Kamuf (London: Routledge, 1994); and Jacques Derrida, 'On Cosmopolitanism', in Jacques Derrida, *On Cosmopolitanism and Forgiveness*, trans. Mark Dooley (London: Routledge, 2001), pp. 1–24.]

18

Jürgen Habermas

A LAST FAREWELL: DERRIDA'S ENLIGHTENING IMPACT

This chapter by Jürgen Habermas was first published in Frankfurter Rundschau *on 11 October 2004, shortly after Jacques Derrida's death. Habermas hails Derrida as one of the most important philosophers of the last decades. He touches briefly on the differences and affinities between his and Derrida's works, which have been the central theme of this volume. Habermas mentions, among other things, Derrida's affinities with Theodor Adorno, the quintessential thinker of the Frankfurt School's first generation who was Habermas's mentor when he first came to Frankfurt.*

Jacques Derrida, like only Michel Foucault, stirred the spirit of an entire generation. He keeps that generation busy to this day. Unlike Foucault, however, although he too was a political thinker, Derrida guided the impulses of his followers onto the tracks of an exercise that for him did not primarily involve doctrinal content, or even the acquisition of a vocabulary that opens up a new world view. Doctrinal content and the acquisition of a world-disclosing vocabulary are also involved. But the practice of micrological reading and the discovery of traces in texts that have resisted the passage of time is an end in itself. Derrida's deconstruction, like Adorno's negative dialectics, is essentially a performative exercise, a *Praxis*.

Jürgen Habermas, 'Ein lezter Gruss: Derridas klärende Wirkung', *Frankfurter Rundschau*, 11 October 2004.

There were many who knew about Derrida's serious illness, which he dealt with confidently. His death was not unexpected. Yet now it strikes us as a sudden, hasty event, shaking us out of the reassuring banality of everyday life. No doubt the thinker who expended all his intellectual energy on the earnest reading of great works and celebrated the predominance of the transmissible written word over the 'presence' of the spoken word will live on in his own works. But now we know that henceforth Derrida's voice and his personal presence will be missing.

For his readers, Derrida is an author who reads each text against the grain until it reveals a subversive meaning. Beneath his unyielding gaze every context fragments. Every apparently firm ground begins to quake, revealing a false bottom. Familiar hierarchies, orders and oppositions disclose a counter-sense. The world in which we seem to be at home is uninhabitable. Not of this world, we remain strangers among strangers. In the end the religious message was hardly encoded any more.

Rarely does one find texts that seem to uncover their author's face so clearly to their anonymous readers. But in fact Derrida belongs to those authors who surprise their readers when they meet for the first time. He was not what one expected. A person of extraordinary kindness, almost elegant, he was certainly vulnerable and sensitive, but had an easy manner and was likeable and friendly, and open to friendship with those he trusted. I am glad I had his trust when we met again six years ago here in Evanston, near Chicago, from where I am sending this final tribute.

Derrida never met Adorno. But when he was awarded the Adorno Prize he gave a speech in the Paulskirche in Frankfurt, which in its train of thought could not have been closer to Adorno's spirit, right down to the secret twists of Romantic dream motifs. Their Jewish roots are the common factor that links them. While Gershom Scholem remained a challenge for Adorno, Emmanuel Levinas became an authority for Derrida. So it is that his œuvre can also have an enlightening impact in Germany, because Derrida appropriated the themes of the later Heidegger without committing any neo-pagan betrayal of his own Mosaic roots.

Translated by Marian Hill

BIBLIOGRAPHY

The bibliography includes all works cited in the introductions as well as everything that is published on the Derrida–Habermas constellation.

Beardsworth, Richard (1996), *Derrida and the Political*, London: Routledge.

Bohman, James (1988), 'Emancipation and Rhetoric: The Perlocutions and Illocutions of the Social Critic', *Philosophy and Rhetoric*, 21:3, pp. 185–204.

Borradori, Giovanna (2003), *Philosophy In a Time of Terror: Dialogues with Jürgen Habermas and Jacques Derrida*, Chicago: The University of Chicago Press.

Bowie, Andrew (2001), 'The "German-French" debate: critical theory, hermeneutics and deconstruction', in C. Knellwolf and C. Norris (eds), *The Cambridge History of Literary Criticism Volume 9*, Cambridge: Cambridge University Press, pp. 121–31.

Coole, Diana (1996), 'Habermas and the Question of Alterity', in Maurizio Passerin d'Entrèves and Seyla Benhabib (eds), *Habermas and the Unfinished Project of Modernity: Critical Essays on* The Philosophical Discourse of Modernity, Cambridge: Polity Press, pp. 221–44.

Critchley, Simon (1999), 'Habermas and Derrida Get Married', in Simon Critchley, *The Ethics of Deconstruction: Derrida and Levinas*, 2nd edition, Edinburgh: Edinburgh University Press, pp. 267–80.

Culler, Jonathan (1988), 'Habermas and Norms of Language', in Jonathan Culler, *Framing the Sign: Criticism and its Institutions*, Oxford: Basil Blackwell, pp. 185–200.

Derrida, Jacques (1986), 'Declarations of Independence', *New Political Science*, 15, pp. 7–15. Also in Jacques Derrida, *Negotiations: Interventions and Interviews 1971–2001*, edited and translated by Elizabeth Rottenberg, Stanford: Stanford University Press, pp. 46–54.

Derrida, Jacques (1988), 'Afterword: Toward An Ethic of Discussion', trans. Samuel Weber, in Jacques Derrida, *Limited Inc*, Evanston: Northwestern University Press, pp. 156–8 (note 9).

Derrida, Jacques (1989), *Memoires for Paul de Man*, trans. Peggy Kamuf, 2nd and revised edition, New York: Columbia University Press, pp. 255–61 (note 44). Also in Jacques Derrida, 'Like the Sound of the Sea Deep Within a Shell: Paul de Man's Flemish Writings', in Werner Hamacher, Neil Hertz and Thomas Keenan (eds),

Responses: On Paul de Man's Wartime Journalism, Lincoln: University of Nebraska Press, 1989, pp. 160–4 (note 44).

Derrida, Jacques (1992), *The Other Heading: Reflections on Today's Europe*, trans. Pascale-Anne Brault and Michael B. Naas, Bloomington: Indiana University Press.

Derrida, Jacques (1996), 'Remarks on Deconstruction and Pragmatism', in C. Mouffe (ed.), *Deconstruction and Pragmatism*, London: Verso, pp. 77–88.

Derrida, Jacques (1998), 'Ich mißtraue der Utopie, ich will das Un-Mögliche: Ein Gespräch mit dem Philosophen Jacques Derrida über die Intellektuellen, den Kapitalismus und die Gesetze der Gastfreundschaft', trans. Andreas Niederberger, *Die Zeit*, 11, 5 march 1998, pp. 47–9.

Derrida, Jacques (2000), *Of Hospitality: Anne Dufourmantelle Invites Jacques Derrida to Respond*, trans. Rachel Bowlby, Stanford: Stanford University Press.

Derrida, Jacques (2001a), "'I Have a Taste for the Secret"', in J. Derrida and M. Ferraris, *A Taste for the Secret*, trans. Giacomo Donis, Cambridge: Polity, pp. 1–92, at pp. 9f. and 53–6.

Derrida, Jacques (2001b), 'On Cosmopolitanism', trans. Mark Dooley, in Jacques Derrida, *On Cosmopolitanism and Forgiveness*, London: Routledge, pp. 1–24.

Derrida, Jacques (2002a), 'Globalization, Peace, and Cosmopolitanism', in *Negotiations: Interventions and Interviews 1971–2001*, edited and translated by Elizabeth Rottenberg, Stanford: Stanford University Press, pp. 371–86.

Derrida, Jacques (2002b), *Positions*, 2nd edition, trans. Alan Bass, London: Continuum.

Derrida, Jacques (2005), *Rogues: Two Essays on Reason*, trans. Pascale-Anne Brault and Michael Naas, Stanford: Stanford University Press.

Derrida, Jacques and Wetzel, Michael (1987), 'Antwort an Apel/ Erwiderungen', *Zeitmitschrift*, 3, pp. 76–85.

Devenney, Mark (2004), *Ethics and Politics in Contemporary Theory: Between critical theory and post-Marxism*, London: Routledge.

Dews, Peter (1995), 'Introduction: The Limits of Disenchantment', in Peter Dews, *The Limits of Disenchantment: Essays on Contemporary European Philosophy*, London: Verso, pp. 1–16.

Duvenage, Pieter (2003), *Habermas and Aesthetics: The Limits of Communicative Reason*, Cambridge: Polity, especially pp. 81–6.

d'Entrèves, Maurizio Passerin and Benhabib, Seyla (eds) (1996), *Habermas and the Unfinished Project of Modernity: Critical Essays on The Philosophical Discourse of Modernity*, Cambridge: Polity Press.

Eriksen, Erik O. and Weigård (2003), *Understanding Habermas: Communicative Action and Deliberative Democracy*, London: Continuum.

Ferraris, Maurizio (1985), 'Note. Habermas, Foucault, Derrida. A proposito de "neoilluminismo" e "neoconservatismo"', *Aut aut*, 208.

Fleming, Marie (1996), 'Working in the Philosophical Discourse of Modernity: Habermas, Foucault, and Derrida', *Philosophy Today*, 40:1, pp. 169–78. Also in Marie Fleming, *Emancipation and Illusion: Rationality and Gender in Habermas's Theory of Modernity*, Philadelphia: Pennsylvania State University Press, chapter 1.

Frank, Manfred (1989), *What is neostructuralism?*, trans. Sabine Wilke and Richard Gray, Minneapolis: University of Minnesota Press.

Fraser, Nancy (1984), 'The French Derrideans: Politicizing Deconstruction or Deconstructing the Political?', *New German Critique*, 33. Also in Gary B. Madison (ed.), *Working through Derrida*, Evanston: Northwestern University Press, 1993, pp. 51–76.

Gasché, Rodolph (1986), *The Tain of the Mirror: Derrida and the Philosophy of Reflection*, Cambridge, MA: Harvard University Press.

Gasché, Rodolph (1988), 'Postmodernism and Rationality', *Journal of Philosophy*, 85:10, pp. 525–38. Revised version as 'Answering for Reason', in Rodolph Gasché,

Inventions of Difference: On Jacques Derrida Cambridge, MA: Harvard University Press, 1994, pp. 107–28 (chapter 4).

Habermas, Jürgen (1987), 'Beyond a Temporalized Philosophy of Origins: Jacques Derrida's Critique of Phonocentrism', in Jürgen Habermas, *The Philosophical Discourse of Modernity: Twelve Lectures*, trans. Frederick G. Lawrence, Cambridge: Polity Press, pp. 161–84.

Habermas, Jürgen (1992), 'Philosophy and Science as Literature?', in Jürgen Habermas, *Postmetaphysical Thinking: Philosophical Essays*, trans. William Mark Hohengarten, Cambridge: Polity Press, pp. 205–27.

Habermas, Jürgen (1996a), 'Modernity: An Unfinished Project', in M. Passerin d'Entrèves and S. Benhabib (eds), *Habermas and the Unfinished Project of Modernity: Critical Essays on* The Philosophical Discourse of Modernity, Cambridge: Polity Press, pp. 38–55.

Habermas, Jürgen (1996b), *Between Facts and Norms: Contributions to a Discourse Theory of Law and Democracy*, trans. William Rehg, Cambridge, MA: MIT Press.

Habermas, Jürgen (1998a), 'Kant's Idea of Perpetual Peace: At Two Hundred Years' Historical Remove', in Jürgen Habermas, *The Inclusion of the Other: Studies in Political Theory*, trans. Ciaran Cronin, Cambridge: Polity Press, pp. 165–202.

Habermas, Jürgen (1998b), 'On the Internal Relation between the Rule of Law and Democracy', in Jürgen Habermas, *The Inclusion of the Other: Studies in Political Theory*, trans. Ciaran Cronin, Cambridge: Polity Press, pp. 253–64.

Habermas, Jürgen (2001a), 'The Postnational Constellation and the Future of Democracy', in Jürgen Habermas, *The Postnational Constellation: Political Essays*, trans. Max Pensky', Cambridge: Polity Press, pp. 58–112.

Habermas, Jürgen (2001b), 'Constitutional Democracy: A Paradoxical Union of Contradictory Principles?', trans. William Rehg, *Political Theory* 29, pp. 766–81.

Habermas, Jürgen (2003), 'On Law and Disagreement. Some Comments on "Interpretative Pluralism"', *Ratio Juris* 16, pp. 187–94.

Habermas, Jürgen (2004a), 'Ein Interview über Krieg und Frieden', in Jürgen Habermas, *Die gespaltene Westen. Kleine Politische Schriften X*, Frankfurt am Main: Suhrkamp, pp. 85–110, especially pp. 86–8. English translation as 'America and the World: A Conversation with Jürgen Habermas', trans. Jeffrey Craig Miller, *Logos*, 3:3 (Summer 2004).

Habermas, Jürgen (2004b), 'Intolerance and Discrimination', *International Journal of Constitutional Law*, 1:1, pp. 2–12.

Habermas, Jürgen (2005), *Time of Transitions*, Cambridge: Polity.

Honig, Bonnie (1993), *Political Theory and the Displacement of Politics*, Ithaca: Cornell University Press, chapter 4.

Honneth, Axel (1995), 'The other of justice: Habermas and the ethical challenge of Postmodernism', trans. John Farrell, in S. K. White (ed.), *The Cambridge Companion to Habermas*, Cambridge: Cambridge University Press, pp. 289–323.

Hoy, David Couzens (1985), 'Interpreting the Law: Hermeneutical and Poststructuralist Perspectives', *Southern California Law Review* 58: pp. 135–76.

Hoy, David Couzens (1996), 'Splitting the Difference: Habermas's Critique of Derrida', in M. P. d'Entrèves and S. Benhabib (eds), *Habermas and the Unfinished Project of Modernity: Critical Essays on* The Philosophical Discourse of Modernity, Cambridge: Polity Press, pp. 124–46. Also in Gary B. Madison (ed.), *Working through Derrida*, Evanston: Northwestern University Press, 1993, pp. 230–51.

Jay, Martin (1992), 'The Debate over Performative Contradiction: Habermas versus the Poststructuralists,' in A. Honneth, T. McCarthy, C. Offe and A. Wellmer (eds), *Philosophical Interventions in the Unfinished Project of Enlightenment*, trans. William Rehg, Cambridge, MA: MIT Press, pp. 261–79.

Landry, Lorraine (2000), 'Beyond the "French Fries and the Frankfurter": an agenda for critical theory', *Philosophy and Social Criticism*, 26:2, pp. 99–129.

Levy, Daniel, Pensky, Max, and Torpey, John (eds) (2005), *Old Europe, New Europe, Core Europe: Transatlantic Relations After the Iraq War*, London: Verso.

Lucy, Niall (2004), *A Derrida Dictionary*, Oxford: Blackwell.

Martin, Bill (1992), 'What is at the heart of language? Habermas, Davidson, Derrida', in Bill Martin, *Matrix and the line: Derrida and the possibilities of postmodern social theory*, Albany: SUNY Press, pp. 65–124.

Matuštík, Martin J. (1995), 'Derrida and Habermas on the Aporia of the Politics of Identity and Difference: Towards Radical Democratic Multiculturalism', *Constellations*, 1:3, pp. 383–98. Revised version as 'Multicultural Enlightenment', in Martin J. Matuštík, *Specters of Liberation: Great Refusals in the New World Order*, Albany: SUNY Press, 1998, pp. 49–64.

Matuštík, Martin J. Beck (1998), 'Specters of Deconstruction and Critical Theory', in Martin J. Beck Matuštík, *Specters of Liberation*, Albany: SUNY Press, pp. 65–96.

McCarthy, Thomas (1978), *The Critical Theory of Jürgen Habermas*, London: Hutchinson.

McCarthy, Thomas (1988), 'On the Margins of Politics', *The Journal of Philosophy* 85, pp. 645–48. Reprinted as 'Postscript: The Politics of Friendship', in Thomas McCarthy, *Ideals and Illusions: On Reconstruction and Deconstruction in Contemporary Critical Theory*, Cambridge, MA: MIT Press, 1991, pp. 120–23.

McCarthy, Thomas (1990), 'The Politics of the Ineffable: Derrida's Deconstructionism', *The Philosophical Forum*, 21, pp. 146–68. Also in M. Kelly (ed.), *Hermeneutics and Critical Theory in Ethics and Politics*, Cambridge, MA: MIT Press, 1990, pp. 146–68; and in Thomas McCarthy, *Ideals and Illusions: On Reconstruction and Deconstruction in Contemporary Critical Theory*, Cambridge, MA: MIT Press, 1991, pp. 97–119.

McCumber, John (2000), *Philosophy and Freedom: Derrida, Rorty, Habermas, Foucault*, Bloomington: Indiana University Press.

Mendieta, Eduardo (2003), 'We Have Never Been Human or, How We Lost Our Humanity: Derrida and Habermas on Cloning', *Philosophy Today*, 47:5, pp. 168–75.

Myerson, George (1995), 'Democracy, Argument and the University', *Studies in Higher Education*, 20:2, pp. 125–33.

Nässtrōm, Sophia (2003), 'What Globalization Overshadows', *Political Theory* 31:6, pp. 808–34.

Norris, Christopher (1989), 'Deconstruction, Postmodernism and Philosophy: Habermas and Derrida', *Praxis International* 8:4. Also in Christopher Norris, *What's wrong with postmodernism: Critical theory and the ends of philosophy*, London: Harvester Wheatsheaf, chapter 1; and in D. Wood (ed.), *Derrida: A Critical Reader*, Oxford: Basil Blackwell, 1992, pp. 167–92.

Purdon, Mark (2003), 'The nature of ecosystem management: postmodernism and plurality in the sustainable management of the boreal forest', *Environmental Science and Policy*, 6:4, pp. 377–88.

Rasmussen, David (1990), *Reading Habermas*, Oxford: Basil Blackwell.

Reader, John (2004), 'Deconstructing Autonomy: Towards a New Identity', *Ecotheology: Journal of Religion, Nature and the Environment*, 9:2, pp. 221–44.

Rorty, Richard (1991), 'Is Derrida a transcendental philosopher?' in Richard Rorty, *Essays on Heidegger and Others: Philosophical Papers Volume 2*, Cambridge: Cambridge University Press, pp. 119–28. Also in D. Wood (ed.), *Derrida: A Critical Reader*, Oxford: Blackwell, pp. 235–46.

Rorty, Richard (1995), 'Deconstruction', in R. Selden (ed.), *The Cambridge History of Literary Criticism. Volume 8: From Formalism to Poststructuralism*, Cambridge: Cambridge University Press, pp. 166–96.

Rorty, Richard (1996), 'Remarks on Deconstruction and Pragmatism', in C. Mouffe (ed.), *Deconstruction and Pragmatism*, London: Verso, pp. 13–18.

Shabani, Omid A. Payrow (2003), *Democracy, Power, and Legitimacy: The Critical Theory of Jürgen Habermas*, Toronto: University of Toronto Press.

Thomassen, Lasse (2005), 'Jürgen Habermas', in T. Carver and J. Martin (eds), *Continental Political Thought*, Basingstoke: Palgrave, 2005.

Trey, George A. (1989), 'The Philosophical Discourse of Modernity: Habermas's Postmodern Adventure', *Diacritics*, 19:2, pp. 67–79.

van Reijen, Willem (1994), 'Derrida – Ein unvollendeter Habermas?', *Deutsche Zeitschrift für Philosophie* 42:6, pp. 1037–44.

White, Stephen K. (1991), *Political Theory and Postmodernism*, Cambridge: Cambridge University Press.

COPYRIGHT ACKNOWLEDGEMENTS

Grateful acknowledgement is made to the following sources for permission to reproduce material previously published elsewhere. Every effort has been made to trace copyright holders, but if any have been inadvertently overlooked, the publisher will be pleased to make the necessary arrangement at the first opportunity.

Polity and MIT Press for permission to reprint Jürgen Habermas, 'Excursus on Leveling the Genre Distinction between Philosophy and Literature,' in idem., *The Philosophical Discourse of Modernity: Twelve Lectures*, trans. Frederick G. Lawrence (Cambridge: Polity Press, 1987), pp. 185–210.

Galilée and Stanford University Press for permission to reprint Jacques Derrida, 'Is There a Philosophical Language?', in idem., *Points . . . Interviews, 1974–1994*, ed. Elisabeth Weber, trans. Peggy Kamuf (Stanford: Stanford University Press, 1995), pp. 216–27. Originally published in Jacques Derrida, *Points de suspension, Entretiens* (Paris: Galilée, 1992).

Revue Internationale de Philosophie for permission to reprint Richard Rorty, 'Habermas, Derrida, and the Functions of Philosophy', *Revue Internationale de Philosophie*, 4 (1995), 437–59.

Polity and MIT Press for permission to reprint Richard J. Bernstein, 'An Allegory of Modernity/Postmodernity: Habermas and Derrida', in idem., *The New Constellation: The Ethical-Political Horizons of Modernity/Postmodernity* (Cambridge: Polity Press, 1991), pp. 199–229.

Blackwell Publishers for permission to reprint Simon Critchley, 'Remarks on Derrida and Habermas', *Constellations* 7:4 (2000), 455–65.

Blackwell Publishers and M. Derrida for permission to reprint Jacques Derrida, 'Performative Powerlessness – A Response to Simon Critchley', trans. James Ingram, *Constellations* 7:4 (2000), 466–8.

Galilée and Fordham University Press for permission to use Jürgen Habermas, 'How to Respond to the Ethical Question' from the English abridgment and translation of Joseph Cohen and Raphael Zagury-Orly (eds), *Judéités. Questions pour Jacques Derrida* (Paris: Galilée, 2003), forthcoming from Fordham University Press.

Blackwell Publishers for permission to use Seyla Benhabib, 'Democracy and Difference: Reflections on the Metapolitics of Lyotard and Derrida', *The Journal of Political Philosophy*, 2:1 (1994), 1–23.

The Modern Language Association of America for permission to reprint the 'Afterword' to Chapter 8.

Sage Publications for permission to use a slightly revised version of 'Dead Rights, Live Futures: A Reply to Habermas's "Constitutional Democracy"', *Political Theory* 29:6 (2001), 792–805.

"A bizarre even opaque practice": Habermas on Constitutionalism and Democracy', © Lasse Thomassen, 2006.

Cambridge University Press for permission to reprint Jürgen Habermas, 'Religious Tolerance – The Pacemaker for Cultural Rights', *Philosophy* 79 (2004), 5–18.

Taylor & Francis and M. Derrida for permission to reprint Jacques Derrida, 'Hostipitality', trans. Barry Stocker and Forbes Morlock, *Angelaki: Journal of the Theoretical Humanities* 5:3 (2000), 3–18.

The Canadian Political Science Association for reproducing, in a slightly shortened and modified version, Martin Morris, 'Deliberation and Deconstruction: Two Views on the Space of a Post-National Democracy', *Canadian Journal of Political Science* 34:4 (2001), 763–90.

Livien De Cauter and the Brussels Tribunal for permission to reproduce Jacques Derrida, 'For a Justice to Come', The BRussells Tribunal (2004), www.brusselstribunal.org. It was originally printed in a shorter version in Dutch in the Belgian Newspaper *De standaard* and in *filosofiemagazine*.

Blackwell Publishers and M. Derrida for permission to reprint Jacques Derrida and Jürgen Habermas, 'February 15, or What Binds Europeans Together: A plea for a Common Foreign Policy, Beginning in the Heart of Europe', *Constellations* 10 (2003): 291–7.

Epoché and Walter Morgan for permission to reprint Martin Beck Matuštík, 'Between Hope and Terror: Habermas and Derrida Plead for the Im/Possible', *Epoché*, 9:1 (2004), 1–18.

M. Derrida for permission to use, in translation, Jacques Derrida, 'Unsere Redlichkeit!', trans. Ulrich Müller-Schöll, *Frankfurter Rundschau*, 18 June 2004.

Jürgen Habermas for permission to use, in translation, Jürgen Habermas, 'Ein letzter Gruss: Derridas klärende Wirkung', *Frankfurter Rundschau*, 11 October 2004.

NOTES ON THE CONTRIBUTORS

Seyla Benhabib is Eugene Meyer Professor of Political Science and Philosophy at Yale University. She is the author of, among others, *Critique, Norm and Utopia*, *The Claims of Culture: Equality and Diversity in a Global Era* and, most recently, *The Rights of Others: Aliens, Residents and Citizens*.

Richard J. Bernstein is Vera List Professor of Philosophy at the New School for Social Research, New York. He has published numerous books, among them *Beyond Objectivism and Relativism*, *The New Constellation: The Ethical/Political Horizons of Modernity/Postmodernity*, *Habermas and Modernity* and *Radical Evil: A Philosophic Interrogation*.

Lieven De Cauter is a philosopher and art historian. He has published several books on art, architecture, Walter Benjamin, and politics. He teaches philosophy of culture in several art schools and universities, among them the Department of Architecture at the University of Leuven, and the Berlage Institute (Rotterdam). His latest book is *The Capsular Civilisation*.

Simon Critchley is Professor of Philosophy at the New School for Social Research, New York, and at the University of Essex. Among his numerous books and other publications are *The Ethics of Deconstruction*, *Very Little . . . Almost Nothing*, *Ethics-politics-subjectivity: Derrida, Levinas and Contemporary French Thought*, *On Humour*, and *Things Merely Are*. He has just finished a book called *Infinitely Demanding – A Political Ethics*.

Jacques Derrida (1930–2004) was Director of Studies at the École Pratique des hautes Études en Sciences Sociales, Paris, and Professor of Humanities at the University of California at Irvine. His numerous books include *Writing and Difference*, *Of Grammatology*, *Limited Inc*, *Specters of Marx*, *Politics of Friendship*, and *Rogues*.

Jürgen Habermas is Professor of Philosophy Emeritus at the University of Frankfurt, and Visiting Professor at Northwestern University. He is the author of, among others, *The Structural Transformation of the Public Sphere*, *Knowledge and Human Interest*, *The Theory of Communicative Action*, *Between Facts and Norms* and, most recently, *Time of Transitions*.

Bonnie Honig is a professor of political theory at Northwestern University and senior research fellow at the American Bar Foundation. She has written extensively on political theory and feminist theory, including *Political Theory and the Displacement of Politics*, *Feminist Interpretations of Hannah Arendt* (ed.) and *Democracy and the Foreigner*. She is currently co-editing the *Oxford Handbook of Political Thought* and is working on a book tentatively entitled *The People, the Multitude, and the Paradoxes of Politics*.

Martin Beck Matuštík is Professor of Philosophy at Purdue University, Indiana. He has written extensively on Critical Theory and Continental philosophy. His books include *Mediation of Deconstruction*, *Postnational Identity: Critical Theory and Existential Philosophy in Habermas, Kierkegaard, and Havel*, *Specters of Liberation: Great Refusals in the New World Order* and *Jürgen Habermas: A Philosophical-Political Profile*.

Martin Morris is Lecturer in Communication Studies at Martin Morris of Windsor, Canada. He is the author of *Rethinking the Communicative Turn: Adorno, Habermas and the Problem of Communicative Freedom*.

Richard Rorty is Professor of Comparative Literature and Philosophy at Stanford University. He is the author of numerous books and papers on comparative literature, and on analytic and Continental philosophy, including *Philosophy and the Mirror of Nature*, *Contingency, Irony and Solidarity* and three volumes of *Philosophical Papers* and, most recently, *A Postphilosophical Politics* and *The Future of Religion*.

Lasse Thomassen is Junior Lecturer in the Department of Politics and Public Administration, University of Limerick. He is the author of articles, chapters and reviews on Habermas and post-structuralist theory and the co-editor (with Lars Tønder) of *Radical Democracy: Politics Between Abundance and Lack*. He is currently working on a research monograph, *Deconstructing Habermas*, to be published with Routledge.

INDEX

Adorno, T., 3, 14–16, 73, 75, 89, 117, 123–5, 307–8
aporia, 5–7, 18, 32, 33n, 77, 89, 132, 140, 189, 192, 208, 211, 213, 223, 225–6, 239,
Austin, J. L., 13, 20–2, 43, 112, 153n; *see also* speech act theory
authority, 112–13, 134–6, 140–3

Benhabib, S., 128–56, 179, 188
Bernstein, R. J., 63n, 71–97, 152n, 154n

communicative action, 3–4, 22–3, 28, 30–1, 34n, 55, 75–6, 78, 89, 96n, 237, 244, 282
communicative reason, 3, 55–6, 76, 79, 235, 242; *see also* reason
community, 58, 123, 136, 142, 181–2, 200–5, 237, 287, 295n, 304
consensus, 4, 6, 24, 90, 184–5, 234, 237–8, 242, 248
constitutional democracy, 139–40, 160–194
constitutionalism *see* constitutional democracy
cosmopolitanism, 143–4, 209, 212, 228, 257–8, 262, 279, 287, 304–5; *see also* international law

Critchley, S., 98–110, 111, 114
Critical Theory, 1, 3, 101, 151, 280, 285, 290–3
  and deconstruction, 101, 150, 188, 243
critique, 3, 17, 78, 88, 125, 130–1, 147, 175n, 245, 249
  immanent, 188
  normative foundations of, 32, 55, 243–4, 250
  of reason, 2, 14–20, 32, 33–34n, 54, 78, 243–4
Culler, J., 19–24, 50–53

decisionism, 138, 151n, 193n; *see also* Schmitt, C.
Declaration of Independence (American), 132–6, 148, 153n
deconstruction, 5–7, 244
  and Critical Theory *see* Critical Theory, and deconstruction
  Derrida on, 41
  Habermas on, 14–20, 307
  as method, 5–6, 81–2, 100, 143–4, 146–7, 188–9, 208–9, 307
  and politics, 6–7, 63, 82–86, 91, 99, 148–9, 250
deliberative democracy, 4, 141–6, 172n, 177, 233–4, 238, 287

democracy
and constitutionalism *see* constitutional democracy
deliberative *see* deliberative democracy
to come *see* democracy to come
democracy to come, 7, 87, 91–2, 107–9, 268, 287, 290
Derrida, J.
Habermas on, 2, 11, 13–32, 47–56, 116–17, 125–6, 307–8
life, 1, 80, 149
différance, 42, 86, 88, 186, 188
discourse ethics, 3–4, 103–4

Enlightenment, 2–3, 74–5, 78–9, 87–8, 100, 146, 148, 280–3, 292
Europe, 130, 150, 249, 270–7, 279–90, 302–5
European Union *see* Europe
exclusion, 6, 136–7, 148, 150n, 197, 204, 247, 250; *see also* inclusion

fiction, 18, 20–2, 24–8, 31, 37–8, 59, 245–6
as solution to paradox of democracy, 144, 187–9, 194n
see also literature *and* poetry
forgiveness, 287, 291
Foucault, M., 53, 55, 57, 62n, 307
Frankfurt School *see* Critical Theory

Habermas, J.
Derrida on, 2, 37, 41, 111–14, 270, 300–6
life, 1, 74–5
Hegel, G. W. F., 57, 134
Heidegger, M., 14–17, 38, 41–3, 79, 116–17, 124–6, 151n, 221–3, 289–90
hermeneutics, 5–6, 23–4, 139, 188
Honig, B., 153n, 161–75, 189–92
hospitality, 6, 208–30, 287–8

inclusion, 137, 167, 197, 200, 203–5, 234, 246–7; *see also* exclusion
international law, 3, 107, 252n, 259–69, 271–7, 282–3, 305; *see also* cosmopolitanism
intersubjectivity, 4, 48, 53–4, 101–4, 204, 233, 235, 239–41
iterability, 185–6, 215

justice, 93, 99–100, 103, 105–6, 108, 118–19, 138, 287
justice to come, 259, 268
social justice, 49, 62n
see also law, and justice

Kant, I., 64n, 65n, 99, 103, 107, 165, 173n, 209–13, 220, 228n, 262, 271, 286, 291, 301, 304
Kierkegaard, S., 119–25, 291–2

language
ordinary, 21, 25, 30, 122–3, 153n
language game, 23–4, 55, 64n, 156, 244
law
international *see* international law
and justice, 99–100, 138, 148
legitimacy, 4, 132–45, 162–3, 177–80
liberalism, 48–50, 58–60, 62n, 118, 148, 162, 172, 201, 205, 238
literature
and philosophy, 16–27, 30–2, 36–8, 41, 50–2, 83, 99, 146, 244–5, 250
see also fiction *and* poetry
logic
and rhetoric, 14–20, 37, 41, 83, 90
logocentrism, 19, 48–9, 81, 96
Lyotard, J.-F., 72, 131–7, 139–45, 151n, 152n, 153n, 154n, 155–6n

Marx, K., 57, 107, 280
Marxism *see* Marx, K.
metaphysics, 14–20, 29, 32, 33n, 38, 42, 47–50, 54, 59–60, 62n, 63n, 64n, 77, 81–2, 84–6, 100–1, 125, 139, 143–5, 155–6n, 239
of presence, 14, 19, 81
see also postmetaphysics
modernity, 1 53, 64n, 73–5, 87, 94n, 100, 103, 131, 236, 285; *see also* postmodernism

nationalism, 142–4, 274, 304
post-national constellation, 276, 282
Nietzsche, F., 16, 47–50, 288, 290, 292, 300–2

performative contradiction, 14–15, 20, 102, 213–14
performativity, 21, 24, 39–40, 101–3, 112–14, 116, 133–4, 136, 138–40, 147, 153n
Philosophical Discourse of Modernity (Habermas), 2, 37, 47, 101, 301

philosophy, 15–20, 29–32, 36–8, 42–4, 54–6, 117–19, 122–3, 146, 188, 264, 301
  of consciousness *see* subject, philosophy of
  and literature *see* literature, and philosophy
  and social science, 92–3, 101
poetry, 25–31, 37, 51–2, 245; *see also* fiction *and* literature
popular sovereignty *see* sovereignty, popular
postmetaphysics, 100–1, 119–23, 143; *see also* metaphysics
postmodernism, 70–3, 87, 93–4, 130, 150–1n; *see also* modernity
power, 16, 113–14, 122–3, 139, 202, 232, 247, 250
private–public distinction, 47, 49–50, 53–4, 57–8, 60, 62n, 98
public sphere, 4, 144–5, 232–3, 271, 279

rational reconstruction, 3–4, 188
rationality *see* reason
Rawls, J., 54, 118, 201, 251n
reason
  communicative *see* communicative reason
  critique of *see* critique, of reason
  Derrida on, 14–20, 32, 33–34n, 108, 146
  instrumental, 3, 75–6, 235
  Kant on, 165, 291, 304
  subject-centred *see* subject, philosophy of subjectivity
reconciliation, 166, 180–4, 187, 189–90
religion, 104, 120, 122, 196–205, 206n, 267–9, 275, 283–8, 291–3
  Judaism, 80, 125, 267, 296
responsibility, 83–5, 91, 102–3, 105–6, 112–14, 218, 248–50, 289
rhetoric, 26–7, 31–2, 37–8, 96, 243–6
  and logic *see* logic, and rhetoric
Rorty, R., 29–30, 33n, 46–65, 102
Rousseau, J.-J., 142, 173n

Schmitt, C., 105–6, 151n, 265; *see also* decisionism
Searle, J., 20–4; *see also* speech act theory
sovereignty, 113, 141–3, 151n, 225, 234, 260–1, 263–5, 277, 287, 290
  popular, 113, 143, 162, 168, 171, 177, 192n
speech act, 20–7, 101–3; *see also* Austin, J. L. and Searle, J.
subject, 38, 48, 226, 240
  philosophy of subjectivity, 14–15, 17, 47–9, 53, 56, 61, 77, 89, 240, 252n
  see also intersubjectivity
supplementarity, 15, 169–70, 180, 194n

terrorism, 198, 267, 281–4, 286
text
  Derrida's conception of, 5, 17–20, 24, 39, 82
tolerance, 195–207, 286–7; *see also* hospitality
totalitarianism, 246, 276
transcendental, 55, 63n, 77, 99–104, 236, 285, 296
  quasi-transcendental, 3–4, 236

undecidability, 84–5, 91, 185–92
universality, 31, 34, 50, 54–9, 61–2, 63n, 76–8, 90–1, 99–103, 106–8, 130–1, 143–5, 197, 209–12, 228n, 238, 242, 244, 248, 284

Wittgenstein, L., 43, 106; *see also* language game